PAPER
BOOM

WHY REAL PROSPERITY REQUIRES A NEW APPROACH TO CANADA'S ECONOMY

by Jim Stanford

co-published by
The Canadian Centre for Policy Alternatives
and James Lorimer and Co. Ltd.
1999

Canadian Cataloguing in Publication Data

Stanford, Jim
  Paper boom

Includes index.
ISBN 1-55028-656-0

1. Canada – Economic policy – 1991- .* 2. Job creation – Canada. 3. Public investments – Canada. I. Title.

HC115S7175 1999   338.971   C99-930335-X

Printed and bound in Canada

Published by
The Canadian Centre for Policy Alternatives
804-251 Laurier Avenue West
Ottawa, Ontario K1P 5J6

James Lorimer & Company Ltd., Publishers
35 Britain Street
Toronto, Ontario M5A 1R7

Critical Acclaim for PAPER BOOM

"*Paper Boom* provides the clearest explanation yet of the inner workings of the world of finance and its destructive impact on the real world economy where most of us live."

– Maude Barlow
Chair, Council of Canadians

"*Paper Boom* makes an important contribution to the development of a progressive economic strategy for our country. This book is essential reading for all those who agree that we cannot afford to surrender control over our economic destiny to the speculators and beancounters."

– Svend Robinson
NDP Member of Parliament

"Forget the *Globe and Mail* (or *National Post*)! Here's the Canadian economy illuminated for you and me! Want to know how it all works? Read Jim Stanford's disturbing, fascinating and really, really readable *Paper Boom*."

– Dorothy Smith
Author of *The Everyday World as*

Problematic

"Working people need to understand capital, if we're ever going to learn how to control it. There's no better place to start than by reading this book."

– Buzz Hargrove,
President, Canadian Auto Workers

"If you thought your financial investments were contributing to improvements in productivity or the quality of our infrastructure, this book will broaden your perspective. Unfortunately, most investors are involved in a big casino operation, with many losers and few gainers."

– Mike McCracken
President and CEO, Informetrica Ltd.

"I never miss a chance to read Jim Stanford. His writing is smart, pointed, informed, funny and–a rare thing from a man of the left–not always wrong."

– William Watson
Editor, *Policy Options*

"Stanford explodes conventional wisdom, on both the left and right, about what is wrong with the Canadian economy and what to do about it…a work of impressive depth and breadth."

– Monica Townson
Chair, Ontario Fair Tax Commission

"Stanford puts it all together—solid economic analysis, concrete applications to Canada today, and a writing style that makes the subject come alive."
– Myron J. Gordon,
Professor of Finance, University of Toronto

"Jim Stanford is the most thoughtful, articulate, sensible policy analyst that Canada's Left has produced in decades. This is a powerful analysis of how to improve productivity and the creation of wealth—a refreshing change from simplistic diatribes about unfair distributions of wealth."
– Avi J. Cohen
Professor of Economics, York University

Table of Contents

Part I–Money in Motion: Investment and Job-Creation

Part II–Slow Motion: How Investment Lost Steam

Part III–A Recipe for Stagnation: Ingredients in the Slowdown

Preface and Acknowledgements

This is a book about investment, real and imagined. Financial investments in paper assets like stocks, bonds, and mutual funds get most of the attention these days from the media and politicians. But on their own these investments are worth no more to society than the paper they are printed on. Rather, it is real investments—in real-world assets that are useful in the actual production of valuable goods and services—which are the crucial source of job-creation and rising incomes for Canadians.

The connection between financial investment and real investment has never been more indirect and uncertain than in the 1990s, as the paper economy boomed but the real economy went nowhere. In fact, the paper boom in many ways has had a perverse impact on real growth and job-creation.

The importance of investment to economic progress is not well-appreciated, in my view, even (or especially) among those who have been very critical of the right-wing direction of economic policy in Canada over the past two decades. It is my view that the left in Canada needs to "reclaim" the issue of investment. Workers and communities, it turns out, may have more at stake in a vibrant and rapidly-growing investment regime than do the private businesses and financiers whose talk about investment is not matched by deeds. Right-wing measures to improve the "business climate" have not revitalized real investment in Canada, and in fact have probably had a negative effect.

Progressives are often uncomfortable talking about "investment," because it is something that is usually done by business. But this book argues that it is possible, indeed necessary, for the left to develop a position on investment that recognizes its importance to economic growth, without buying into counterproductive demands for still more belt-tightening and still more concessions on the part of average Canadians.

The arguments contained here will be very controversial, not least of all within the left itself. If the book sparks thinking, discussion, and debate among trade unionists, community activists, and anyone else concerned about job-creation and living standards, it will have truly served its purpose. I welcome feedback on any of the positions and ideas expressed here (stanford@caw.ca).

To avoid cluttering up the book with too many endnotes and citations, I have formally cited data sources only for the numerous tables and graphs that are presented. An appendix describing the major statistical sources used in the book is provided at the end. Interested readers are welcome to contact me for further information on sources, where necessary. All direct quotations which appear in the book were obtained from already-published sources; these references are also available on request.

Literally dozens of individuals have contributed in one way or another to this project, and their assistance and encouragement is profoundly appreciated. The initial enthusiasm and ongoing encouragement of Bruce Campbell and Sam Gindin were absolutely essential to the book's completion, and I thank them both for their insight and support. The editorial talents of Kerri-Anne Finn and Ed Finn at the Canadian Centre for Policy Alternatives, and the research and technical assistance of Maureen Gale and Dana Grant at the CAW office in Halifax, are well reflected in the quality of the final product, and are most gratefully acknowledged.

Many other individuals gave generously of their time with research support, reviews of draft chapters, brainstorming, and other forms of input. Without incriminating them in the final product, a partial alphabetical list of those individuals includes: Greg Albo, Donna Baines, Bob Baldwin, Kathy Bennett, Neil Brooks, Kirk Falconer, Myron Gordon, Jo-ann Hannah, Anders Hayden, Doug Henwood, Andrew Jackson, Seth Klein, Marc Lavoie, Hugh Mackenzie, Brian MacLean, Lars Osberg, Mario Seccareccia, Yvonne Stanford, and Coro Strandberg. I apologize to anyone inadvertently left off this list.

Helpful comments on material presented here were obtained from seminars and conferences organized at Dalhousie University, Laurentian University, Simon Fraser University, and the B.C. branch of the Canadian Centre for Policy Alternatives. The enthusiastic response of CAW members and other community activists to this material at innumerable workshops and panel discussions in recent years encouraged me to develop the arguments in book form.

My economic thinking was shaped by the many free-thinking professors who taught me over the years at the University of Calgary, Cambridge University, and the New School for Social Research. I owe a special personal and intellectual debt to my Ph.D supervisor at the New School, the late David M. Gordon.

Financial assistance from the Canadian Centre for Policy Alternatives and the Canadian Auto Workers is also gratefully acknowledged. And I stress that the views expressed here are my own, and not official positions of these two fine organizations.

By far my greatest thanks go to my partner, Donna Baines, and our daughter Maxine Baines, not just for their generous patience and support during the writing of this book, but more importantly for the vim and verve they bring to our life together, which energizes and inspires me in everything I do.

Jim Stanford
Halifax
April 1999

Chapter 1
Lots of Money, Not Enough Jobs

Each year, Canadians collectively go through a bizarre national ritual known as "RRSP season."

The federal and provincial governments offer generous subsidies to taxpayers who make deposits into official Registered Retirement Savings Plans (RRSPs). But the deadline for deposits, for those who want to receive the tax credit with their next tax return, is the beginning of March. For the financial companies which sell and manage RRSPs, January and February are the most important sales season of the year—the equivalent of the pre-Christmas rush at Toys 'R' Us. So, as soon as the Boxing Day sales signs have been taken down, a barrage of advertising from banks, stock-brokers, and other financial institutions is unleashed on a winter-weary public.

"We'll put your money to work for you!" the ads trumpet. Various psychological strategies are pursued in the effort to reel in RRSP customers. Some promise freedom and leisure as the rewards for frugality and smart decision-making; these might typically feature a happy, healthy sixtyish couple strolling along a tropical beach. Others paint a dire picture of life for those who do not invest early and invest often. A bold headline flashes across the TV screen: "THE AVERAGE CANADIAN WILL NEED $800,000 TO PAY FOR AN ADEQUATE PENSION."

These ads consciously attempt to capitalize on the heightened insecurity that many Canadians feel in the wake of cutbacks to social programs and public pensions. They promise an individual escape from these social woes—but only for those who pick the right mutual fund.

Another set of ads highlights the real products and services that might be produced, possibly with the very same dollars that you might deposit in your RRSP. One ad shows a shiny new compact disk, under the heading: "Imagine if you'd invested in this when it was just an idea." A retro TV commercial portrays a brave mutual fund manager personally inspecting a factory where an early prototype jet aircraft was being produced. She asks the test pilot to take her up in the prototype. "But what if it doesn't fly?" someone warns. "Then we don't invest," she replies—quite happily prepared to put her life on the line for the sake of our RRSPs.

Of course, not all companies pass muster under the watchful eye of the fund managers, who possess the same rugged tenacity that in earlier decades was embodied in cowboys or private investigators. Another TV spot shows a team of investigators inspecting a factory. Poking around in a corner, a fund manager quietly pulls out a Swiss Army knife to scrape the grime off an old machine, and finds that it was made in the 1960s—far too old, it seems, for this factory to be considered a credible investment. The ad concludes with the team silhouetted against the setting sun as they stride quickly out of the financial life of this company. Don't worry, the ad suggests: our private investigators won't give any of YOUR money to inefficient, dirty companies like this one.

This strand of RRSP advertisements carries an implicit but important theme: an investment in a mutual fund is much more than just a deposit in a bank account. It is an active, productive, real contribution to the creative activity of real companies. Yes, the goal for individual investors is to get more money back than they put in. But the mutual fund industry portrays itself as doing this by putting money to "work" in real factories, inventing amazing new technologies and incredible new products like CDs and jet airplanes. This leaves customers with greater confidence that their paper investments have a solid foundation. And it leaves a more general impression—namely, that financial investments like mutual funds play a big role in economic growth and technological change.

Lots of Money

Canada's financial industry devotes millions of dollars to this annual blitz of RRSP advertising. One Toronto advertising executive estimated the annual spending on RRSP ads to exceed $125 million per year. In contrast, the federal government spends only about $200 million per year on the total cost of administering the entire Canada Pension Plan—a program that covers more than twice as many participants as do mutual funds.

Amazingly, then, it doesn't cost much more to administer a universal public pension program than it costs to *advertise* the private pension industry.[1] Yet the argument is still made that governments are "inefficient" when it comes to administering our money.

Even these hefty advertising costs, however, are just a drop in the bucket compared to the flood of money that comes pouring back to the mutual fund brokers. During the 1997 RRSP season, for example, Canadians purchased $25 billion worth of mutual funds in just three months. Enticed by a booming stock market, Canadians deposited a record $27.4 billion in RRSPs during the whole 1997 tax year—costing the federal government about $10 billion in foregone tax revenues, and costing the provinces another $5 billion.

Total investments in Canadian mutual funds have grown more than 700% during the 1990s, to an incredible total of almost $350 billion by the middle of 1998.

Indeed, the phenomenon of "personal investing" has become more than just a lucrative industry for the banks and brokerages which dominate it. It has become a powerful cultural force (see sidebar, *Ticker Tape*). In a bygone era, subway commuters opened their morning papers to check last night's hockey scores; now they are more likely to turn to the mutual fund listings to see if their personal funds rose or fell by a fraction in yesterday's trading.

Even young people are getting in on the action. In 1998, the *Globe and Mail* reported on the "young bulls" of personal investing—individuals in their twenties or even their teens who view their personal portfolios as defining features of their very personalities. Eschewing government handouts (which are pretty hard to get these days, anyway), this new generation of investors began building their stockpiles of personal wealth early, well-versed in the long-term magic of compound interest.

"My generation wants to be in charge of its own destiny," one 26-year-old investor stated bravely. This spirit of self-reliance is admirable—but our young investor has forgotten that the true destiny of his portfolio depends mostly on the unpredictable, uncontrollable swings of the stock market, not his own frugality and financial smarts.

A 1997 editorial in the *Financial Post* endorsed a pro-business campaign to teach economic "fundamentals" in elementary school, suggesting that schoolchildren could learn valuable lessons about stock markets through managing their own pocket money. Mutual fund powerhouse GT Global pitched in with a series of comic books and child-sized T-shirts featuring a financially savvy Henry Hedgehog. Henry cheers: "It's fun to have FUNDS with friends!"

In short, a financial juggernaut has rolled through Canada during the 1990s—with powerful economic, political, and cultural implications. Incredible new wealth has become concentrated in the hands of the financial industry. Indeed, the boom in RRSPs and mutual funds has been just the tip of this iceberg. The total financial assets of the country grew by almost $2 trillion between 1990 and 1997, a growth of over 60% in just seven years. For comparison purposes, the

Ticker Tape

One annoying manifestation of the modern culture of personal investing is the ubiquitous display of stock market tickers in all sorts of public places. Stock tickers list the three-letter trading symbol of a company (such as BNS for the Bank of Nova Scotia, or NTL for Northern Telecom), followed by its up-to-the-minute share price.

Given this code-language, only knowledgeable "insiders" can really understand the ticker displays—and, indeed, this probably explains much of their appeal to the initiated. Like carrying a cell-phone or hanging out in the executive lounge of an airport, knowing (and showing) that you can comprehend ticker displays helps to reinforce that smug sensation that you must be a really, truly important person.

Perversely, however, almost nobody actually looks at these ostentatious symbols of the omnipotence of the market. For example, right on the northwest corner of King and Bay streets in Toronto, a massive marquée has been erected outside the headquarters of the Bank of Montreal, whose multicoloured chrome- and-light display rivals any of those in Toronto's flashy theatre district. The display surely cost millions of dollars to build, and more to operate.

Current share prices and exchange rates flash endlessly along the marquée, 24 hours a day. But does anyone really think that the marquée constitutes a useful public service to the investing pedestrians rushing by outside? Consider the results of a recent (unscientific) survey: of the thousands of pedestrians who passed while this author watched the street-corner one busy noon hour in 1998, not one stopped to watch the marquée for late-breaking market news.

But no matter. Whoever decided to build that expensive sign was under no illusions that some red-suspendered trader, munching a hot dog on the street-corner, might one day spot an emerging investment opportunity and quickly rush back to his trading desk to seal the deal. The purpose of that sign, rather, is quite different: to create the impression in the minds of pedestrians that this bank is on top of market developments, and thus qualifies as a good place to store one's money. A side-effect of this and similar displays is the broader cultural understanding that is created: namely, that markets are everywhere, all-knowing, all-powerful, irresistible.

The casual restaurant in the lobby of Toronto's Sheraton Hotel is appropriately named "Traders Bar and Grill," and it features a 10-foot long moving ticker display hanging over the bar. While lunching there one day in 1999, this author didn't spot a single one of the restaurant's dozens of clients even give the monotonous lights a second glance. Why is it there? Image, pure and simple. With stock prices flashing uselessly in the background, perhaps the restaurant managers are promoting the idea that this is a place where important deals are made.

At least we can credit the Canadian Broadcasting Corporation with dispensing with the myth that anyone actually reads ticker displays. Some news broadcasts on CBC's Newsworld channel have a superimposed live-action stock ticker displayed to the right of the announcer. But the symbols are so small and fuzzy that no viewer can possibly read them. Why take up so much screen-space with information that is virtually useless even when it *can* be deciphered? Like the Bank of Montreal, the CBC clearly wants to promote the image of being top of all the news that matters— and, in an era ruled by the stock market, all news is business news.

size of Canada's entire economy (measured by our gross domestic product) grew by less than one-tenth as much during the same period.

By the end of 1997, the financial industry shepherded $171,000 worth of financial assets on behalf of each and every Canadian. (Have you got yours?) Millions of Canadians have entrusted their savings and their very futures to the realm of finance, hoping that good personal investing can offset the fear and insecurity they feel as a result of corporate downsizing, government cutbacks, and uncertain job prospects.

A powerful ideology of "playing the markets" has infiltrated every important decision our society now makes, ranging from how we'll pay for retirement, to how we finance our mortgages, right down to how we educate our children. For instance, the federal government's much-touted Millennium Scholarship program for university students will be managed by three groups of private bond-traders.

Underlying it all is the implicit faith that, when we put our money into play in those markets, we are in fact putting it to "work:" funding good companies, inventing new products (like compact disks and jet airplanes), and creating jobs, all the while generating a healthy return for the original investor.

Not Enough Jobs

The financial juggernaut which dominated Canada's economy through most of the 1990s stumbled badly later in the decade. Beginning with some seemingly unrelated events—big real estate losses for some Japanese banks, an increase in interest rates in the U.S. in March 1997, and the devaluation of Thailand's currency three months later—a disastrous storm quickly erupted in global financial markets that now operate 24 hours per day at the speed of light.

Trillions of dollars of paper wealth quite simply disappeared, as panicked investors stampeded back into the relative safety of government bonds in the major economies (especially the U.S.), abandoning higher-risk ventures in developing countries and the stock market.

Many economies—in East Asia, Eastern Europe, and Latin America—experienced Depression-like contractions of output and employment in the wake of this financial chaos. Others, like Canada, escaped with milder slowdowns. By early 1999, it seemed that the worst had passed in most of the industrialized world's financial markets; indeed, America's Dow Jones index was setting new all-time records again by January of that year, and other markets were close behind, seeming to signal that the Asian debacle was a mere hiccup. Nevertheless, the world's wild and destructive experience with the "down-side" of the financial roller-coaster has sparked a widespread questioning of the economic effectiveness of private finance.

Policy-makers will obviously be preoccupied with understanding the causes and consequences of the 1997-98 financial crisis, and doing what they can to prevent this catastrophe from occurring again. But the shorter-term ups and downs of the markets should not make us lose sight of a longer-term, more fundamental problem. Even when the private financial industry was doing *well*, its success was not being translated into growth and job-creation in the rest of the economy. In other words, even when stock markets were booming and Bay Street bonuses were sky-high, this financial success contrasted surprisingly with the continuing poor performance of Canada's overall economy.

Judging by numerous crucial economic measures, such as job-creation, growth in output, and household incomes, the 1990s were already the worst decade for the Canadian economy since the Great Depression, long before the effects of global financial chaos reached our shores.

Let's start with the crucial issue of employment and unemployment. Canada's official unemployment rate has averaged almost 10% during the 1990s. That's higher than in any other decade since World War II. In fact, average unemployment rates have steadily increased in Canada, decade after decade (see Figure 1-1). To make matters worse, the official unemployment rate significantly understates the true extent of joblessness. It excludes hundreds of thousands of Ca-

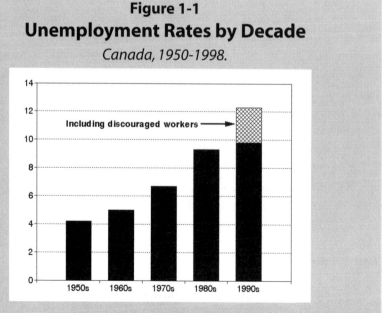

Figure 1-1
Unemployment Rates by Decade
Canada, 1950-1998.

Source: Author's calculations from Statistics Canada Catalogue, *Canadian Economic Observer*, and *Canadian Social Trends*, annual labour force estimates.

nadians who would like to work, but who have given up looking because of chronically poor job prospects.

This phenomenon of "discouraged workers" is evident in a long decline since 1990 in the proportion of adult Canadians who consider themselves to be part of the "formal" labour market—that is, either working in a job or else actively looking for a job. This rate, which economists call the *labour force participation rate*, fell from a high of 67.5% in 1989 to about 65% 1995, reversing a decades-long trend of increased work activity by Canadian adults.

The decline in labour market participation corresponds to the withdrawal of 600,000 potential workers from Canada's economy. If the official unemployment rate is adjusted to reflect this hidden pool of unutilized labour, the numbers look much worse: average unemployment of over two million throughout the decade, and an average unemployment rate of over 12%.

Even by the end of 1998, when the official unemployment rate finally slipped below 8% (its lowest level in a decade), the true rate of unemployment (counting these discouraged workers) was still in excess of 11%.

Another perspective on Canada's weak employment performance during the 1990s can be gained by looking at the slow rate at which new jobs were created. For starters, hundreds of thousands of jobs were destroyed during the 1990-91 recession—the result of very high interest rates, the fallout from the 1989 Canada-U.S. Free Trade Agreement, and global uncertainty arising from the Persian Gulf war.

This recession (which was much deeper in Canada than in the U.S. and our other trading partners) cast a pall over the whole decade. But even *after* the recession bottomed out in 1992, the pace of job-creation in Canada was historically weak, and much slower than during other periods of economic recovery. Employment expanded at an average rate of just 1.5% per year during the upswing of the 1990s, barely enough to keep up with our growing population, and just one-half the pace of job-creation during previous post-war booms.

And even this comparison probably makes the 1990s look better than they actually were for Canada's job market. To an unprecedented degree, job-creation in the 1990s was concentrated in part-time jobs and nominally self-employed occupations. Much of this nominal "self-employment" consists of marginal attempts at self-reliance by workers displaced from corporations and government—low-productivity, low-wage jobs like home-based sales or temporary contract work.

Between 1992 and 1998, close to one-quarter of all new jobs were part-time, and a full 40% were self-employed. Both of these job categories include many Canadians who would rather be working full-time in paying jobs; therefore, the official job-creation numbers once again significantly underestimate the true depth of the problem.

Table 1-1 **Financial Success versus Real-World Stagnation** Cumulative change in selected indicators, 1990 to 1997.			
In the Financial World:		**In the Real World:**	
Growth in financial assets per Canadian	47%	Growth in real Gross Domestic Product per Canadian	4%
Growth in the total stockpile of financial capital	61%	Growth in the total stockpile of real fixed capital	13%
Growth in market capitalization of the Toronto Stock Exchange	81%	Growth in total employment	6 %
Growth in after-tax profits of the five largest banks	101%	Growth in real disposable income per Canadian	-7%
Growth in average salaries, brokerages and investment banks	102%	Growth in average salaries, all industries	18%
Source: Calculated from Statistics Canada, *Annual Estimates of Employment, Earnings and Hours, National Balance Sheet Accounts, Fixed capital Stocks and Flows,* and *Canadian Economic Observer;* company annual reports; *Toronto Stock Exchange Review.*			

It is not just Canada's labour market which suffered during the 1990s. Other crucial indicators of economic well-being also paint a picture of prolonged stagnation and falling expectations. These gloomy indicators from the realm of real-world productivity, income, and living standards provide an incredible contrast with the booming world of finance, as summarized in Table 1-1. Adjusted for inflation, the value of the goods and services produced by Canada's economy (our GDP) barely grew at all during the 1990s, in per person terms: by a grand total of 3.8% between 1990 and 1997, for an average annual growth rate of just 0.5 percent.

Disposable income for Canadian households actually fell over the decade: after inflation, the typical Canadian had $1,300 less to spend in 1997 than they did in 1990, a decline of 7.5%. Job-creation inched along at a snail's pace during the decade—and so did the earnings of the average worker, which grew by 2.4% per year, barely enough to keep up with inflation.

In sharp contrast, the growth of sales, profits, and salaries in Canada's financial industry during the 1990s was nothing short of stunning. And, even in the wake of the 1997-98 financial downturn, it is still clear that the financial world has done far better than the real world. Clearly, the incredible 1990s boom in finance—the money flooding into mutual funds, the record-breaking performance of stock markets, the lucrative profits enjoyed by financial institutions, and the salaries and bonuses enjoyed by financial professionals—was not mirrored in the progress of the rest of the economy (see sidebar, *Follow the Bouncing Buck*).

Advertisements for mutual funds imply that this flood of money is soundly invested in real industries, creating innovative products like CDs and jet aircraft, and presumably generating good jobs in the process. But Canada's economic record suggests a schism between the hyperactive world of finance and the chronic fatigue of today's labour market.

The Two Worlds of Investing

How do we explain the contrast between the spectacular expansion of finance and the continuing austerity and pessimism of the rest of the economy? Canada has more money than ever before. Why isn't it being used to put Canadians back to work? What really happens to the gigantic sums of money flowing into the coffers of the banks and investment brokers? Where is the weak link in the economic chain that is supposed to connect financial investment with real-world economic progress?

This book is about investment. It will argue that Canada's economic system has been unsuccessful at translating its growing financial wealth into concrete, job-creating investments in real industries—and hence important changes will be needed in order to better put finance to work. To understand what has gone wrong with our system of finance and investment, we need to get more specific about what we mean by "investment."

Influenced by the annual barrage of advertising for mutual funds and other financial products, most people think of an investment as something they do with extra money they may have. [In fact, contrary to the advertising of the mutual fund companies, most Canadians do not have extra money to make personal investments; this problem will be explored further in Chapter 12.] The goal of a personal investment is simple: to get more money back, at some point in the future, than was initially invested.

This popular understanding of "investing" can be defined more precisely as a *financial investment*. Specifically, a financial investment represents the purchase of a financial asset (such as a company share, a unit in a mutual fund, a guaranteed investment certificate, or a savings bond) in the anticipation or hope of earning a monetary profit at some point in the future. The investor puts money up, for the sake of getting more money back. Money in, money out.

Economists, however, have something very different in mind when they think about "investment." In terms of the real economy, and its capacity to produce goods and services and support a real standard of living, investment has nothing to do with "money." In the economic sense, investment refers to the greater use of machines, tools, computers, buildings, or other real-world equipment in the course of day-to-day economic activity.

Why do we use these things (which we can think of broadly as "tools") in our work? Because they make us more productive. A farmer ploughing a field performs much more work using a modern tractor than using a horse-drawn plough, which in turn was more productive than a simple hand-held hoe. A typist using a modern word-processor can prepare many more business letters, with greater quality and accuracy, than with a manual typewriter, which in turn was more productive than old-fashioned manual typesetting or hand-writing.

Follow the Bouncing Buck

The RRSP ads make it seem as if every penny deposited into a mutual fund is destined for a wise, sound investment in an entrepreneurial but financially responsible company. The well-informed (and well-paid) research staff of each mutual fund select the best-managed companies with the most innovative products. That way, you know your money is not only earning a good return, but is also contributing to job-creation and economic progress.

In reality, however, virtually none of the hundreds of billions of dollars of government-subsidized mutual fund contributions ever finds its way into actual new investment spending by companies in the real economy.

To dramatize this, let's imagine an "average" RRSP investor in the 1990s. Call her Freda Frugal. Freda contributes an "average" amount—about $3,500 per year—into an "average" mutual fund (consisting of the same rough distribution between equities, bonds, and other assets as the overall universe of mutual funds). We will assume that she receives an "average" rate of return, based on the average experience of all mutual funds.

Between 1990 and 1997, Freda's fund grew to a total of $43,000, for an enviable average annual rate of return of about 12%. But, since RRSPs are subsidized by the federal and provincial governments, the actual personal cost to Freda was much smaller than the $3,500 annual contributions. If we assume that she received an "average" RRSP tax deduction of $1,400 each year, then her *personal* rate of return was much higher: over 25% percent per year. [In fact, most RRSP contributions are made by higher-income Canadians, who receive even larger tax subsidies for their investments, so this illustration is on the conservative side.]

This was clearly a good *financial* investment for Freda. But where did all the money actually go? How much ended up actually being employed in the production of important new products like CDs or jet aircraft? Was this investment an important one in real terms, not just financial terms? Did the investment pay off for *society*?

Don't forget that the mutual fund company deducts an "average" management expense ratio—equal to about 2.25% of her total assets each year—from Freda's account, totaling $3,800 over the eight years (or 13.5% of her total contributions). We also have to eliminate money that the mutual fund invested in government bonds and other investment vehicles that have no connection to real investment by Canadian businesses. Based on typical mutual fund holdings, only about 40% of Freda's account would have been invested in Canadian corporate equities (with the rest invested in bonds, money markets, foreign shares, and other assets).

The per-share value of the stock market portion of Freda's account grew rapidly during the 1990s, at an average annual rate of about 13%, and this powered much

In general, the more tools we use to assist us in our work, the more productive we will be—assuming, of course, that we are trained in how to use those tools efficiently. The entire process of economic development through human history has been driven primarily by the discovery and use of new technologies and new tools, which allow workers to produce more output with less human effort. These technologies almost always require the use of increasingly complex and expensive machinery, structures, buildings, and computers.

of the rise in the value of her overall portfolio. But most of that rise was due simply to the rapid growth in stock market prices (that is, the run-up in the value of existing equities), rather than to the creation of new real wealth by firms.

Between 1990 and 1997, for example, the total market value of the Toronto Stock Exchange grew by an incredible $647 billion. New issues of new shares by TSE companies during this time totalled just $86 billion, and much of that was offset by share retirements due to takeovers, mergers, and share buy-back programs. On a net basis, then, no more than 10% of the rise in the TSE's value during this time resulted from new equity actually being pumped into the market; the rest resulted from stock market inflation, pure and simple.

We can conclude, then, that about one-tenth of the equity purchases made by Freda's fund managers (which in turn made up just 40% of her total contributions) were used to purchase brand new shares, hence generating new funds for the coffers of real companies. In other words, just 4% of Freda's contributions were used to purchase new equities. But about half of all new issues sold on the TSE during this time were issued by banks, brokerages, income trusts, and other financial companies (see Chapter 3 for more details on this surprising trend). These firms are also players in the paper economy, rather than being producers of real goods and services which undertake real investments in the real economy.

Therefore, only about $560 of Freda's total RRSP contributions (or just 1.3% of the closing value of her portfolio) ended up as new cash in the hands of companies which undertake real investments, rather than financial ones. All the rest of Freda Frugal's investment was siphoned off in management fees, investments in non-business assets, inflated payments to the investors who sold their stocks to Freda's mutual fund, and investments in other financial companies. Stunningly, for every dollar that Freda provided to a real business, she provided $7 to the well-paid managers of her own mutual fund.

In short, the link between Freda's successful financial investment and real investment by the corporations she partly owns is so indirect and weak as to verge on being irrelevant.[1]

---

[1] Freda is still richer at the end of the day, despite the near-irrelevance of her financial investments to the expansion of the real economy. How is this possible? Largely because of pure inflation in the price of her securities (the rise in the market value of which is not matched by any underlying expansion in the real assets underlying those securities). Whether that higher paper worth ultimately translates into an ability by Freda to buy something of real value (after she retires, for example, and begins cashing in her account) depends on the willingness and ability of other investors to continue paying those inflated prices. As described in Chapter 13, the stability of this process, which increasingly resembles the Ponzi schemes of financial con-artists, is very much in doubt.

But these tools, so important to any job performed in our economy today, do not simply fall from the sky. They have to be produced in their own right. Indeed, there is a whole set of industries in the economy—called the *investment goods* sector—whose purpose is to produce the machinery, tools, buildings, and other sorts of equipment which in turn enhance the productivity of the people who work in other industries.

Therefore, it *costs* an economy something to use modern tools in production, as opposed to old-fashioned, "hand-made" techniques. Someone in the economy must first take the time and effort to manufacture the tools which are subsequently used to produce the other final goods or services which were desired in the first place. When a society takes something that it has produced, and doesn't immediately consume it but instead dedicates it as a "tool" for producing something else, then that society is making an investment—in the economic sense of the word.

Understanding Investment

One way to understand the real economic meaning of investment (as opposed to its financial meaning) is to consider an example of a real, productive enterprise. Imagine a farm that produces one commodity: corn. There are two things that can be done with that corn: it can be eaten (consumed), or it can be replanted as seed to grow new corn. When the farmer replants corn as seed to start a new crop, she is investing that corn (in the economic sense) instead of consuming it. A real commodity goes into the system: corn as seed. And a real commodity comes out: more corn. The investment is real, and so is its return.

Note that the farmer has to reinvest a certain share of her total output just to stay in business as a farmer. If the farmer consumed all of the corn she produced in any given year, she would have no seed left to plant the next spring, and her farm would collapse. Some investment is thus required simply to keep a business operating at its current level. Suppose that her existing fields produce 1,000 bushels of corn, and she must replant 100 bushels as seed for next year. She and her family can then consume 900 bushels over the year, setting aside 10% percent of the crop for replanting.

In economic terms, this investment is called *depreciation*: the amount of ongoing investment required just to offset normal wear and tear, and maintain a business in its current state.

But an ambitious farmer might actually be interested in expanding the farm, so that more corn can be grown on nearby land that is not currently being used. So, in addition to the 100 bushels required to replant the existing field, the farmer sets aside (or *saves*) an additional 50 bushels to re-invest in planting a second smaller field.[1] Now she and her family have only 850 bushels to consume. Their consumption must be smaller in the short term. But the pay-off will be extra corn production next year.

The farmer's total (or *gross*) investment is now 150 bushels of corn. But 100 bushels of that investment are required to offset depreciation. The other 50 bushels

To differentiate this concrete definition of investment from the financial investments discussed above, we will use the term *real investment*. Specifically, real investment refers to the current production that is set aside to be used as an input in the course of further production (rather than being consumed). There are many complex definitional issues encountered in trying to define real investment (some of which are pursued in more detail in Chapter 5). But the general principle should be clear: a real investment involves the decision to postpone the consumption of a share of the economy's current output, with the goal of increasing the level of production in subsequent periods through the use of more "tools" (see sidebar, *Understanding Investment*).

There are crucial differences between a financial investment and a real investment. The success of a financial investment is measured in terms of money: did the investors receive more money back than they originally advanced? The success of a real investment, in contrast, can be measured in terms of real output and productivity: did the investment allow some sector of the economy to

represent a *net* investment that contributes to actual economic growth: even more corn production in future years.

There's another way in which the farmer might invest corn in order to increase production—a more complex way, but one which will soon prove to be far more effective and important in economic growth than merely taking over more land. Suppose that over several years the farmer manages to set aside 200 bushels of corn, which she then gives as food to a skilled tool-maker for one year. During that year, the tool-maker manufactures a new plough for the farmer. [In a modern economy, the farmer would simply sell the corn for money, and then use the money to buy a new plough.]

By using the plough to make her own work more efficient and productive, the farmer might be able to increase the output from her first field to, say, 1,100 bushels per year. The 200-bushel investment is paid off with two years of extra production; the subsequent fruits of the farm's higher productivity are all "profit" to the farmer. By investing in a plough—which economists call *real capital equipment*—the farmer expands her future productive potential.

In the real-world economy, of course, the process of investment is vastly more complicated than it is on this farm. But the essential principles—production, consumption, saving, and investment—are all at play underneath the complex machinations of production, trade and high finance. Real investment is as crucial to the growth and well-being of the modern economy as it is for this farmer.

The core problem is that we have let money—and the financial institutions and conventions which create and control money—disrupt and confuse the link between real savings, real investment, and real productivity.

---

[1] In this particular example, the farmer's saving and investment are one and the same act. This is not the case in a modern monetary economy, in which saving and investment can occur at different times, and be undertaken by different agents. See Chapter 10 for a discussion of this distinction and its implications.

produce more final goods and services than it did using an older, less sophisticated method of production?

Of course, in a modern economy, even real investments usually have monetary values attached to them. For example, imagine that a company decides to invest in a new computer system to improve the efficiency of its widget assembly operation. The company pays for that computer equipment with money, and the company hopes to generate additional money by selling the extra widgets which come off the assembly line. If the extra money from the increased production more than offsets the cost of the computer equipment, then the investment is a monetary success for the company.

It is important, however, to keep track of the concrete economic relationships which underlie the firm's financial transactions: it was computer equipment (not money) which constituted the real investment, and it was greater production of widgets (not money) which was the favourable outcome of that investment. A financial investment is characterized by a process of money in, money out. In contrast, a real investment might be characterized as a process of "production in, production out."

There are many similarities between real and financial investments—similarities which add to the widespread confusion concerning these two distinct concepts. Both financial and real investments involve an up-front "sacrifice" in the interests of a longer-term gain. Both are often described as the outcome of smart, "frugal," self-restraint—whether individually or collectively.

An individual who invests money, instead of spending it on consumer goods today, is said to deserve a higher standard of living tomorrow; the same is said of a whole society which "lives within its means" and invests for the future. But, despite this common rhetoric of sacrifice and deferred gratification, financial and real investments differ markedly in their concrete economic effects. In particular, the well-being of particular individuals or groups can be improved by successful financial investments: getting more money back than was originally advanced. But the economic well-being of society as a whole requires successful *real* investment. In other words, without new tools, new productivity, and new jobs, the real economic standard of living of a society cannot improve—no matter how "bullishly" the stock market might be performing.

An analogy can be made to bets on a horse race. Some individuals will come away from the track richer than they went in, but some must also come away poorer. By definition, the economic well-being of the whole betting population cannot be improved: not everyone can come away from the track a winner. [In fact, losers must outnumber winners; the difference between losses and winnings represents the "take" of the race-track owner.]

Similarly, the ups and downs of the stock market—in and of themselves—must produce as many losers as winners. Without an underlying and vibrant process of real investment to increase the real productivity of the real-world economy, even the most sophisticated system of financial investment boils down to a high-tech parimutual game. Money may be redistributed from losers to winners, but the well-being of the collective is not increased and may even be reduced.

Like the owners of the race-track, the only consistent winners in this process are those who "own" the betting establishment—in this case, the money-managers and traders who pocket a healthy commission on each trade, win or lose. Understanding the links between financial investment and real investment, and developing policies which promote the latter (and not just the former), will be an important step in getting Canada's economy back on a strong, long-term growth path in the wake of its miserable performance during the 1990s.

Overview of this Book

This book argues that, while financial investments may produce profits, it is real investments which create jobs. And the chain of economic relationships which is supposed to link financial investments with real investments has been broken in many places. This helps to explain the ironic juxtaposition of Canada's booming financial sector with a lacklustre labour market, sluggish productivity, and stagnant or even declining living standards.

Once we better understand the importance of real investment to economic growth, and the failure of our current financial system to generate that real investment, then we can start to think about alternative investment systems which might be more effective in putting our money to work.

The rest of this book is organized into the following broad sections.

Part I, titled *Money in Motion*, further explores the difference between a financial investment and a real investment, and explains why real investments are central to the process of creating new jobs.

Chapter 2 explains the contrast between Canada's booming paper economy and the stagnant real economy.

Chapter 3 discusses the paper economy in more detail, and considers what it is that the financial industry actually *does*. Chapter 4 provides an overview of how a new job in the real economy is actually created, and the important role of real investment spending in that process.

Chapter 5 defines the concepts of "investment" and "capital," and introduces the different ways in which we can measure these important variables. It then discusses the economic benefits of real investment, and compares the words and deeds of different economic actors regarding investment and investment policy.

Chapter 6 then discusses the issue of real investment in relation to the small business sector, which *seems* to have been responsible for most job-creation in Canada in recent years. But it turns out that a crucial weakness of small business is precisely its lack of capital investment, and this accounts for many of the problems associated with small business employment: low productivity, poor compensation, and rapid turnover. Rejuvenating real investment—by big firms and small firms alike—is thus a crucial precondition for the creation of *good* jobs.

Part II of the book is titled *Slow Motion: How Investment Lost Steam.* It presents a range of empirical data showing a profound slowdown in real investment spending in Canada, starting in the early 1980s. This slowdown contrasts obviously with the boom in financial investment that has been experienced in Canada during the same epoch.

Chapter 7 portrays the extent of the investment slowdown.

Chapter 8 considers the various possible causes for this slowdown. Many of the factors that are often advanced as explaining slower investment (and hence slower job-creation) turn out to be not so important after all—such as the "globalization" of the world economy, or a supposedly "unfriendly" business climate. Other factors turn out to be critically important in explaining the slowdown: a turn to high-interest-rate anti-inflation macroeconomic policies starting in 1981, persistent unemployment and excess economic capacity since that time, and—surprisingly—a steady decline in corporate profitability.

Part II is the most technical section of the book; it can be skipped without loss of continuity by readers who are not interested in some of the economic details of the investment slowdown.

In Part III, titled *A Recipe for Stagnation*, the key factors which have contributed to the investment slowdown are explored in more detail. First we look at *interest*, and the impact of Canada's interest-rate policies on financial and real investments since the era of high interest rates began in 1981. Then we consider *savings*: the relationship between savings and investment, and whether or not real investment is held back by Canadians' poor savings performance.

Chapter 11 examines *profits*, and shows that corporate profitability has fallen substantially in Canada (contrary to the popular conception). This helps to explain the slower pace of business investment, and raises some difficult but important questions for those concerned with the seemingly increased power of corporations in Canadian society.

We consider *ownership* in Chapter 12, and show that the heavy reliance of Canada (and other "Anglo" countries) on stock markets and other mechanisms of "securitized" ownership has held back our real investment performance.

Finally, in a chapter on *fragility*, we look in more detail at the destabilizing internal logic of the financial industry, and explore the causes and consequences of its perpetual boom-and-bust cycle.

The concluding Part IV of the book is titled *Kick-Start: Putting Money Back to Work*, and it presents suggestions for policy directions that would contribute to revitalizing real investment and job-creation.

Chapter 14 synthesizes our understanding of the investment process and the gap between the financial and real worlds, and considers a range of policy measures that would help to put finance back to work in a "real" job.

Chapter 15 critically evaluates various proposals that have been advanced for making financial investment a more socially responsive undertaking—including ethical investment funds, so-called "labour-sponsored" funds, and the more pro-active use of pension monies by unions

Finally, one complete model for a new system of social investment and community entrepreneurship is presented in Chapter 16. This model provides one example of how the collective creativity, energy, and frugality of Canadians could be harnessed for the sake of job-creation and productivity, without being so dependent on the wheelings and dealings of private finance.

Part I
Money in Motion:
Investment and Job-Creation

Chapter 2
Money and Reality:
Canada's Two Economies

Canada's economy has had two personalities during the 1990s.

The realm of money and finance has enjoyed an unprecedented expansion of revenues, profits, and influence. Records have been broken and broken again: stock market values, bank profits, trading of bonds and equities, the growth of mutual funds and derivatives. The salaries and bonuses paid to top performers in the financial sector have reached astronomical levels. For those who live and work in this realm—centred around Toronto's Bay Street—things have never been better.

But for the rest of the economy, and the rest of Canadian society, the 1990s were unquestionably the worst decade since the 1930s. The growth of sales and employment in most non-financial industries has been slow and uncertain. Some important sectors (like the public sector and the construction industry) actually contracted through most of the decade. Unemployment has remained stubbornly and painfully high. Even workers who have kept their jobs have experienced continuing insecurity and stagnant earnings. The real purchasing power of household incomes has declined, even as the productive power of Canada's economy has grown.

According to economic theory, the inherent purpose of the financial sector is to act as an *intermediary*, or a lubricant, for production, sales, investment, and growth throughout the rest of the economy. In theory, finance plays a supporting role in the economy, making it easier and more productive for us to make and exchange the real things that our material life depends on. After all, money itself is supposed to be just a means to an end: we can't eat the paper that money is printed on, we can only use its symbolic and institutional spending power to transform that paper into the things that we really want.

Sand in the Wheels

"The banking system, chartered and private, was of little value to industry. In fact it was a positive hindrance."
—Tom Naylor
The History of Canadian Business 1867-1914

Money makes it easier for people and companies to trade goods and services, money makes it easier to account for the real productivity and profitability of industry, and money makes it possible for those with wealth to store their wealth in an abstract form (rather than in sacks of gold, jewels, or other precious items) and keep track of it. An economy without money is one which could never develop beyond the production and barter of very simple products within small regional communities.

Similarly, the financial industry does not actually produce anything of inherent value: we can't eat stocks and bonds, a derivative has no intrinsic artistic merit, and few money managers can fix your car's transmission. The financial industry exists, in theory, to lubricate the growth and development of those parts of our economy which *do* produce things of inherent value (namely, the goods and services on which our standard of living is based, like food, art, and transmission repair services).

The financial sector is supposed to link up individuals who save money with those who wish to borrow it—a macroeconomic match-making service. It is supposed to ensure that capital is invested in its most productive potential uses. And it is supposed to make sure that companies are managed in the most efficient and productive manner, by using the stock market to reward good managers and punish bad ones.

To the extent that the financial industry does indeed perform these useful and productivity-enhancing tasks, then finance "adds value" to the rest of our economy. But to the extent that its activities are irrelevant (or, worse yet, even destructive) to the rest of the economy, then the financial industry is inherently wasteful—no matter how well-paid its top employees or how rich its corporate coffers.

In reality, of course, the mystique and attractive power of money can indeed take on a life and appeal of its own, quite apart from money's role as an economic lubricant. Greedy people become infatuated with money, and try to accumulate it for its own sake. In the same way, the financial industry can take on a life of its own, independent of its intended role as a supporting player in the production and exchange of the goods and services we actually need and use.

Given the huge contrast that has emerged between the financial sector and the rest of Canadian industry in the 1990s, it has to be asked whether the eco-

nomic link which is supposed to join these two halves of our economy has been
broken.

The Two Faces of Canada's Economy

This chapter will explore the important distinction between the *financial economy*
and the *real economy*. [This distinction corresponds in many ways to the distinction between financial investments and real investments that was introduced in
Chapter 1.]

The financial economy (also called the "*paper economy*") represents the huge
industry that has developed around the creation, purchase, and sale of money
and other financial (or paper) assets: stocks, bonds, loans, mortgages, mutual
funds, derivatives, foreign currency, annuities. The wheelings and dealings of
the paper economy have an incredibly high profile. Daily fluctuations in stock
markets, bond prices, interest rates, and exchange rates are followed extremely
closely by economists, journalists, and politicians, and are often held to be a
barometer of the general well-being of the economy.

Yet, despite the apparent importance of finance, in a fundamental sense its
operations are *tangential* to the economic life of a country. This is because the
activity of the financial sector—its "output"—does not directly contribute to the
material well-being or productivity of Canadians. It is the *real economy* that
produces the products and services that contribute concretely to our material
standard of living.

The output of the real economy includes the things that Canadians consume
in their homes and communities (such as food, clothing, transportation, entertainment). It includes the products and services that Canadian governments or
public institutions generate through their operations (such as health care services and supplies, schools and textbooks, road construction). And it includes the
raw materials, spare parts, and machinery that Canadian companies must purchase in order to maintain and grow their businesses.

Most Canadians work in the real economy, and most "value-added" is produced there. If the real economy is not functioning well, then the real standard
of living of Canadians will suffer correspondingly. But Canada's real economy
has not done well at all in the 1990s. Real job-creation, real growth, and real
investment have all languished during the decade. The stagnant production of
real goods and services has failed miserably to keep up with the explosive growth
of finance.

Despite its high profile and overall political and economic influence, the
financial sector's contribution to real economic progress is actually quite unim-

portant—at least in a direct sense. To be sure, many Canadians are employed in the paper economy; a total of 500,000 people worked in the broader financial and insurance industries in 1997. But that accounted for less than 5% of the total paid workforce (see Table 2-1).[1]

And, far from creating new jobs during its period of most frenetic expansion, the paper economy actually *destroyed* jobs faster than in the rest of the economy. New banking technologies and other cost-cutting innovations have allowed the overall financial sector to downsize as fast or faster than any other segment of corporate Canada, despite its booming profits and paper valuations.

Similarly, the paper economy makes only a small contribution to Canada's overall GDP (the value of all the goods and services produced in the economy). GDP in the paper economy grew twice as quickly as in the rest of the economy during the 1990s. But even at the end of this period of hyperactivity, the financial sector still accounted for just 6% of total Canadian GDP. No, the paper economy is not primarily about generating real work and providing services of real value. Rather, the financial economy is driven by the urge to buy and sell paper. Huge profits can be generated in this pursuit, but not many jobs, and not many services of concrete use for Canadians.

In one particularly important area, the general unimportance of the paper economy to real economic growth is starkly visible. The financial sector undertakes almost none of Canada's real investment in machinery, buildings, factories, homes, and infrastructure. In other words, almost all of Canada's tangible, non-financial investment is undertaken by companies, individuals, and public bodies operating in the real economy. Just 6% of tangible investment was undertaken in the financial sector itself (in such forms as new office towers or computer systems for banks). This dramatizes the schism between the two worlds of investing that we considered in Chapter 1.

Financial investments (such as stocks, bonds, and mutual funds) are purchased and managed through the paper economy, and they have been booming. But the paper economy itself undertakes almost no *real* investment of its own. Therefore, there is no guarantee that the funds flooding into the paper economy will be translated into tangible, job-creating investments in real industries. For that to occur, the supportive, intermediary role of the financial sector must be fulfilled—and this is precisely what did not seem to be happening in the 1990s.

In the realm of paper and profits, however, the financial sector reigns supreme. Business profits are disproportionately high in the paper economy. About one-quarter of all business operating profits were generated by the financial sector in 1997, and one-fifth of all after-tax business net income. Operating profits for banks and insurance companies grew by an incredible 200% between 1990 and 1997, four times as fast as profits in the real economy.

Table 2-1 **A Tale of Two Economies**		
	Paper *Economy*	*Real* *Economy*
"REAL OUTCOMES"		
Share total paid employees, 1997	4%	96%
Change in employment, 1990 to 1997	-2.6%	-0.5%
Share of total GDP (at factor cost), 1997	6%	94%
Share of total real investment, 1990 to 1997	6%	94%
"PAPER OUTCOMES"		
Share of business operating profits, 1997	25%	75%
Share of after-tax business net income, 1997	20%	80%
Growth of operating profits, 1990 to 1997	+200%[1]	+55%
Average rate of profit on equity, 1990 to 1997	13.3%[2]	5.5%[3]
Share of total business assets, 1997	58%	42%
Growth of business assets, 1990 to 1997	+75%	+31%
Share of business asset-creation, 1990 to 1997	71%	29%

Source: Author's calculations from Statistics Canada, *Canadian Economic Observer; Employment, Earnings and Hours; Quarterly Financial Statistics of Enterprises, Gross Domestic Product by Industry*; and *National Balance Sheet Accounts.* Paper economy includes broad finance and insurance industries (but excludes real estate), unless otherwise noted.
1. Banking and insurance only.
2. 5 major banks and 185 investment dealers.
3. Total economy.

Profits have been consistently higher in the financial industry than elsewhere in the economy. Canada's major banks earned an average rate of profit on their shareholders' equity of 12.9% during the 1990s, while investment dealers (stock brokers, investment bankers, and other high-finance participants) earned an average 17.8% on equity. On the other hand, return on equity in Canada's economy as a whole averaged just 5.5% during the same period.

Other "paper" measures verify the disproportionate size and influence of Canada's financial industry. By the end of 1997, the financial sector (which accounts for a very small share of total business employment and real GDP in Canada) accounted for a startling 58% of all business assets. The assets of financial companies grew by 75% between 1990 and 1997, versus a growth of 31% in the total assets of all non-financial businesses. During this time, the paper economy accounted for over 70% of all asset-creation by business in Canada. In other words, for every dollar of total investment by business (both real and financial) in the 1990s, over 70 cents of it occurred in the paper economy.

To further illustrate the different directions taken by the paper and real economies in Canada over the past decade, consider the following six "vignettes." Each of them highlights, in a different way, the growing gap between money and reality in Canada's economy.

Vignette #1: Financial Business and Real Business

Canada's private sector reached a turning point in 1990, one that would fore-shadow the growing dominance of finance that would characterize the rest of the decade. For the first time in history, the total assets of financial corporations in Canada exceeded the total assets of non-financial corporations. In other words, finance had finally become king; and, since its inauguration, the financial sector has never looked back.

Figure 2-1 illustrates the total assets of financial and non-financial businesses in Canada (both expressed as a share of Canada's GDP for perspective). In 1961, when Statistics Canada first started gathering this data, non-financial businesses had total assets of $80 billion, compared to total assets of $49 billion in the private financial industry. The relative importance of finance grew slowly but steadily during the next three decades until 1990, when the financial industry finally eclipsed non-financial businesses (with each owning, at the time, about $1.35 trillion in total assets).

In just seven years since then, the asset gap *between* the financial and non-financial spheres of business grew dramatically, to an incredible $650 billion. By the end of 1997, the total assets of financial companies equalled $2.4 trillion, versus about $1.75 trillion in the non-financial sector.

There is another way of thinking of this fundamental shift in the relative importance of the two sides of the economy. Remember that the financial sector

Figure 2-1
Total Assets of Canadian Corporations
1960-1997

Source: Statistics Canada, *National Balance Sheet Accounts.*

is supposed to be just a lubricant for the real production of goods and services. Back in 1961, it took about 60 cents worth of corporate assets in the financial industry to "lubricate" the creation of a full dollar of business assets in the real economy. By 1990, this ratio had grown to one-to-one: it took a full dollar of finance to lubricate each dollar of the assets of non-financial companies.

Today, our economy requires almost $1.40 in finance for each dollar of assets in real business. In other words, this "lubrication ratio" has more than doubled since 1961; Canada's economy has become dramatically more dependent on finance in its day-to-day operations.

When the owner of a car needs to put in a litre of oil every time she fills up her car with gas, she usually recognizes that something is wrong: her car is requiring far too much lubrication. The same is now true of Canada's economy. This financial lubrication is costly, we are injecting ever-greater amounts of it, yet the real economy is running more sluggishly than ever. It is definitely time for a tune-up.

Vignette #2: Book Value and Paper Value

Another startling feature of Canada's business community also reflects the huge schism between paper and reality. The decade-long boom in high finance drove up the stock market value of Canadian companies to an unprecedented degree. Markets retreated substantially during 1998, but recovered again in 1999. They will certainly finish the decade far richer than they began it.

For example, the total market value of the 300 largest firms on the Toronto Stock Exchange, which together account for about two-thirds of the value of all publicly-traded companies in Canada, soared by 105% between the end of 1990 and the end of 1997 (for an average annual growth rate of 11%). Factors contributing to this impressive performance by Canada's stock markets included declining interest rates, rebounding corporate profits, and the ongoing flow of new funds into tax-subsidized RRSPs and other pension funds.

But this rapid expansion in the market value of Canada's leading companies was not matched by equivalent growth in the underlying real value of those companies. Rising share prices did not primarily reflect new investment in tangible assets (such as equipment, factories, buildings, or land) by those companies. Rather, rising stock markets mostly represented pure increases in the share prices of those companies.

In other words, the rising TSE resulted mostly from a process of asset price *inflation* rather than from growth in the inherent value of the represented companies. Financial commentators usually rail against inflation as Economic Enemy No. 1. But it seems that stock market inflation is one type of inflation that does not cause the financial community to lose sleep.

As indicated in Figure 2-2, the book value of the 300 companies that make up the TSE's main index grew by only 21% during the same seven years—from the end of 1990 to the end of 1997. "Book value" is an accounting concept that measures the total capital that investors invest in a company, either directly (through purchases of newly issued shares) or indirectly (through retained earnings that are kept within the company, rather than being distributed as dividends).

For a non-financial business, book value will roughly equal the value of its tangible assets, recorded at their actual purchase costs, after deducting the company's net debt and other liabilities. In short, a company's book value will grow if it uses profits and other sources of funds to expand its real business through reinvestment in expanded facilities and equipment.

The book value of Canada's leading corporations grew very slowly through the 1990s, at an annual rate of less than 3% per year (or only about 1% per year after inflation). Yet the market value of these same companies grew by nine times as fast (after inflation). Put differently, for each dollar rise in the value of the TSE 300 between 1990 and 1997, just 21 cents was due to a rise in the inherent book value of the companies represented. The other 79 cents was due to stock market inflation, pure and simple.

There is another way of understanding this data. If a company is worth more on the stock market than it is worth on the accounting books, it is said to

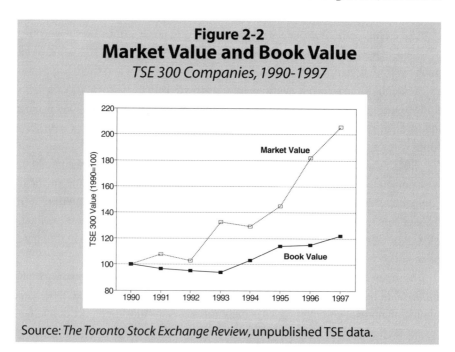

Figure 2-2
Market Value and Book Value
TSE 300 Companies, 1990-1997

Source: *The Toronto Stock Exchange Review,* unpublished TSE data.

trade at a market premium. This premium indicates that the company is worth "more than the sum of its parts." Thanks to good management, brand-name recognition among consumers, proprietary technology, or other assets, the company is worth more on the stock market than its actual tangible assets would otherwise suggest.

But the average market premium exhibited by Canada's leading corporations has grown exponentially during the 1990s. At the end of 1990, the TSE 300 companies were trading at about $1.25 for each dollar of book value. By the end of 1997, that premium had grown to over $2.00 per dollar of book value. The market premium on Canada's largest corporations had quadrupled—from 25% to over 100%.

It is impossible to believe that improved management and brand-name recognition, or other improvements in general business performance, can account for this rise. Clearly the market value of Canada's corporate sector has come unglued from its book value.

Vignette #3: Paper Assets and Real Assets

The shifting balance between the accumulation of real assets and financial assets by Canadian companies is mirrored in the changing composition of wealth in our economy as a whole (including the wealth of governments and individual households). Figure 2-3 illustrates the trend of Canada's stockpile of tangible, non-financial wealth—embodied in such forms as capital equipment, factories, buildings, physical infrastructure, homes, and land.

Measured as a share of Canada's economy, this non-financial wealth has held remarkably steady over time, at about 3.5 times the annual output of the economy as a whole. In other words, Canada's accumulation of real wealth has roughly kept up with our economic growth over the past four decades. Indeed, it is quite natural that real wealth and real output should rise in step: we need higher income in order to accumulate more wealth, while that real wealth itself contributes to the subsequent growth of incomes (thanks to the productivity of investments in assets such as factories, computers, and infrastructure).

In contrast, however, the growth of financial wealth has completely taken flight relative to the slow progress of the real economy. Like our real wealth, Canada's stockpile of financial wealth was roughly constant at about 3.5 times our GDP until about 1980. That was when Canada's top economic officials (in the federal government and the Bank of Canada) first adopted tough policies of high interest rates to slow down real growth and control inflation. Since that time (and particularly during the 1990s), the financial industry has boomed and the

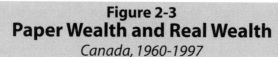

Figure 2-3
Paper Wealth and Real Wealth
Canada, 1960-1997

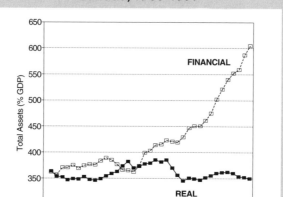

Source: Author's calculations from Statistics Canada, *National Balance Sheet Accounts.*

stockpile of financial wealth has risen steadily, in contrast to the comparative stagnation of the real economy.

By the end of 1997, total financial assets in Canada equalled some six times the value of our total GDP. In other words, until 1980 it took about $3.50 worth of accumulated finance to "lubricate" each dollar of GDP that our economy produced in any given year. Now it takes $6 worth of finance to "lubricate" a dollar of real output. Once again, it's time to stop the car, look under the hood, and figure out why it is requiring so much "lubrication."

The separate paths taken by real wealth and financial wealth in Canada highlight another problem. Prior to 1980, there was roughly one dollar in real wealth for every dollar of financial wealth in this country. In other words, it was safe to conclude that each financial asset had something "real" underlying it: a house, a factory, or a parcel of land. Since that time, however, the link between real wealth and financial wealth has been broken. By 1997, there were only 58 cents of real wealth underlying each dollar of financial wealth.

While many Canadians may look "wealthy" on paper, thanks to the growing value of their financial assets, the concrete value of that paper wealth is increasingly uncertain. Even the value of tangible assets can fluctuate over time, of course, but there is always something real underpinning it—land, buildings, equipment—that, if properly maintained, will retain some inherent worth. The same cannot be said of wealth held in the form of stocks, bonds, and other types of paper.

The great global fluctuations in stock market and foreign exchange values that dominated the economic landscape during the latter part of the 1990s are testimony to the fact that paper wealth can, when times are tough and markets break down, be worth little more than the paper it is printed on.

Canada's dramatically increased reliance on financial assets with shrinking real underpinnings leaves us collectively vulnerable to financial panics and collapse. Far from being a cushion for Canadians to fall back on when their incomes decline, this kind of wealth may be a fair-weather friend: likely to disappear just when it is needed the most (see sidebar, *What is Wealth?*).

Vignette #4: The Mirage of Financial Wealth

Another great irony related to Canada's growing stockpile of paper wealth is the fact that Canada collectively has not become any better-off in terms of its national net worth, despite the mountains of finance that have been built up in our bank accounts and mutual funds.

There is a curious aspect to financial wealth that will be familiar to anyone who has ever studied the "double-entry" system of book-keeping that is used by most accountants. Every new financial asset is indeed an *asset* (or positive value) for the person or company who buys it, but it also represents a *liability* (or negative value) for the person or company who issued it. For example, a bond is a financial asset. The person who owns it has the right to receive the initial investment plus interest back at specified time periods. The owner of the bond is in the "black." But that same bond is also a liability for the institution (usually a company or government) which issued or sold the bond. By so doing, they are promising to pay back the initial capital plus interest; they are in the "red."

The net wealth of the whole community is unchanged by the increase in financial assets which accompanies the creation of a new bond. Like the horse-racing track, some people go home richer, others go home poorer, but the community itself is no better or worse off.

The same is true of every other sort of financial asset. For example, someone who owns a share in a company, purchased on a stock market, has an asset. But the company which initially issued that share (in return for an investment of new equity capital, usually at some point in the distant past) has a liability. It transferred a small piece of the company's ownership to the shareholder, along with a promise to pay future dividends.

Similarly, a loan or mortgage is both an asset for the bank which approved it, and a liability for the customer who undertakes to pay it back. Even cold hard money itself is both an asset and a liability: an asset for the person who owns it, and a liability for the federal government (or, more accurately, the Bank of Canada, Canada's central bank) which has promised to guarantee that money.[2]

What is Wealth?

Easy come, easy go. That motto might aptly describe the creation (too often followed by the destruction) of financial wealth via the operations of stock markets, bond traders, and other financial intermediaries.

As shown in the text, there is little direct connection between the financial assets that Canadians have been accumulating at a record pace and the much slower accumulation of concretely valuable real-world assets (such as homes, land, or capital equipment). With a large and worrisome gap between financial assets and their real underpinnings, concern naturally emerges about the true value of the apparent wealth that so many Canadians are counting on.

During a time of crisis—when buyers suddenly become no longer willing to pay for financial assets what their owners thought they were worth—the near-imaginary nature of financial wealth becomes painfully visible.

For example, on October 1, 1998—a particularly bad day during the global financial panic of that year—world stock markets from Tokyo to Toronto lost an astounding trillion dollars' worth of their apparent value. In other words, financial wealth equivalent to about US$200 for every human being on the planet simply disappeared.

Of course, most of the world's citizens didn't own that much wealth in the first place, so they would hardly notice the disappearance of "their share" of it. Indeed, for perhaps a full third of the world's population, their per capita "share" of the wealth lost in a single day of trading was worth more than their income for an entire year.

The real companies whose share values plunged that day are still there, for the most part, and so are the real economic assets (machinery, mines, offices, technology) which ultimately underpin their share prices. So one could be forgiven for asking what had really changed between October 1 and October 2.

Nevertheless, the instantaneous disappearance of so much apparent wealth cast a pall over the sentiments and hence the spending decisions of companies and consumers around the world, with real economic consequences.

October 1, 1998 was just one bad day in a very bad week for one of Canada's flagship corporations: Northern Telecom Ltd. (or Nortel), a global manufacturer of telephone and electronic communications equipment. On September 29, the company held a briefing for the New York stock market analysts who report on the high-tech industry. Near the end of that briefing, Nortel's chief financial officer implied—apparently mistakenly—that the company's third-quarter revenues for 1998 would be lower than previously expected.

Analysts stampeded out of the briefing room, using cell-phones to instruct their companies to sell Nortel shares immediately. The company's shares fell by almost 25% in the next four days, cutting an incredible $9 billion from its market value (and from the paper worth of the investors who owned those shares, either directly or through their mutual funds).

It turned out that investors had little to worry about. Nortel's ultimate third-quarter earnings were acceptable, and the company's share price actually *tripled* over the next six months (quite contrary to the initial panic of the assembled analysts). When a company official bungles a news conference, the company must obviously expect to pay a certain price. But a *$9 billion* price? What is financial wealth, when so much of it can disappear simply because of the misinterpretation by a handful of investment advisors of a misstatement by a single corporate leader?

In short, the apparent growth of financial wealth is really a "wash" for the community as a whole. Each piece of paper issued becomes an asset for someone, but a liability for someone else—and hence the aggregate net worth of collective society is unchanged.

This basic fact is recognized in the design of official wealth statistics. Canada's total wealth is determined almost completely by its stockpile of real (tangible) assets. Only a relatively small financial adjustment is made for the country's net financial position with the rest of the world. Since Canada is a net debtor to the rest of the world (due to the foreign ownership of many Canadian companies and some of our government's debt), this adjustment for Canada's net financial balance is negative. Thus, Canada's total wealth at the end of 1997 equalled our stockpile of tangible assets (about $3 trillion) less just over 10% ($340 billion) for our net foreign debt.

Incredibly, then, the fantastic growth of financial wealth in Canada has had *no impact* on our bottom-line net worth as a nation. As illustrated in Figure 2-4, the stockpile of financial assets has grown rapidly since 1980 relative to the size of our real economy. Yet Canada's bottom-line net financial worth has remained roughly constant—at a slight negative value, equal to just over one-third of GDP, reflecting our net foreign indebtedness. And the growth of Canada's overall net worth (both financial and real) has actually slowed, thanks to the very slow accumulation of real assets.

If it hasn't contributed to our overall net worth, what does the explosive growth of finance actually represent? It means that more individuals and com-

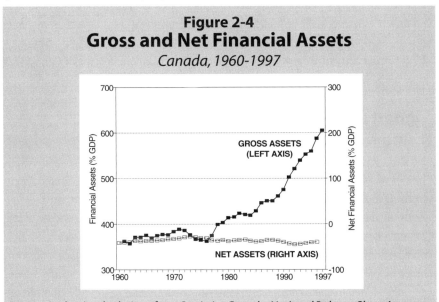

Figure 2-4
Gross and Net Financial Assets
Canada, 1960-1997

Source: Author's calculations from Statistics Canada, *National Balance Sheet Accounts.*

Table 2-2 **The Growth of Canada's Wealth** *Annual growth rates (percent per year)*				
	Tangible Assets		Financial Assets	
	Nominal	After Inflation	Nominal	After Inflation
1960s	8.6	5.5	9.8	6.7
1970s	14.4	5.9	14.2	5.7
1980s	7.1	1.1	9.5	3.3
1990s	3.1	1.1	7.0	4.8

Source: Author's calculations from Statistics Canada, *National Balance Sheet Accounts, Canadian Economic Observer.* Wealth series deflated by growth in CPI. 1990s average calculated to end-1997.

panies in Canada are shuffling more financial paper back and forth between themselves. It means that the business of managing that shuffling process—the business of bankers, brokers, traders, and money managers—has become bigger and more lucrative. It means that more Canadian individuals and institutions look rich on paper. But it has not translated at all into the development of Canada's real wealth, which has stagnated.

In fact, the accumulation of real wealth in Canada was slower in the 1990s than in any decade since statistics began to be collected: an average growth rate of just 3.1% per year, or just 1.1% per year after inflation (see Table 2-2). Meanwhile, paper assets have been piling up as fast as ever: almost five times as fast in the 1990s, after inflation, as the accumulation of real wealth.

Indeed, the emergence of a huge financial bubble—vast quantities of financial assets existing without an adequate underpinning in real assets—may have actually undermined the accumulation of real wealth, by creating uncertainty about the stability of wealth and by diverting the creative energies of Canadians away from more concretely useful economic undertakings.

Vignette #5: Disappearing Savings and Rising Net Worth

The net worth of Canada's household sector (that is, the aggregate personal net worth of individual Canadians) has been increasing more rapidly than the net worth of the Canadian economy as a whole.[3] We can verify this trend only for Canada's household sector as a whole. Some households, of course, have become richer, while others have become poorer. Unfortunately, Canada does not currently collect data on the distribution of wealth between households.[4] So we can only ascertain the overall trend, and not the differing patterns exhibited by different segments of the population. [The issue of wealth distribution will be considered in detail in Chapter 12.]

The growth in the net worth of Canadian households has been primarily driven by growth in the net financial wealth of those households (that is, the value of financial assets less the value of financial liabilities). Real household assets (represented mostly by ownership of homes and land) grew by 30% between 1990 and 1997, but net financial assets grew more than twice as fast: 63% over the same seven-year period. Net financial wealth now accounts for 45% of total household net worth, up from 35% in 1980.

The amazing thing about the growth of household wealth during the 1990s is that it has occurred despite an absolute stagnation in the income of those same households, and the consequent collapse of household saving (see Figure 2-5). Chronic unemployment, record-low wage and salary increases, and large cutbacks in government social programs all contributed to the very slow growth of personal incomes in Canada during the decade.

After inflation, in fact, real incomes per person in Canada were 5% lower by 1998 than they were in 1990—despite seven consecutive years of so-called economic "recovery." When the growing bite of taxes is taken into account, average real after-tax income declined by 7.5% during the same period.

Typically, the growing wealth of households has depended on their ability to *save* from their current income: pay off their mortgages, build up their savings

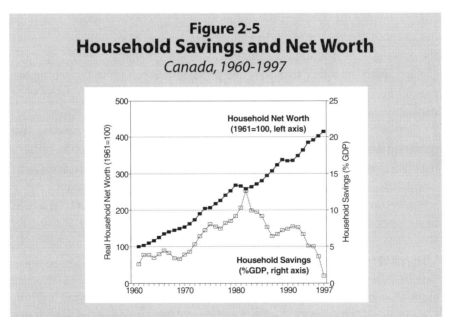

Figure 2-5
Household Savings and Net Worth
Canada, 1960-1997

Source: Author's calculations from Statistics Canada, *Canadian Economic Observer* and *National Balance Sheet Accounts*.

accounts or retirement funds, and purchase other assets. Indeed, as shown in Figure 2-5, until 1980 the growth of household disposable incomes and the growth of household net worth were closely correlated.

But, since 1980, during the epoch of finance, that link has been broken. Household incomes have gone nowhere. Household savings rates have collapsed as a natural result; in fact, by 1998 the personal savings of Canadians (as measured in our national income statistics) turned *negative* for the first time in our post-war history. [The causes and consequences of the collapse in personal savings are explored further in Chapter 10.] Yet paradoxically, household wealth has continued to grow.

How can household wealth be growing if Canadian households are no longer (on average) saving? Part of the answer lies in what statisticians would call a "composition effect." There are great differences between Canadian households, and these differences can be lost when we look only at an overall average. Statistics on income distribution suggest that, while average real incomes have declined in Canada, the incomes of the highest-income households have grown during the 1990s. Yet it is these same high-income households that account for the bulk of household wealth, especially financial wealth (as will be shown in Chapter 12). Most lower- and middle-income households don't accumulate financial wealth even in the best of times.

Growing incomes at the top of society, therefore, have financed the continued accumulation of wealth for those lucky households, despite the decline in overall average incomes and the evaporation of aggregate household savings. In this sense, the contrast between falling incomes and rising net worth reflects the growing maldistribution of income and wealth in Canada.

But there is another feature to the problem that relates to the schism between the real and financial sides of Canada's economy. The growth in the financial net worth of Canadian households has been driven by the explosive expansion of the financial sector during the 1990s: booming stock markets, skyrocketing asset values. But the stagnation of real household incomes reflects the corresponding stagnation of the real economy where most Canadians earn their living. Thanks to the booming paper economy, many Canadians look richer on paper, even though their real incomes have been falling. One doesn't have to be an economist to know that this illusion cannot continue forever.

Vignette #6: Of Brokers and Burger-Flippers

Statistics Canada publishes a monthly survey of employment and wage levels in Canada, titled *Employment, Earnings and Hours.* One section of this report provides an exhaustive breakdown of average earnings (for both waged and salaried workers) in about 400 different industries in Canada. If an interested reader runs a finger down the average weekly earnings column, it turns out that one particular industry ranks far above all the others in this detailed comparison. That industry is assigned number 741-749, and carries the rather innocuous title: "Other financial intermediaries."

Behind the Corporate Veil

Vignette #4 showed that Canada's net financial wealth has not grown, despite the explosive creation of new financial assets. But Vignette #5 showed that net financial wealth in Canada's *household sector* has indeed grown, despite the decline in average incomes. This leads to an interesting question: Why has the net worth of households been rising, while the net worth of the country as a whole has not?

It turns out that the rising net worth of individuals, which consists increasingly of financial wealth, is perfectly offset by the rising indebtedness of other sectors of our economy. We all know about the huge debt loads of our governments, which totalled some $568 billion (on a net basis) by the end of 1997. In fact, the debts of Canadian businesses are even larger: the business sector carried net financial obligations of almost $1 trillion at the same time.[1] These net financial debts almost completely offset the total real assets owned by Canadian businesses. On a bottom-line basis, their net worth is just $182 billion—or only 4% of the value of their total assets.

Who owns the wealth, then, if not the seemingly all-powerful corporations? Despite their economic power, corporations are beholden to the genuinely well-off individuals who "own" them (either directly through shares, or indirectly through loans and other forms of lending). Statistics Canada's official wealth statistics help us to lift this "corporate veil," which discreetly conceals the true nature of wealth in Canada. Despite their power, corporations are abstract legal entities which are not actually wealthy in and of themselves. They are, rather, the institutional vehicle of choice through which wealthy *individuals* conduct their economic affairs.

For this reason, many critics of the recent evolution of Canadian society are quite wrong when they place blame for conservative policy changes and the general polarization of our economy solely with large corporations. To be sure, those corporations are influential, and they constitute a powerful and self-interested constituency. But, in and of themselves, the corporations have no net worth: they are beholden to those who own them. If there is a fundamental dispute over the future direction of society, it is not so much between corporations and "the people." Rather, it is between the people who own corporations and those who don't.

---

[1] Interestingly, then, the net financial obligations of Canada's business sector are almost twice as large as the net debt of Canadian governments. It is seen as quite appropriate for private businesses to take on a certain level of debt in order to finance growth. When it comes to government, however, fiscal conservatives strangely demand a zero-debt strategy. The author is indebted to Myron Gordon for assistance in clarifying the discussion in this section.

In plainer English, this refers to a range of non-bank companies involved in Canada's booming paper economy: stock brokerages, mutual fund companies, and other financial investment specialists. This industry has the honour of paying the highest average earnings of any industry in Canada: just over $1,600 per week in 1997, or almost $85,000 per year. Keep in mind that this is an *average* figure only, and includes the much-lower wages offered to the secretaries, clerks, janitors, and other support staff who also work in this industry. The average income for the professional staff in this industry is well over $100,000 per year. And even this excludes the value of non-salary bonuses such as stock options, which can add hundreds of thousands of dollars to the total income of financial professionals.

Amazingly, there is no other industry in Canada which is even in a position to challenge the stock-brokers for top spot. The second-best-paid sector in the country (the oil and gas industry) lags almost 25% back of our leader, at a mere $1,250 per week (or $65,000 per year). Average earnings for "other financial intermediaries" in 1997 were 2.7 times higher than average earnings in Canada's economy as a whole—and eight times higher than average earnings in Canada's worst-paid industry (the food service industry, where weekly earnings average just $200).

Stock-brokers have always been relatively well-paid, of course, but their income advantage over other Canadian workers expanded rapidly in the 1990s. Figure 2-6 shows the relative growth of average earnings paid by "other financial

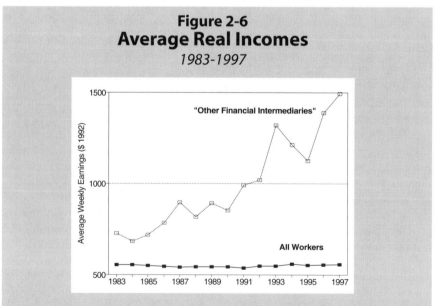

Figure 2-6
Average Real Incomes
1983-1997

Source: Author's calculations from Statistics Canada, *Canadian Economic Observer, Employment, Earnings and Hours*.

Market Rule

"Behind the abstraction known as 'the markets' lurks a set of institutions designed to maximize the wealth and power of the most privileged group of people in the world, the creditor-rentier class of the First World and their junior partners in the Third."

—Doug Henwood
Wall Street: How it Works, and For Whom

intermediaries," compared to average earnings in the economy as a whole, beginning in 1983 (when Statistics Canada first began gathering this data).

Throughout the 1980s, the stock-brokers typically earned less than 1.5 times as much as the average worker. This gap doubled during the 1990s, driven by booming salaries in the paper economy, as well as by unemployment and wage stagnation in the real economy. Little wonder that the best and brightest graduates of Canada's management schools head straight to Bay Street with their resumés. The financial industry can well afford to hire the most talented young minds that Canada produces. But society as a whole might be better off if we put this creativity and ambition to work on more important projects: finding better environmental technologies, cures for new diseases, or better ways to produce real goods and services.

Conclusion

The vignettes in this chapter have highlighted several of the ways in which Canada's paper economy has apparently become unhinged from the real economy which it is supposed to serve. The creation and sale of paper assets seems to bear less and less relationship to the creation and sale of the real goods and services on which our material life is based.

The accumulation of paper wealth has accelerated far beyond the accumulation of real assets which should underpin that wealth. Business has boomed, and incomes have soared, for those who manage paper assets. In each case, the gap between the paper economy and the real economy either opened up or widened dramatically starting in about 1990. This has truly been the decade of finance in Canada. Meanwhile, the growth and development of the real economy has been slower and less certain than at any time in the past 60 years.

Subsequent chapters of this book will explore in more detail how the artificial boom in finance has actually helped to undermine the process of real investment in capital machinery, equipment, and infrastructure that is so crucial to economic growth and rising living standards.

Chapter 3
What Does the Paper
Economy Actually Do?

October 1998 was not a month for the faint-of-heart, especially for anyone who reads the financial pages. The crisis that wracked world financial markets beginning in 1997 reached a turning point that month. In the wake of the default by the Russian government on much of its foreign debt, continuing turmoil in Asia, and signs that major investment houses in the U.S. and Europe might be brought down by huge losses in hedge and derivative trading, there was real fear that what had started a year earlier as a serious but regional crisis might become a truly global catastrophe.

Despite their supposed economic rationalism, many financial professionals superstitiously believe that October tends to be the "worst month" of the year for stock markets. The historic market crashes of 1929 and 1987 both occurred during October. What would October 1998 bring?

World finance ministers convened an emergency summit in Washington. The usually slow-moving U.S. central bank, the Federal Reserve, cut its main interest rate three times in six weeks to stabilize markets. Policy prescriptions which only months previously would have been dismissed as leftist claptrap began to be bandied about freely by Nobel prize winners and heads of state alike: emergency controls should be imposed to limit international capital flows; central banks should print money to bail-out shaky banks and boost the purchasing power of worried consumers; beleaguered debtors should declare unilateral moratoria on their obligations to international banks.

This represented an astounding intellectual turnaround. Global economic policy in the 1990s had been dominated by the so-called "Washington consensus," which demanded deregulation (especially financial deregulation) and public sector restraint in developing countries in return for financial support from the IMF and other international lenders.

Suddenly, in the wake of this most spectacular failure of private finance in almost 70 years, all bets were off. Even countries which had followed the Washington prescription to a fault (such as Mexico) were hammered by the panicked flight of investors buying U.S. dollars—fearing that *any* emerging economy, no matter how "responsible," could be the next Indonesia or the next Russia.

The panic even battered the currencies of smaller developed countries such as Canada, Australia, and Norway. In the wake of this unpredictable and destructive financial havoc, the free global reign that had been granted to private finance was open to serious question for the first time in decades. It was no longer accepted that the unconstrained, self-interested actions of the financial industry were even rational, let alone economically optimal.

At this critical juncture, Canada's *Globe and Mail* carried a front-page analysis by economics reporter Bruce Little proposing how the world might emerge from this financial mess. Ambitiously titled "How greed can save the world," the article described how global markets had been hammered by a sudden shift in the intangible, subjective sentiments of investors. In recent years, money had been sucked into hot markets—whether to the emerging economies in Asia or to conventional markets like New York's Wall Street—by "greed." The expectation or hope of rising prices motivated more and more investors to crowd in on the action.

This herd mentality in itself produced the rising prices that investors sought. But when "greed" turns to "fear," the whole process reverses itself. Fearing a downturn, investors try to make sure they are the first ones to bail out. In so doing, however, they themselves bring the market crashing down around them. Little quoted knowledgeable experts exhorting investors to rediscover a healthy sense of "greed." Only in this manner, the article suggested, could the crisis of confidence that had humbled world markets be resolved and reversed.

This almost metaphysical explanation of the global crisis was striking, for several reasons. Perhaps most notable was the fundamental acceptance by the quoted experts that the subjective emotional state of private financiers is an acceptable, logical, or at least somehow "natural" foundation on which to erect the institutional superstructure of global finance.

In the bizarre world of modern finance, the economic well-being of the entire human race seems to depend on mood swings among that small subset of the population which owns most of the financial wealth. Even more bizarre is that this state of affairs is not fundamentally questioned; discussion is limited to thinking about how to "cheer up" investors, how to once again stoke their hunger for vast but illusory paper gains.

One is reminded of the Queen of Hearts in *Alice in Wonderland*, who orders the beheading of selected subjects for trivial offenses, based solely on her daily mood. In analyzing this predicament, her poor subjects will understandably devote considerable energies to trying to predict (and where possible improve) the mood of their leader. But at some point they will want to ask a more fundamental question: why it is that one person's mood should determine whether they live or die?

Even if greed should replace fear, as the *Globe and Mail*'s experts fervently hoped, allowing financial markets to begin their ascent once again, it seems that a few other important questions remain unanswered. What is to stop fear from suddenly erupting again in the future? How many economies will be devastated in the next bad-mood panic? More fundamentally, can't human beings find a more predictable and efficient way of organizing important financial transactions than on the basis of primeval and unreliable instincts like greed and fear?

Strangely, the notion that existing private financial markets may *not* be fulfilling an inherently useful, economically efficient function has not infiltrated most policy discourse, even in the wake of the recent global calamity and the consequent broadening of the spectrum of economic debate. For example, that same *Globe and Mail* article described the economic *raison d'être* of the financial system in the following matter-of-fact terms:

Financial markets are the vehicle for money to get from people who save (call them creditors or lenders or investors) to people who want to invest in expanding their businesses or build the infrastructure to encourage economic growth.

What could be simpler? What could be more efficient and productive? The fact that financial markets demonstrate a repeated tendency to gyrate wildly between "greed" and "fear," causing massive dislocation and human suffering in their wake, should not divert readers from an understanding of the basic and supposedly useful function these markets play. We need financial markets to match savers with investors and thereby fuel the process of economic growth itself. Even in the course of explaining how the fate of the global economy was hanging on the subjective whims of private investors, the *Globe and Mail* could continue to report—as seeming self-evident fact—a textbook version of what it is these markets actually do.

Needless to say, the major players in the financial industry take a similarly rosy, self-important view of their own activities.

What does the stock market do? "The Toronto Stock Exchange is Canada's foremost capital market. As the centre for the issue and trading of Canadian equities and related investment products, it plays a vital role in the Canadian economy." Or so claims the Web page of the TSE.

What are banks? "Banks are society's financial intermediaries. Banks make a significant contribution to economic growth and national employment. Banks provide financing for Canadian businesses to produce their own goods and services, and help consumers to buy them." So says the Canadian Bankers' Association.

Barter in Asia

The expensive costs of financial intermediation are justified on grounds of the important role of finance in facilitating or lubricating real trade and investments. The parable for this function is the role of money itself: without money to act as intermediary between buyers and sellers, a modern economy would soon be mired in a sluggish and complex process of barter. A supplier with goods to sell would need to meet not just someone who wanted those particular products, but someone who simultaneously wanted to sell something in exchange that the initial vendor wanted. With money as the "middleman," a supplier can sell a product for cash to *anyone* who wants to buy it, and then use that cash in another completely separate transaction to buy something that they genuinely want or need.

The real problems of a barter system led to the invention of money centuries ago; but society clearly does not require anything like our modern hyperactive financial industry in order to enjoy the benefits of money. Ironically, the hyper-sophistication and resulting instability of modern financial institutions can even undermine that old, simple function of money.

For example, as a result of the collapse in Asian financial systems during 1997 and 1998, many still-viable real businesses in several Asian countries (including Korea and Indonesia) found themselves completely starved for cash. The inability to locate funds for even the most straightforward purposes—buying raw materials and spare parts, or financing valuable export shipments—meant that many of these companies had to shut down. This made the economic effects of the financial crisis all the worse.

One outcome of this widespread "credit crunch" was the spontaneous re-emergence of barter trade in Asia. Companies worked out arrangements in which they would trade their own products for another commodity, which they could then trade again to other purchasers or try to sell in world markets for hard currency. An industry of trade brokers sprung up, with a particular concentration in hard-hit Indonesia, whose sole function was to arrange and oversee these increasingly complex and tangled barter transactions.

The notion of conducting trade and investment in sophisticated industries on the basis of barter seems ludicrous; and the real inefficiencies associated with this type of intermediation are huge. Yet, perversely, it was discovered that even the oldest, simplest use of money—to facilitate real trade—could no longer be fulfilled by the speed-of-light financial system we have inherited at the end of the 20th century. Who is intermediating whom?

Even financial regulators seem to accept this description of the *raison d'être* of the paper economy. For example, the 1998 report of the MacKay Task Force on the Canadian financial services industry prefaced its review with a textbook profile of the object of its inquiries: "The effectiveness of any economy depends significantly on how well its financial services sector functions. Economic growth and job creation require the efficient intermediation of capital from savings to investment, and allocation of capital among investors."

Typical economics textbooks describe the process of financial intermediation in similar terms, as an essential and fundamentally productive task. Savings and investment are undertaken by different economic agents at different times and in different places. The efficiency of the whole economy is improved by a sophisticated system for channelling savings into investments. Some economists have even claimed that economies with more financial intermediation are the ones which grow faster.[1]

In the wake of recent global financial instability, not to mention the longer-run slowdown in the processes of real investment and capital accumulation that the financial industry is supposed to facilitate, it is worth questioning these claims at a very fundamental level. Of course, every modern economy needs financial intermediation. We need money to facilitate valuation, exchange, and accounting. And we need financial institutions which manage the flow of money and credit through the economy in an efficient and productive manner. But we must always remember that this service is not an end goal in and of itself. Rather, as its name suggests, financial intermediation is an *intermediate* function which is only valuable to the extent that it promotes some other inherently valuable outcome (such as real investment, production, or job-creation).

If we can produce as much or more real output while reducing our reliance on costly financial services and inputs, then our economy would become fundamentally more efficient. Of course, the notion that Canada's economy might actually be better off with a few less stock brokers is heretical on Bay Street. But in light of the contrast between our ever-more dynamic and sophisticated financial sector and the decline of real savings and investment in Canada, it is time to ask a very basic question: what does the financial industry actually *do?*

Do Stock Markets Raise Capital?

The stock market, of course, is the glamourous star attraction of the financial sector. This is where the shares of real companies (known as corporate equities) are bought and sold. The Toronto Stock Exchange (TSE) accounts for about 85% of the value of all publicly listed companies in Canada. The value of stock trading on the TSE during 1998 equaled a record $500 billion—an average of about $2 billion per business day.

The aggregate market value of all the companies traded on the TSE reached an all-time record of $1.4 trillion in April 1998 (or about one-quarter of all financial assets in Canada), before falling off in the wake of the global financial crisis. In 1998 about 30 billion shares changed hands on the TSE, nearly one-half of all the shares of all companies listed there. On average, then, the whole equity base of the TSE "turns over" every two years.

In short, the stock market is a place of frenetic buying and selling. Each stock trade generates new business (and corresponding commissions) for the brokers, money managers, analysts, and other financial professionals who carry such economic and political clout in Canada. But what is the connection between this hyperactivity and the real economy?

In theory, the stock market is supposed to be a sophisticated system for raising new financial capital for private businesses. A new or growing company will issue new shares, each representing a small piece of the company's ownership. The net worth of a company is called its "equity," hence company stocks are also called "equities" since each share represents a tiny share of a company's net worth.

Individual investors buy the new shares, in the anticipation that they will receive dividends from the company's future profits, and also that the price of their shares will rise as time goes by. These two sources of profit—dividend income and a rising share price (or capital gain)—constitute the total return which lures prospective investors.

Canada's tax system provides added incentive, since both dividend income and capital gains are taxed at a lower rate (for most investors) than other sources of income (such as wages), further enhancing the after-tax rate of return on stock market investments. [See sidebar: *The Subsidized Casino*.] In this manner, the stock market is supposed to be the intermediary through which the savings of individual private investors are channeled into the coffers of companies, which in turn put that money to work in real business undertakings.

The picture is complicated, however, by the fact that issues of new shares actually constitute only a tiny fraction of total stock market activity. Most of the buying and selling that occur on the TSE and other stock markets represent the exchange of already existing shares from one owner to another. The company whose shares are being traded is not involved at all, and receives no proceeds from this after-market activity.

New issues of shares are actually a rather infrequent event on the stock market. During the 1990s (up to mid-1998), new issues sold (or "floated") by TSE-traded companies accounted for just 5% of the value of all shares bought and

What's It All About?

Number of TSE-traded firms which issued 10,000
or more new shares to acquire new assets in 1998:   262

Number of TSE-traded firms which issued 10,000 or
more new shares to compensate executives in 1998:   655

Number of TSE-traded firms which eliminated 10,000 or more
shares through buy-back programs or takeover bids in 1998:   283

sold on the TSE during that same time. In times of market turbulence, new issues virtually cease altogether, since companies and investors are unwilling to shoulder the risks associated with launching new shares when the whole market might tumble at any time.

During the last four months of 1998, for example, following the Russian bond default and other global turmoil, just 17 new share issues were floated on the Toronto Stock Exchange, compared to 80 new issues during the same period of 1997. Those 17 new issues raised $2.4 billion, equivalent to barely a single day's share trading, or some 1.5% of total TSE activity during that tumultuous autumn.

Even these numbers *overstate* the importance of the stock market for the financing of new investment projects. From the total value of new issues, for example, we must deduct the value of existing shares that are regularly repurchased and then retired by companies (through mergers, acquisitions, or share buy-back programs). In the first half of 1998 alone, 148 TSE-traded companies announced that they were buying back their shares, including major firms such as Canadian Pacific, Imasco, Imperial Oil, and most of the major banks (compared to just 93 companies which issued new equity on the TSE during the same period).

A share buy-back is often announced during periods of stock market weakness, when a company wants to support the value of its share price (by reducing the outstanding supply of its shares). The fact that executive compensation is now closely linked to share prices (through the prevalence of stock option plans and other market-based incentives) might also have something to do with the popularity of share buy-backs among CEOs. In some periods, the net supply of equity capital represented by the stock market can actually *shrink*, when these share retirements outweigh the value of new issues.

Moreover, not all of the funds raised by new stock market issues are connected to real investment projects in the real economy. In many cases, the money raised when a company issues new shares is used to buy out the stake of the company's existing owner. For small businesses entering the stock market for the first time, the existing owner is usually the entrepreneur who first started the company. As often as not, "going public" by issuing shares to the stock market is a convenient and potentially lucrative "exit strategy" for that entrepreneur: a means of converting their existing sweat equity in the company into cold hard cash. These pay-outs may be an important motivating factor in the dynamics of small business development; for example, the founders of numerous small high-technology companies have become instant multi-millionaires in recent years when their newly-issued shares zoomed to lofty stock market heights, or when they received special "dividend pay-outs" from their companies prior to going public. But that is quite distinct from the process of raising money for new investment.

Another large share of the funds that are raised on stock markets is dedicated to the creation of cutting-edge *financial* instruments, rather than being put to use in the *real* economy. In this manner, a sophisticated and expensive financial institution—the stock market—is used to lubricate the expansion of still more sophisticated and expensive layers of financial activity, and the process becomes ridiculously circular.

For example, one of the most popular new financial products during the booming mid-1990s were known as "income trusts." These are equity-like assets sold by existing companies on the stock market. They reflect the capitalization (or securitization) of the future income stream that is expected to be produced by an *existing* productive asset (such as a hotel, a coal mine, or a gas pipeline).[2]

Income trusts were intended to be a relatively low-risk form of stock market investment that provided steady income (in the form of dividends) to their purchasers. There was also a tax incentive behind the popularity of income trusts; since they are not technically "corporations," they do not have to pay corporate income taxes.

As an investment vehicle, income trusts were considered an appropriate way for companies with a more-or-less steady income profile to convert that future income into an up-front sum of cash. In reality, however, many investors did not fully understand the risks that were still associated with income trust units, and were unpleasantly surprised during 1998 when the collapse in world prices for coal, oil and gas, and other resource commodities drove down the value of most income trusts.

The trusts quickly lost their lustre, but while they were "in fashion" they accounted for a large share of new equity issues in Canada. But the conversion of an existing productive asset into an income trust does not represent any new *real* investment in the Canadian economy, since the productive asset itself is unchanged by the transaction. The rise of income trusts, far from representing a new way to match "savers" with "investors," actually represented a process of pure financial entrepreneurship. Some clever brokers invented a new form of paper asset, and profited mightily from its design and initial sale. But the rise (and fall) of income trusts had almost no connection to growth or investment in the real economy.

Similarly, a large proportion of other equity issues during the 1990s represented new shares in red-hot financial companies themselves: mutual fund dealers, hedge fund managers, holding companies, and other investment specialists. These issues raised new capital for their sponsoring companies—and commissions for their underwriters. But those financial companies do not themselves engage in the production of real goods and services in their own right. So again, these equity issues represent another case of finance fuelling still more finance, rather than facilitating real growth and job-creation.

Another important source of new stock issues in the 1990s has been the privatization of Crown corporations and other previously non-profit firms (including some cooperatives such as the Saskatchewan Wheat Pool and the Surrey Metro Savings credit union). In line with the general tendency by governments to favour downsizing and private-sector-led development strategies, a number of major public companies were sold to private investors during the 1990s, usually by issuing new shares on the stock market.

Companies sold off in this manner have included Air Canada, Petro-Canada, Canadian National Railway, and Manitoba Telephone; indeed, the $2.3 billion sale of CN Rail by the federal government in 1995 still constitutes the largest single public offering of shares by any corporation in Canadian history.

Once again, these privatizations generate valuable business for the brokers who handle the share issues, and they also offer a potentially lucrative investment opportunity (since governments, anxious to make the privatization look "successful," typically price the new shares far below their true value).[3] But the connection between these issues and new investment undertakings in the real economy is unclear at best.

Newly-privatized but long-standing companies are sold lock, stock, and barrel by government to their new owners; the company may not even retain any of the newly-raised funds, which are handed over instead to the government vendor. Indeed, many troubled Crown corporations are sold off precisely so that private owners (rather than more politically-sensitive governments) will preside over their downsizing and retrenchment. The privatization of the Cape Breton Development Corporation, announced by the federal government in 1999, is a classic example of this strategy. It is hard to believe that new share issues related to privatization, despite their importance to the stock market, will produce sudden bursts of investment spending by their newly-rationalized sponsoring firms.

In sum, hardly any of the activity of the stock market has any direct relationship to the stated function of raising capital for real industry. New equity
issues account for no more than 5% of the day-to-day operation of the stock
market. And even a good portion of these new issues has nothing to do with real
investment projects undertaken by companies which produce goods and services in the real economy.

Consider the major new equity issues undertaken by Canadian companies
during 1995, 1996 and 1997. Fuelled by the great bull market of the 1990s, this
three-year period constituted the biggest rush of new equity financing in the
stock market's history. If there was ever a time to measure the stock market's
contribution to economic growth, this would be it. And, since each new issue of
equity generates a valuable bundle of new business for the underwriters, law-

The Subsidized Casino

Nothing symbolizes the economic and cultural power of capitalism more
than the stock market. The stock market—with its bulls and bears, its top-hatted
executives, its wining and dining—is the epitome of the self-made entrepreneur. How ironic, then, that the modern stock market is actually a major benefi-
ciary of government aid. The following table summarizes some of the expensive government subsidies that benefit the stock market:

Public Subsidies to Stock Market Activity		
Program	Effect on Stock Market	Cost to Federal Government
Dividend tax credit	Taxes dividend income at a lower rate than other income (like wages); enhances after-tax return on stock market investments.	$995 million per year
Partial taxation of capital gains	Provides exemption from taxes on a share of profits received from capital gains (including rising prices for stock market investments).	$1.0 billion per year
Capital gains, small business	$500,000 lifetime capital gains exemption for shares in small businesses.	$620 million per year
Treatment of stock options income	Executive stock options gains are treated as capital gains rather than income.	$115 million per year
Deduction of carrying charges	Allows deduction of investment-related costs (management fees, interest costs, etc.).	$590 million per year
Registered Retirement Savings Plans (RRSPs)	Defers taxes on money contributed to RRSP investments, and on income derived from those investments.	$11 billion per year
Registered Pension Plans (RPPs)	Deduction for contributions to workplace RPPs, and tax sheltering of investment income of the plans.	$10 billion per year
GST exemption, financial services	Investment-related services (brokerage fees, etc.) are excluded from GST.	$150 million per year
Canada Pension Plan reform	Starting in 1999, new CPP premiums will be invested in commercial securities markets, providing a major boost to share prices.	$60 billion or more over 10 years
Source: Dept. of Finance, *Government of Canada Tax Expenditures 1998*, Alternative Federal Budget. [1]		

[1] The author is particularly indebted to Hugh Mackenzie for assistance with this table.

	Table 3-1				
	Gross Funds Raised Through New Equity Financing				
	Canada, 1995-1997				
	Resource & Income Trusts	Finance & Holding Companies	Privati- zations	Other "Real" Business	TOTAL
Number of Issues	70	58	5	216	349
Total Funds Raised ($billion)	$12.8 b	$10.1 b	$5.4 b	$37.7 b	$65.9 b
Share Total Funds[1]	19%	15%	8%	57%	100%

Source: Author's calculations from Financial Post Datagroup, *Record of New Issues*.
1. Total does not add to 100 due to rounding.

yers, analysts, and brokers who oversee its birth, the flood of new issues was a major source of the booming business—and bonuses—which Bay Street experienced during most of this time. [In fact, the high overhead cost of equity financing is another of its fundamental weaknesses: up to 10% of the total funds raised through a new issue will be siphoned off in various administrative costs associated with the exercise.]

Table 3-1 provides a breakdown of those funds which were raised from new equity issues in Canada between 1995 and 1997. Surprisingly, just over one-half of the gross funds raised through new issues was collected by private companies active in the real economy. The rest of the new funds were raised to support various types of financial intermediaries (especially income trusts, which alone accounted for one-fifth of all funds raised), and through the privatization of existing Crown corporations and other non-profit firms.

The funds raised on Canada's stock markets by companies active in the real sector thus account for less than 10% of the total real investment spending by Canadian business during this same time—and that is before deductions for brokerage and underwriting fees, and payments to existing owners of the companies in question.

The stock market is obviously an important institution in Canada's economy, and its ups and downs have broad ramifications for real businesses. But the stock market has much less to do with the financing of real investment and growth than its proponents claim.

How do companies pay for their new investment projects, then, if not through the stock market? In fact, Canadian companies fund the vast majority of their investment projects through their own internal cash flow—that is, from the cash generated by their own ongoing operations. As shown in Figure 3-1, internal financing typically accounts for about 95% of gross fixed investment expenditure by Canadian businesses. This process of internal financing will be explored in more detail in Chapter 10 (dealing with national savings). In fact, corporate cash flow (consisting of both retained profits and depreciation expenses, which are deducted from a company's profits to reflect the cost of worn-out capital equip-

ment) constitutes the most important single source of *national* saving, accounting for about one-half of total domestic saving in Canada through the 1990s.

The very notion, therefore, that the expensive process of stock-market-based
financial intermediation provides an essential link between savers and the companies which undertake real investment projects is already looking somewhat
questionable. As far as business is concerned, the saver and the investor are for
the most part one and the same entity: the corporation which generates cash through
its existing business, and then allocates that cash to its new investment projects.

In financial theory, there should be no relationship between a firm's internal cash flow and its investment spending: if an enterprising firm has a good
investment idea, it should be able to raise money for that project independently
through the "efficient" intermediation of financial markets. In practice, however, there is a very close link between corporate cash flow and investment spending. Most modern theories of business investment have focused on the importance of internal cash flow as a determinant of corporate investment projects.[4]

This all suggests that, despite the hype associated with today's hyperactive
stock market, it does not function, first and foremost, as a vehicle for channelling capital from flush personal investors to growing real companies.

Do Money Managers Pick Winners?

The fastest-growing segment of stock market activity has been the booming mutual fund industry. A mutual fund is a means through which numerous investors

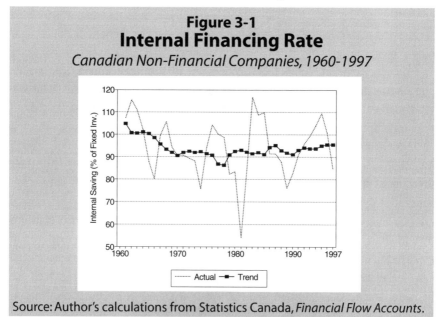

Figure 3-1
Internal Financing Rate
Canadian Non-Financial Companies, 1960-1997

Source: Author's calculations from Statistics Canada, *Financial Flow Accounts*.

Permutations and Combinations

Number of companies listed on the Toronto Stock Exchange, end-1998:	over 1,300
Number of mutual funds in Canada, end-1998:	over 2,000

pool their funds, providing for a larger base of finance, which can then be used to hire professional investment managers and diversify the investors' combined portfolio. It is a way of reducing and pooling risk. The cost for this risk-reduction, however, is the management cost associated with running the fund.

The first mutual fund was formed in Canada in 1931, but the industry didn't really start booming until the late 1980s. By 1998, over 2,000 Canadian mutual funds were in existence, with an accumulated total of $325 billion in total assets. Up to 40% of that total (or about $125 billion) is invested in Canadian stock markets. The rest is invested in a variety of other types of assets, including government bonds, short-term money market assets, and foreign investments.

Despite their high profile, therefore, mutual funds only account for about 10% of total holdings of corporate equities in Canada. Most stocks are still owned directly by individuals, primarily—as will be shown in detail in Chapter 12—by a small proportion of very well-off families. Nevertheless, the convenience and lower risk of mutual funds have certainly helped to "popularize" stock market investing, and this has accentuated the trend away from traditional savings deposits in favour of so-called "personal investing."

It is now estimated that approximately 35% to 40% of adult Canadians have made some kind of mutual fund investment, although for most Canadians the amount of money invested remains small.

The job of managing the money invested in mutual funds has become a multibillion-dollar business. Each mutual fund levies a management fee on its clients, which is charged as a share of the client's total investment each year. This is true even of so-called "no-load" funds, which do not charge any initial commission when an investor first puts up money; these funds still charge an annual management expense fee.

Annual management fees vary with the type of mutual fund being considered. In 1998, the typical Canadian equity mutual fund (invested in Canadian corporate shares) charged an annual management fee equal to 2.35% of total assets. Fees for specialty funds—such as those focusing on smaller companies, labour-sponsored venture funds, or international mutual funds—can be much higher. For bond-based or money-market mutual funds, management fees are lower, presumably reflecting the less intensive research and analytical functions required for these types of investment.

All told, the mutual fund industry charged management fees in 1998 of approximately $7 billion. To put this in perspective, the Canada Pension Plan (CPP), which covers twice as many Canadians as mutual funds, costs only about $200 million per year to administer. In other words, it costs the government less than 3% as much to administer a virtually universal pension plan as it costs the private money management industry to manage a program that covers only a minority of Canadians.

Mutual fund management fees account for about three-quarters of a percentage point of Canada's entire GDP, and are thus more important than each of the following industries in Canada (measured by their respective contributions to our total GDP): forestry, mining, steel production, machinery manufacturing, aerospace manufacturing, railway transport, and pipelines.

A large and well-heeled community of money managers, analysts, and advisors has sprung up, concentrated in Toronto, and funded by these hefty administration tithes. Indeed, so many mutual funds have been designed that there are now considerably more mutual funds in Canada than there are companies listed on the Toronto Stock Exchange. Some mutual funds even invest in different combinations of the shares of other mutual funds. The permutations and combinations of investments served up by the mutual funds industry—each one with its own secret philosophy for how to beat the market—now far exceed the complexity of the stock market itself.

It is interesting how financial investors will rail against any measure that erodes a portion of their accumulated wealth, whether it be a small Tobin tax on internatonal financial transactions (equal to perhaps 0.05% of asset value), or an annual tax on accumulated wealth (of perhaps 0.1% per year, which would put Canada on par with most other industrial countries in terms of its level of wealth taxation), or even a small uptick in the rate of inflation (which eats away the real wealth of financiers).

Yet investors quite voluntarily cough up amounts dozens of times greater than these supposedly onerous taxes through their annual management expense fees. Surprisingly, surveys indicate that three-quarters of mutual fund owners don't even know the meaning of the term "management expense ratio" (which is the percentage of their assets which they forfeit each year in fees to their money managers). The mutual fund industry prides itself on its efforts to promote a more "educated investor," yet most investors don't even know what their management fees are, let alone understand whether they receive good value (in terms of investment decisions) for those fees.

Amazingly, the economic evidence indicates overwhelmingly that mutual fund managers, on average, actually do more harm than good. Returns on most mutual funds consistently fall below the average rates of return generated by the "benchmark" markets in which those mutual funds compete. Consider, for example, the *Financial Post's* roundup of 1998 mutual fund performance. Of the 295 large-cap and diversified Canadian equity funds listed there, just 109 (barely one-third) matched or beat the total return of the Toronto Stock Exchange's top 300 index for the year.

On average, these mutual funds (with total assets of $80 billion) lost more than 3% of their unit value in 1998; that was almost twice as large as the 1.6% decline in the TSE 300 total return index. That negative differential translates into a loss to investors of $1.1 billion, compared to what they would have received had they simply "bought" the TSE 300.

This underperformance is repeated over time and across markets. For example, out of 177 large-cap and diversified U.S. equity funds in the *Financial Post* roundup, just 21 (or 12%) matched or beat the 1998 rise in the major U.S. stock market index, the S&P 500. And over time, the TSE 300 total return has outperformed the average Canadian equity mutual fund in seven of the past ten years. If an investor had put $1,000 per year over the past decade into the TSE 300, rather than actively managed funds, they would have had $19,275 by 1998, instead of $17,360 in the typical mutual fund.

Why do investors purchase mutual funds, when the evidence overwhelmingly suggests they underperform stock market averages? Many investors have obviously been asking themselves this question, especially in the wake of the poor financial returns that accompanied the global financial crisis of 1997 and 1998. "No-brain" index funds—which invest in baskets of stocks mirroring major stock market indices like the TSE 300, rather than picking and choosing between individual companies—have grown steadily in popularity, in large part because their administration fees are much lower (as low as 0.25 per year).

A new financial product called "index participation units" can do the same thing for no annual management fee whatsoever, ensuring that investors will precisely match the overall return of the market. An investor simply pays a one-time commission up-front to a broker who purchases a bundle of stocks exactly mirroring the weighting of the stock index in question (such as the 35 largest companies on the TSE).

Strangely, the growing popularity of index-related investment products implies that a company's share price can receive a major boost just by virtue of being included in a major stock market index. For example, there was fierce jockeying among Canada's largest companies to be included in a new index (dubbed the TSE S&P 60) which the Toronto Stock Exchange introduced in 1998. This competition was not solely because of the added public profile which might be generated for companies included in the index; in fact, most investors have no idea which firms are included in which stock market indices. More importantly, real demand for the shares of companies included in the new index would be strengthened by the demand of investors who want to be sure they "match the market." Needless to say, when a company's share price depends on the purely arbitrary construction of statistical indices, this casts further doubt on the idea that stock market prices are an accurate indicator of corporate efficiency.

Despite this evidence, however, actively-managed mutual funds still constitute the lion's share of the mutual fund industry: about 95% of mutual fund assets in Canada, and slightly less in the U.S. (where no-brain index funds have been more popular).

Why do investors continue to pay high mutual fund fees, even though mutual fund returns consistently fail to justify those hefty expenses? Investors seem to view mutual funds in the same light as less well-heeled Canadians look at lottery tickets. Even though the expected return on a lottery ticket is always negative—that is, on average, purchasers will receive back less in winnings than they pay for tickets—lottery players continue to hope that they will be the exception. *Their* ticket will be the one that pays off. In the same way, purchasers of mutual funds hope that *their* money managers will be among the few to beat the market.

And that is why the industry devotes such effort to advertising the supposed investigative and analytical skills of their managers. By showcasing money managers as modern-day private investigators—scraping the grime off machines in neglected factories, leaping into the cockpit for test flights of prototype aircraft—the money management industry aims to shore up the blind faith of millions of small investors that their management fees are well spent.

The failure of mutual fund managers to actually earn their large salaries is proof of more than just an ongoing disservice to their clients. It also throws cold water on the important claim that the stock market—by rewarding efficient companies and punishing inefficient ones—is an efficient means of allocating capital among competing investment prospects.

The stock market, in theory, raises capital for real investment. And successful companies with high share prices get the cheapest capital on the stock market (because their new issues are the easiest to sell). We have already seen that raising new capital is almost irrelevant to the stock market's true activity. And now we have seen that the high-paid analysts whose informed judgments are reflected in stock market trends cannot keep up with market averages.

Years of ruthless corporate downsizing and government cutbacks are supposed to have cut the "fat" from our economic system. Yet here is an industry which spends $7 billion per year on money management fees, with absolutely no positive economic outcome. The supposed rationality of the financial industry is once again open to question.

Can Banks Change?

The biggest players in Canada's financial industry, of course, are the five major banks. The proposed mergers among four of those banks—the Royal Bank and the Bank of Montreal in one marriage, and the Toronto Dominion Bank and CIBC in the other—focused public attention on the banking industry for over a year, until the federal government turned down the mergers late in 1998.

Most public debate centred on whether the larger merged banks would hold too much market power, thus undermining competition and reducing service in the consumer banking business. Ironically, however, even prior to the mergers the major banks had indicated a definite shift in the emphasis of their activities away from bread-and-butter neighbourhood banking services: managing household chequing services, maintaining personal savings deposits, and issuing residential mortgages. These traditional banking functions were already being downplayed in favour of higher-profile (and higher-profit) activities elsewhere within the booming paper economy. In fact, an examination of the evolving nature of the banks' true business provides an interesting insight into the changing face of finance in Canada.

Canada's banks have faced growing pressure from competing segments of the financial business. The growing popularity of mutual funds and the blossoming of the culture of "personal investing" have deprived banks of much of their traditional base of household savings deposits. Fierce competition from "near-banks" (such as trust companies and credit unions) has pushed down profit margins in traditional neighbourhood banking services. And sophisticated new forms of investment banking and underwriting have undercut the high-margin services of the banks to their corporate clients.

Faced with pressure in most of their traditional business areas, Canada's banks responded like any other large corporation under attack: they bought out the competition. Thus, the 1990s saw a wave of takeovers as established banks acquired major competitors, ranging from trust companies to stock brokerages. Today the largest brokerage houses in Canada are each owned by a major bank. This process of simultaneous concentration and diversification has allowed the major banks to rebuild and consolidate their overall share of total financial assets (the chartered banks together account for about one-sixth of all financial assets in Canada), after some earlier slippage in the 1980s.

The banks were further helped by a macroeconomic environment during the 1990s that was tailor-made for bank expansion and profitability. Low inflation, low nominal interest rates,[5] and slow but continuing economic growth (and hence a low rate of default by lenders) all assisted the banks in pushing new loans out their doors as fast as possible.

The bottom-line result: the five largest Canadian chartered banks expanded their total assets by an incredible $700 billion (or 150%) between 1990 and 1998. At the same time, the banks also radically reoriented their businesses, away from the bread-and-butter savings-and-loan activity that had been their mainstay, in favour of more high-tech, high-margin niches of the booming paper economy.

In 1990, almost three-quarters of the banks' total assets were held in the form of traditional loans. By 1998, that ratio had declined to barely one-half. Indeed, 1998 was a watershed year in the banks' effort to remake themselves in the image of the modern casino economy. That year, for the first time, the non-lending business activities of the five largest banks exceeded their net interest income from traditional lending (see Figure 3-2).

This massive reorientation of the fundamental business of these huge corporations paid off in spades. Between 1994 and 1997, the five banks collectively set a new all-time profit record with each passing year. Coincidentally, the size of their profits happened to match the last year of each fiscal year in question: $4 billion profits in 1994, $5 billion in 1995, $6 billion in 1996, and $7 billion in 1997. [The numerologists and other quacks who populate the broader community of stock market "analysts" must have had a field day with this result!]

These nice round numbers couldn't keep growing forever, of course, and the record-breaking trend was broken in 1998 when the five banks' collective profits

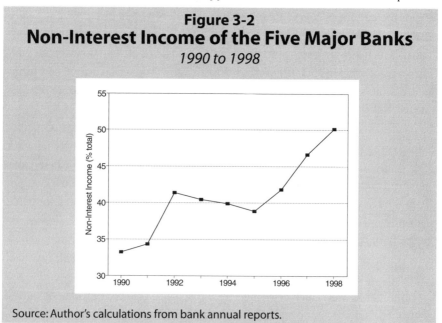

Figure 3-2
Non-Interest Income of the Five Major Banks
1990 to 1998

Source: Author's calculations from bank annual reports.

fell to "only" $6.7 billion, mainly thanks to losses on securities trading associated with the global market turmoil of that year. Nevertheless, every one of the banks earned over $1 billion in after-tax net profit for the year (it used to be extremely rare for a Canadian corporation to earn a billion dollars in a year, but no longer), and three of the five set all-time profit records.

The Royal Bank, with a 1998 net profit of $1.82 billion, is even closing in on the $2 billion mark; in 1999 it may be the first publicly-traded company to earn a profit (excluding extraordinary items) in excess of $2 billion in Canadian history. During the five years between 1994 and 1998, the five banks earned a cumulative average return on their shareholders' equity of almost 15%. Businesses are typically doing very well to earn a rate of profit on equity of 10% in a good year, let alone for several years in a row.

These five banks alone accounted for approximately 12% of the total after-tax corporate profits generated in all of Canada during that period. And the banks' cumulative return on equity is by far the highest over time of any major sector of the Canadian economy.

A breakdown of the banks' total revenues and sources of profit in 1998 provides an interesting insight into the changing nature of their fundamental business. This information is summarized in Table 3-2. The largest area of bank revenue is still the net interest income generated by bank loans to home-owners, consumers, businesses, and even governments. This represents the income received by banks on those loans, less the interest paid out by the banks on savings deposits and loans which the banks themselves take out, less an allowance for losses and defaults on non-performing or "bad" loans.

This is the area of the banks' business that perhaps comes closest to the traditional description of financial intermediation as a process of matching savers (those who have excess funds they can deposit in the bank) with investors (those who need to borrow those excess funds). It might seem as if the bank simply sponsors a convenient meeting-place for these disparate constituencies: customers with excess money deposit it in the bank, and the bank (after carefully scrutinizing the credit-worthiness of competing applicants) lends that money out to the best prospective borrowers.

But this is not actually how the banks' savings-and-loans business works. If the banks relied on individuals coming in to deposit existing surplus funds before they were able to extend that money in new loans (which would presumably be limited by the amount of deposits on hand), the banks would be a fraction of their existing size. Instead, banks are actually allowed to *create* new loans far in excess of the funds they have on hand from initial depositors.

A bank starts with a certain injection of funds (from the bank's owners, in the form of equity, as well as from its first depositors). It can then issue loans equal to several times the value of that initial money, on the assumption that not all of the banks' clients will come in to demand their money back at the same time. When that occurs, in what is known as a "run" on the bank, the bank cannot convert the paper accounts of its customers into real cash, and the bank usually collapses like a house of cards (unless government regulators step in to ensure the value of deposits).

Banks get a further boost for their expansion of loans when most of those initial loans are redeposited into the banking system—either by the customers who borrowed the money, or by individuals or companies who received that money second-hand when the bank's initial customer used their loan to purchase a product or service, thus putting new money into the pockets of individuals and businesses who had nothing to do with the initial loan. Banks can then re-lend this additional money out to additional customers, starting the whole process over again.

In fact, larger banks have a better chance of receiving back more of these "downstream" or "recycled" deposits, leaving them with all the more power to create still more new loans. Even banks which don't receive a healthy share of those downstream deposits can actually borrow money from other banks to allow for the continued expansion of their own lending.[6]

Table 3-2 **Sources of Bank Income** *Five largest banks, fiscal 1998*		
	Income Source ($ billion)	Share of Total Income (%)
Traditional Lending		
Interest income	67.0	
Interest expense	46.2	
Loan loss provision	2.2	
Net interest income	**18.5**	**49.4**
Non-Interest Income		
Banking and credit card service charges	4.9	13.1
Investment banking	6.5	17.5
Wealth management	2.4	6.3
Trading and derivatives profits	2.1	5.5
Insurance and other	3.1	8.2
Total non-interest income	**19.0**	**50.6**
Source: Author's calculations from bank annual reports.		

This process of creating new loans—called the creation of credit—is actually the source of most new money in the economy. Actual printed or coined currency accounts for a small share of the total money in circulation in Canada (only about 5% of the broadly-defined money supply in 1998). The rest is composed of deposits of various forms in banks and other financial institutions, now including mutual funds and other non-bank companies.

The engine pushing this explosive but fragile process is the power of the banks to create new loans far above and beyond the actual cash they have received from the savings of their customers. It is therefore not an exaggeration to claim that banks literally have the power to create money. This power is embodied in the charters which banks receive from the federal government, and which they must utilize according to the terms of the Bank Act.

This process of ongoing credit creation is absolutely central to growth in any modern economy. It fuels the spending power of both households and businesses, and facilitates job-creation during times of expansion. This is one aspect of the paper economy which is directly and centrally relevant to the functioning of the real economy. In this sense, credit creation is almost like a public *utility*: it is a fundamental service that must be provided before almost anything else can occur in the economy.

Private banks have been granted the power by our governments to perform this essential (and lucrative) task. To be sure, they must do this carefully and efficiently: they must screen borrowers carefully to avoid excessive defaults, and they must compete successfully for market share among banking consumers so that they can maximize "downstream" deposits and hence their power to create new credit by recycling those deposits. So merely holding a bank charter is no guarantee of super-profits. Still, it is the unique power of banks (and similar non-bank financial institutions) to literally create credit out of thin air that is the key ingredient in their incredible financial success.

This credit-creating power is conceptually quite distinct from pure intermediation, in which a bank merely positions itself between two parties and assists in the exchange of existing resources between them. In reality, banks are actually *creating* the resources, not simply facilitating their exchange.

Net interest income on this lending and depositing business has declined markedly as a share of total bank revenues over the past decade, and now accounts for just under one-half of total revenues. Moreover, the interest rate "spread" collected by banks—the gap between the interest rates charged on loans and the interest rates paid out to depositors—has also declined, from a difference of as much as three percentage points in the late 1980s to two points or less by the late 1990s.[7]

Both these trends are symptoms of the broad structural pressures faced by the banks in the 1990s. Fierce competition for the bread-and-butter banking business drove down profit margins on basic lending. And the shift by households away from traditional savings accounts in favour of mutual funds and other forms of "personal investing" undermined the extent to which initial loans could be recycled (through what economists term the "money multiplier" process) several times over.

It was these pressures that pushed the banks to enter other financial service businesses (such as mutual funds and investment banking), as well as moving more aggressively into global financial markets. For example, all of the five major banks invested heavily in takeovers of smaller banks and other financial institutions in the U.S. and other countries during the 1990s (but sometimes, as in turbulent 1998, with disastrous consequences).

A breakdown of the various sources of non-interest income is also provided in Table 3-2. About 13% of total bank income, or close to $5 billion in 1998, is provided by service fees collected by banks for their basic consumer banking services (such as account management, statement processing, cheque clearing, and credit card fees). These activities are part of traditional banking, of course: indeed, the provision of these mundane, concrete services is as close as banks come to directly providing a real service that is actually "consumed" by Canadians. Service fees have increased in recent years, sparking much ire among bank consumers.

Consumer activists focused largely on service fees during the debate over proposed bank mergers in 1997 and 1998, claiming that greater concentration of the banking industry would lead to higher service fees. Ever-larger banks would take advantage of their increased market power to gouge their customers. This complaint was well-intentioned, but misguided. In fact, the increase in bank service charges in recent years actually reflects the growing *competitiveness* of the banking industry.

In previous years, economically-comfortable banks would subsidize the cost of basic banking services through a small portion of the income that they collected on their lending business. In the 1970s and early 1980s, it was not uncommon for basic banking services to be free of charge, even for customers with small balances and no mortgages or other loans from their bank. These basic expenses were financed from a portion of the "cream" siphoned off from the banks' lending business. But, as the banking industry became more competitive, banks could no longer afford this practice (which economists call "cross-subsidization").

Specialty lenders, which did not have to bear the cost of the expensive personal banking services offered by banks, could undercut the interest rates charged on mortgages and other loans, stealing much of this traditional business away from the banks. So banks were forced by increasing competition (not by a lack of competition) to begin charging full-fare for their basic personal banking services.

Consumer activists are quite right to be concerned about access to basic banking services for poor people, young people, and residents of certain underserviced regions of Canada; banks and other lending institutions should be required to offer low-cost services to these constituencies as a condition of their license to bank.[8] But there is no evidence that consumers, in general, are being "soaked" by banks through basic service charges; indeed, most reports indicate that banks still do not collect enough service charges to fully cover the cost of the basic but costly services which are provided in return. Hence it would be quite wrong to conclude that bank mergers would lead to increased service charges. And the converse assumption—that retaining a supposedly more "competitive" market structure with numerous smaller banks would lead to lower service charges—is equally unjustified.

Most of the banks' non-interest income is now generated by a range of businesses related to the creation, management, and trading of paper assets in private financial markets. Close to one-third of the banks' total income now comes from a variety of activities related to the management of existing wealth rather than to the creation of new credit. This includes high-level investment banking, brokering mergers and acquisitions, profits earned from the trading of securities and derivatives, and fees collected for the management of mutual funds and other investment portfolios.

In these functions, the banks are positioned more genuinely as "intermediaries," in which they act as middlemen between the owners of various financial assets and the companies and other end-users which need access to those assets. This growing income from wealth management represents the fruit of the banks' efforts to climb aboard the paper boom, and reorient their business away from the important but mundane supply of credit to real businesses and real consumers. Indeed, the banks which have positioned themselves most effectively to profit from the paper boom are the ones most in favour with shareholders and investors.

Of course, an investment in any of the major banks paid off handsomely during the high-flying 1990s; propelled by soaring profits, share prices for the large banks rose far faster than for other companies, not to mention the healthy dividends that are paid out each quarter to bank shareholders. But those banks with the greatest emphasis on investment banking, wealth management, and other forms of paper activity—such as the Toronto Dominion Bank, with its highly successful discount stock brokerage—have been the hottest tickets in the eyes

Buying or Building?

Rather than go to the trouble of building up new business activities through new investments, many companies find it more profitable to grow simply by taking over other existing firms. The sums of money spent on mergers and acquisitions have exploded through the 1990s. Indeed, a turning point in the "buy or build" debate was reached in Canada in 1998. That year, the value of Canadian corporate takeovers soared to $148 billion, up 47% from the previous year, and an all-time record. [This total does not include the two huge proposed bank mergers which were turned down by the federal government late in 1998, nor the Canadian portion of global mergers by firms with major investments in Canada–such as Exxon's takeover of Mobil, and the merger between Chrysler Corp. and Germany's Daimler-Benz.]

For the first time ever, Canadian companies spent as much on mergers and acquisitions as they did on real investment in machinery, equipment, factories, offices, and new homes. Real fixed investment expenditure by business totalled $149.7 billion for the year, up by a rather less spectacular 7%.

Since takeovers involve the simple purchase of an existing company and its facilities, there is little connection between mergers and the growth of real investment (and real jobs) in Canada's economy. For the financial industry, however, the distinction is irrelevant: financiers earn healthy commissions for brokering mergers (up to 2% of the value of a successful merger, which can translate into hundreds of millions of dollars for a successful large deal).

Brokers are also needed to facilitate the loans and new share issues which accompany mergers. So, for the paper economy, the boom in mergers and acquisitions is simply more of a good thing.

of stock market investors and analysts. Indeed, by early 1999, the stock market value of the Toronto Dominion Bank—the smallest of the big five in terms of assets—actually surpassed that of the much-larger Royal Bank, making it the most valuable bank in Canada.

In summary, then, Canada's major banks have indeed changed radically during the 1990s. Their new focus on wealth management and paper trading has little to do with the allocation of real capital to real economic undertakings. Their older, less profitable function—the creation of new money to finance the expenditures of households and non-financial businesses—still plays a crucial role in facilitating real economic growth and job-creation. In fact, to the extent that the attention of the banks is unduly distracted by the lucrative but fleeting profits of paper asset trading, their ability to continue to perform this more mundane but crucial task may be impaired. As will be discussed further in Chapter 13, lending to households and businesses can be cut back dramatically by banks which have incurred big losses in other more speculative lines of business.

And even when it is performed well, this essential credit-creating function of the banks does not really accord with their self-depiction as "intermediaries." Banks do not, for the most part, match thrifty savers with cash-hungry investors. In their basic lending business, which has declined to now account for only about one-half of their total activity, banks literally create new money to finance real economic growth. And this crucial function is more the result of society's collective willingness to grant banks their unique financial capacities than it is the product of the ingenuity and productivity of the bankers themselves.

Does the Financial Industry Match Savers with Investors?

The image of a macroeconomic match-making service, in which savers with spare money are hooked up with clever and productive investors who need it, is pervasive in both academic descriptions of financial intermediation and in the self-promotion of financial institutions. In reality, however, the degree to which spare funds are funnelled across and between different sectors of the economy is actually quite modest.

We can think of Canada's real economy as being composed of three general sectors: non-financial companies, private households, and government. Companies receive income from their business activities, and require discretionary funds to support new investment projects. Households receive income from employment (including self-employment), income from personal investments, and various government programs (such as pensions or unemployment insurance). They require discretionary funds to finance major purchases (such as homes), and to provide for future retirement income (on top of whatever income they will receive from government and workplace pension plans). Governments receive income from current tax collections; they may require discretionary income to fund deficits (which occur when the cost of government programs and interest payments exceeds incoming tax revenue).

Given these complex flows of funds, what role does the financial industry truly play in mediating the contrasting financial requirements of different sectors in different parts of the country? In other words, how hard is it to match savers with investors, channelling discretionary funds to those economic players who can put them to work? This task may not be nearly as demanding as is typically implied in the economics textbooks or the corporate mission statements of major financial institutions. For, in reality, the vast majority of "savings" are generated in exactly the same sectors of the economy in which they are ultimately "invested"—and often by exactly the same economic actors.

Consider the sectoral distribution of savings and investment flows in Canada, summarized in Table 3-3. This table presents average annual incomes, savings, and investments in real (non-financial) assets by the three major players in Canada's real economy, during the three-year period between 1995 and 1997.

As was illustrated above, corporations active in the real economy finance most of their investment activities from their own internal funds, especially the cash flow that is provided by depreciation allowances (which reflect the wear and tear on existing real capital equipment). Of an average of $78 billion per year of real capital acquisition during this three-year period, $76 billion (or 97%) was financed from internal sources of cash. Net flows of funds to corporations from other economic players, undertaken to finance real investment, are very small: equal to about 3% of real business investment.

In the household sector, over 80% of personal savings are invested in residential home purchases and other real investments undertaken by that same household sector. In other words, households in general save only somewhat more than would be required to gradually pay off their own mortgages. The notion that careful personal investors in Canada—through their purchases of mutual funds and other assets—are financing the whole process of economic growth is not borne out by the economic evidence.

The net financial outflow from the household sector equaled just 1.8% of total personal income and less than one-fifth of total household savings. Obviously, some financial intermediation is required to match those households which are just buying their homes (and thus need a mortgage) with those who are pay-

Table 3-3
Income, Savings and Investment by Sector
$Billions, annual average, 1995-1997

	Non-Financial Business	Households	Government	Domestic Total[1]
Income and Savings:				
Gross "income"[2]	69.9	680.6	377.7	824.8
Taxes and other deductions	34.1	163.0	-	-
"Disposable" income	35.8	517.6	377.7	824.8
Gross savings	75.9	61.2	4.5	146.9
(Of which: depreciation)	(60.0)	(26.1)	(16.4)	(105.7)
Gross investment (non-financial assets)	78.4	49.2	18.9	150.3
Financial Balances:				
Financial surplus (deficit)	-2.5	+12.0	-14.4	-3.4[3]
As share income	-3.6%	+1.8%	-3.8%	-0.4%
As share real investment	-3.2%	+24.4%	-76.2%	-2.3%

Source: Author's calculations from Statistics Canada, *Canadian Economic Observer, National Economic and Financial Accounts*, and *Quarterly Financial Statistics for Enterprises*.
1. Total differs from sum of three columns due to exclusion of financial and non-resident sectors, and to the double-counting of some flows.
2. Equals operating profit for business, personal income for households, total revenues for government, and GDP for Canada.
3. The financial deficit of the country as a whole corresponds to net lending to Canadians by non-residents.

ing off their debts (and thus reducing their mortgages). But this task need only require a network of neighbourhood credit unions or saving-and-loan institutions, rather than the hyperactive and overdeveloped network of stock markets, money managers, and other middlemen who constitute the bulk of today's financial industry.

So the household and non-financial business sectors are, for the most part, surprisingly autonomous and self-sufficient in financial terms. It turns out that government, on average, has had the largest net financial requirements of any sector during the 1990s—and even this requirement has evaporated completely in the wake of Canada's attainment of overall balanced budgets in 1997 (so that government itself now is a large net saver).

But governments are able to raise most of the funds they require directly from investors, whether from individuals purchasing Canada Savings Bonds or larger institutions buying other government bonds. Not much intermediation is needed in order to finance government debt. Government has high visibility, and most investors have a general idea of the government's credit-worthiness (indeed, despite endless conservative rhetoric to the contrary, governments are still considered by bond-raters to be the lowest-risk borrower in the whole economy).

So the task of recruiting funds for government is not generally a difficult one, and it certainly does not require a huge and costly administrative apparatus. In many cases (such as the sale of savings bonds to the public, and other direct bond auctions for private investors), the government finances its debt without any direct financial intermediation whatsoever.

Canada as a whole was a slight net dis-saver during the period covered by Table 3-3. Since the extra savings of Canadian households were not sufficient to cover the (small) net financial deficits of governments and non-financial businesses, an additional "wedge" of financing had to be obtained from outside of the country. This overall national financial requirement—equal to an annual average of $3.4 billion, or about 0.5% of Canadian GDP—resulted in a slight increase in Canada's net foreign debt during the period.[9]

In summary, it appears as if the much-vaunted process of matching savers with investors is not nearly as difficult as the self-descriptions of financial institutions make it appear. The financial imbalance experienced by any particular sector of the economy is invariably tiny: just a percentage point or two of the sector's total income. The vast majority of funds invested in Canada's economy are raised in exactly the same sectors (and often by the same actors) where they are ultimately placed.

Only small flows of discretionary funds travel across sectors, from households and non-residents (the net savers) to non-financial businesses and governments (the net borrowers). In the big picture, then, it appears that the financial industry actually plays a surprisingly marginal role in putting money into the hands of those who invest it in the real economy.

Financial Intermediation and Real Growth: International Comparisons

For a country of its size, Canada has a clearly overdeveloped financial industry. Accounting for 5% of employment, one-fifth of total corporate profits, and more assets in total than the entire non-financial corporate sector, Canada's financial industry has become much more than just a handmaiden to real growth (as the textbook stories suggest). Instead, finance has become a powerful, self-interested centre of investment and entrepreneurship, with its own agenda and its own momentum.

In this aspect, Canada is similar to other countries of English colonial heritage:[10] the U.S., Australia, Hong Kong, and of course Britain itself. The so-called "Anglo-Saxon" financial model features large and influential stock markets, arms-length relationships between financial intermediaries and the real companies which they supply with capital, and the aggressive securitization of assets (that is, the conversion of as much wealth as possible into tradeable assets such as stocks and bonds which can be quickly disposed of by investors when desired).

While this approach certainly creates many employment opportunities for financial professionals, and promotes the profile and political influence of a set of constantly-churning asset markets, it is not the only way for a country to organize its financial affairs. Alternative models stress banks as sources of new capital for real investment projects (rather than stock markets), and promote closer institutional and cultural links between the suppliers of financial capital and their end users.

In continental Europe, for example, it is common for banks to hold large equity positions in companies active in the real economy, and to be represented actively on boards of directors. This implies a degree of cooperation and participation by financiers in the operation of the real economy that is quite rare in the U.S., the U.K., and Canada. The implication is that financiers are forced to adopt a longer-term planning horizon in their financial decisions. Rather than focusing solely on how much a company's share price will rise over the coming months, capital investors (funnelled largely through banks rather than stock markets) identify more closely with the long-run interests of the companies they have supported.

Indeed, they have to: since their holdings cannot be disposed of on a moment's notice in a highly liquid equity market, investors need to "make it work" for the companies they have financed, rather than bailing out at the first sign of trouble.

Supporters of the "Anglo-Saxon" approach argue that its arm's-length relationships and intense pressure for short-term results enforces more discipline and great efficiency on the end-users of capital. Critics claim that it produces an economically damaging myopia on the part of companies in the real sector. Anxious to keep their shareholders happy, firms favour measures which may boost share prices in the short term (downsizing their employees, carefully conserving cash instead of spending it on new investment projects, or even buying back their own shares), but which can hamper real economic growth.

Similarly, when volatile asset markets dominate the process of capital accumulation and allocation, investors become more interested in short-run changes in the prices of those assets rather than the ultimate real economic use to which those assets are put.

Is there a relationship between financial intermediation and economic growth? Consider Figure 3-3, which compares the size of the financial industry in several OECD countries with their longer-run investment performance. The degree of financial intermediation is measured by the value of trading on the major stock market of each country in 1994, expressed as a proportion of each country's GDP.[11] Real investment is captured by the average proportion of GDP that was allocated to gross real fixed capital formation between 1990 and 1995.[12]

The correlation in this graph is actually *negative*: that is, the larger and busier a country's stock market, the less successful its record of actually putting money

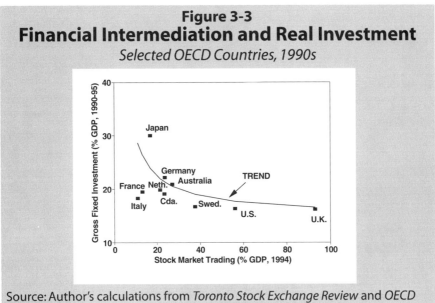

Figure 3-3
Financial Intermediation and Real Investment
Selected OECD Countries, 1990s

Source: Author's calculations from *Toronto Stock Exchange Review* and *OECD Economic Outlook*.

High Performance

"[The] financial system performs dismally at its advertised task, that of efficiently directing society's savings towards their optimal investment pursuits. The system is stupefyingly expensive, gives terrible signals for the allocation of capital, and has surprisingly little to do with real investment."
— Doug Henwood,
Wall Street: How it Works and For Whom.

into motion in the real economy. The more attention and resources a country devotes to paper trading in corporate equities, the less attention and resources it is likely to devote to the accumulation of real capital in the real economy.

In short, like the mutual fund managers who are paid good money to *reduce*, on average, the value of their clients' portfolios, it is not entirely clear that the commercial financial industry serves a productive economic purpose at all.

Conclusion

This chapter has critically reviewed a few of the most common claims regarding the real economic functions that are supposedly fulfilled by modern financial institutions. It is clear that the connection between the hyperactivity of the paper economy and the progress and development of the real economy is tenuous at best, and downright counterproductive at worst. The next chapters of this book will now focus on the process of *real* investment, and its crucial leading role in creating jobs and improving productivity in the real economy.

Chapter 4
Money Into Motion:
How is a Real Job Actually Created?

Every time an election is held in Canada, the voting public is subjected to what usually turns out to be a painful anti-climax: the televised leaders' debate. After interminable negotiations regarding the format, the venue, the questions, and even the placement of the speakers' podiums, the debate finally takes place.

Voters and journalists alike wait with bated breath for a legendary knock-out punch, but it rarely occurs. John Turner's passionate opposition to free trade during the 1988 debate was a rare exception—but then he lost the election, anyway.

The 1997 federal leaders' debate was no exception to this generally dull record. The analysts and commentators couldn't seem to agree on which leader won, and the debate proved to be unimportant in the overall campaign (which saw the Liberal party, led by Prime Minister Jean Chrétien, returned to power with a reduced majority).

Many observers agreed, however, that the most interesting exchange of the three-hour debate occurred when Reform leader Preston Manning asked Chrétien to explain precisely how it is that a new job is created. In the context of a mini-debate over chronic unemployment and what the Liberal government had or had not done to reduce it, Manning put the focus on the Prime Minister's economic expertise—or lack thereof.

"I do not see from what I've heard you say in the House of Commons that you have an understanding of how a job is actually created in the modern economy," Manning challenged. "I think you owe it to Canadians to show or to tell them: How do you see a job created in today's economy?"

Chrétien stumbled, offering a few motherhood statements about reducing the deficit and Canada's strong economic "fundamentals." He hadn't yet managed to utter a grammatically complete sentence before he was cut off by the Conservatives' Jean Charest, who proceeded to give a lengthy speech on the scintillating subject of payroll taxes.

The incident didn't especially damage Chrétien: in a perfect reversal of the experience of his predecessor, John Turner, he did poorly in the debate but won the election, anyway. Nevertheless, the exchange highlighted something that should be of interest to Canadians of any political persuasion. Political leaders on both the right and the left wax eloquent about how their policies will "restore confidence" and improve the economic "fundamentals." But it is seldom specified how the policies involved would have any bearing on the nitty-gritty economic processes through which a new job vacancy is created, advertised, and eventually filled by some needy and thankful unemployed Canadian.

Consider Chrétien's first response to Manning's question: "We reduced the deficit." Well, yes, the Liberals under Finance Minister Paul Martin did indeed reduce the deficit—dramatically, rapidly, and painfully. In a period of three short years, Martin turned a $37.5 billion deficit in fiscal 1994 into an outright surplus (the first in a generation) by fiscal 1997. This was years ahead of Martin's own deficit-reduction timetable, and faster than even his most ambitious supporters dreamed the deficit could be eliminated.

But what does this have to do with job-creation? In reality, rapid deficit-reduction, especially when accomplished primarily through spending cuts (rather than on the strength of economic growth), destroys jobs rather than creating them. Even conservative economists agree that the unprecedented spending cuts implemented by the Liberal government, starting with Paul Martin's watershed budget of 1995, exacted a heavy toll from Canada's labour market. Literally hundreds of thousands of jobs were destroyed by the huge fiscal demands (rising taxes combined with spending cutbacks) that were imposed on an already-sluggish economy.[1]

Supporters of the Liberal approach might have argued that the previous fiscal path was unsustainable, and that failing to eliminate the deficit would ultimately lead to financial crisis and even larger job cuts down the road. Yet even if that highly debatable claim were indeed the case, it still could not be argued that deficit reduction *per se* had anything to do with creating jobs. Yet the Prime Minister of the country felt he could list deficit reduction first among his government's dubious job-creation achievements. And confusion is so widespread about how a capitalist market economy actually generates new employment opportunities that literally millions of Canadians might very well have nodded sagely in agreement with Chrétien's preposterous claim.

This chapter will try to dig beneath the fuzzy slogans of election campaigns, and the self-interested proclamations of business and financial leaders, whose prescriptions for tax cuts and deregulation are designed to enhance the economic position of a limited community of investors and entrepreneurs, but are invariably advanced as huge job-creators and hence beneficial for everyone.

Abstract concepts such as "business confidence," "entrepreneurial spirit," "appropriate incentives," and "economic fundamentals" do not provide a very convincing explanation of how jobs are actually created in the real economy. Surely we can be more precise about the concrete economic mechanisms that produce that most optimistic of all economic indicators: a "Help Wanted" sign hung in the window.

Two Paths to Job-Creation

Almost all jobs in Canada can ultimately be traced to one of two general chains of economic decision-making. As of the end of 1998, some 14.5 million Canadians were working in the formal, paid labour market.[2]   Slightly over two million of those workers were employed in the broader public sector of the economy. This includes direct government workers, and also those employed in the huge range of public and quasi-public service providers: schools, hospitals, social service agencies, and other non-profit undertakings.   The remaining 85% of Canadian workers were employed in the private business sector, by companies and enterprises which are motivated by the pursuit of private profit.

Public service employment is an important source of relatively high-quality and high-wage jobs, and the expansion of the public sector workforce during previous decades played an important role in the rising standard of living of working people in the first decades after World War II. Conversely, public sector layoffs and cutbacks can obviously make a bad labour market even worse, as has been the case more recently.

Public sector employment in the economy has declined markedly in relative terms during the past two decades, from 20% in 1977 to less than 15% in 1997. Indeed, after the deep government spending cuts of the late 1990s, the absolute number of public-sector employees is no higher than it was in the early 1980s. This may finally be about to change: after cutting their workforces to the bone, public employers ranging from governments to hospitals to schools are now finding they have no choice but to once again hire new employees to keep up with the demand for their services.

Nevertheless, it is *private-sector* hiring and firing decisions that have been (and will continue to be) by far the dominant influence on overall employment and labour market conditions. Public-sector employment conditions remain an important but secondary ingredient in the economic mix. In short, as private-sector employment goes, so too goes the overall labour market.

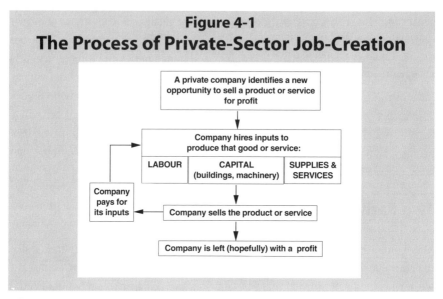

Figure 4-1
The Process of Private-Sector Job-Creation

The Private Sector

These two general sources of employment are the outcome of fundamentally different economic factors and motivations, as illustrated in Figures 4-1 and 4-2. Let us start with the more important private sector decision-making process. Why and how does a private business create a new job? Private companies are motivated by the hope or anticipation that they can earn a profit by selling a product or service to a certain group of customers for revenues which exceed the cost of producing that product or service.

An existing company or a new entrepreneur first identifies what they think will be a profitable new market opportunity. This could involve selling a newly-designed or improved product or service, or selling an existing product or service into a new market. It may also involve using a new production technique to sell an existing product or service into an existing market, but at a lower price than other suppliers, thus capturing more customers. In every case, the firm thinks it can produce and sell something better and more successfully than is currently being done, generating profits in the process.

How does the private company concretely position itself to take advantage of that identified opportunity? First, it needs to obtain the resources which are required to produce and sell the product or service in question. Companies utilize all kinds of different productive resources—or "inputs"—in the course of their business.

The most important of these inputs include labour (the workers who are hired to produce the product or perform the service being delivered), capital (the buildings, equipment, and machinery which are necessary for the firm's workers to productively perform their work), and a whole range of other supplies and services (such as raw materials, spare parts, and various financial, advertising, and other business services purchased from sub-contractors).

The company must thus advance money "up-front" to purchase these inputs and get its new venture off the ground. Typically, the first and largest of these initial investments will be expenditures on new facilities: office or factory space, production equipment, computers, and a whole range of other essential real capital assets which will constitute the fundamental physical environment within which the business's work will be performed.[3]

This real investment "comes first" in terms of timing: that is, the company will want to have those fixed productive facilities in place *before* it begins paying the salaries of new workers and the costs of other supplies and services once production begins. But these concrete investments also "come first" in *economic* terms. Fixed capital investments by business largely determine the quality of the product or service destined for sale, and the productivity with which it is produced. More than any other input to production, these real assets embody the current state of technological knowledge of society.

New investment spending by real businesses thus represents the "cutting edge" of private-sector economic activity. Growing investment is a sure sign that private companies are preparing themselves to produce more goods and services, of higher quality and sophistication—and, in most cases, hiring new workers to do it.

Once a company's new or improved productive facilities are in place,[4] fully supplied with the machinery and equipment that will be required in the course of production, it will then begin hiring new workers and purchasing supplies of raw materials, spare parts, and business services. Production of the good or service in question begins. Revenue is generated by its sale.

After the company pays for the cost of its various inputs, the moment of truth arrives: did the company earn enough on the sale of its output to cover the cost of its numerous inputs, and still provide a profit for the company's owners at the end of the day? If not, then the company will have a limited time in which to turn around its operations and attain profitability—before either its owners decide there are better things they can do with their money and energy, or until the company is driven into outright bankruptcy. If the company is indeed profitable, then it will be encouraged to consider further expansion of its operations. And, conveniently, the profits it earns on its existing business provide an important source of revenues with which additional expansion could potentially be financed.

Several features of this private-sector job-creating process are worth highlighting. First, note how complex and risky the whole undertaking can be. A private company must invest, up-front, significant sums of cash in order to position itself to take advantage of a market opportunity which it has hypothesized exists, but the real potential of which remains unproven.

To generate a profit from a real economic activity, a private company must identify a new product, service, or production technique, buy equipment, hire workers, oversee the production process itself (which can be difficult and uncertain, especially when unproven technologies are being used), deal with interminable labour-management issues (including, conceivably, negotiating with a union or even experiencing a strike), market its product, and hope that it takes in enough cash at the end of the day to cover costs, let alone generate a profit.

This litany of the trials and tribulations of private companies and entrepreneurs is not provided to elicit sympathy: the successful segments of Canada's private sector perform these complex functions quite nicely, thank you, and do very well for themselves as a result. The intent of this discussion, rather, is to contrast what is required of a *real* business investment with the infinitely simpler process of making a *financial* investment.

A financial investor merely advances money to purchase an asset, and then hopes that the value of that asset grows over time. In many cases, such as purchases of government or blue-chip bonds, there is virtually no risk associated with the investment at all. Even in other cases (such as purchases of equities and other less predictable financial assets), there is very little actual "work" involved.

If the expected return on a real business investment is not significantly higher than risk-adjusted returns on financial assets, it is not hard to understand why someone with money would steer clear of the complex, uncertain world of real business, hitching their wagon instead to the relatively straightforward paper economy. Far from lubricating or facilitating real investment and real growth, the super-profits of financial investments can lure away both financial resources and entrepreneurial creativity that could be better used to produce goods and services of real value.

The job-creation process illustrated in Figure 4-1 requires the firm to advance money well before it starts to receive income back from the subsequent sale of its output. This is obviously true of the cost of fixed capital structures and equipment. But it is also true even of the initial payments for wages and salaries, raw materials, and other inputs (all of which economists call "variable" inputs, because their utilization varies with the level of output of the business).

Workers and suppliers need to be paid from the time production commences (give or take a week or two). They cannot wait for revenues to come flowing

Why Bother?

"Why would you pour a foundation, buy machines, hire employees, if you can make as much money buying bonds?"
— Frank Stronach, Former CEO
Magna International
July 1994

Average return on equity, Canadian business, 1990-97: 5.5 percent
Average interest rate, long-run Canadian bonds, 1990-97: 8.5 percent

back in before they receive compensation for their own contributions to the firm's activity. Thus the firm needs to advance significant sums of money for these initial business expenses (paid for from an ongoing reserve fund of *working capital*) long before it receives payment for its output from final customers.

This highlights the absolutely central need of private business for *credit*: in most cases, even established firms will need credit of some kind (loans, lines of credit, or other forms of indebtedness) to finance those up-front expenditures. Indeed, the creation and supply of that credit is the most important function which the financial industry performs.

The growth of business credit—when firms are demanding it, and when financial institutions are supplying it—is a sure sign that employment will also soon be growing. But, as was discussed in Chapter 3, the financial industry in general (and banks in particular) have become less and less focused on the supply of credit to real economic undertakings, and more concerned with capturing profits and commissions through the administration and trading of paper assets.

Another interesting feature of the private-sector employment-generating mechanism is that the price of the firm's output, in general, is determined by supply-and-demand conditions in whatever end-market the business is attempting to penetrate. This creates another element of uncertainty and discipline facing the firm. With the exception of a handful of private industries in which prices are determined through public regulation rather than private competition,[5] the vast majority of private producers have little power to directly pass on their production costs to consumers.

Ultimately, of course, average prices for any good or service must cover the average costs of producing it, or else suppliers in the industry would be driven out of business. For individual producers in a competitive market, however, the prevailing market price imposes a fairly binding constraint within which that company must constrain its own production costs.

The social and economic impacts of corporate cost-cutting (usually involving downsizing and layoffs) have become painfully apparent in recent years, of course. But in most cases it is wrong (or at least misleading) to blame blatant corporate "greed" for the problem. The true source of the difficulty lies in the nature of the competitive markets within which those companies are operating. Firms must match the costs of their competitors to survive.

Even huge corporations can be quickly driven into bankruptcy if their business is fundamentally uncompetitive. In some cases, rules and structures can be put in place to limit socially destructive forms of cost-cutting (such as chopping wages or neglecting environmental responsibilities), thus channelling competitive pressures in more socially useful directions (such as efforts to reduce costs through changes in technology or genuine efficiencies in organization and management). Otherwise, however, market competition is likely to produce endless downward pressure on the wages and working conditions of employees, and the social and environmental condition of their communities.

Given this competitive market structure which shapes and constrains most private-sector business activity, a new job created by one particular company may not translate into a new job created for the economy as a whole. Firms compete with each other for slices of a certain economic pie. If that pie is growing, thanks to rising incomes and an expanding economy, then all firms can conceivably share in economic success, expanding their output and employment across the board.

At the same time, however, companies also engage in a zero-sum battle over market share: each tries to increase production (and thus employment) at the expense of its competitors. A firm may identify a profitable opportunity to expand output by introducing a new, lower-cost production method which allows it to underbid its competitors and increase market share.

In this case, each new job in the growing firm is offset by a lost job in a declining firm. In times when the overall market is stagnant or even declining, this zero-sum battle of position between companies will dominate. For this reason, we cannot identify the success or growth of a particular company with the success of a whole industry or economy. Many "job-creation" announcements by companies can more accurately be described as "job-reallocation" announcements. Employment may rise at the company in question, but probably at the expense of employment at competing firms.

Consider, for example, a developer who announces the construction of a new shopping centre, and claims that it will employ 250 new retail clerks. If the overall population and income level of the surrounding community is growing, hence generating higher levels of consumer spending which would "justify" that new mall, then perhaps it is safe to conclude that 250 new jobs have indeed been created. [Note, however, that it was not the shopping mall itself which "created" the 250 jobs; it was the underlying growth in the purchasing power of the regional economy, only a tiny portion of which has to do with the construction of

Labour-Saving Technology and the Benefits of Investment

For the most part, injections of private business investment exert a strong positive influence on labour markets. More investment by businesses almost always means stronger growth, rising incomes, and healthier labour markets.

There is one sense, however, in which more private investment can translate into *fewer* jobs, not more. Most firms will utilize the latest technology when they expand or refurbish their production facilities with new capital equipment. In many cases, this technology may reduce the firm's need for workers. This is especially the case in industries such as mining and manufacturing, in which the automation of various stages of the production process can significantly reduce the labour content of those processes. The upside of these investments is typically a higher-productivity and higher-quality operation. The downside is that automation often implies downsizing and layoffs.

How do workers respond to this dilemma? On one hand, private investment is crucial to the creation of new jobs and the preservation of existing ones. On the other hand, the technology embodied in new investments may reduce the demand for labour in any given facility.

One response is to try to expand the size of the total economic pie being produced—through measures which promote faster economic growth and hence faster-growing markets. That way, companies will be more likely to use their expanded productive capacity to increase their total output, rather than laying off workers.

Policies to reduce average working time can also help to preserve jobs in the wake of technological change. With these measures, the negative effects of labour-saving technology can be moderated, while preserving the positive benefits provided by the injections of new investment spending.

A good example of how to attain this fine balance is provided by Canada's auto industry. The industry experienced an unprecedented wave of new investment during the 1990s, as virtually every auto plant in the country was refitted with new technology to produce new models of cars and trucks. Auto-makers invested over $10 billion in new plant and equipment in the five years ending in 1997—an absolutely unprecedented pace of expenditure which cemented Canada's status as perhaps the leading auto manufacturing nation in the world (relative to the size of our population).

Unfortunately, however, each time a plant was refurbished, an average of about 200 jobs would disappear in the wake of new labour-saving technology. Was investment thus a good thing or a bad thing for workers in the auto industry?

Clearly it was a good thing. While the jobs lost to new technology offset some of the benefits of the investment, Canada's situation was far preferable to that of other jurisdictions, such as the U.S., where auto investments were much slower, and where total auto industry employment declined significantly as a result.

The fact that Canadian auto production increased during this time (driven mostly by strong exports) helped to preserve Canadian auto jobs. So did measures negotiated by the Canadian Auto Workers to reduce average working time in the industry, thus creating some 2,000 high-wage jobs during the decade. The end result: total auto employment increased modestly in Canada during the 1990s, in sharp contrast to the experience of most other auto-manufacturing countries, and despite the unending introduction of labour-saving technology by the auto-makers.

the mall itself; this is an important distinction that will be explored further in Chapter 6.]

If the overall economy is not growing, however, then are 250 new jobs really going to exist for long? Not likely. The existence of a new shopping mall can hardly force local residents to spend more. If the mall is more convenient and appealing than existing shopping facilities, residents may *redirect* their spending to the new facility, thus making the development a success and guaranteeing the jobs of the retail clerks who work there. But simultaneously, 250 jobs (if not more) are likely to disappear from other existing retail establishments in the region—perhaps the old-fashioned stores located on the main street of a small city, now being undermined by a modern suburban mall complete with Wal-Mart, food court, and 10-screen cineplex.

Let us summarize the main features of how a new job is created in the private sector of the economy. A private firm, hoping to generate a profit, identifies a new opportunity: a new product or service, a new market, or a new production technique. First, it must invest in the fixed production facilities where this business activity will take place. It then hires workers, raw materials, and other inputs to complete the actual work. After selling the final product, it hopes to receive a final profit. If so, it may be encouraged to consider a further expansion; if not, it is likely to cut-back production and lay off at least some of the newly-hired workers.

The key ingredients in the recipe are the existence of a market into which the company can sell its output, and a set of economic and institutional conditions such that it can do so at an adequate level of profitability. In order to stimulate private-sector employment, therefore, policy-makers need to somehow "strengthen" one or more links in this economic chain. They might try to identify or stimulate new markets (by adopting expansionary macroeconomic policies, for example, or opening up foreign markets through free trade agreements). Or they might try to make it easier for firms to conduct their existing business in a more profitable manner (by cutting business taxes, for example), in hopes that more private-sector employment would be created.

It is a complex brew, however, and the brew-master needs to be wary that fiddling with one part of the recipe might mess up another part. For example, suppose that a government wanted to stimulate private-sector production by reducing the cost of labour (through measures such as reducing the minimum wage or erecting greater barriers to union activity). Yes, this might help to enhance the inherent profitability of private production. But it would simultaneously weaken a significant market—the consumer spending of workers themselves—into which those private firms aim to sell their output. The net effect of such a move on private business activity is thus not at all apparent.

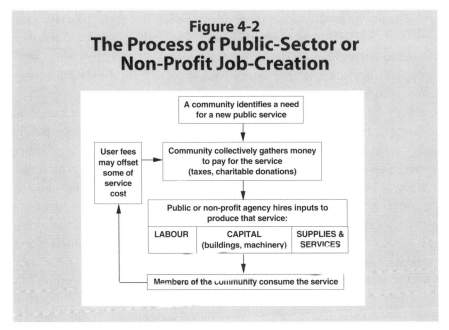

Figure 4-2
The Process of Public-Sector or Non-Profit Job-Creation

The Public Sector

An entirely different job-creating mechanism exists in the public or non-profit sector of Canada's economy, with different motivations and different end results. This alternative chain of causation is summarized in Figure 4-2. In this case, it is not the search for private profit, but rather a collective desire on the part of some community to provide a needed public service, which sets the whole process in motion.

The members of this community may be responding to a newly-identified social problem. Or they may simply be deciding to utilize some of society's economic resources to provide for a new high-quality service (such as Internet services at public libraries) that would be delivered on a non-profit or even free-of-charge basis, thus supplementing their consumption of privately-purchased goods and services.[6]

In either case, the community makes a collective decision to allocate sufficient resources to provide for the desired service—most commonly by empowering an elected government to collect taxes, but alternatively by collecting resources on a voluntary basis (such as through charitable donations). An appropriate public or non-profit agency is charged with using these funds to deliver the service in question. Just like a private company, that agency must use its resources to construct facilities, purchase capital equipment, hire workers, and purchase raw materials and other inputs.

Also like the private sector, expenditures on real fixed capital facilities and equipment will tend to precede new hiring. The service is produced and then consumed by the public which paid for it (sometimes with the collection of additional user fees to supplement the revenues obtained from taxes or donations), and the process starts again.

Both the private-sector and public-sector forms of employment have their respective costs and benefits, strengths and weaknesses. In one sense, public-sector activities are inherently more democratic. They represent a collective choice by society to deliberately allocate a portion of its resources to particular end goals. This differs fundamentally from the decision-making of private markets, which is driven by *money*: consumers with money to spend determine what gets produced (through their effective demand for those goods and services), and employers with money to invest in a real business determine how it is produced (through their control over the processes of investment and production).

On the other hand, public-sector service delivery also encounters problems of its own, especially in terms of the accountability and efficiency of management decision-making. To be sure, every public sector agency is ultimately accountable to some democratically-elected body. But the structures of that accountability may be so diffuse or non-transparent as to effectively eliminate it; hence some public agencies operate inefficiently or ineffectively for years, no matter how frustrated its consumers or workers may be, without any change in management practices.[7]

Most private companies, on the other hand, are quickly and powerfully "accountable," in a very specific but limited sense. If a company is not generating profits, the whip will be cracked and changes will be made—and quickly, too. The fundamental problem is that the cost-benefit accounting which guides that private accountability and responsiveness often does not accord with the real economic well-being of human society. Contrary to what the proponents of the free market would have us all believe, just because a company is making profits does not mean its operations are inherently "valuable."

Similarly, the fact that an enterprise does not generate profit does not imply that its operations constitute a net loss for society. An optimum compromise might be to somehow combine the responsiveness, flexibility, and transparency of private firms with the democratic accountability and collective goal-setting embodied in the operations of public and non-profit agencies. [Perhaps the model of social investment outlined in Chapter 16 of this book provides some hints of how this combination could be obtained.]

Investment, Jobs, and Growth

The decision by a private firm to undertake new expenditures on real capital facilities and equipment is usually a precursor to subsequent increases in that firm's workforce. That real investment has additional benefits in increasing the value and productivity of the work performed in the firm; these benefits will be described more fully in the next chapter.

But the benefits of investment spending by a particular company do not stop at the borders of that company. Rather, real investment spending generates powerful and beneficial economic waves which are propelled throughout the entire economy, resulting in additional and ultimately even more important job-creation.

These important economic links are illustrated in Figure 4-3. The initial direct effects of a private investment decision are shown in the solid black lines. An expanding company—let's call it the Far-Out Software Design Company—invests in new plant and equipment. This immediately generates new business for the corresponding companies which in turn produce those capital goods (computers, machinery, and office construction).

The initial company, Far-Out Software, then hires workers to work in its new facility. Those workers immediately spend their new income on consumer goods and services, thus generating new business for the companies which supply those goods and services—everything from housing to autos to clothes to take-out food. The initial investment by Far-Out led to new jobs being created within that company. This in turn generates new demand, investment, and job-creation throughout the economy, through a snowball effect which economists call the *investment multiplier*.

Think of the capital goods suppliers pictured in the top right corner of Figure 4-3. One might be the Massive Mainframes Company, which will supply Far-Out with its computer hardware. In response to new business, they too will consider expanding their own facilities and hiring new workers. That decision would lead to more demand for capital goods by the investing companies, and more demand for consumer goods and services by their newly-hired employees.

Similarly, new business is also generated for consumer industries. Perhaps a company called Peter's Pocket Protectors might enjoy a sudden surge in business from the newly-hired programmers at Far-Out. This stimulates new investment spending and new hiring in that important segment of the economy.

The process cycles around and around until the initial burst of demand created by Far-Out's investment is finally dissipated. The initial business expansion by Far-Out Software sent a diverse and far-reaching surge of job-creating demand cascading through the entire economy. Far-Out's purchases of raw materials (floppy disks), business services (the graphic designers who design Far-Out's flashy web site), and other supplies and services add further fuel to this expansionary economic fire.

One company's new investment alone cannot singlehandedly lead economic growth, of course. But, if Far-Out's story is repeated often enough by other companies, then an expansion of overall business investment will literally set an entire economy into motion.

How powerful is this investment multiplier process? In previous years, when regional or national economies were more self-contained or "closed" systems, the investment multiplier was very powerful, indeed. More recently, however, numerous factors have combined to undermine the extent to which an initial injection of investment spending courses through the economy, creating more and more jobs with each go-around.

None of these factors has been more important than the globalization of the world economy. As import and export flows have grown, relative to the size of national economies, a larger proportion of new spending—whether by companies on investment projects, or by workers on consumer goods and services— now tends to "leak" out of the national economy where the initial injection of investment occurred. This undermines the job-creating multiplier effects experienced in the local and regional economies, with some of the benefits of higher investment "exported" to that region's trading partners.[8]

For Canada, international trade flows have always undermined the power of the investment multiplier process, since Canada has always imported a majority of the capital equipment which is purchased for private investments. Cana-

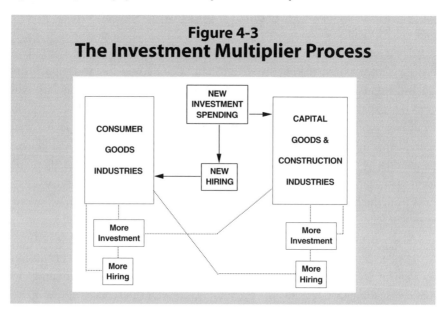

Figure 4-3
The Investment Multiplier Process

A Two-Way Street

Figure 4-3 illustrated the investment multiplier process by which an initial injection of investment spending is transformed into an overall expansion of income and employment throughout the economy. That broader expansion, in turn, fuels more investment spending by companies anxious to meet new demand–and the cycle begins all over again. Investment causes growth, and growth causes more investment, in a virtuous circle of job-creating expansion.

We can illustrate this beneficial two-way relationship with a statistical technique called "Granger causation" analysis. This technique compares two data series, to see if one variable seems to "explain" a significant portion of the other variable–or vice versa. One must always be cautious about equating "correlation" with "causation": just because two variables are empirically linked doesn't necessarily imply that one logically causes the other. Nevertheless, if there is good reason to suspect a logical connection between two variables (as is clearly the case with investment and economic growth), then Granger causality tests can help to confirm which variable causes which.

To consider the two-way relation between investment and growth, Granger causation tests were performed between changes in both gross and net fixed investment, on the one hand, and changes in total GDP on the other. [The difference between gross and net investment will be explained further in the next chapter; it turned out that test results were not really affected by the choice of investment measure.] Details of the tests are reported in Appendix IV of this book, and are summarized in Table 4-1.

Table 4-1
Granger Causality Tests: Investment and GDP

Number of Years Considered	Causation Conclusion
1	Investment strongly causes growth.
2	Growth strongly causes investment.
3	Growth weakly causes investment.

Source: Author's calculations from Statistics Canada, *National Income and Financial Accounts*.

These Granger test results confirm the expected two-way linkage between investment and growth that was described in this chapter. Granger test results depend on the number of years (or "lags") considered in the test. If we consider only a one-year lag, investment is found to strongly cause faster growth. But if a two-year lag is considered, then the positive feedback effects of stronger growth on investment predominate, and growth is found to cause investment. Finally, over a three-year time horizon, the effects of the initial investment stimulus begin to peter out, but growth is still found to weakly cause investment.

da's relatively underdeveloped machinery and high-tech industries necessitated a heavy reliance on foreign suppliers for this technology.[9]

On the other hand, most of the residential and non-residential construction work that still makes up the bulk of total fixed investment spending must of necessity be completed right in Canada. And, despite free trade and the growing importance of imports in consumer goods markets, the clear majority of consumer spending is also still destined for the purchase of made-in-Canada goods, and especially services.

So, despite globalization, any increase in business investment spending in Canada still generates a strong demand impulse which creates spin-off jobs and investments elsewhere in the economy.

Other factors influencing the strength of the investment multiplier process include how much of the new spending stimulus leaks out of economic circulation in the form of taxes and savings, rather than being spent and re-spent to generate further demand and employment.

The end result will vary from one type of investment project to another, but as a rule-of-thumb it is safe to conclude that a $1 billion increase in business investment spending will ultimately generate in excess of $2 billion in total new spending power in the domestic economy. And, again depending on the particular industry involved, every job created in a new business venture is likely to be matched by between one and two additional spin-off jobs created in other sectors of the economy.

Other sources of new spending stimulus to the economy can also generate their own multiplier effects; growing exports and changes in government spending patterns are especially important. But none are as powerful in creating new work and boosting incomes and productivity as is business investment.

Business, Profits, and Jobs: Rhetoric and Reality

This chapter has attempted to provide a better understanding of the specific mechanisms through which a job is actually created in the real economy, and the leading role of real investment expenditure (especially real investments by private companies) in that process. We have described in detail the complicated and difficult obstacle course which a private company must negotiate in order to attain the hoped-for pot-of-gold at the end of the rainbow.

The policy implications of our collective reliance on the profit-seeking investment decisions of private firms are complex and difficult. Obviously, a company has to have a reasonable opportunity to generate a profit from its activities, or else it will cease those activities and lay off its employees. [The causes and consequences of the declining profitability of business investment in Canada will be considered in detail in Chapter 11.]

Private profitability is thus an important constraint on economic and social policies in any economy which is dominated by private profit-seeking firms. This poses a difficult challenge for advocates of a more socially and environmentally responsible economy, since many of the measures which might help to enhance

What Goes Around, Comes Around

The Polish economist Michal Kalecki was a contemporary of his more famous British colleague, John Maynard Keynes.[1] Indeed, Kalecki and Keynes simultaneously developed the theory underlying the investment multiplier process described in this chapter. But Kalecki had a much better understanding of how the process was affected by the distribution of income and economic decision-making power between different groups in society.

Kalecki had an apt image which summed up his description of the investment multiplier: "Workers spend what they get, but capitalists get what they spend." Assume, for now, a private-sector economy with no government and no foreign trade.[2] Also assume that workers, on average, do not save anything from their current income; as will be described in Chapter 12, this assumption is actually quite close to present-day economic reality. All saving is thus undertaken by the higher-income individuals who also happen to be the main owners and managers of private businesses. They save a share of the profit income produced by those businesses, either directly within the firm (in the form of retained earnings) or within their households (setting aside a portion of the dividend income distributed by companies to their shareholders).

The production process is started by an initial business investment. The new workers hired by the firm spend their income, generating new business for consumer industries. The whole process stops when the savings from profits by companies and their owners perfectly offset the initial investment by those companies. The economy attains a macroeconomic balance between savings and investment, while the business sector attains a financial balance between outlays and inflows. Workers spend virtually every penny they receive, while companies get back every penny they spend.

The moral of Kalecki's parable is clear: business must be aggressive and growing if it wants to generate high profits. If business investment declines, then so, ironically, will business profits–not just for the particular companies which reduced their own investment spending, but indeed for the whole private sector which is dragged down by the stagnation of the broader economy.

---

[1] Kalecki's most-important English-language writings are contained in *Selected Essays on the Dynamics of the Capitalist Economy* (Cambridge, U.K.: Cambridge University Press, 1971).

[2] These assumptions were never fully valid, of course, and hence the real multiplier process never worked as "purely" as Kalecki's stylized depiction. But the assumptions make it easier to picture the still-dominant underlying processes at work

that degree of responsibility—such as higher wages, corporate taxes, or the full costing of natural resource usage—would seem to potentially cut into corporate profitability.

There are other measures, however, that could be taken to enhance the profit motive for private firms in the real economy, without imposing hardship on the working people and their communities for whom the economy is supposed to function. Some of these measures (such as more expansionary macroeconomic policy, lower interest rates, and a shift of the burden of capital taxes from users to owners of capital) are discussed in later chapters of this book.

In the long run, society might very well wish to reduce its dependence on the private profit motive as the dominant motivation for economic activity. In the meantime, however, one can recognize the fact that in a private market system profit literally makes the economic world go around, without buying into the self-defeating idea that society must give business everything it asks for, or else face the consequences.

Indeed, the credibility of conservative arguments that our economic and social policies need to become more "business-friendly" if Canada's miserable job-creation performance is to be turned around is wearing very thin. Non-stop business propoganda about the "bloated" and "inefficient" role of government in our economy has shifted most of the blame for our poor labour market performance onto government policy.

Too many rules and regulations "interfere" with the activity of private employers, we are told. Government debt and deficits create "uncertainty" for investors. Overly-generous social programs have diminished the "incentive" to work, and thus contributed to joblessness. The best thing policy-makers can do

Table 4-2 **Pro-Business Policy Changes** *Canada, 1980-1997*	
When	**What**
The Macroeconomic Environment	
1981	Implementation of high interest rates and deliberately slow growth; full employment abandoned in favour of the "natural rate of unemployment."
1981-1986	Inflation cut in half (to 5% or less).
1989-1992	Interest rates increased even further; Bank of Canada adopts official inflation targets; inflation falls to 2% or less.
1995	Paul Martin budget launches war on deficit; federal program spending cut by one-third (as share of GDP).
1995-1996	Most provinces balance their budgets.
1997	Federal budget balanced.
1998	Canada experiences deflation in the domestic economy for the first time since the Great Depression.
Role of Government in the Economy	
1983 to 1997	Public sector employment falls steadily to 15% of total Canadian employment.
1985	Energy industry deregulated.
1986-87	Initial deregulation of finance, allowing banks to purchase stock brokerages and other financial intermediaries.
1987	Airline and trucking industries deregulated.
Late 1980s-1990s	Privatization of most major federal Crown corporations (Air Canada, @@@ Petro-Canada, @@@ CN Railway).
Late 1980s-1990s	Continuing deregulation of telecommunications.
1992	Further deregulation of the banking industry.
1992 to 1997	Program spending by all Canadian governments falls from 44% to 36% of GDP.
Late 1990s	Widespread provincial deregulation and privatization.

to create jobs is to simply get out of the way—through spending cuts, deregulation, and balanced budgets—and let the private sector solve the unemployment problem (or so the story goes).

In reality, however, it is getting harder and harder to accept the view that the private sector will cure all that ails our job market, if only government will leave it alone to do its job. The role of the state in Canada's economy has been shrinking for two full decades, and the retreat of government from our economic lives accelerated dramatically during the late 1990s. For example, total program spending by all levels of government in Canada declined from 44% of GDP in 1992 to 36% of GDP in 1997—and is still falling.

Canada used to rank squarely in the middle of the G7 countries in terms of the role of government in the overall economy. Now, however, we are second only to the U.S. in the extent to which our economy is dominated by the private sector—and the gap between Canada and the U.S. is narrowing rapidly. Even the right-wing Fraser Institute lists Canada among the handful of countries in the world with the most extreme free-market, pro-business economic policies.

Table 4-2 (continued)	
International Trade	
1985	Restrictions on foreign investment eliminated; Foreign Investment Review Agency (FIRA) abolished.
1989	Canada-U.S. Free Trade Agreement.
1994	North American Free Trade Agreement.
1996	World Trade Organization formed; Canada a member.
1996	Canada-Chile free trade deal paves way for NAFTA expansion throughout Latin America.
1997	Multilateral Agreement on Investment negotiated in secret, then defeated.
Taxes	
Late 1980s	Federal corporate tax rate cut from 36% to 28%; federal income tax rates for high-income earners cut from 35% to 29%.
1991	GST replaces the "job-killing" Manufacturers Sales Tax.
1996-98	Income tax cuts favouring high-income earners implemented in various provinces, and promised at the federal level.
Labour Relations	
1983 to 1997	Real hourly wages *fall* (after inflation) by 3%, even though real productivity per employee in Canada *grows* by 16%.
1986 to 1997	Federal minimum wage is frozen at $4 per hour, and loses 35% of its value to inflation; many provincial minimum wages also lag inflation.
1990 to 1997	Percentage of unemployed Canadians receiving UI benefits is cut from 85% to 40%.
1995	Ontario eliminates anti-scab laws, weakens union organizing and decertification procedures.
1990s	Welfare "reforms" introduced in numerous provinces, including workfare, welfare-to-work, and wage subsidy schemes--all of which increase the effective supply of low-wage labour for employers.
Late 1990s	Various provinces weaken or eliminate pay equity and employment equity schemes.

Table 4-2 lists just some of the more important pro-business economic policy changes that have been implemented in Canada during the 1980s and 1990s— ever since government abandoned the goals of full employment and the "just society," and instead set about disciplining the population to become more amenable to the demands of private corporations.

By any standard, Canada now has a more free-wheeling, deregulated, and business-friendly economic environment than has been the case for decades. In the wake of the dramatic pro-business shift in our policy environment, it is hardly credible to blame government for the continuing failure of a private-dominated economy to create enough jobs for a population that is hungry to work.

It is time to shift scrutiny back to the performance of the private sector that dominates the economy. We need to ask: what is it about our free-market system that continually generates chronic high levels of unemployment and permanent insecurity for its workforce? If anything, the private sector is responding to its more favourable economic environment with a distinct lack of economic effort.

Real investment spending by Canadian business has been significantly lower during the 1990s, as a share of total GDP, than during previous decades; this will be described in detail in Chapters 7 and 8 of this book. Perhaps the policy changes summarized in Table 4-2 were more about redistributing the economic pie, and less about actually "growing" it.

Canadian society has made unprecedented concessions to business demands for more accommodating economic and social policies since 1980, and yet the real contribution of the business sector to capital accumulation and hence economic growth has diminished. The rest of this book will focus on explaining the decline in real private-sector investment activity, analyzing its consequences, and proposing a range of potential remedies.

Chapter 5
Real Investment:
What is It, Why Does it Matter, and Who Wants It?

In the most general sense, any investment represents an addition to some exist-ing stockpile of capital. We have earlier defined *real capital* as the collection of buildings, structures, equipment, tools, and machinery which Canadian workers use on a day-to-day basis to aid their work effort and enhance their productiv-ity. A *real investment,* therefore, is a decision to add to that collection of build-ings, structures, and tools. Ongoing real investment thus corresponds to a proc-ess of *capital accumulation*, in which the stockpile of real capital grows over time. Therefore, a real investment occurs when a decision is made to construct or manufacture new buildings, new structures, and new tools, and then to mobi-lize them into economic action in the subsequent production of other goods and services.

These real investments play a key and direct role in the production of the goods and services which people actually need and consume in their daily lives. In this they differ fundamentally from *financial* investments, which simply rep-resent new purchases of paper instruments (such as stocks and bonds) by inves-tors hoping for a paper profit.

The preceding chapter described the leading role of real investment deci-sions in the process of job-creation in the economy. When a private company identifies a potentially profitable new business opportunity and positions itself to take advantage of that opportunity, its expenditures on real capital assets are usually the first sign of the firm's coming expansion. That initial investment spending, followed by subsequent hiring within the firm, spurs spin-off demand in other parts of the economy: first for the companies which make capital goods, and later for companies which sell goods and services to the newly-hired work-ers.

In the public sector, too, new investments in real capital equipment and structures play a leading role in the creation of new jobs in public services.

This chapter will now consider in more detail the different faces of real investment: the different ways it can be measured, the different forms it can take, and the different ways it contributes to economic growth, job-creation, and productivity. It turns out that the benefits to general society of a real investment expenditure are likely to exceed the benefits to the individual company or agency which undertakes that investment.

In other words, real investment spending is so important to the well-being of the overall economy, that society as a whole may have more at stake in strong investment than the investors themselves do. [In economic lingo, the *social return* to real investment is higher than the *private return*.]

Private investors, not surprisingly, are well aware of this asymmetry. Companies possess considerable bargaining leverage to extract concessions from local governments or unions in return for new investment spending. Like unskilled parents holding out candy to bribe their young children into better behaviour, investors know that their decisions to invest or not invest carry huge economic implications for the communities in which they do business, and so they use this "goodie" to press for "better behaviour" on the part of those communities.

An important policy implication of the fact that the social benefits of investment exceed the private benefits is the conclusion that governments should take active, interventionist measures to promote real investment spending. Without those measures, the level of investment forthcoming from purely self-interested private companies will be lower than the investment level which would be optimal from a broader social viewpoint. Investment, in short, is too important to be left to the investors.

Kinds of Capital

Investment, in general, is an addition to a stock of capital. But the real capital assets considered above—buildings, structures, machines, tools, and computers—are not the *only* kind of capital that matters to economic growth and well-being. Other types of non-financial capital are also important ingredients in the overall economic recipe. Hence other types of investment, in addition to real investment in capital assets, are also likely to play an important economic role.

For example, economists of all stripes have long recognized the importance of what has come to be known as *human capital*. This refers to the accumulated knowledge, skills, and capabilities of individual workers. An investment in human capital, therefore, represents the expenditure of energy and resources in an attempt to enhance those personal skills and capabilities. Education is the most common example of an investment in human capital. When an individual expends time and money to gather training so that they can subsequently perform their job more efficiently and productively, this is conceptually very similar to an investment in any productivity-enhancing tool or piece of machinery. The key difference is that, instead of being embodied in a concrete capital asset, the human capital is reflected intangibly in the skills and capabilities of the individual.[1]

Conservative economists have long used "human capital theory" to explain—and in many cases to *justify*—the large inequalities in income distribution which are typical of unregulated free-market economies. Why are some people rich, and others poor? Because some people frugally chose to invest in their own human capital (in the form of additional education and training), and are more productive and hence better-compensated as a result.

Conversely, the poor job and income prospects faced by many Canadians have been blamed on their alleged failure to invest in their own skills and training. This is hardly a complete or fair assessment of the link between education and incomes, nor is it a satisfactory explanation of Canada's poor labour market performance. In many jobs, the status of a particular degree is more important than the actual training the degree-holder may or may not have received; the degree is merely a *credential* which allows its holder to gain access to a particular and better paid sub-section of the labour market. And, as has been all-too-evident in Canada's economy during the 1990s, investment in human capital through education and retraining is certainly no guarantee of well-paid employment upon graduation.

Canada's labour force is one of the best-educated in the world, and average education levels have climbed steadily during the post-war era. For example, in 1995 Canada boasted more post-secondary students, relative to population, than any other country in the world, and allocated a higher proportion of GDP to public spending on higher education than any other industrial economy. Yet Canada's labour market performance during the 1990s was one of the least impressive in the industrialized world.

A "kinder, gentler" interpretation of human capital theory is advanced by the advocates of greater public support for education, health care, and other programs. By contributing to the development of a healthier, better-educated workforce, these programs constitute an economic "investment" as legitimate and important as any real investment undertaken by a private company. And this public investment in human capital should pay off down the road in higher productivity and a lower incidence of social problems.

Recent economic research has confirmed that, to a certain degree, public investment in education, health care, and other public services is indeed a precursor to stronger growth and higher living standards. This argument is absolutely valid, and plays an important ideological role in refuting the conservative stereotype of government programs as inherently wasteful and economically damaging.[2] But even this interpretation of the benefits of human capital should not take away from a focus on *tangible* capital investment as a central source of economic growth and job-creation.

To be sure, investments in education, skills, and health are highly beneficial, for more than just economic reasons. But even a highly-educated workforce needs jobs, and, with the important exception of jobs created within the education sector, education in and of itself does not create those jobs. A taxi driver who possesses a Ph.D is not much more "productive" than one who doesn't, hence the economic and social pay-off from education depends heavily on the existence of good jobs for the graduating class.

Moreover, to fully utilize their skills, most highly-educated workers also need sophisticated tools and equipment with which to perform their jobs. In this sense, investments in human capital and investments in real tangible capital are not *substitutes*; rather, they tend to *complement* each other.

A related concept is the notion of *social capital.* Just as a healthy and well-balanced individual is likely to be more productive in the long run, so too is a healthy and balanced society. There are real economic costs to the poverty and inequality which tend to arise in economies which lack adequate social insurance schemes and other measures to enhance the economic opportunity and participation of all social classes. Those costs include poor health, crime, higher policing and insurance expenses, chronic turbulence in families and neighbourhoods, and a breakdown of trust in human relationships (which can affect all kinds of economic outcomes ranging from household mortgage lending to the provision of in-house training by employers).

At the same time, there can be real economic benefits to social policies which promote equality, security, safety, and participation.[3] Investments in social capital, therefore, can have a real economic payoff. But once again, a healthy "stockpile" of social capital alone is not a sufficient condition for job-creation and economic growth. A healthy unemployed worker, living in a safe and clean neighbourhood, is still unemployed. And, while public investments in the types of programs and facilities which are likely to enhance social capital certainly make a positive contribution to growth and social well-being, a healthy economy also needs the accumulation of real capital—throughout the economy, not just in public services. As with human capital, therefore, social capital can be seen as complementary in its effects to investments in tangible capital assets.

Another type of intangible capital investment which plays a very similar role to real investment spending is the research and development activity of high-technology companies and scientific agencies. Learning how to produce new kinds of goods and services, and how to produce them more efficiently, is a crucial part of economic development. Indeed, this technological progress is intimately tied up with investment in real capital assets. Most technological improvements involve the utilization of new and more complex forms of capital equipment. And the R&D process itself uses capital equipment intensively: computers, laboratories, simulation and experimentation facilities, and so on.

The spin-off economic benefits of R&D spending are very similar to those resulting from real investment spending. The decision by a firm to increase its research activity is usually a precursor to the future growth of its output and its workforce. Hiring scientists and researchers, and buying the sophisticated equipment they need to work with, pumps important new purchasing power into a local or regional economy, generating exactly the same positive multiplier effects that were described earlier for traditional capital investments.

The end result of R&D investment is a "stock" of technological knowledge. This stock is not embodied in a concrete machine or tool, so much as it is reflected in a collective base of knowledge. For this reason, R&D investments are inherently quite risky. In the first place, if they don't successfully "produce" new knowledge, the R&D sponsor is left with nothing tangible as a result of the investment. [With real capital assets, on the other hand, the investing firm at least has some used capital equipment it can sell off should its investment not pan out.]

In addition, the intangible nature of "knowledge" in many cases raises the possibility that it could be used by someone other than the investor who paid for its creation. That's why technology-intensive companies place so much emphasis these days on stronger intellectual property and copyright laws: they do not want the fruits of their research investments to be captured by competing firms. Because of the continuing difficulty of fully enforcing "private ownership" over knowledge, there is strong economic evidence that private companies will tend to underinvest in R&D (because the *private* benefits of those investments may be reduced if competing firms gain access to the resulting knowledge base).

As with real investment spending, this suggests that government should play a strong role in fostering R&D activity. Indeed, particularly in cases in which the dissemination of new knowledge is clearly beneficial in social terms (as with new prescription drugs, for example, or new advancements in basic science), there is a strong case that R&D should be undertaken by public agencies, with the resulting new knowledge given away "free."

In general, the impacts of R&D investments on productivity and employment are otherwise very similar to those of real investment spending. And Canada's poor record of R&D investment has hampered our economic progress as surely as has the slowdown in our real investment in tangible capital. Despite generous tax subsidies for private R&D activity, Canada has by far the lowest rate of R&D investment of any major industrial economy.

To a large extent, this is due to the continuing importance of foreign-owned multinational corporations in Canada's high-tech manufacturing industries. These companies tend to conduct their R&D activities at head offices in their "home" countries, rather than in their branch plants in Canada and other technologically "dependent" countries.

In summary, the concept of "investment" is obviously a rich and multi-faceted one, even if we exclude the purely *financial* investments which play such a secondary and questionable economic role. By zeroing in on the importance of investments in real capital assets (structures, machinery, and tools), it is not the intention of this book to negate or downplay the other important forms of investment—human, social, and technological—which are also crucial to the development of the real economy. Simply spending billions of dollars to build factories and fill them with equipment is no guarantee of successful economic growth. We also need healthy, well-educated people to operate those facilities, and we need an expanding base of technical knowledge to ensure that our economic capacity continues to grow over time.

Nevertheless, real investment expenditure on tangible capital assets still constitutes the most important leading edge of growth and job-creation in the economy. Indeed, these real investments tend to go hand-in-hand with the human and social investments favoured by many social justice proponents. Ensuring that individuals are healthy and well-educated, and that communities are safe and secure, almost always entails significant real investment spending (usually by public agencies) on schools, hospitals, and neighbourhoods. Moreover, to be ultimately productive and well-compensated, those healthy and well-educated workers also need well-equipped and modern workplaces. That, too, requires real investment spending.

Even investment in something as intangible as "know-how" also requires a growing stock of real capital assets—to aid in the discovery of that knowledge, but, even more importantly, to allow for its application in real production. So

Formula for Success

"The best single predictor of the growth of an economy remains its investment rate."

—Dani Rodrik
Harvard University, 1997

for all of these reasons, the state of real investment spending is perhaps the most important single factor in economic growth and job-creation.

Defining and Measuring Real Investment

Real investment has many faces: there are many different things that can be made or built in the process of making an investment in real capital. And real investment spending has many different economic benefits. Which type of benefit is produced depends, to some extent, on which type of real investment is undertaken.

Components of real investment spending

Real investment spending is usually broken down into four broad categories.[4] These categories are illustrated in Figure 5-1. *Public investment* is undertaken by governments and public agencies such as transportation authorities, school boards, or hospitals. Public investment is conceptually distinct from private investment in that it is not motivated by the hope of private profit, but rather is explicitly mandated by some social desire for a particular service or facility. Public investment has declined significantly during the 1990s, and now accounts for barely one-tenth of all real investment spending in Canada: about $18 billion in 1997.

Private firms account for most real investment, and there are three broad categories of real investment by these firms. *Machinery and equipment* investment refers to the purchase and installation of machines and tools: anything ranging from computers to assembly lines to aircraft to the furniture in a hotel room. It has been the fastest-growing component of total investment spending.

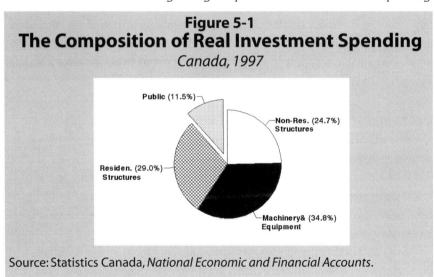

Figure 5-1
The Composition of Real Investment Spending
Canada, 1997

Public (11.5%)
Non-Res. (24.7%) Structures
Residen. (29.0%) Structures
Machinery& (34.8%) Equipment

Source: Statistics Canada, *National Economic and Financial Accounts.*

This growth reflects the more intensive use of high-technology equipment by companies. Machinery and equipment purchases now account for over one-third of all real investment in Canada, or some $55 billion in 1997.

Non-residential structures represent buildings such as factories, offices, and shopping malls, and other permanent structures such as pipelines or railways. Cost-conscious companies have shied away from traditional "bricks-and-mortar" expansion plans in recent years, and hence these non-residential structures account for a dwindling share of total investment: about one-quarter of all real investment spending in 1997, or slightly less than $40 billion.

The final component of private real investment is expenditure on the construction of *residential structures* (including homes, town-houses, and apartment buildings). Even though the bulk of these assets end up being owned by individuals (not businesses), residential investments are still included in economic statistics as a form of business investment.[5] Residential construction was especially hard hit by the recession and high interest rates of the early 1990s. It accounted for about 30% of total real investment in Canada in 1997 (about $45 billion).

Each of these categories of investment spending has different motivating forces, and different end results. All are important in stimulating job-creation in their initial phase, since all require the employment of workers who manufacture the equipment and build the residential and non-residential structures. In this sense, all forms of real investment have important immediate benefits for job-creation. Labour-intensive construction projects (such as residential and non-residential structures, and public works such as road construction) may have the biggest initial employment impacts.

In terms of the longer-run effects of investment on productivity, however, and hence on incomes and living standards, investment in machinery and equipment may be the most crucial. Economists have also zeroed in on machinery and equipment investment as the crucial leading indicator of economic growth; a pick-up in machinery and equipment spending seems to be the most accurate signal that business expansion is around the corner.[6]

Gross investment and net investment

Another important distinction needs to be made between that share of real investment which merely replaces capital assets that have been worn out or used up in the course of day-to-day business and that share which adds to the final stockpile of real capital assets actually in use at any point in time. In this context, *gross investment* refers to the total expenditure in a current year on real investment goods and structures.

A portion of this spending will offset what economists and accountants call *depreciation*: the value of the existing capital stock which is lost each year be-

Sector	Gross Investment ($ billion)	Share Canada Total (%)	Depreciation ($billion)	Depr. as Share Gross	Net Investment ($billion)
Households	$49.9	31%	$27.1	54%	$22.8
Non-financial businesses	$86.6	54%	$63.0	73%	$23.6
Financial businesses	$3.9	2%	$3.4	87%	$0.5
Government	$18.2	11%	$16.8	92%	$1.4
Total Canada	$158.9	100%	$110.2	69%	$48.7

Table 5-1
Gross and Net Investment by Sector
Canada, 1997

Source: Author's calculations from Statistics Canada, *National Economic and Financial Accounts.*

cause of day-to-day use and deterioration. A certain flow of ongoing investment spending is thus necessary merely to maintain the capital stock in its current state; without replacing that depreciation, the capital stock would run down over time, and the economy's productive potential would decline.

Any investment spending which occurs over and above depreciation, however, represents an actual net addition to the capital stock. It is called *net investment*, and represents an increase in the total value of real capital being used in the economy.

The relative importance of depreciation and net new investment in the real investment spending of different sectors of the economy is summarized in Table 5-1. In total, more than two-thirds of all real investment spending in Canada simply represents the replacement of existing capital assets which have worn out. Less than one-third of total investment spending—under $50 billion in 1997—constitutes a net addition to the nation's capital stock.

Companies active in the real economy are the most important investors. They accounted for 54% of gross investment spending in 1997. But almost three-quarters of their investment spending was required just to offset depreciation of their existing assets.

The household sector (which includes unincorporated small businesses) accounts for just under one-third of gross investment in Canada. Depreciation charges account for a smaller proportion (just over one-half) of household investments, so the net investment rate of the household sector is somewhat higher than that of non-financial businesses. Financial businesses and governments are small investors, especially on a net basis.

One important and worrisome piece of information is contained in Table 5-1. Governments allocated barely enough to investment spending in 1997 to cover the depreciation of existing public assets. On a net basis, then, Canada's total government sector added almost nothing (just $1 billion) to the public capital stock that year. This is an ominous symptom of the underinvestment in public capital by fiscally-pressed governments in Canada during the 1990s.

Anyone who has visited a school or hospital in recent years is probably all-too-familiar with the deterioration of most of these public facilities. On a net basis it is clear that public investment is far from adequate to meet the needs of a growing, changing society.

Both gross and net investment are beneficial for the economy. Even if an economy invested only enough to offset the depreciation of its existing capital stock (so that net investment was zero), that gross investment would still be economically beneficial. Gross investment still represents a decision by companies to spend on real capital, and that decision still courses through the entire economy, spurring the job-creating multiplier process described in Chapter 4. And, merely by replacing old machines and equipment with new versions, the economy is likely to experience benefits in terms of productivity and technological progress, since those newer "vintages" of capital assets will incorporate the latest technology.[7]

The pace at which an economy adds to its net capital stock, however, is also of concern. It is only through net investment that an economy can become, on average, more *capital-intensive* in its production techniques. In other words, it is only by investing in new equipment faster than old equipment wears out that the total amount of capital equipment available to aid each individual in his or her work can increase. This growing capital intensity can be measured with a number called the *capital-labour ratio*; this ratio measures the amount of capital, on average, that supplements the labour effort of each individual worker in an economy.

In general, the higher the capital-intensity of production, the higher the productivity. Higher productivity, in turn, translates into economic growth, and offers at least the potential for higher incomes. There is no guarantee, of course, that higher productivity will automatically translate into higher wages and salaries; whether higher incomes are actually paid out by more productive employers depends on many factors, such as the level of unemployment and the strength of unions. But, without higher productivity, the chances of winning higher incomes are slim indeed.

It turns out that the slowdown in net investment in Canada, and hence in the capital-intensity of production, has been even more pronounced than the slowdown in gross investment, as will be explored in detail in Chapter 7.

Nominal and price-adjusted investment spending

One final measurement and conceptual issue worth exploring is the extent to which each dollar of investment *expenditure* by a company or agency translates into the concrete purchase and installation of new capital assets on the ground.

This depends, of course, on the going purchase prices of those capital goods and structures.

A good analogy can be found in the purchasing power of a consumer. A consumer's total spending on consumer goods and services, measured in dollars, may grow in a particular year. But are they actually consuming more in real terms, or is it simply that the average price of their purchases has increased due to inflation? To determine the *real* spending of the consumer, the purchases must be adjusted to reflect changes in the consumer price index.

Similarly, to determine the real "investing power" represented by the investment expenditures of companies, we might also want to adjust them for prices, to reflect changes in an "investor price index."

The pattern of price inflation varies dramatically across different investment goods sectors, as illustrated in Figure 5-2. The average price of constructing a residential structure was about twice as high in 1997 as it was in 1980. The cost of home-building has thus roughly paralleled the experience of inflation in the economy as a whole; average consumer prices were also about twice as high in 1997 as they were in 1980. To perform the same "real" quantity of residential construction, therefore, investors would have to spend twice as much (in dollars) in 1997 as they did in 1980.

For other investment goods, however, prices on average have increased significantly less quickly than in the economy as a whole. The average "price" of government investments has stayed roughly constant since the early 1980s, re-

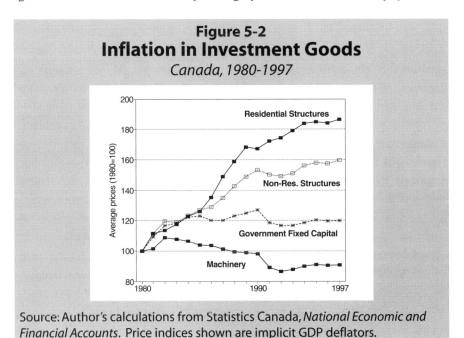

Figure 5-2
Inflation in Investment Goods
Canada, 1980-1997

Source: Author's calculations from Statistics Canada, *National Economic and Financial Accounts*. Price indices shown are implicit GDP deflators.

flecting both improvements in the efficiency of public works construction and severe wage restraint imposed on public sector workers during the 1990s.

In the all-important machinery and equipment sector, prices actually seemed to *decline* substantially during the 1980s and early 1990s. This means that purchasers of this equipment are getting more "bang for the buck": they can purchase more machinery and equipment today with a given investment budget, measured in nominal dollars, than was the case a decade ago.

This result must be interpreted with extreme caution. There are extremely difficult methodological issues encountered in the calculation of average price indices for technologically sophisticated products such as capital goods. The most important problem is how to adjust prices to reflect the improved quality of more recent vintages of a particular product. Think of computers. To purchase the same "real" computing power in 1980 as is presently embodied in a Pentium II desktop computer selling for $2,000 would have required the purchase of large main-frame computers totalling many millions of dollars.

Does this mean that the "price" of computers has fallen by 99% percent since 1980? Well, yes and no. The nominal prices of typical personal computers have actually been surprisingly stable in recent years: "cheaper" ones are available for $1,000 to $2,000, "top-of-the-line" models sell for $6,000 or more. What has changed dramatically is the computing power embodied within each class of desktop computer. Even a bargain-basement computer today possesses far more computing power than the cutting-edge models of just five years ago.

Trying to capture these fundamental changes within an average price index results in bizarre and unintended outcomes. It could be argued that the "real" value of a $2,000 Pentium II computer today is actually several million dollars if measured in, say, "1986 dollar terms". While it is true that the Pentium desktop possesses computing power that would have cost millions of dollars a few years ago, this hardly implies that its owner is a "multi-millionaire" in 1986 dollars!

More recent statistical techniques have attempted to address this problem. For example, statisticians are now starting to use what is known as "chain" price indices which are rebalanced to reflect quality improvements each year (rather than once every several years). On this basis, the "average" price of machinery and equipment has kept closer pace with the overall level of inflation.

Some economists have pointed to the apparent fall in the prices of some investment goods in an attempt to minimize the importance of the apparent slowdown in real investment spending by Canadian business in the 1980s and 1990s. Since investors are getting more "real" investment effort for each dollar of investment spending, that investment effort may not have slowed down at all, after adjusting for the fall in the average prices of investment goods.[8]

This argument is not convincing, for several reasons. First, while it is certainly the case that modern machinery and equipment are more efficient and productive than ever before, the depiction of these quality improvements as major price decreases is the anomalous result of faulty statistical techniques. Investment goods are better than ever, but they are not really "cheaper" than ever.

Moreover, if investment goods were indeed genuinely less expensive, this does not necessarily imply that investors would spend less money on them, in total. In some cases, a fall in prices can lead purchasers of a particular product to *increase* their total spending on that product. Like the bargain-hunting shopper who "saves" so much by buying cut-rate goods that they exhaust their credit limit, some buyers will be so encouraged by lower prices that they will actually increase their total spending. [In economic terms, total spending will increase if the price elasticity of demand is greater than one.]

This has clearly been the case with computers: their lower prices have elicited more spending on computers, not less. It isn't clear why the same result could not be true of capital equipment as a whole.

Finally, in relation to the importance of investment spending for job-creation and purchasing power in the economy, it is the injection of actual dollars that matters most, not the abstract price-adjusted value of that spending. If investment spending, in current dollar terms, declines, then the individuals who are employed in the manufacture and construction of capital assets will likely lose their jobs. They will hardly be comforted by the knowledge that the "price-adjusted" investment effort of companies has not declined as much as their falling investment budgets would suggest.

One way to avoid this conceptual problem is to steer clear of measuring investment in dollar terms. In fact, the most common measurement of real investment in an economy, and the one that will be generally utilized in later chapters of this book, is current investment spending measured as a share of the total output of the economy. This measure, known as the *investment share*, indicates the share of current output which an economy allocates to real investment.

The "price-adjusted" investment effort which is reflected in that allocation is not a direct concern. It is obviously relevant to note that many forms of capital investment—especially in machinery and equipment—have become incredibly more productive and efficient thanks to technological change. And, if anything, one would think that this trend would *enhance* the appeal and importance of real investment as a leading force in economic growth.

The Economic Benefits of Investment

Economic growth and job-creation

The discussion in Chapter 4 highlighted the crucial importance of real invest-ment spending as the engine of economic growth and job-creation in Canada's economy. This importance is verified by statistical data regarding the close rela-tionship between investment and the overall expansion of the economy.

Total purchasing power in the economy depends on a number of different components: business investment, consumer spending, exports, and the real purchases of governments and public agencies. In theory, an increase in any of these variables should translate into an increase in total economic output and hence, ultimately, into new jobs. But it turns out, as suggested in Chapter 4, that investment spending is by far the most closely correlated with employment growth.

The statistical "co-variance" between two variables measures the extent to which they tend to follow one another over time. Table 5-2 indicates the co-variance between the different components of total purchasing power in the economy and the expansion of total employment. That correlation is signifi-cantly higher for investment spending than for any other component of expendi-ture. And it turns out that the co-variance is slightly higher for gross investment spending (including depreciation) than for net investment; this confirms the ear-lier suggestion that, in terms of current job-creation benefits, it is gross invest-ment which is the more relevant measure.

The positive impact of investment spending on economic growth is also vis-ible in international comparisons. Figure 5-3 plots the average annual growth of total per capita GDP (after inflation) in each of about 25 different industrialized

Table 5-2 **Demand Growth and Job-Creation** *Covariances by component of GDP*, 1960-1997	
Component of Expenditure	**Covariance with Employment Growth**
Gross Investment	.813
Net Investment	.773
Exports	.595
Household Consumption	.565
Government Consumption [1]	.289
Source: Author's calculations from Statistics Canada, *National Economic and Financial Accounts*. Covariances compare first-differenced natural logs, and hence are a comparison of proportional changes in the paired variables. [1] Government purchases of current goods and services; excludes transfer payments and investment spending.	

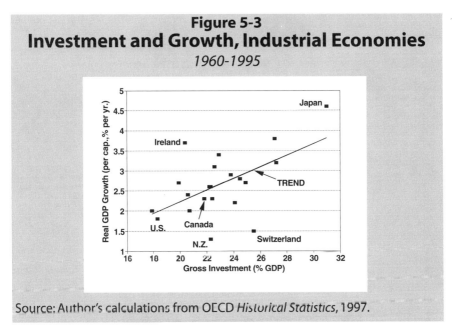

Figure 5-3
Investment and Growth, Industrial Economies
1960-1995

Source: Author's calculations from OECD *Historical Statistics*, 1997.

economies between 1960 and 1995, and their corresponding levels of real investment (measured as a proportion of total GDP). Faster investment is obviously
not the only factor explaining economic growth: some countries (such as Ire-
land) have grown quickly despite only average rates of investment, while others
(such as Switzerland) have grown relatively slowly despite having relatively strong
rates of investment.

Nevertheless, the positive correlation between investment and growth on
average is clear. In general, allocating four more percentage points of GDP to
investment over this period produced an average rate of real economic growth
that was more than one-half percentage point higher. Over a sustained period, a
half percentage point of economic growth each year can translate into a significantly higher standard of living in the long run.

Productivity and incomes

Industries in which the work effort of individual employees is aided and supplemented by larger amounts of real capital equipment also tend to be industries in
which the productivity of those workers is higher. There are obvious reasons for
this correlation between capital-intensity and higher productivity. The quality
and quantity of work performed is enhanced by the use of more and better tools,
equipment, and structures. And the final price of a good or service must incorporate a proportional share of the cost of the capital assets tied up in its production. Hence the total value of output will be higher for industries which use
capital more intensively.[9]

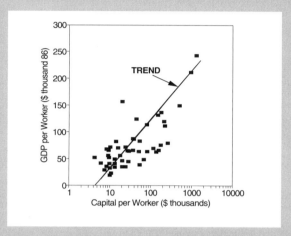

Figure 5-4
Productivity and Capital Intensity
Selected Canadian industries, 1994

Source: Author's calculations from Statistics Canada, *Fixed Capital Flows and Stocks, Employment, Earnings and Hours,* and *Gross Domestic Product by Industry.* Capital measure equals net capital stock per employee in current dollars, geometrically depreciated, at the end of 1994.

This relationship is illustrated in Figure 5-4. This figure plots the average output per worker in some 50 different Canadian industries against the average capital-intensity of those industries (measured by the value of real capital assets used in the industry, per employee). Once again, capital-intensity is obviously not the only factor influencing productivity, but it is probably the most important. Indeed, differences in capital-labour ratios across industries can single-handedly explain over half of the differences in productivity across those same industries. (See sidebar, *Crunching the Numbers.*)

The slowdown in real investment in Canada, and the resulting stagnation in the capital-intensity of the whole economy, has been an important factor behind the slowdown in productivity growth which has generated so much concern among policy-makers in the late 1990s. Indeed, as will be considered further in Chapter 7, there is some evidence that the average capital-labour ratio of Canada's economy actually *fell* during the 1990s—that is, that our net investment in real capital was not even sufficient to keep pace with the growth of our labour force.

In the preceding sense, then, it is the rate of *net* investment which is most important to productivity growth, since it is only net investment (after depreciation is paid for) which adds to the value of the outstanding capital stock. In another sense, however, even strong rates of *gross* investment can contribute to technological change and productivity growth. Every time the capital stock "turns

Learning by Doing

"Each new machine produced and put into use is capable of changing the environment in which production takes place, so that learning is taking place with continually new stimuli."

— Kenneth Arrow
Nobel Prize Winner in Economics, 1962

over," with older worn-out machinery replaced with newer versions, an immediate productivity gain is experienced, thanks to the updated technology embodied in those more modern machines.

But a potentially more important dynamic is then also set into motion. Economists have identified that technological progress tends to be associated with a process of problem-solving which depends on individuals being confronted with ever-changing sets of stimuli. This process is called "learning by doing" (see sidebar).

When a given company or agency starts to produce a certain good or service using a certain technique, it will naturally encounter certain problems or bottlenecks which it will attempt to solve. Managers and workers alike will identify certain ways in which the quality of the product, or the efficiency of the production system, can be improved. But, once those changes are made, a whole new set of problems will be encountered, and a whole new set of possible improvements can be identified and implemented.

In this manner, a company or even a whole country which is already investing, producing, and hence growing, enjoys the opportunity to "learn" more from the growth—fixing problems, devising ever more improvements—and hence tending to grow and progress even faster. Thanks to this virtuous circle of innovation, growth tends to breed growth. Companies or countries which get a head start in producing one or more particular products will have the opportunity to cement their leadership as they improve on their own production techniques.

In this sense, every investment—even one which merely replaces old machines with a similar quantity of new ones—represents an opportunity for new learning by doing, because it has changed the economic environment in which work takes place and hence opened up a whole new vista of potential problems to be solved and improvements to be made.

Public investment can enhance productivity in a unique way. Obviously, the productivity of public service delivery will tend to increase when the workers producing those services are employed in better facilities with more modern and efficient equipment. But there are also spin-off productivity effects from many public investments that are felt throughout the economy, even by private firms.

In particular, investments in public *infrastructure* are believed to be important, to a certain point, in enhancing the productivity of general economic activity. An economy with good roads, advanced communication systems, and other facilities which are needed by virtually any company or agency, is one in which virtually every task can be performed more quickly and efficiently. Indeed, to the extent that this efficiency is translated into more output in the private sector, and more profits for private investors, public investment can produce a "crowding-in" effect, by which public investment stimulates private investment.[10]

While these linkages between public investment and the productivity of private firms are certainly valid, their importance should not be overstated, especially in the case of a developed country like Canada, where it is difficult to believe that the activities of private firms are held back in any significant way by a lack of basic infrastructure (although it is certainly the case that much of Canada's infrastructure is now crumbling).

Many well-meaning advocates of greater public investment attempt to buttress their argument with over-ambitious claims about the benefits of those investments to private investors. A more convincing case for those investments can be made on the basis of their direct value to the public at large.

There is another important sense in which investment contributes to higher productivity. The preceding discussion has focused on the positive impact of

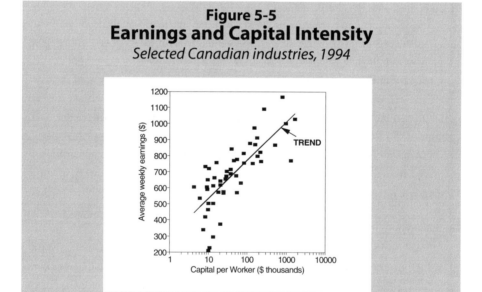

Figure 5-5
Earnings and Capital Intensity
Selected Canadian industries, 1994

Source: Author's calculations from Statistics Canada, *Fixed Capital Flows and Stocks, Employment, Earnings and Hours,* and *Gross Domestic Product by Industry.* Capital measure equals net capital stock per employee in current dollars, geometrically depreciated, at the end of 1994.

investment and capital accumulation on the *capacity* of Canadian workers to produce more: with more technology and more tools to aid their work effort, the workforce is able to churn out more goods and services with less effort. But real investment expenditure also helps to determine the extent to which that productive capacity is actually *utilized.*

As we have seen, investment spending is the "team captain" of economic growth in a market economy: when investment is strong, purchasing power will grow, employment will expand, and the economy will be generally busy. When investment is strong, therefore, it is not just that more capital is available to help workers work more productively. Equally important, strong investment makes it more likely that those workers have a job in the first place—and this is an obvious precondition for their being able to work productively. [In the language of economics, strong investment carries both *supply-side* and *demand-side* benefits for productivity.]

As suggested earlier, higher productivity opens up the possibility of rising incomes. And, as illustrated in Figure 5-5, this possibility, in most cases, becomes a reality. There is a strong positive link between the capital-intensity of an industry, which allows for higher levels of productivity, and the wages and salaries paid in those industries.

As with productivity, differences in capital-intensity across industries can "explain" over half of the differences in wages between those same industries. Industries which typically utilize less real capital in production—retail, hospitality, and business services are the stereotypical examples—are also the industries which tend to offer the lowest average incomes. In contrast, capital-intensive industries such as high-technology manufacturing, communication, utilities, and many transportation sectors pay wages and salaries much higher than the Canadian average.

There are several possible explanations for the correlation between capital-intensity and earnings. In general, workers in high-tech industries are likely to possess higher levels of skills and training, required for them to efficiently operate the expensive capital equipment which they work with and are responsible for. These higher skills help them to command higher incomes. The higher productivity of these industries allows more room for employers to pay higher wages and salaries, without unduly impinging on the profitability or viability of their companies.

The bargaining power of workers also tends to be higher in more capital-intensive industries, for various reasons. The importance of wage costs in an employer's overall expenses will decline as that employer invests more capital in production; this makes it easier for employers to "afford" wage increases for their workers.

Crunching the Numbers

Economists often use a statistical technique called "econometrics" to investigate and verify the links between two or more economic variables. Econometric results cannot "prove" a particular economic theory. But if there are strong logical reasons for believing that one variable affects another in a certain way, econometric tests can strengthen the case for that belief.

Simple econometric tests were performed on the data that are illustrated in Figures 5-4 and 5-5: the varying capital-intensity of different Canadian industries, and their corresponding levels of productivity and average earnings. The results of these tests, summarized in Table 5-3, support the argument presented in the text that investing more in capital structures and equipment in an industry is likely to enhance both the average productivity of the industry, and the living standards of the people who work there. [For more details on the tests, see Appendix IV.]

Table 5-3
Capital-Intensity, Productivity, and Earnings
Summary of econometric tests, 51 Canadian industries, 1994

Issue	Econometric Finding	Explanatory Power
Impact of capital-intensity on productivity.	An increase of 10% in the capital-labour ratio of an industry is associated with an extra $4000 per year per worker of labour productivity.	Capital-intensity explains 53% of differences in productivity.
Impact of capital-intensity on average earnings.	An increase of 10% in the capital-labour ratio of an industry is associated with an extra $5400 per year in average wages and salaries per worker.	Capital-intensity explains 58% of differences in earnings.

Source: Author's calculations as explained in Appendix IV.

Similarly, employers with expensive investments in capital equipment and structures will desperately want to avoid having those investments tied up unproductively due to a strike or work stoppage. Hence they are more likely to agree (up to a point) to worker demands for higher incomes.

Finally, the skill and complexity of work in most capital-intensive industries makes it difficult for employers to fire "uncooperative" or militant workers (including workers who may be on strike) and replace them *en masse* with unemployed workers recruited on short notice from the community. This also strengthens the bargaining position of workers.

For all these structural reasons, therefore, average incomes are higher in industries which use more capital-intensive production techniques, and the long-term rise in the capital-intensity of the overall economy which accompanies strong real investment provides the economic underpinning for rising living standards.

At the same time, as with productivity, strong investment is also highly beneficial for shorter-term "demand-side" reasons. When business investment is strong, labour markets also tend to be strong. This gives workers in *all* industries—not just those which receive the bulk of the new investment spending—a much better chance of getting a raise.

Equality

It seems that strong investment performance may actually be associated with a more equal *distribution* of income, not just with higher income *levels*. This association must be interpreted cautiously: it is not entirely clear whether stronger investment "causes" more equality of income distribution, or whether more equality "causes" greater investment—or both.

The stronger economic growth and employment conditions associated with stronger investment would certainly seem to contribute to greater income equality: lower unemployment and expanding economic opportunities will tend to reduce the incidence of poverty.

At the same time, there are some ways in which greater equality of income distribution might help to spur on more investment. For example, if unemployment is low and wages are growing, then the domestic market for private businesses is also growing, hence spurring more investment. Alternatively, to the extent that strong investment performance is associated with state interventions in the areas of financial regulation and public investment (as has been true in continental Europe and East Asia), then one might also expect to see equality-

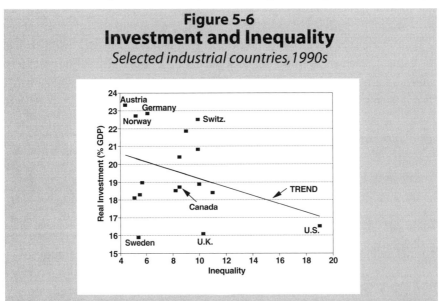

Figure 5-6
Investment and Inequality
Selected industrial countries, 1990s

Source: Author's calculations from World Bank, *World Development Report*; and International Monetary Fund, *International Financial Statistics*. Investment share is average for 1990-97. Inequality measure is the ratio of top to bottom decile income shares, selected years in 1990s.

promoting state interventions in the area of income distribution (through measures such as progressive income taxes and stronger minimum wage legislation).

Figure 5-6 illustrates this correlation for a group of 17 industrialized economies. This figure plots the level of real investment spending in each country (measured as a share of total GDP) against the degree of income inequality in that same country. Income inequality is measured by the ratio of the income received by the richest 10% of the population to the income received by the bottom 10% of the population. [In a "perfectly" equal society, this ratio would be 1: the richest 10% would receive exactly the same income as the bottom 10%. As inequality rises, the ratio also rises.]

There is a weak negative correlation in this graph: as inequality tends to rise, the real investment expenditure of an economy tends to fall. Not too much should be made of this finding: it is weak in statistical terms (technically speaking, the correlation is not "statistically significant"), and largely results from the fact that one country—the United States—is both by far the most unequal economy in the industrial world and also one of its weakest investors.

High degrees of income equality are no guarantee of strong and sustainable investment pattens, as evidenced by the poor investment performance of Sweden. On the other hand, it is clearly the case that economies can exhibit high degrees of income equality combined with strong investment. Austria, Norway, and Germany all fall into this category.

At a minimum, even if we do not accept the notion that equality alone actually *promotes* stronger investment, it is certainly not *inconsistent* with strong investment. Hence the conservative argument that we must cut public programs and labour market regulations in order to fashion a better "investment climate" is not supported by international evidence.

Exports and competitiveness

A final general benefit of strong investment for overall economic performance is the positive impact of real investment on the ability of an economy to compete in international markets. Economists have found a strong correlation between the rate at which a country invests in real capital assets (especially in those industries which are most sensitive to international pressures, such as manufacturing) and the general performance of that country in international trade.[11]

Strong investment makes a country's products more saleable in export markets for two reasons: 1) the new technology embodied in new equipment usually reduces the unit cost of production, but 2) perhaps more importantly, it is also associated with the output of higher-quality cutting-edge products which command a premium on world markets.

The link between investment and exports has been especially clear in Canada's economy during the 1990s. Strong growth in exports was one of the few bright spots in Canada's general economic performance during the decade. After inflation, total exports grew by 72% between 1990 and 1997, compared to real growth of just 13% in the economy as a whole. Sales to the U.S. economy, which grew more strongly than Canada's throughout this time, were the most important destination for these expanding exports.

To be sure, many of the new exports were offset by higher imports in the wake of the Canada-U.S. Free Trade Agreement (FTA) and the subsequent inclusion of Mexico in the North American Free Trade Agreement (NAFTA), and hence their impact on employment has not been one-sided. Job losses in import-sensitive industries have offset some of the new hiring by successful exporting companies.

Nevertheless, new hiring by export-oriented manufacturing industries was one of the few sources of strength in an otherwise spineless economic recovery, and the net impact of foreign trade on Canada's labour market in the 1990s was undoubtedly positive. Not coincidentally, the industries most responsible for Canada's export boom are also the industries in which real investment spending by companies has been the strongest.

The auto industry has been the clear leader in this regard. Real investment expenditures by auto assemblers and auto parts manufacturers has averaged over $4 billion per year during the 1990s, more than twice as high as during the previous decade. At the same time, Canada's total auto exports more than doubled between 1990 and 1997 (to over $70 billion).

The emergence of a large trade surplus in autos and auto parts, totalling over $10 billion by 1997, single-handedly accounts for almost one-half of the total improvement in Canada's overall merchandise trade balance during the 1990s. The outstanding success of Canada's auto industry is a prime example of the virtuous circle that can exist between strong investment and export success. Modern, high-technology production facilities make a country's products more attractive internationally. But this, in turn, encourages companies to invest even further in new and updated production facilities to meet the growth of export demand.

Investment breeds investment, growth breeds growth, and jobs breed jobs. The end-result: the broader auto industry added some 20,000 mostly high-wage jobs between 1990 and 1997, a welcome exception to the general pattern of lay-offs and downsizing that marked much of the rest of the economy.

Investment: Who Wants It?

A strange cognitive dissonance tends to cloud discussions about real investment spending, its effects, and the sorts of policies which might help to promote it. We have indicated the crucial importance of real investment to economic growth, job-creation, productivity, and incomes. Curiously, however, many progressive constituencies (e.g., labour activists, social justice advocates, and others) tend to shy away from discussing the importance of real investment spending.

Thinking perhaps that investment is something mainly done by businesses, it is often concluded (wrongly) that being "pro-investment" means being "pro-business." Hence much more attention is typically devoted by these constituencies to issues like tax fairness, opposing government cutbacks, and criticizing the increasingly polarized distribution of income in Canada.

To be sure, these are crucial economic and social problems which progressives need to confront. But the revitalization of investment spending and hence economic growth would make a huge contribution to the resolution of these other issues. And, far from implying that society needs to become more "business-friendly" in order to encourage more investment by private firms, the failure of businesses to respond sufficiently to an increasingly attractive economic and institutional context with more real economic effort actually provides progressives with a powerful platform from which to *critique* the dominant role that private business plays in our economy.

As was summarized in Chapter 4 (see especially Table 4-2), Canada's economic and social policies have become significantly more "business-friendly" in recent years. The extent of this policy shift, and its general failure to elicit a positive response in terms of investment spending, will be explored in more detail in subsequent chapters of this book.

If business is still not delivering the investment our economy and society needs, despite these changes, this raises some pretty fundamental questions about policy and strategy. Should private firms really be assigned virtually sole responsibility for this crucial economic function?

On the other hand, there is also a contrast between the words and deeds of those constituencies which tend to identify with the interests of private business. In words, we are lectured *ad nauseum* that a strong and attractive "investment climate" is a crucial precondition for growth and job-creation. All sorts of painful social and economic measures are justified on these grounds: government spending cutbacks, tough anti-inflation policies, corporate downsizing, anti-union "reforms" in labour law.

It is not actually clear what many of these policies have to do with real investment in the first place. In many cases—anti-inflation policy being the most important—the clear motive is to enhance the returns on *financial* investments, not to boost the incentive for *real* investment. And, as we have seen, the connection between the booming financial economy and the development of the real economy is not apparent at all.

In fact, despite endless jargon about improving the "investment climate," there is every indication that real companies are actually concerned more with strictly *conserving* their real investment expenditures than with expanding them. Like any other cost input, the more that companies can save on their purchases of real capital assets, the higher their profit per unit of output will be at the end of the day.

Every new investment expenditure needs to be carefully justified on grounds that it will enhance profitability. Growth for the sake of growth, a maxim which guided some corporate executives in the booming 1950s and 1960s, has gone the way of the Edsel. Profits, not growth, is what matters to shareholders in the 1990s, and these two variables do not necessarily move in the same direction. Yet it is growth, more than profits, which matters to job-creation and incomes in the broader economy. Thus a potential conflict is created between the need of the community for more investment and more jobs, and the desire by companies to strictly limit their investment spending in the interests of maximizing profits.

The fact that macroeconomic policies have shifted away from an emphasis on job-creation in favour of placing top priority on controlling inflation and protecting financial returns (more on this in Chapter 9) has reinforced the extreme caution with which any company in the real economy will consider an expansion of its investment program. No company wants to be caught having just expanded its physical capacity when the central bank suddenly decides to clamp down on economic growth in the interests of preventing an uptick in inflation.

Constant (and perverse) warnings from the guardians of financial stability that growth might be "too strong," and job-creation might be getting "out of hand," are internalized by corporate executives. Even in the event of a relatively strong short-term expansion in demand and sales, most real businesses today will be very slow to respond to those favourable conditions with more investment.

They know that growth is being tightly regulated at the macroeconomic level by monetary officials far more concerned with price stability than with job-creation and real growth. So they are more likely to respond to strong demand conditions—for a considerable time, at least—by pushing existing factories to the limit and demanding excess overtime from existing workers, rather than taking the risky step of investing in permanent expansion.

But this reluctance of real businesses to undertake real investment itself holds back the growth of the economy, and indeed the expansion of physical capacity, turning the initial paranoia of financial officials about inflation into a self-fulfilling prophecy. If capacity does not respond quickly to increased demand, due to the fear of real businesses that the demand will be cut off by the anti-inflation actions of central bankers, then that demand (if sustained long enough) may indeed induce the inflation that the central bankers fear.

If, on the other hand, real investment was stimulated (indeed, a commitment by the central bank to foster sustained real growth would ease the fears of companies that their contemplated capacity additions might become white elephants), then capacity would grow in step with demand and there would be little reason to expect higher prices.

To invest, or not to invest? As usual, financial analysts are blunt about which side their bread is buttered on (see quote, *Prophets and Profits*). They will be extremely wary of any move by corporate managers to "over-invest" in new projects, no matter how beneficial those projects may be to the communities which host them.

Investment growth can be a good thing if it indicates an effort to capitalize on a particularly appealing new opportunity. But if it tends to depress a firm's average rate of profit, new investment can depress share prices and hence must be resisted. This may be true even if the new project being considered is itself likely to be profitable—that is, its revenues will exceed its costs. If the *rate* of profit on that investment is lower than the "hurdle" rate of return which shareholders demand of all new projects, then they will firmly oppose the move.

One prominent New York investment house even conducted a study to show that companies which invest less, tend to be more profitable over the long haul.[12] The odd stock-picking strategy which is suggested by this observation can be

Prophets and Profits

"Accumulate! Accumulate! That is Moses and the prophets."
—Karl Marx
Capital, Volume I, 1867

"Some strong fundamentals underpin the optimism about profits embedded in stock prices. One that's often overlooked is the stinginess with which companies are approaching capital investment. Many companies, out of concern for their stock price and greater management discipline, are instead making strategic acquisitions or repurchasing their own stock. The money they do spend on capital investment has gone heavily into cost-cutting technology...rather than new buildings and factories that add capacity."
—Greg Ip, Business Reporter
Wall Street Journal, March 23 1998

summed up as follows: financial investors should buy shares in those companies which invest the *least* in capital equipment!

"This is clearly one of the most easily investible and logical anomalies in the entire stock market," the study concluded. "Investors ought to be very cautious about companies with very ambitious capital spending plans." This anomaly might be "logical" from the point of view of a stock-broker. But for a society which needs investment to spur job-creation, it is clearly perverse.

Even the prestigious Organization for Economic Cooperation and Development (OECD) recently stamped its seal of approval on this general philosophy, with a major 1998 report on corporate governance. The report urged all countries to adopt U.S.-style methods of corporate management, in which company decisions are linked clearly and directly to the interests of shareholders. The report's lead author, prominent New York corporate lawyer Ira Millstein, lambasted companies (such as many of those in East Asia) which placed more importance on growth and job creation than on the paper profits of their shareholders.

"Nobody was watching management; they were growing for the sake of growth with no concern for shareholder value," Millstein complained of companies in Asia and elsewhere which did not follow the U.S. governance model. The fact that the extremely rapid pace of real investment between 1960 and 1990 by companies in Japan, Korea, and the other Asian "tigers" was the primary cause of the greatest and fastest increase in living standards that the world has ever seen should hardly be relevant when a few extra percentage points of shareholder return are at stake.[13]

Indeed, institutional changes in corporate governance have been important in reorienting corporate managers away from real investment and growth as their priorities. Corporate executives are far more sensitive to the bottom-line demands of their shareholders for maximum profitability, and hence higher share prices, than was the case in previous decades.

The rising importance of stock options and other market-contingent forms of executive compensation have been important in this regard. Ironically, so too have been efforts by large institutional investors (including trusteed pension funds) to demand greater accountability by corporate executives to their shareholders.

In this context, the movement for improved "corporate governance" and "shareholder democracy" has probably had negative implications for that majority of the population which does not own shares, and hence is excluded from this "democracy." By emphasizing profitability over growth, private businesses and their shareholders undermine the vibrancy of job-creation and purchasing power in the broader economy. That this result was obtained in part due to a narrowly-

Who Cares?

"In the development of mainstream economics over the past 30 years, the analysis of investment has gradually shifted from centre stage to side-stage, if not into the wings."

—Malcolm Sawyer
Leeds University, 1984

defined "activism" on the part of pension funds (some of which are jointly managed by unions) is surely one of the most ironic and perverse outcomes of the paper boom of the 1990s. (This issue will be considered further in Chapter 15.)

The strange attitude toward real investment spending within the financial and corporate communities—which ranges from benign neglect to outright hostility—is also reflected within the economics profession itself. (See quote: *Who Cares?*) Mainstream "free-market" economists do not share the concern with job-creation and purchasing power that motivates most of the arguments presented in this book.

In free-market economic theories, a shortage of purchasing power is never a lasting constraint on an economy. In their theoretical models, the operation of free markets is supposed to ultimately ensure that all available resources—including all willing and able workers—are fully and productively employed in the economy. [The thinking behind this "supply-side" view of how the economy works is explored further in Chapter 10.]

For these theorists, then, investment is just one source of spending among many equals. An economy that doesn't "spend" a lot on investment will "spend" its extra resources on something else. Investment plays no special role in job-creation, which is taken care of by the self-adjusting supply and demand forces of a "free" labour market.

This approach, again, is surprisingly at odds with the stated emphasis of "free market" politicians on the need to improve the "investment climate." In the economic theories which—nominally, at least—are supposed to guide the thinking of conservative politicians, investment actually plays no special role.[14]

Alternative economic theories, which recognize the limitations on growth and employment that normally result from a lack of sufficient purchasing power in the economy, place a much greater emphasis on the role of investment in kick-starting the creation and expansion of purchasing power. [Some of these theories will also be explored in Chapter 10.] Strangely, it may be these theories, not the free-market view of the world, that provide the strongest argument in favour of the need to improve the investment climate—although most have quite different measures in mind for accomplishing this goal than do the conservative politicians who make investment such an important theme of their election platforms.

In conclusion, we are left in a bit of a muddle. Free-market economic theories suggest that real investment spending is not particularly important. Financial analysts, and the corporate executives who are increasingly beholden to those analysts, are fearful that too much investment will reduce profitability and hence share prices. Yet the conservative politicians—who supposedly follow free-market theories, and whose campaigns are funded by financial and non-financial businesses alike—wax eloquent about the need to take socially painful measures to improve the "investment climate."

The muddle extends to the other side of the political spectrum, too. Left-wing critics of business seem fearful that talking too much about "investment" implies the advocacy of even more policies favouring business. Hence they overlook the investment slowdown and its economic and social consequences, even though this slowdown has been perhaps the most important single factor behind the economic stagnation which most Canadians have experienced for two decades.

Perhaps it is time to publicly proclaim the nudity of the economic emperors. Despite conservative rhetoric about investment, the fact of the matter is that companies and financiers are not especially interested in investment, and conservative policies in many ways may have undermined the conditions for successful investment.

The essentially *anti-investment* bias of much conservative thinking (in the realms of both economic theory and applied practice) should be identified and denounced. It is the rest of society—not private businesses, and certainly not financiers—which has the most pressing interest in restoring vibrant rates of real investment. This recognition that faster investment will likely have to be accomplished over the objections of the private investors who currently control it will obviously shape the nature of the measures that need to be considered.

In Defense of Growth

Throughout this book, one of the primary benefits of real investment spending is held to be its positive impact on the rate of economic growth, and hence job-creation. On the other hand, many progressive critics in recent years have questioned the very desirability of economic growth, for a variety of reasons. It is sometimes argued that growth has done little to produce new jobs (as evidenced by Canada's "jobless recovery" of the 1990s) or to reduce poverty. Hence we should focus more on redistribution than on growth.

It is also argued that growth is incompatible with environmental protection; to respect the increasingly binding environmental constraints which we are collectively encountering (such as resource depletion or global warming), perhaps we should deliberately aim for a low-growth or even no-growth economy.

Both of these views are motivated by well-founded concerns about growing inequality and looming environmental catastrophe. It is far from clear, however, that an absence of economic growth would solve either of these problems; more likely, it would make them worse.

Consider the links between growth, unemployment, and poverty. High levels of unemployment and poverty have persisted in Canada during the 1990s despite the economic "recovery." But this has not been because of a breakdown in the link between growth and prosperity; more important, rather, is the fact that the recovery was so weak that it hardly deserved the term. Growth is still a powerful force in creating new jobs and reducing poverty. It's just that we need a lot more of it.

Canada's labour force grows by about 1.5% per year. Thanks in part to vibrant immigration, we have the fastest rate of population growth of any major industrial economy. At the same time, average labour productivity grows (thanks to new technology and capital investment) by about 1% per year. [It *could* grow much faster if investment were stronger and unemployment lower.]

That means that Canada's total economic output—our Gross Domestic Product (GDP)—must grow by 2.5% per year (after adjusting for inflation) just to keep up with population growth and technology. Any less, and unemployment rises. And when unemployment rises, poverty rises.

Poverty can move somewhat independently from the unemployment rate for a while; for example, big cutbacks in social programs can create higher pov-

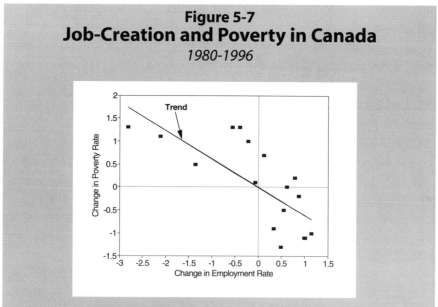

Figure 5-7
Job-Creation and Poverty in Canada
1980-1996

Source: Author's calculations from Statistics Canada, *Canadian Economic Observer* and *Income Distributions By Size After Tax.*

erty rates even if unemployment does not change (this happened, to some extent, in Canada in the mid-1990s). In the long run, however, there is a stable, virtually one-to-one relationship between higher unemployment and higher poverty.

This relationship is illustrated in Figure 5-7, which plots the change in the poverty rate each year since 1980 against the change in the employment rate. [The employment rate measures the proportion of working-age Canadians who are employed; it is roughly the inverse of the unemployment rate.] Without exception, if the employment rate falls, poverty grows. And in every year but one (1987), every time the employment rate increased, poverty fell.

A "trend line" calculated on the basis of this data passes exactly through the "cross-hair" origin of the graph: zero change in the employment rate implies zero change in poverty. The key explanation for the rise in poverty in Canada during the 1990s, therefore, is the sharp decline in the employment rate during the recession (from 62% in 1990 to 58% in 1993), and its slow and halting recovery since then.

Better social programs would make a huge contribution to reducing poverty, to be sure. But there is still no more powerful anti-poverty force than strong job-creation—and this will occur virtually any time real economic growth exceeds 2.5% in a year. Conversely, when economic growth falls short of that 2.5% hurdle, a very strong tendency is triggered for higher poverty that would eventually overwhelm even the most ambitious income redistribution policies.[15]

The environmental constraints on economic growth are more complex and probably more difficult to solve. But here, too, it is far from clear that a lack of growth is the answer. Some types of pollution (not all) are negatively associated with income levels—that is, some types of pollution are worse in the poorer economies which have fewer resources to allocate to environmental protection. In this sense, economic growth can free up resources which can be used in the interests of environmental protection.

Other types of pollution, however, tend to become more severe as economies grow; most worrisome, it is the richest economies which emit the largest quantities of greenhouse gases, by virtue of their more intense use of fossil fuels. In this sense, growth has clearly been associated with environmental degradation.

But it is probably possible to channel and regulate economic growth so as to minimize or eliminate its environmentally destructive side-effects. Investments in environmental protection—such as energy-saving retrofits of houses and other buildings, the clean-up of toxic wastes, the creation and maintenance of parks— are all forms of economic growth, too. In general, public and "caring" services (education, day-care centres, and other community projects) tend to be relatively benign in environmental terms; this suggests a larger role for public services in the transition to a more environmentally sustainable economy.

By mandating environmental investments on the part of private business, government can actually spur investment spending (more on this in Chapter 16). And for political reasons as well as economic, it is unlikely that trying to suppress growth could solve the problem. Given the clear connection between slow growth, high unemployment, and rising poverty, few citizens are likely to support environmental protection if joblessness and poverty are the price they have to pay.

Properly defined and measured, economic growth simply means more employed people producing more goods and services of higher value. There are plenty of things that need to be done in Canadian society: more and better housing, more and better services, more and better cultural and outdoor facilities. Growth does not necessarily imply the more extensive consumption of natural resources; it can also imply the process of producing more value from those resources, in a sustainable and socially beneficial manner.

The issue is not whether or not to grow. The issue is how to channel and regulate that growth so that it enhances the well-being of society and the natural environment, rather than undermining it.

Chapter 6
Behind the Boondoggle:
Investment, Jobs, and Small Business

Who do Canadians most respect? According to a 1998 Angus Reid public opinion poll, no group is held in higher regard by their fellow Canadians than the overworked, underpaid neighbourhood small business operator. The poll found that lawyers are reviled; no surprise there. Politicians are distrusted; we all knew that. Journalists, corporate executives, and, yes, even trade union leaders all have an image problem. But not the corner dry-cleaner, the private-practice accountant, or the door-to-door Amway salesperson.

The poll put small business owners right at the top of the heap of Canadian professions, in the level of respect their work elicited from the population at large. A full 67% of respondents said they had a "great deal of respect" for small business owners, putting them miles ahead of any other profession, even priests, doctors, and police officers. Another 30% of respondents had a "fair amount" of respect.

Like Rodney Dangerfield in reverse, virtually no one in Canada holds any *disrespect* for these self-made entrepreneurs. The long hours, the spirit of self-reliance and the generally modest habits of most small business operators have clearly touched a sympathetic nerve with most Canadians.

A little bit of envy might even be colouring these poll results. Following the poll, one newspaper article quoted the owner of a small gift basket company in Mississauga enthusing: "A little part of everyone dreams of being their own boss."

As will be indicated in this chapter, however, if Canadians knew more about how hard small business operators work, and how little they typically get paid for it, a little bit of the lustre might chip off this rugged, individualist dream. Public respect may be one thing, but bottom-line success, it seems, is quite another. Many small entrepreneurs would happily trade in some of their public esteem for a little more money.

In general, small business is a surprisingly unproductive, poorly compensated undertaking. Indeed, the low productivity and low incomes of the rapidly-growing small business sector have helped to drag down overall productivity and income growth in Canada. And a poor record of investing in real capital equipment by most small businesses is an important reason for this poor performance.

A well-oiled lobby machine has effectively translated the almost universal high regard for capitalism's "little guy" into formidable political clout with governments of all political stripes. Small business representatives are among the loudest, and typically most conservative, of the lobbyists pressing hands on Parliament Hill and in the provincial capitals. And the most powerful ammunition in their campaign for small-business-friendly policies is the evidence that small businesses have been the most important source of job-creation in Canada's economy. This would seem to suggest that measures to help small business would result in a stronger labour market and lower unemployment, and many policy-makers have accepted this argument.

A closer look at the economic evidence, however, suggests a different conclusion. Perhaps the growing importance of small business in Canada is more a symptom of economic weakness than evidence of a growing, vital, entrepreneurial spirit among Canadians. Small businesses have become the most important source of new jobs largely *by default*, simply because larger companies and governments—which offer better-paid, more productive, and more secure jobs—have not been hiring or, worse yet, are downsizing.

Bluntly put, many small business undertakings are marginal low-productivity undertakings that would not be carried out if their proprietors had access to more productive and well-paid work in a "real" job. Part of the policy response to the growth of small business employment will require actions to improve productivity and income levels within those small businesses. But part will also involve taking measures to rejuvenate employment opportunities in larger, more productive firms and public agencies.

It turns out that economic policies to encourage more rapid investment in real capital can help to solve both problems: leading to faster job-creation in larger firms, and better productivity and compensation in small ones.

Small Business Rhetoric and Reality

"Get government off our backs," is the typical refrain of the Canadian Federation of Independent Business (CFIB) and other small business lobby groups. They fight for lower taxes, fewer regulations, weaker social programs, and tougher rules against unions. For example, a 1996 survey undertaken by the CFIB found that the following five policy measures were deemed most important by small business owners for improving the economic climate for their job-creation efforts (listed in order of their degree of support among survey respondents):

- Reduce payroll taxes (like UI premiums)
- Cut taxes for consumers (like personal income taxes)
- Cut government spending
- Reduce the employment "paper burden"
- Cut social assistance payments

At the same time, however, not to let consistency stand in the way of a good lobby campaign, the small-business sector has also been successful in winning a wide range of attractive government subsidies for smaller companies. Table 6-1 lists several of the special tax breaks enjoyed by small businesses in Canada. Their total cost runs to several billion dollars in forgone revenue at both the federal and provincial levels each year. In addition, small business also benefits from a range of other subsidy programs which involve the actual payment of hard money by governments, such as special job-creation grants, cash subsidies to self-employment through the unemployment insurance program, federal guarantees for small business loans by commercial banks, and numerous other measures.

Small businesses pay notably lower wages and fewer benefits to their employees, as well as lower taxes to government, than do their mega-corporate counterparts. Despite this, however, they are consistently less profitable, to the point in numerous cases of being marginally viable.

Many small business operators are personally conservative; but it is not just a "redneck" social attitude which fuels the small business community's demands for lower taxes, passive government, and weaker unions. Rather, these demands also stem from the fundamental economic conditions which most small business operators face: unending fierce competition from other small firms, a chronic lack of purchasing power in the domestic markets which most small businesses serve, and low levels of productivity and profitability.

Admittedly, some of the more right-wing views of the small-business community may be motivated more by conservative personal outlook than by real economics. For example, why should small businesses be such vocal supporters of cutbacks in government spending and welfare programs, when governments and welfare recipients are important customers of small businesses?

Table 6-1
Small Business Tax Subsidies

Subsidy	Explanation	Estimated Annual Cost[1]
Lower income tax rate: federal	Small business taxed at 12% instead of 28%.	$3 billion
Lower income tax rate: provincial	Provinces also charge lower corporate taxes for small businesses, with rate reductions of between 5.0 and 9.5 points.	$1 billion[2]
Capital gains exemption for small business shares	Investors receive a $500,000 lifetime capital gains exemption on small business investments.	$620 million
Enhanced R&D tax credit	Rebate of 35% of R&D spending, instead of 20% for other companies.	$195 million[3]
Labour-sponsored venture fund tax credit	Rebates 30% of investments in labour-sponsored small business mutual funds.	$150 million[4]
Small business GST exemption	Exempts very small businesses from collecting and forwarding GST.	$130 million
Allowable business investment loss	More generous treatment of capital losses incurred on small business investments.	$117 million
Small business stock option subsidy	Allows deferral of tax on stock options for small business executives and employees.	$93 million
Deduction of home office expenses	Allows home workers to deduct a portion of total household operation costs for businesses run partly or wholly from home.	Unknown
Exemption from workers' compensation premiums	Allows small businesses to avoid WCB premiums in many provinces.	Unknown
Other payroll tax exemptions	Allows small businesses to avoid or pay lower rates for other employer-paid payroll taxes (such as public health insurance premiums) in many provinces.	Unknown

Source: Department of Finance Canada, *Tax Expenditures*, 1998; *Report of the Technical Committee on Business Taxation*, 1997.
1. Federal government only, unless otherwise specified.
2. Provincial costs only.
3. Estimated difference between 35% small business rate and 20% normal rate.
4. Federal and provincial costs.

The long hours and modest incomes of small business owners may promote a certain bitterness toward others who lack the inclination or the opportunity to be equally entrepreneurial: "If I have to work so hard to make a lousy buck from my own business, why should I pay taxes to finance the cushy existence of public sector workers and welfare bums?"

But there is also a deeper economic underpinning to the conservative views of small business. As will be shown below, wages are typically much lower in small companies than in large corporations or public agencies. Hence these small businesses depend on a pool of available workers who will accept low pay, few benefits, and insecure job prospects.

History has shown that, when social programs are generous, workers are less willing to put up with such conditions. This makes life more difficult for small employers who are struggling to pay the bills, but who are also prevented from passing on higher costs to their customers because of the hyper-competition which dominates most small business industries. Hence the typical small employer hates social security programs for "rational" economic reasons, not just knee-jerk personal ones.

The bitter economic constraints facing most small businesses make any additional business cost—no matter how socially or morally justifiable it may be—a very bitter pill to swallow. Thus small business resistance is fierce to taxes, unions, minimum wages, and government regulation governing anything from consumer protection to worker rights to environmental guidelines. Larger businesses, too, tend to hate these things, but, thanks to their superior productivity and flexibility, they can usually adjust their operations accordingly.

That's why larger, more productive companies have been more fruitful targets for policies aimed at improving the social and environmental conditions of employment and production. Unions have been far more successful organizing and bargaining with large companies than with small ones. Government regulations on anything from worker safety to environmental protection are typically more effective with larger companies which possess discretionary resources to invest in safer, cleaner workplaces. Indeed, many government regulations on these issues explicitly exempt small business out of fear that the administrative and operational burden of the new rules would bankrupt some smaller employers.

Increasing the minimum wage by 15 cents rarely draws more than a peep from large companies, most of whom employ few if any minimum wage workers anyway, yet it sparks a near-rebellion from legions of low-productivity retailers and restaurants and other small businesses which depend on ultra-low wages for their very existence.[1] For small businesses scrambling desperately to stay afloat, every new effort by governments or unions to improve social and economic conditions for workers and communities is seen as potentially the last straw.

Thus it is not surprising that the small-business sector tends to be one of the most solidly entrenched conservative constituencies in the whole economy. This stems at least as much from the marginal, hyper-competitive economic conditions that most small businesses face as it does from the personal views of small business owners—many of whom, of course, are enlightened and compassionate people.

In this light, it is somewhat odd that the small-business sector's strong public cachét is often endorsed by progressives who would otherwise be critical of business, and who would support the types of social and economic interventions that are invariably denounced by small business. Perhaps it is a knee-jerk concern for the underdog that leads many left-wing commentators to express solidarity with small businesses, even as they denounce the power and influence of large corporations (which, ironically, tend to have much better records in labour relations, social responsibility, and environmental protection).

Even Canada's federal New Democratic Party has tried to jump on the small business bandwagon; in 1998 several party leaders expressed a desire to shift the party's policies to appeal to the small business community. The political logic of this repositioning seems far-fetched, given the stated conservative views of most small business owners (although, to be sure, some individual entrepreneurs hold progressive personal views and may vote NDP).[2]

More worrisome is the economic thinking underlying such an approach. If the goal is to generate a high-wage, productive, and egalitarian economy, then the growth of small business must be seen as a negative development, not something to be encouraged with even more favourable policies.

The Economic Performance of Small Business

Small companies may indeed have been the source of most new employment during the grim 1990s. But they have not, in general, been a source of *good* jobs. And the sub-par productivity and compensation levels which are all-too typical of this sector suggest that both the quality of small business jobs needs to be improved, and traditional sources of job-creation (by larger companies and public agencies) need to be revived.

Job-Creation and Job-Destruction

The evidence is clear that small companies have indeed produced a share of new jobs in Canada that is far out of proportion to their overall role in the labour market. At present, there are over one million private companies in Canada. Most of them are very small: 75% of them employ fewer than five workers, and 98% employ fewer than 50 workers.

Large employers are still the most important source of paid work in the private sector. Firms with more than 500 employees make up a tiny fraction—just 0.2%—of all companies in Canada, yet they still provide 40% of all private sector work. [Large employers are even more important in the public sector.] But the share of large companies in the total workforce has been declining in recent years, thanks both to their own sluggish hiring and to the much stronger growth in small business employment.

Firms with fewer than 50 employees accounted for about 60% of all net job creation in Canada during the 1980s and 1990s. They now employ about 35% of all private-sector workers. Medium-sized companies, with between 50 and 500 employees, accounted for 20% of job growth during the same period, and now make up another one-quarter of all private-sector employment. There is some indication that the importance of larger firms in job-creation has picked up some-what as Canada's economic recovery gathered steam later in the 1990s. During 1997, for example, workplaces with over 500 employees accounted for over 25% of all job growth, significantly more than in previous years.[3]

The generally positive job-creation record of small firms hides a lot of churn-ing and turmoil under the surface of the aggregate employment statistics. In addition to being the largest creators of jobs in the modern labour market, small businesses are also the largest *destroyers* of jobs. Rapid job turnover, the fre-quent bankruptcy of small firms, and other sources of instability mean that em-ployment with small firms is generally quite insecure.

As indicated in Table 6-2, the *gross* job-creation rate is extremely high in the small-business sector. The smallest companies typically create about one "new" job each year for every four jobs currently in existence: a phenomenal rate of job-creation. Unfortunately, however, almost as many jobs (about one in five each year) simultaneously *disappear* from the small- business sector thanks to layoffs and bankruptcies. Thus the net bottom-line job creation of small busi-nesses is much more modest. Even on a net basis, however, small firms have still been the most important source of new employment.

One consequence of this ongoing job turmoil in the small- business sector is that smaller firms and their workers are by far the heaviest "users" of Canada's unemployment insurance program. Statistics Canada studies indicate that workers at companies with less than 20 employees are about four times more likely to lose their jobs in a given year than employees of firms with over 500 workers.

Table 6-2
Gross and Net Job Creation by Size of Firm
Canada, private sector, 1978 to 1992, annual averages

	Size of Company[1]				
	Under 20 Workers	20-50 Workers	50-100 Workers	100-500 Workers	Over 500 Workers
Job creation (% per year)	23.4%	15.9%	14.4%	12.2%	6.8%
Job destruction (% per year)	20.2%	14.2%	13.0%	11.2%	6.6%
Net job creation (% per year)	3.3%	1.7%	1.4%	1.0%	0.1%
Share total employment	24.2%	11.9%	8.3%	16.0%	39.6%

Source: "Have small firms created a disproportionate share of new jobs in Canada? A reassessment of the facts," by Garnett Picot, John Baldwin, and Richard Dupuy, Research Paper #71, Analytical Studies Branch, Statistics Canada, November 1994.
1. Weighted according to average current size of firm.

As a result, the small-business sector draws far more out of the unemployment insurance system (in the form of UI benefits for workers who have lost their jobs at small companies) than it contributes (in the form of premiums collected from currently employed workers and their small business employers). One federal government study indicated that companies with less than five employees and their workers, on a relative basis, received back $2.60 in UI benefits for every dollar of premiums they paid. In contrast, large companies on average are net payers to the system, by virtue of the fact that they lay off their workers far less often. The same study indicated that companies with over 500 employees and their workers receive, on a relative basis, barely 50 cents of UI benefits back for each dollar of premiums paid into the system.

In this context, it is especially ironic that the small-business constituency remains the most vocal critic of UI premiums and other payroll taxes. The failure of small businesses to create *stable* jobs has clearly added to the cost of Canada's unemployment insurance system.[4]

Wages and Benefits

Jobs with small companies tend to offer significantly lower compensation than those with larger firms, in terms of both wages and salaries and the provision of non-wage employment benefits. Recent data on this subject is provided in Table 6-3. Wages and salaries for employees in large workplaces (those with over 500 workers) are between 60% and 70% higher than for those working at sites with fewer than 20 employees. Part-time employees of small businesses fare even worse: average earnings for part-time workers with large firms are twice as high as for those in the smallest workplaces.

Large employers also offer a far more extensive package of important non-wage benefits, such as health care benefits and pension coverage, which may be even more important to the economic and social security of their employees. Workers at the largest firms are between two and six times more likely to receive these non-wage benefits as part of their total compensation.

Lower union activity in small companies is an important factor explaining the lower wages that are paid there, and especially the absence of standard employment benefits. The unionization rate in firms with less than 20 employees was just 8% in 1996, compared to over 50% in the largest companies.

Self-Employment

The dramatic expansion of self-employment in Canada has been the most striking form of small business growth. Self-employment grew by one-third between 1990 and 1997, accounting for over three-quarters of all job growth during this

	Size of Company				Gap: Largest versus Smallest Companies
	Under 20 Workers	20-100 Workers	100-500 Workers	Over 500 Workers	
Wages and Salaries (1997):[1]					
Average hourly wage	$12.27	$15.35	$17.69	$20.59	$7.82 (+61%)
Average weekly earnings	$453	$568	$665	$771	$318 (+70%)
Non-Wage Employment Benefit Coverage (1995):					
Supplementary health insurance	23.1%	56.9%	69.5%	79.5%	56.4 points
Dental plan	19.7%	50.9%	63.8%	78.0%	58.3 points
Paid sick leave	27.7%	46.9%	61.7%	71.2%	43.5 points
Pension plan[2]	9.8%	29.1%	45.8%	65.7%	55.9 points
Unionization (1996)					
% of workers rep'd by a union[3]	7.8%	14.7%	32.5%	52.6%	44.8 points

Table 6-3
Earnings and Benefits by Firm Size

Source: Author's calculations from Statistics Canada, *Labour Force Information*; "Recent Canadian evidence on job quality by firm size," by Marie Drolet and René Morissette, Research Paper #128, Analytical Studies Branch, Statistics Canada, November 1998; Statistics Canada, *The Evolving Workplace: Findings from the Pilot Workplace and Employee Survey*, May 1998.
1. Wage and salary data compiled by size of workplace, not size of firm.
2. Male-female weighted average based on average gender composition implicit in other employment benefit data. Data covers private sector only.
3. Longer-service employees only.

time. Self-employment accounted for 18% of all jobs by 1997—much higher than in most other industrial economies, even the U.S. (where just 10% of all workers are self-employed).

By 1995, self-employment exceeded total employment in the public sector of the economy for the first time in Canada's post-war history. This symbolized the extent to which Canadians, in the wake of the government downsizing and stagnant labour markets which dominated the economy during the 1990s, had truly become a nation of ruggedly self-reliant entrepreneurs. But is this a good thing?

Statistics Canada published a unique survey of the incomes and working conditions of self-employed Canadians in 1997.[5] The data contained in this survey painted an interesting—and worrisome—picture of the nature of this most rapidly-expanding form of small business activity. Some highlights of the survey include:

- 90% of the growth in total self-employment during the 1990s consisted of "own account" self-employment, in which the self-employed individual has no additional employees other than him- or herself.
- By 1997, these "own account" workers accounted for 60% of total self-employment.

- On average, self-employed workers earn less than paid employees. This is especially true for "own account" self-employed individuals, who had average earnings of $22,900 in 1995—just two-thirds the level of average earnings for employees. Self-employed individuals who in turn employ other workers earn almost twice as much as own-account self-employed individuals: an average of $41,000 in 1995.[6]
- Incomes among the self-employed are far more polarized than in society as a whole. At the top end, almost 5% of the self-employed earned over $100,000 in 1995, versus just 1% of paid employees. At the bottom end, over 35% of all self-employed individuals earned less than $15,000 the same year, compared to just 17% of paid workers.
- Self-employed individuals worked an average of 42 hours per week in 1996, about six hours more per week than paid employees. One-third of all self-employed individuals work over 50 hours per week.

This portrait of long hours and relatively low pay does not exactly suggest that self-employment is the path to an easy, prosperous life. The expansion of self-employment, and the apparently difficult conditions of work for the self-employed, have sparked considerable discussion about what motivates the self-employed to incur the personal costs and risks that seem to be associated with running one's own business.[7]

There are two general categories of motivation that might explain the growth of self-employment. Self-employment might be a desirable occupation in and of itself, for both financial and personal reasons: think of these as "pull" factors which attract new entrepreneurs. On the other hand, conditions in the paid labour market might be so bleak that many individuals feel compelled to strike out on their own: think of these as "push" factors motivating an exodus into self-employment by individuals who feel they have few other options.

There are many positive features of self-employment which continue to attract hopeful entrepreneurs: more personal freedom and independence, greater flexibility of work schedules (although it is difficult to be too flexible when you are working more than 50 hours per week), the desire to carry on a family business inherited from one's parents.

The Statistics Canada survey referenced above reports that desire for greater independence was the greatest single motivation identified by self-employed individuals for their own career choice; 42% of all self-employed listed that as their primary motivation. Just 12% explicitly identified a lack of alternative work options as their primary motive (although for a number of reasons this response is likely to underestimate the true extent of "push" factors in motivating self-employment).

Figure 6-1
Paid Employment and Self-Employment
Canada, 1990 to 1997

Source: Author's calculations from Statistics Canada, *Canadian Economic Observer.*

Other economic evidence, however, suggests that the motivation for being self-employed tends to become much stronger when developments in the paid labour market are negative; in other words, that self-employment in many cases is appealing only by default.

Figure 6-1 compares the annual changes in self-employment in Canada in the 1990s with corresponding changes in the level of paid employment. The years of strongest self-employment growth—1990, 1993, 1996, and 1997—were also years in which paid employment grew by less than 0.5% in the year. Conversely, years in which paid employment growth was strong enough to bring about a significant reduction in the unemployment rate—1994, 1995, and 1998—are also the years in which self-employment growth was less.

For women, the fastest-growing types of self-employment are traditional low-paying child care and home-cleaning occupations; it is hard to believe that "being your own boss" could be a major incentive for the rebirth of these traditional domestic service jobs. There is clearly an increasing structural trend toward greater self-employment; but the extent to which this reflects the free choices of the self-employed, and the extent to which it reveals a chronic lack of opportunity elsewhere in the labour market, remains to be determined.[8]

Profitability

The harsh market conditions faced by most small businesses, and their underinvestment in productivity-enhancing capital equipment, means that they tend to be consistently less profitable than larger firms. Companies with over $75 million per year in total revenues earned an average rate of profit in their

Generous Spirit

"These provisions result in Canada's income tax treatment of small business being among the most generous in the world."
—Technical Committee on Business Taxation,
Dept. of Finance Canada, 1997

total assets of 5.5% between 1992 and 1997; companies with revenues under $5 million, on the other hand, earned just 3.5% percent on assets.

Larger companies thus tend to be about 60% more profitable than small ones. Ironically, the poor profitability of small businesses tends to reinforce the low productivity and labour-intensity of their operations, which in turn is a fundamental underlying cause of their poor profitability.

With few internal cash resources to allocate to new investments, and with a high rate of bankruptcy and default which discourages lenders and outside investors from supplying capital, smaller firms typically do not have sufficient funds to allocate to new investments, even if their businesses might be more profitable as a result.

Strangely, the small business lobbyists stridently blame the consistent financial underperformance of their constituency on onerous government taxation. Given the range of lucrative tax subsidies which are provided to small business (and which were summarized in Table 6-1), this claim is laughable. Large companies pay far more in taxes than small businesses, yet they are still more profitable at the end of the day.

Indeed, it appears that the tax loopholes provided for small businesses may, perversely, be one of the key factors motivating their relative growth in recent years. This should come as no surprise: a fundamental principle of public finance states that if you want more of something, subsidize it.

The range of subsidies available to small business has expanded in recent years, even as average tax rates imposed on regular paid workers have increased. Perversely, this can only reinforce the shift toward relatively poorly-compensated small business activities. The ability to write off a significant share of normal household expenses as business costs is often the greatest compensation that operators of home-based businesses ever receive.

Some economic studies have even linked the growth of self-employment to the rising incentive to evade personal taxes. Since many self-employment occupations offer ample opportunity for proprietors to under-report cash income and hence reduce their taxes, the relative appeal of self-employment rises when the tax rates paid by regular paid employees also increase.[9]

Investment and Productivity

Unfortunately, no direct firm-level data are yet available on the real investment expenditures by private companies of different sizes. The evidence regarding the low and perhaps declining productivity of small businesses suggests strongly that they invest far less in real capital equipment than do their larger counterparts. Sectoral analysis of the sorts of industries which are dominated by small business—retail and wholesale trade, food and beverage services, personal and business services—also indicates the highly labour-intensive pattern of most small-business production (see Table 6-4).

The average value of capital equipment used by each worker in Canada's retail industry, for example, is just one-fifth as large as that of the manufacturing sector. Put simply, if an industry does not require much capital investment for a firm to get started, then it is precisely those industries which will be dominated by smaller companies.

Where capital investment is strong and growing is also where productivity levels, as well as the rate of productivity growth, tend to be highest. And, as indicated in Table 6-5, these favourable trends are concentrated in industries which are dominated by larger companies. Productivity growth in many labour-intensive sectors such as business and hospitality services—precisely the industries dominated by smaller firms—has actually been *negative* in recent years, as smaller companies spring up using little capital equipment and offering primarily low-wage, often part-time or temporary employment.

The relative growth of employment in these industries through the 1980s and 1990s, which coincides with the rising importance of small firms and self-employment in the total economy, is thus an important factor in Canada's poor productivity performance.

Table 6-4 Fixed Investment by Sector Canada, 1994			
Sector	Net Fixed Capital per Worker[1]	GDP per Worker[2]	Growth in GDP/Worker, 1994-97
"Small Business" Industries			
Business services	$4,250	$52,600	-2.0%
Retail trade	$7,500	$28,700	5.7%
Wholesale trade	$9,300	$56,200	-1.6%
Accommodation & food services	$11,000	$22,600	-3.4%
"Big Business" Industries			
Manufacturing	$38,000	$65,000	4.0%
Transportation	$52,000	$62,900	6.3%
Communication & utilities	$228,000	$111,000	12.7%
Oil & gas	$790,000	$430,000	7.8%

Source: Author's calculations from Statistics Canada, *Fixed Capital Stocks and Flows, Gross Domestic Product by Industry*, and *Employment, Earnings and Hours*.
1. Net capital stock, current dollars, geometric depreciation.
2. In real 1992 dollars.

Table 6-5 **Investment in Training and Technology by Firm Size** *Canada, private sector, 1978 to 1992, annual averages*				
	Size of Company			
	Under 20 Workers	**20-50 Workers**	**100-500 Workers**	**Over 500 Workers**
Percent of employees covered by in-house training programs	26.9%	31.1%	45.4%	48.3%
Percent of firms conducting ongoing R&D[1]	19.1%	32.3%	42.2%	52.7%

Source: Statistics Canada, *The Evolving Workplace: Findings from the Pilot Workplace and Employee Survey,* May 1998; and "The importance of research and development for innovation in small and large Canadian manufacturing firms," by John Baldwin, Research Paper #107, Analytical Studies Branch, Statistics Canada, September 1997.
1. Manufacturing sector only.

Other tangential evidence also confirms the slow pace of investment by small companies. Surveys have been completed on investments in technology or human capital by private firms, and they also indicate that investment slows down dramatically as company size decreases. Table 6-6 summarizes survey results on the prevalence of ongoing R&D investments, and regular in-house training programs, by firms of different sizes.

Not surprisingly, the largest companies are approximately twice as likely to invest in regular in-house training of their staff, and close to three times as likely to invest in regular research and development activity. These findings are surely mirrored in a much higher rate of real capital investment by these same large companies.

Base and Beyond: The Economic Role of Small Business

Most small businesses in Canada are destined to play an inherently secondary or subsidiary role in the economic progress of the nation as a whole, by virtue of the fundamental nature of the goods and services which they produce. Most smaller firms depend on sales to one of two markets: either the consumer purchases of individuals who already have jobs with other companies, or else purchases by those other companies of supplies and services used in their own operations.

Most small businesses need some *other* employer to do something *first*, therefore, before they can sell their own product and create their own jobs. In this sense, most small businesses cannot "lead" the development of the broader economy. They can only follow it.

Consider the following not-so-hypothetical example: a mining development located in a remote region of northern Canada. Prior to the discovery and development of the mine, there were few residents of the region (perhaps mainly Aboriginal peoples supporting themselves through traditional activities such as hunting and trapping). With the development of the mine, many hundreds of paying jobs are created at the new facility (let's assume optimistically that Aboriginal land claims were settled agreeably before the mine was built, and hence a significant share of the new jobs go to the Aboriginal peoples on whose land the mine is being built).

A whole town soon springs up. Subsequent spin-off jobs will be created in the town, mostly by small businesses which are set up to meet the needs of residents for a whole range of goods and services: everything from home construction to auto repair facilities to restaurants and retailers, to doctors and dentists, to personal services like hair-stylists and accountants. Other small businesses will focus on meeting the needs of the mine for supplies and services, ranging from fuel to machinery repair services to stationary to computers.

Finally, public sector jobs will be created to provide services like schools, hospitals, electricity and sewage services.

The initial investment in a new mine has sparked an ongoing "multiplier" effect which creates a total volume of new employment far in excess of the number of jobs created at the mine itself—much like the investment multiplier process illustrated in Chapter 4 (see especially Figure 4-3). Indeed, at the end of the whole process, the mine itself will likely account for a minority of total employment in the new community.

Depending on the type of industry which sparked the initial boom, the spending and sourcing patterns of local consumers and businesses, and the economic characteristics of the surrounding region, each initial job at the town's major employer could spur the creation of as many as two other jobs elsewhere in the community. Once that has occurred, the combined employment of small businesses in the town may actually constitute the majority of all jobs.

Does this mean that the town's economy is being "led" by small business? Hardly. Demand for the goods and services produced by the town's many small businesses depends completely on the prior decision by the mining company to locate the mine there. This is true of "upstream" jobs with supply and service contractors which sell fuel, spare parts, and services to the mine itself. It is also true of the "downstream" jobs: consumer-oriented businesses whose market depends first and foremost on the spending power of employed mine-workers.

Either way, if the initial surge of spending power which resulted from the location of the mine were to be withdrawn, the spin-off jobs would ultimately disappear as well. The mine goes, and the town dies: it's as simple as that. And sadly, this is exactly what has occurred in numerous resource-dependent "one-industry" towns in Canada's hinterland.

Regional economists explain this jobs-multiplier effect with a concept called the economic "base" of a community or a region. The economic base refers to that industry or group of industries which generates an initial surge of investment, employment, and purchasing power coursing through a local or regional economy. That initial expenditure in turn stimulates spin-off production and employment, both upstream and downstream.

The circular process of employment-creation stops once the new spending has exhausted itself. How many jobs are created in the interim depends on many different factors. If the region in question is very remote, it likely has to import almost all goods purchased by consumers and businesses; this will limit the spin-off job creation, since so much of the initial injection of spending power "leaks out" of the local economy in the form of spending on imports. Similarly, if a large portion of the income generated by the mine is collected by far-off governments in taxes, and this revenue is not reinvested in the provision of local services, then the jobs-multiplier effect will also be limited.

On the other hand, if taxes are re-invested in the provision of local public services, then the job-creation effects of the initial investment may be accentuated by new hiring in local public agencies. And, if the local or regional economy is relatively diversified, so that more local needs can be met through local production, then again the jobs-multiplier of the initial investment will be all the stronger.

When you move from a mining town to Canada's large cities, economic life naturally gets more complicated. In any modern urban economy, there are likely to be numerous different industries which function as an economic "base." The fluctuating investment and employment decisions of those different industries will send shock waves through the urban economy—sometimes offsetting one another, sometimes reinforcing one another.

A large, diverse, and permanent collection of small businesses will exist to service both the supply needs of those "base" industries, and the consumer needs of the community. It thus becomes very difficult to determine which industry came "first." But this does not alter the fact that the survival of most small businesses still depends on the success of those base industries which delivered the first injections of investment and spending power to the urban economy.

For example, most citizens of the greater Toronto area do not work in the industries which ultimately constitute that city's strong and diverse economic base: its financial complex, its still-strong manufacturing base (in key industries such as auto assembly and aerospace), the provincial government headquarters, or its tourism and convention businesses.

These and other base industries independently located in and around Toronto for autonomous and sometimes purely accidental reasons. Their exist-

The Shopping Mall Economy

Newcomers to Halifax might be forgiven some confusion. If they follow the signs to the Bayers Lake Industrial Park (not-so-affectionately known to many locals as the BLIP), they don't really come across much industry. They actually enter a surreal satellite community of retail stores and restaurants, located miles from any significant residential development.

For the consumer, the BLIP is a convenient, if soulless, agglomeration of strip malls, chain stores, fast food restaurants, cinemas, and other mostly small business outlets. That explains why the one road into the complex is jam-packed every Saturday, necessitating the provision of traffic cops to guide the crowds. Even tourists now make the drive out to what has become Halifax's most important, and certainly strangest, retail centre.

How did this "industrial park" come to be a magnet for shoppers, given its strange location in the midst of a largely uninhabited, rugged forest? Anxious to attract new businesses to the city, local government offered significant incentives, including virtually free land, to any company which set up shop in the park.

An unintended consequence of the subsidy program was that many retail businesses also stepped up to take advantage of the subsidy. Why pay high rents downtown when land is virtually free at the BLIP? A phenomenal relocation of retail investment occurred. As the BLIP's unexpected retail boom gathered momentum, even more stores and restaurants clambered aboard the bandwagon, since the weekly pilgrimage of thousands of consumers out to the Bayers Lake forest constituted a new and lucrative market for everything from construction materials to cappuccinos.

Opinion is divided as to whether the BLIP is a cultural and economic disaster, or a source of vibrant new growth. One thing is certain: the word "industrial" should be removed from the development's name, in the interests of fairness in advertising. There is very little industrial development at this industrial park. Indeed, the park's star industrial tenant—a small auto assembly operation run by the Swedish auto giant Volvo—closed its doors in 1998, laying off its 200 workers. Perhaps they can apply for work at the new Second Cup coffee shop which opened shortly afterward.

The planners who conceived of the BLIP forgot the important distinction considered in this chapter: between the economic "base" of a region and the other businesses which depend on that base. Clearly, no economy can be built on the strength of shopping malls alone.

ence and growth spurred the development of a huge and thriving metropolis, most of whose residents work in activities aimed at serving the large local market which grew along with the city itself. But if the city's base industries disappeared, Toronto's fortunes would surely flag in their wake—no matter how hardworking or persistent the city's corner store operators, auto mechanics, and hairstylists might be.

It is not impossible for small businesses to contribute to the economic base of a regional or even national economy; it is just unlikely. Some small businesses clearly contribute to the initial investment or export demand which is required to set the jobs-multiplier in motion. A good example is the high-tech, export-oriented production of highly specialized tools, dies, and machine parts. This industry was historically dominated by smaller, often family-run manufacturing firms (although larger corporations are now becoming more important). These companies are highly productive, their investment in sophisticated capital equipment contributes to all-important real investment spending in an economy, and their successful export sales further enhance the jobs-multiplier process described above. In some countries (such as Germany and Italy), industrial complexes composed of smaller but high-tech machinery and tool manufacturers have been an important ingredient in overall economic success.

These examples are exceptions, however. Despite the rhetoric of "self-reliance," most small businesses are fully dependent on the investment and purchasing decisions of larger companies, governments, and their respective workers.

Indeed, much of the rapid growth in small business employment can even be attributed to changing patterns of supply purchasing by large companies and governments; current research indicates that a significant proportion of self-employment is accounted for directly by the decisions of larger enterprises to outsource services that were formerly provided by in-house staff.

Similarly, the continued popularity of franchising in many industries (including retail, restaurants, and business services) is another factor behind the creation of jobs which are technically located within small businesses, but which in reality depend immediately and directly on the investment decisions of large ones.

For all of these reasons, if disproportionate attention is paid to the economic prospects and hiring decisions of small business, policy-makers will be neglecting the dog in order to watch over its wagging tail. If the economic base of a region or country is growing—if investment is strong, if exports are up, and if government is expanding the provision of public services—then the small-business sector will undoubtedly share in that success. Rising consumer incomes, along with vibrant demand from large companies for supplies and services, will ensure the birth and development of the small businesses that every economy needs.

Economic policy should obviously keep an eye on the continuing viability of small business operations; it should also do what it can to push the small-business sector toward more socially and economically beneficial business practices. But targeting small business as the engine of future economic growth is clearly a mistake.

Even if small business continues to account for a disproportionate share of new jobs created, that job-creation is itself dependent on prior expansion in the base industries whose performance ultimately determines the rise and fall of the economy as a whole. In the vast majority of cases, those base industries are dominated by large companies and public agencies.

Conclusion

The owners and operators of small businesses in Canada have a well-deserved reputation for their hard work, self-reliance, and frugality. Their long hours and typically low pay have won small business owners the respect of their fellow citizens. But we shouldn't confuse respect with prosperity, and we shouldn't make a virtue out of the economic necessity that most small business owners face.

The independence of "being your own boss" obviously motivates many entrepreneurs (if they're in it for the money, most will be sorely disappointed). Yet most small businesses face a brutal set of economic conditions which controls their actions and limits their flexibility as surely as the most dictatorial boss in a *Dilbert* cartoon. Any manager who could get paid employees to work for as long in return for as little pay as the typical small business owner would be hailed as a genius in the corporate clubroom.

Clearly, the self-exploitation of small business owners (and often their families) has been crucial to the survival of their companies; much economic evidence suggests that, when regular paying jobs are more abundant, then the apparent "appeal" of self-employment is dramatically reduced. Long hours and low pay hardly constitute a model for future economic growth. The whole point of economic development is presumably to support a *higher* standard of living with *less* work, not more.

The low productivity, below-average incomes, and marginal profitability of small business suggest that Canada's increased reliance on this sector for most job-creation is one of our greatest economic weaknesses, not one of our strengths.

All of this reinforces the importance of taking measures to revitalize real investment spending—both by the small businesses which currently don't invest much, if at all, in real capital equipment, and also by the larger, more productive employers whose contribution to job growth has flagged during the last two decades.

The current condition of Canada's hard-pressed small-business sector reveals the downside of trying to create new jobs in an economy *without* investing adequately in productivity-enhancing capital equipment. Chapter 4 of this book, dealing with how jobs are created in Canada's economy, stressed the important leading role of real investment spending in job-creation. But, in the absence of sufficient real investment in an economy, it is still possible for jobs to get created. In fact, "jobs" of one sort or another must inevitably be created in any economy, due to the simple imperative that individuals must find some way to support themselves. This is especially true when social programs are unavailable or inadequate to protect the unemployed.

Think, for instance, of an underdeveloped economy in Latin America or Africa. A desperate unemployed person there might lay out a blanket on a street corner selling gum or trinkets, to earn a few dollars a month with which to buy a few necessities. This person is "employed," and his or her "job" has required virtually no investment in capital equipment. Millions of jobs just like this one explain why the official rate of unemployment in a country like Mexico is significantly lower than it is in developed countries like Canada. With no unemployment insurance or other social benefits to fall back on, if you're unemployed, you starve. Period.

Not surprisingly, then, unemployment (at least as strictly defined by the statisticians) can thus be relatively low. But this hardly implies that the economy is utilizing the full productive potential of those "employed" trinket-sellers, nor that their creative self-reliance should be promoted, let alone subsidized.

The unprecedented growth of low-wage, low-productivity small business employment in Canada, especially prominent during the 1990s, in many ways represents a shift toward a third-world pattern of economic development. The number of well-paying, productive jobs available in the "core" of the economy (larger firms and public agencies) has stagnated, thanks in large part to the slowdown in real capital accumulation by those same employers. Through economic necessity more than choice, many Canadians have responded to the dearth of "good" jobs by trying to make their own jobs. Government has promoted this trend with tax breaks and outright subsidies, as a relatively cheap way of dealing with the overall unemployment crisis.

Conservative politicians and economists herald the trend as evidence of an entrepreneurial spirit. But the low incomes, low productivity, and pressing insecurity of small business employment has clearly held back the progress of the economy as a whole.

It might be argued that a low-wage, insecure job with a small firm is obviously better than no job at all. But, even if this argument is accepted, economic policy needs to address the underlying structural problems which have pushed many Canadians into such marginal forms of economic activity. Stimulating more investment spending in Canada—by big companies, small companies, and public and non-profit agencies alike—would make an important contribution to this goal.

Faster investment would create more jobs with the larger companies which offer the best jobs. It would produce stronger macroeconomic conditions, and hence increase the sales and profits of those small businesses which depend on the general state of domestic purchasing power. And, by encouraging the adoption of more productive, capital-intensive production techniques by small businesses themselves, a more pro-investment policy regime would also assist in the conversion of small business from a ghetto of lousy jobs into a source of true value-added production and employment.

Part II
Slow Motion: How
Investment Lost Steam

Chapter 7
Measuring the Slowdown

Chapter 8
Explaining the Slowdown

Chapter 7
Measuring the Slowdown

It will come as a surprise to many Canadians to learn that the pace of real investment in Canada's economy slowed considerably during the 1980s, and even more in the 1990s. After all, the explosion of the financial industry and the omnipresent culture of "personal investing" make it seem as if Canadians were born to invest. As we have seen, however, a wide and growing chasm divides real investment in things that make a difference to the real economy from the innumerable paper representations of that real wealth. Ironically, by any measure, real investment spending has lost considerable steam in Canada even as the paper boom reached hyperspeed.

In most cases, the investment slowdown can be dated to about 1981, when Canada's policy-makers explicitly abandoned the goal of full employment as their top economic priority. Instead, they imposed punitive high interest rates in an effort to restrain inflation. Those high interest rates (when correctly measured) have become a more-or-less permanent feature of Canada's economic landscape. [This issue will be discussed in detail in Chapter 9.] Real investment spending was among the first casualties of this shift in policy; slower economic growth, chronic unemployment, and a virtually permanent atmosphere of recession have been its long-term results.

Portraits of the Slowdown

The discussion in Chapter 5 indicated that there are numerous different ways of defining and measuring real investment. Similarly, there are numerous different methods of charting its slowdown. The most common way to measure real investment spending is as a share of an economy's total GDP. This measure is often called the *investment share*.

Figure 7-1 illustrates the historical trend in the investment share in Canada during the post-war era. Two measures are presented: one is for gross investment as a share of GDP, while the other is for net investment, measured after the deduction of that portion of investment spending which is required to replace the depreciation of the existing capital stock.

Net investment, then, represents an addition to the capital stock (above and beyond day-to-day wear-and-tear). During the first 35 years after World War II, Canada consistently allocated between 20% and 25% of total GDP to real investment. Net investment consistently averaged between 10% and 15% of GDP.

All this changed, however, with the advent of conservative macroeconomics in the early 1980s. Since then, gross investment spending has declined by about 5 percentage points of GDP—to between 15% and 20% of total output. Net investment has declined by a similar amount. Indeed, during the 1990s net investment has averaged barely 5% of GDP—less than half its typical levels prior to 1981.

In fact, the slowdown in net investment is slightly greater, in terms of its share of GDP, than the slowdown in gross investment. As indicated in Table 7-1, this reflects the slight increase in depreciation charges over time, again measured as a share of GDP. Depreciation costs have increased by about one percentage point of GDP, from around 11% prior to 1980 to 12% or slightly higher subsequently.

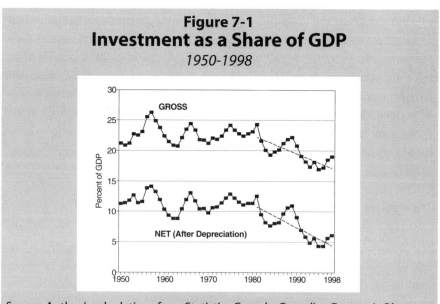

Figure 7-1
Investment as a Share of GDP
1950-1998

Source: Author's calculations from Statistics Canada, *Canadian Economic Observer*.

Table 7-1
The Investment Slowdown: Gross and Net
Percent of GDP, 1950-1998

	1950s	1960s	1970s	1980s	1990s[1]	Change: 1970s to 1990s
Gross Investment	23.2%	22.2%	22.6%	21.4%	18.4%	-4.3 points
Depreciation	10.9%	11.7%	11.3%	11.7%	12.5%	+1.3 points
Net Investment	12.3%	10.5%	11.4%	9.7%	5.8%	-5.5 points

Source: Author's calculations from Statistics Canada, *Canadian Economic Observer*. Totals may not add due to rounding.
1. 1990 to 1998 only.

The growing expense of depreciation has cut further into the rate of net investment: not only has the initial injection of gross investment spending slowed down, but the amount required to keep the existing capital stock in good working order has increased. Net investment, therefore, has experienced a two-fold decline.

Higher depreciation charges (measured as a share of GDP) could result from two factors: either the *rate* of depreciation can increase (so that a greater proportion of the existing capital stock wears out each year), and/or the economic cost of a given rate of depreciation can grow if the size of the initial capital stock, relative to GDP, also grows. Both factors have played a role in pushing up slightly the total importance of depreciation charges in Canada.

Many types of modern capital (especially technologically sophisticated machinery and equipment) have shorter service lives than was true of typical capital assets in previous years (especially the non-residential structures which now make up a decreasing share of the total capital stock). Hence the annual expense of maintaining and ultimately replacing capital assets grows over time.

In this sense, the increasing technical sophistication of capital equipment suggests that a high-tech economy should be investing *more* over time, in gross terms, not less, because of the rising cost of maintaining that more sophisticated capital stock. Canada's economy, however, has done the opposite. Even as investment goods become more complex and easily outdated, we have decreased the share of our economy devoted to gross new investment, which means that the slowdown in *net* capital accumulation is all the more pronounced.

Much of the decline in the average investment share during the 1990s is attributable, of course, to the painful recession experienced at the beginning of the decade, and the unusually slow economic recovery experienced since then. Throughout the post-war era, the investment share has revealed a cyclical trend: investment is stronger in periods of expansion (when a growing economy elicits extra investment from optimistic companies), and weaker during downturns.

The recession, alone, however, cannot explain the extent of the investment slowdown during the 1990s. There was a painful recession in the early 1980s, too; in fact, that downturn was even worse than the 1991-92 recession. And, even by 1998, when the "recovery" was several years old, the pace of investment spending in Canada was anything but stunning. Real investment that year equaled just 19% of total GDP, only slightly above the average for the whole decade. And, on a net basis, investment totalled just 6% of GDP, half its pre-1981 levels.

Only business investment in machinery and equipment showed a vitality in 1998 that would qualify as notable from a longer-term perspective: machinery and equipment spending totalled 7% of GDP in 1998, its strongest performance since 1981. Whether that mini-boom in machinery investment will translate into a broader expansion of investment and ultimately output remains very much in doubt.

Even by 1998, then, total investment in Canada remained well below the cycle-peak levels experienced just a decade earlier. Clearly, deep structural factors underlie the investment slowdown, not just the gloomy day-to-day state of the economy.

Another way of measuring real investment is as a share of the existing stock of capital assets. This measure—called the *investment rate*—captures the speed at which an economy is replacing and growing its total stockpile of capital assets and equipment. If the current value of the accumulated capital stock (after making appropriate deductions for past depreciation) was $100 billion, and current gross investment equalled $10 billion, then the investment rate would be 10%. Indeed, gross investment consistently equalled about 10% of the outstanding real capital stock each year until about 1980. Since then, the gross investment rate has declined by about two percentage points.

In *net* terms, the decline in the investment rate is once again somewhat more pronounced. During the 1990s, annual net investment in Canada has been

Figure 7-2
Investment as a Proportion of the Capital Stock
1950-1997

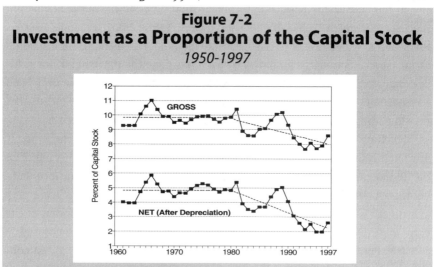

Source: Author's calculations from Statistics Canada, *Canadian Economic Observer* and *National Balance Sheet Accounts*.

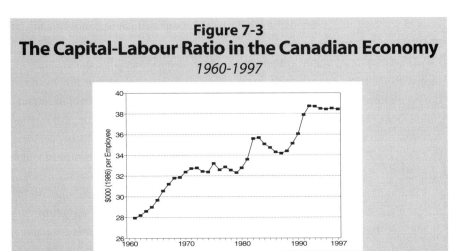

Figure 7-3
The Capital-Labour Ratio in the Canadian Economy
1960-1997

Source: Author's calculations from Statistics Canada, *Canadian Economic Observer, Fixed Capital Flows and Stocks.*

equivalent to only about 2% of the outstanding capital stock, compared to net investment rates of 5% or more prior to 1980. In other words, Canada's net stockpile of capital equipment is now growing at only a snail's pace.

The data illustrated in Figure 7-2 once again indicate the rising importance of depreciation charges. The gross investment rate has declined by about two points since 1980, while the net investment rate has fallen by about three points. This implies that the average depreciation rate—that is, the average proportion of the existing capital stock which must be replaced each year—has increased by about one percentage point over the same time period.

Once again, given the increasing technical sophistication of the capital stock in Canada, and its increasing concentration in machinery and equipment (rather than longer-lived structures), it seems that the economy needs to invest at a faster pace just to maintain a given trajectory for growth in the net capital stock, and hence in the economy. This makes the visible slowdown in Canada's real investment effort all the more worrisome.

A troubling consequence of the very slow growth of the net capital stock in Canada's economy is illustrated in Figure 7-3. This figure illustrates the rise in the net capital stock, expressed relative to the number of employed workers in the economy. This ratio is known as the *capital-labour ratio* (introduced in Chapter 5), and is a simple way of capturing the extent to which each individual employee's labour is supplemented and aided by a collection of tools, equipment, buildings, and structures.

The rising capital-labour ratio over time indicates the growing capital-intensity of the economy, and is strongly correlated with increases in average labour productivity and hence in living standards. Astonishingly, the capital-labour ratio has not increased at all in Canada during most of the 1990s; in fact, it has *declined* slightly.[1]

The ratio grew rapidly at the end of the 1980s and the early 1990s. This was largely the perverse result of the mass layoffs which accompanied the onset of the recession; with fewer workers employed in the economy, the capital-labour ratio "looks" higher, even if no capital has been added. Since the end of the recession, there has been no increase in the average capital intensity of Canada's economy. The snail's pace of net investment has only been enough to keep up with the ongoing growth of the labour force.

The stagnation of capital-intensity in Canada is a stunning contradiction to the whole notion that fantastic technical change and the dissemination of sophisticated new technologies are the hallmarks of a "new" economic paradigm. Strangely, thanks to the very slow pace of real investment spending, Canada's economy has actually become *less* capital-intensive, not more. This bizarre trend—along with other trends depicted earlier in this book, such as the rise of low-productivity self-employment—highlights the degree to which Canada's economy has moved in the direction of *underdevelopment* during the grim 1990s.

Of course, in some industries, technology is more advanced than ever, and productivity is high. In the economy as a whole, however, our failure to mobilize capital in the form of real investments is clearly hampering the extent to which we are able to take advantage of the productive possibilities of new technical ideas and practices. Indeed, the lack of growth in the general capital intensity of Canada's economy during the 1990s is certainly one of the prime factors behind the simultaneous slowdown in productivity growth.

There are many factors which affect productivity, of course, and no one-dimensional explanation of the productivity slowdown is possible. The absence of growth in the average capital-labour ratio during this decade, however, is surely a key contributing factor.

Non-technical factors (like more intense supervision, stronger workplace "discipline," new management techniques, and so on) can improve productivity to some degree, for a certain period of time. In the long run, however, true productivity growth stems from advances in technology which must be embodied within new and more modern capital equipment. In this context, the outlook for future Canadian productivity growth is gloomy indeed.

The link between rising capital-intensity and rising productivity is visible in historical Canadian data, as illustrated in Figure 7-4. Improvements in average productivity levels traditionally depend on previous increases in capital-intensity. [Figure 7-4 compares current productivity growth, the solid line, with changes in the capital-labour ratio from two years previous, the dotted line.]

Figure 7-4
Capital-Intensity and Productivity
1950-1997

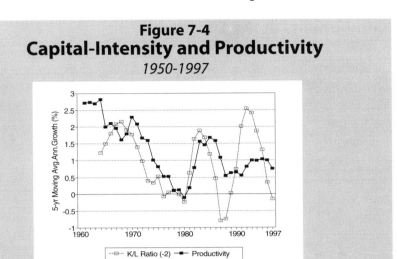

Source: Author's calculations from Statistics Canada, *Canadian Economic Observer*, *Fixed Capital Flows and Stocks*.

Both have fluctuated around relatively low average levels during the 1980s and 1990s. If anything, the almost non-existent growth of the net capital stock in Canada during the 1990s has yet to fully show up in productivity; thus the decline of capital-intensity in this decade is probably an ominous sign of further coming weakness in Canada's productivity performance.

Data from 1998 on the expansion of employment and output in Canada reinforce the concern over slowing productivity. Real GDP grew during 1998 by just under 3% percent: a decent but hardly overpowering performance. Incredibly, however, average employment grew by almost as much: 2.8%, representing close to 400,000 new jobs.

While this job growth was welcome news to a labour market that has remained chronically depressed for most of the decade, its flip-side was a message that productivity growth in Canada has almost stopped dead in its tracks. In the context of a level of economic growth that was positive but modest, Canada's economy created "too many" jobs during 1998. The implied rate of productivity growth during the year was just 0.2%. This reinforces the suspicion that, while jobs have indeed been created in Canada during the latter stages of the 1990s recovery, they have not generally been "good" jobs.

With growing part-time work, marginal forms of self-employment, and other low-value occupations for our nation's underutilized workers, the rising employment numbers are not translating into corresponding increases in productive capacity and living standards. For this to occur, more Canadians need to be employed in high-value, high-technology occupations, which in turn requires a great improvement in Canada's lacklustre record of real investment.

Components of the Slowdown

The slowdown in real investment in Canada has been experienced in a surprisingly uniform fashion across all of the different categories of real investment spending that were introduced in Chapter 5. In other words, no major component of investment spending has escaped the deterioration in Canada's overall investment performance.

Trends over the last five decades in real investment spending by category are summarized in Table 7-2. The table also illustrates the extent of the slowdown experienced within each component, comparing average gross investment (as a share of GDP) in the 1990s with investment in the 1970s—the last decade before the deceleration of investment spending began in earnest.

Investment spending by private companies accounts for about three-quarters of the total slowdown, measured in terms of percentage points of GDP. Total private investment spending fell by over three points of GDP between the 1970s and the 1990s. The worst decline was experienced in the construction of non-residential facilities: factories, offices, shopping malls, and other structures.

As firms shifted away from the traditional "extensive" expansion of physical capacity in favour of the more "intensive" use of high-technology machinery and equipment, non-residential construction budgets experienced the worst spending cuts. Gross non-residential spending declined by over one-quarter, as a share of GDP, between the 1970s and the 1990s. In contrast, machinery and equipment investment fell by less than half as much, just 0.6 percentage points of GDP. Investment in residential facilities also declined, by one full point of GDP between the 1970s and the 1990s.

The steepest proportional cutback in investment spending, however, has been experienced in the public sector. Measured as a share of GDP, public in-

Table 7-2						
The Investment Slowdown by Component						
Percent of GDP, 1950-1998						
	1950s	**1960s**	**1970s**	**1980s**	**1990s**[1]	**Change: 1970s to 1990s**
Private Investment						
Residential Structures	6.1%	5.3%	6.4%	5.9%	5.3%	**-1.0 points**
Non-Residential Structures	6.9%	6.2%	6.2%	6.1%	4.6%	**-1.6 points**
Machinery and Equipment	6.9%	6.2%	6.5%	6.5%	5.9%	**-0.6 points**
Total Private	19.9%	17.7%	19.1%	18.6%	15.7%	**-3.2 points**
Public Investment	3.3%	4.5%	3.6%	2.8%	2.5%	**-1.1 points**
Total Investment	23.2%	22.2%	22.6%	21.4%	18.4%	**-4.3 points**
Source: Author's calculations from Statistics Canada, *Canadian Economic Observer.* 1. 1990 to 1998 only.						

vestment fell by almost 30% between the 1970s and the 1990s. The public investment slowdown thus accounts for about one-quarter of the total fall-off in Canada's investment share (even though public investment accounted for only 14% of total investment spending during the 1990s).

Curiously, the largest decline in public investment spending was experienced in the 1980s, years before the more radical budget-cutting by most governments in Canada began in earnest in the latter 1990s. Remember, though, that most Canadian governments were already hard-pressed fiscally in the 1980s, thanks to the dangerous combination of high interest rates and a weak economy.

Many governments probably felt at that time that it was easier to cut *capital* spending budgets as their first response to emerging deficits. This would help them to preserve the more politically-sensitive jobs and services which depend immediately on *current* public programs. But merely cutting back their investment budgets hardly solved the underlying fiscal problem, however,[2] and hence by the mid-1990s governments started slashing away at current programs, as well.

The cumulative total of two decades of severe underinvestment in public capital is now becoming readily and painfully apparent in communities across Canada, in the form of a rapidly deteriorating stock of schools, hospitals, libraries, and other public facilities.

In the 1990s, however, the continuing slowdown in public investment has been outweighed by the more rapid fall-off in private investment spending. The private sector has accounted for over 90% of the total decline in Canada's investment share during this decade.

Another interesting factor to consider in analyzing the investment slowdown in Canada is the special role that has been played over time by energy-related investments. The production and distribution of energy is the most capital-intensive major industry in Canada. The capital cost of the immense investments that have been made in oil and gas wells, electricity-generating facilities, refineries, pipelines, and transmission lines is stunning. Together, these facilities account for about one-quarter of Canada's total net capital stock.

Energy investments have always been an important part of Canada's overall investment activity, but they have also been subject to more severe cyclical patterns as a result of the rise and fall of energy prices and other unpredictable factors.

In particular, energy investments surged dramatically in Canada during the late 1970s and early 1980s. This was partly in response to the two massive increases in world oil prices that were experienced about that time, which resulted from the efforts of the Organization of Petroleum Exporting Countries

Figure 7-5
Energy and Non-Energy Investment
1960-1997

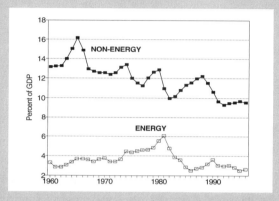

Source: Author's calculations from Statistics Canada, *Canadian Economic Observer, Fixed Capital Flows and Stocks*. Energy includes coal, oil & gas, refining and chemical processing, pipelines, and electricity generation and distribution.

(OPEC) to increase prices at a time when oil supplies were disrupted because of wars and other factors.

The policy response of the Canadian government to those oil price shocks contributed to the subsequent expansion of energy-related investment. In an effort to enhance Canada's energy self-sufficiency, the federal and some provincial governments implemented generous investment subsidy programs which offset much of the cost of new investments in new energy sources.

The energy investment boom peaked in 1980, with total gross investment equalling some 6% of Canada's GDP that year. Investment spending in the energy industry has fallen off significantly since then, to levels half that peak level or lower. The decline in world oil prices back to pre-OPEC levels in 1986 (where they have languished ever since), along with the subsequent elimination of many government energy subsidies, help to explain the subsequent decline in energy investments since then.

The comparative trends in energy and non-energy investment in Canada's economy are illustrated in Figure 7-5. The build-up in energy-related investments during the latter 1970s helped to "mask" a simultaneous and more modest fall-off in non-energy investments. The post-1980 decline in energy investments then exacerbated the decline in non-energy investing, which simultaneously became more pronounced in the wake of high interest rates and other adverse economic conditions in the 1980s.

Nevertheless, the negative structural trend in real investment spending is clearly evident in the data on non-energy investment. Hence Canada's declining investment performance cannot be attributed wholly or even significantly, as some observers have suggested, to the falling importance of energy-related investments since 1980. If anything, the decline in investment spending in Canada appears more marked and consistent over time when energy investments are excluded.[3]

Canada's Slowdown in an International Context

Canada is not the only country to have experienced a noted slowdown in investment since the early 1980s, nor the only country to have experienced a corresponding deceleration of economic expansion and income growth. Many of the same factors which have negatively affected real investment in Canada—and in particular the shift toward high-interest-rate macroeconomic policies early in the 1980s—have also produced slower investment and slower growth in other industrialized market economies. But Canada's performance on both counts has been significantly worse, on average, than those of its peers. The investment slowdown has been more pronounced in Canada than in most other developed countries, and by any measure Canada's overall economic performance has also been sub-par.

Table 7-3 summarizes the extent of the investment slowdown, once again comparing the 1990s with the 1970s, in the seven largest industrial countries (known as the "G7" economies). Average figures for the richest 21 industrial countries are also presented. Prior to 1980, Canada spent more on real investment (measured as a share of total GDP) than did other industrial countries, on average. Not coincidentally, Canada's economy also grew notably faster than did the

	Table 7-3 **The Investment Slowdown: Home and Abroad** *Selected industrial countries, 1990s*			
	Average investment 1990s[1] (% GDP)	**Change from 1970s (points of GDP)**	**Average annual growth, GDP, 1990s[1]**	**Change from 1970s (points)**
U.S.	16.5%	-2.7 points	2.1%	-0.7 points
Japan	30.1%	-4.4 points	2.1%	-3.1 points
Germany	22.9%	-0.7 points	2.1%[2]	-0.4 points
France	18.9%	-6.6 points	1.5%	-2.2 points
Italy	18.5%	-7.3 points	1.3%	-2.6 points
U.K.	16.1%	-3.8 points	1.6%	-0.9 points
Canada	**18.7%**	**-5.2 points[3]**	**1.6%**	**-3.2 points**
21 Industrial Countries	**19.8%**	**-3.5 points**	**2.1%**	**-1.3 points**

Source: Author's calculations from International Monetary Fund, *International Financial Statistics Yearbook*.
1. 1990 to 1997 only.
2. Excludes 1991 (German reunification).
3. This differs from the data presented in Tables 7-1 and 7-2 because of definitional differences between the Statistics Canada sources used there and the IMF data used in this table.

industrial world as a whole: by 4.7% per year (after inflation) in the 1970s, compared to an average of 3.4% in all industrialized countries.

Indeed, it was the very rapid pace of investment in many Canadian industries—manufacturing, resources, and services—that powered years of impressive economic growth and structural change, during which time Canada emerged as one of the wealthiest economies in the world.

Unfortunately, Canada has fared significantly worse than most other industrialized economies since 1980, the point at which growth and job-creation were deposed from the podium of macroeconomic priorities in favour of inflation-control and financial profitability. Real investment spending in Canada declined by over five points of GDP between the 1970s and the 1990s. That is among the worst declines in investment experienced in the developed world.

Correspondingly, economic growth has also deteriorated more in Canada than has been the case elsewhere. Canada's average real GDP growth from 1990 to 1997 ranks in the bottom quarter of all industrial economies. And the *drop-off* in our economic growth—from significantly above-average in the 1970s to significantly below-average in the 1990s—has been the worst of any G7 economy, and the second-worst (next to Iceland) of any industrialized economy.

Canada now invests significantly less than other industrialized countries, on average, and partly as a consequence we now grow significantly slower than average. From a leader of the industrial world, there is no doubt that Canada is now a laggart.

The poor performance of Canada's economy is actually worse than is implied by these figures. Thanks in part to vibrant immigration, Canada's population is growing faster than that of any other industrialized economy. This implies that Canada's total economy needs to expand (after inflation) at a faster rate than elsewhere, just to preserve living standards at their current levels.

Relatively slow GDP growth (of, say, 2% per year after inflation) still translates into rising living standards in countries with low or even zero population growth (such as most European countries and Japan). In Canada, however, where the population grows by 1.5 percent per year, slow growth of the type experienced in the 1990s implies virtually no improvement in living standards at all. Indeed, the fact that Canada's population growth is unusually rapid would normally suggest that Canada should be investing *more* in real capital assets (including residential structures and community infrastructure) than other countries—not less.

The fact that investment spending has slowed down significantly in most industrialized economies suggests that there are deep structural forces (and not just particular national circumstances) behind Canada's slowdown. But this should not imply that the investment slowdown is universal, inevitable, or somehow "natural." The fact of the matter is that the same conservative, belt-tightening macroeconomic policies that were pursued in Canada in the 1980s and 1990s were also implemented in most other economies—although perhaps with not quite as much vigor and vengeance, on average, as was the case here.

And the same potential conflict of interest between the owners of financial capital on the one hand, and the companies, workers, and communities which want to put that capital into motion in the real economy on the other, is also at play in other countries (although again, to varying degrees).

Many countries have managed to sustain much more rapid real investment rates than Canada. Some continental European countries (such as Germany) have actually increased their real investment spending in the 1990s, despite the difficult transition to a single European currency—a transition which entailed the imposition of higher interest rates than would otherwise be expected, with consequent negative effects on investment and overall economic growth.

The pro-investment nature of financial systems in continental Europe (where there is more reliance on banks than on stock markets to supply finance, and closer organic links between financial suppliers and the companies which put capital to work in the real economy) help to explain this result. Even in hard-hit Japan, real investment spending has maintained momentum in the 1990s. This is one reason why real growth in Japan—while slower than the spectacular expansion experienced there in earlier decades—still managed to exceed the performance of many other industrialized countries (including Canada) despite a deep and prolonged financial crisis.

It is interesting to note that the U.S. economy invests even less in real capital than does Canada's. This is perhaps a surprising result, given the incessant discussion in Canada in recent years about the "virtues" of the U.S. economic model, and the increasing pressure to implement U.S.-style policies governing everything from labour markets to stock markets.

To be sure, economic growth and job-creation have been consistently stronger in the U.S. through the 1990s than in Canada; but that does not imply that the U.S. expansion has been especially strong from a historical or international perspective. The U.S. economic system is even more oriented towards finance and paper speculation than is Canada's. One consequence may be that firms there are even less interested in expanding their physical capacity with ambitious real investment programs. This has not stopped the U.S. economy from creating jobs; but, with relatively lower levels of average capital-intensity, many of these jobs tend to be lower-wage, lower-productivity positions.

In countries with a less free-wheeling regulatory environment, and where stock markets play a smaller economic role, real investment has been notably stronger than in the U.S. And, in many of these cases, economic growth has also been stronger, especially when measured in per capita terms. [U.S. population growth is also higher than in Europe or Japan, although not as high as in Canada, and hence per capita economic growth there is also significantly slower than suggested by the expansion of aggregate GDP.]

For various reasons, it may not be feasible or even desirable to return to the extremely rapid investment of previous decades, when real investment could account for 25% or even more of Canada's total GDP. But it is nevertheless clear that Canada needs to invest more than it does now, in order to facilitate faster economic growth and job-creation, and to keep up with the needs of an expanding population.

International experience shows that sustained rates of more rapid investment contribute to economic growth and higher productivity. We can learn from some of the policies which have been successful in stimulating real investment in other countries; we can also experiment with unique made-in-Canada solutions to our investment slowdown. To solve a problem, however, one must first understand it better. And hence the next chapter of this book will examine the causes of the investment slowdown in more detail.

Chapter 8
Explaining the Slowdown

By any measure, real investment spending in Canada has declined substantially over the past two decades, despite the flood of finance into Canada's paper markets. The implications of the investment slowdown for growth, jobs, productivity, and incomes have been negative and serious. What are the key factors which explain the slump in the real investment effort of Canadian companies?

This chapter will summarize some empirical tests which indicate that three factors have been particularly important in explaining the investment slowdown: 1) the high interest rates which have prevailed in Canada since 1981, 2) the resulting fall-off in economic growth, and 3) a longer-term decline in the profitability of private business.

On the other hand, the empirical evidence does not seem to be consistent with the alleged importance of two other purported causes of the investment slowdown which have been emphasized by analysts and commentators on the right and left of the political spectrum, respectively. An "unfriendly" business climate cannot be linked empirically to the investment slowdown, contrary to the slogans of conservative politicians. In fact, by a key measure presented in this chapter, Canada's economic environment has never been friendlier for business. Meanwhile, the omnipresent bogeyman emphasized by so many commentators on the left—the all-pervasive force of "globalization"—is similarly found to be of secondary importance, at most, in explaining the overall decline of investment activity in Canada.

The Basic Story: A "Core" Model

Economists commonly use a statistical technique known as *econometrics* to investigate the links between different economic variables. The key idea is to perform various statistical tests on two or more series of economic data, in order to shed light on the extent to which one variable "causes" or "influences" another. The technique is often misused, and hence has faced increasing criticism in recent years. In particular, it is seldom the case that econometric evidence alone can "prove" a particular economic theory; analysts have to be careful to distinguish between a statistical correlation that may be visible between two variables, and a logical chain of causation which might link them in a behavioural sense.

Carefully used, however, econometric techniques can help to verify or disprove theories that are developed on the basis of theoretical or qualitative research. This chapter will use some of these techniques to investigate the causes of the investment slowdown in Canada. Only conceptual summaries of the tests are provided in the text of the chapter; readers interested in a more complete technical description of the tests should consult Appendix IV.

Economists over the years have identified a wide range of different potential influences on real investment expenditure. The factors emphasized by different studies tend to reflect the prior theoretical orientation of their authors. Economists in the "free-market" tradition (also known as *neoclassical* economics) focus on the relative costs of different types of economic resources used by a company: labour, capital, energy, and other inputs. Firms will respond to changes in the relative prices of these inputs by adjusting the "mix" of inputs they use in production. Their adjustments in capital use translate into higher or lower capital investment, accordingly, and hence investment is related back to relative price variables such as interest rates and wages. Free-market thinkers also link changes in investment over time to the savings performance of an economy.

Researchers in the *Keynesian* tradition, following the theoretical approach of the British economist John Maynard Keynes, tend to emphasize factors related to the vitality of purchasing power in the aggregate economy, and the two-way feedback that can occur between investment and growth. More investment means more growth (Keynesians call this the "multiplier" effect), but more growth also breeds more investment (which is called the "accelerator" effect). As discussed in Chapters 4 and 5, this two-way virtuous circle explains why real investment spending is such an important factor in motivating economic growth and job-creation.

Finally, a whole school of thought known as *structuralist economics* considers the importance of institutional variables such as income distribution, the profitability of private investment, and the nature of government regulations in promoting or restraining private investment expenditure. The structuralists tend to agree with Keynesians on the importance of purchasing-power or "demand" variables in motivating investment. But they also recognize that the structural and institutional features of the economy—government, regulations, labour market institutions, even politics—will shape and potentially constrain those "demand-driven" forces.[1]

This chapter will adopt the following rather "eclectic" approach. A "core" econometric model is constructed, based on three variables which seem to be especially important in explaining Canada's investment performance in the post-war era. First, we consider the pace of economic growth itself: if the economy is growing rapidly, straining at the bounds of its physical capacity, then companies will be motivated to invest more in expanding that capacity. [As explained in Appendix IV, the measure of economic growth utilized in these tests is equivalent to a measure of capacity utilization.]

Second, the seemingly permanent rise in long-term interest rates that was imposed in Canada starting in 1981 has clearly been a crucial factor behind the investment slowdown. Some of this influence has been felt indirectly, via the negative impact of interest rates on economic growth. But some has also been felt directly: higher interest rates make it more difficult for firms to raise money for new investment projects, and encourage companies to use "cheaper" inputs (including low-wage labour) instead of more capital in the production process.[2]

Third, economic evidence suggests that private business investments in Canada became markedly less profitable as the post-war era wore on. [These trends will be addressed in Chapter 11.] And so it would seem to be appropriate to include a measure of business profitability as an indicator of the incentive for new investment.

Each of these three measures could in fact be utilized, with differing interpretations, by each of the three broad schools of economic theory listed above. For example, a neoclassical explanation of investment would interpret interest rates and profits as components of the cost of capital services. It would also allow for economic growth to affect investment simply by virtue of the requirement for a given capital stock (accumulated in the context of a given set of relative prices) to "keep up" with overall economic growth.

Similarly, a Keynesian theory might incorporate the impact of interest rates on grounds of their large impact on overall purchasing-power conditions in the economy. Business profitability might be considered on grounds that real companies are often constrained in their investment plans by the amount of internal funds that are generated through corporate cash flow.

Finally, a structuralist model would interpret profitability as a measure of the impact of changing income distribution on the incentive for private capital accumulation, and would see the interest rate as an indicator of the "opportunity cost" of placing one's money in a real investment rather than in a financial one.

In short, then, there are ample arguments in economic theory to consider these three variables to be crucial factors influencing the pattern of real investment in Canada. And so a simple "core" econometric equation consisting of these three variables was assembled and tested with Canadian data on net private investment spending between 1960 and 1997. By choosing net investment rather than gross investment as the object of this inquiry, we are in essence assuming that firms will normally want to fully replace the wear-and-tear of their existing capital assets. The crucial decision for firms, therefore, is how fast they want to increase their *net* stock of capital assets. And, by excluding public investment from the test, we are trying to focus attention on that component of total investment spending which should most closely reflect economic (rather than political) factors. These econometric tests confirmed that each of these three "core" variables was indeed a significant determinant (in statistical terms) of real net investment spending by Canadian businesses over this time.

The findings of these initial econometric tests are summarized, in non-technical terms, in Table 8-1. We find that an increase in overall GDP (measured relative to the ongoing expansion of the potential output of Canada's economy) is ultimately reflected in an increase in real private net investment equal to about two-thirds of one percentage point of GDP. The positive impact of GDP growth on investment spending is not fully felt immediately: the econometric tests suggest that it takes two years (the current year, and the following year) for the positive feedback effect of growth on investment to exhaust itself.

A sustained one-point increase in real long-run interest rates reduces investment by about one-third of one point of GDP. This effect, too, is felt over a two-year period: the year in which the interest rate is changed, and the following year.

Table 8-1
Core Private Investment Equation

Variable	Finding	Time Lags	Level of Importance[1]
Growth of GDP (Capacity utilization)	An increase of 1 percentage point in GDP spurs an increase in investment of two-thirds of one point of GDP.	Current year, previous year	1.024
Real long-run interest rates	An increase of 1 percentage point in the real long-run interest rate spurs a decrease in investment of one-third of one point of GDP.	Current year, previous year	0.489
Business profits	An increase in business profits of one point of GDP spurs an increase in investment of one-quarter of one point of GDP.	Two years previous	0.282

Source: Author's calculations as explained in Appendix IV.
1. Value of "beta" statistic equals coefficient adjusted for relative variability of independant variable; see Appendix IV for details.

Finally, an increase in before-tax corporate profits of one percentage point of GDP is ultimately reflected in an increase in investment equal to about one-quarter of one point of GDP. This effect takes somewhat longer to be fully felt: the econometric results suggest that an increase in profits is not fully translated into higher investment until two years afterward.

Based on the specific numerical results of the econometric tests, we can evaluate the relative importance of these three different factors in explaining the overall post-war evolution of real business investment in Canada. The relative importance of each factor is indicated by the number in the right-hand column of Table 8-1. This number is the "beta" coefficient corresponding to each of the three separate causal variables; as explained in Appendix IV, a higher "beta" coefficient means that investment tends to be more sensitive to the particular variable being considered. Over the whole period covered by the test, the rate of economic growth was the most important influence on investment, followed by the level of real interest rates, and then by the level of business profitability.

We can also use these findings to retroactively decompose the overall decline in investment spending which has been experienced since 1980 into its different component causes (see Appendix IV for details). By this criteria, we estimate that the slowdown in economic growth since 1980 has been the most important cause of the prolonged slump in investment activity, explaining 43% of the cumulative slowdown between 1980 and 1997. Higher real interest rates were a second important factor, explaining 33% of the investment slowdown. Falling business profitability was the least important of the three major causal variables, explaining 11% of the cumulative slowdown between 1980 and 1997. [The remaining 13% of the slowdown was attributable to unexplained causes and statistical error.]

The overall importance of these three factors—growth, interest rates, and profitability—in explaining the post-war evolution of real investment spending in Canada is illustrated in Figure 8-1. This figure depicts the actual evolution of private investment (measured as a proportion of potential GDP, the solid line) against the level that would be predicted by our "core" econometric model on the basis of changes in economic growth, interest rates, and profitability. Clearly these three factors provide a relatively comprehensive explanation of the slowdown in real investment spending since about 1980.

This, however, does not necessarily rule out the possibility that other factors may have also played a role in the decline in investment. To consider the possible significance of those additional factors, the following methodology was adopted. The "core" model presented above was supplemented with a variable which might be a significant additional determinant of investment. If this revised econometric equation performed better than the original "core" equation,

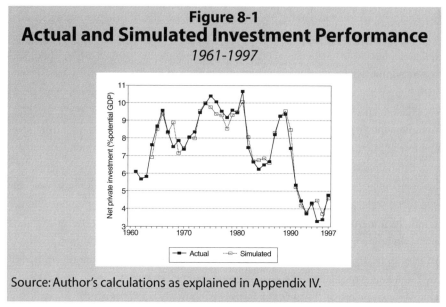

Figure 8-1
Actual and Simulated Investment Performance
1961-1997

Source: Author's calculations as explained in Appendix IV.

then the significance of this additional variable would be accepted. If not, then we go back to the original "core" equation.[3]

We report here on two sets of these experiments: one to consider the relative statistical importance of the "investment climate" so emphasized by conservative policy-makers, and another to consider the extent to which real investment spending has been undermined by Canada's increasing integration into a global economy.

The Business Climate

The architects of the conservative policy revolution which has painted over so much of Canada's economic landscape during the past two decades consistently claim that their policies will enhance "investor confidence" in Canada and hence spur a boom in private investment spending. The scope and reach of these pro-business policy changes is considerable, as was summarized in Chapter 4 (see especially Table 4-2). Indeed, the extent to which Canada's economy now reflects the imperative of "let the market rule" is sometimes shocking, especially for those Canadians used to thinking of Canada as a "kinder, gentler" version of capitalism. By any measure, the dominance of private market forces over economic decision-making has been radically enhanced in the 1980s and 1990s.

Even in the eyes of the ultra-conservative Fraser Institute, Canada is something close to a free-market Nirvana. That institute has attempted to rank the countries of the world according to the extent to which their governments protect private property rights and otherwise keep out of economic life; by their reckoning, Canada ranked among the 10 most pro-market jurisdictions in the entire world in 1995.[4] In this context, it is difficult on *a priori* grounds to accept the notion that an unfavourable business climate could be holding back real investment spending in Canada.

This section will consider some empirical dimensions to the issue of the "business climate" and its impact—real or imagined—on the investment effort of Canadian businesses. To test for the statistical importance of the business climate, of course, we need to develop some way of "measuring" it. This is not a self-evident undertaking. Obviously, there are many different factors which will collectively affect whether a particular economy is business-friendly or not. The approach followed here is to construct a composite "index" of investment risk, based on changes in the underlying factors which together determine that risk. We choose the following five "raw" data series as the inputs to this composite index. Each of them corresponds with one particular complaint of the business community regarding some problem (usually identified with the actions of governments or unions) which allegedly undermines Canada's appeal as a site for investment:

- *Taxes*: We measure tax collections by all levels of government, as a proportion of GDP. This measure has grown fairly steadily through the post-war era, even during the 1990s when government programs were being cut back dramatically; tax hikes during this time paid for deficit reduction and debt-servicing costs, rather than new public programs. Taxes, of course, became Public Enemy No. 1 during the latter part of the 1990s, as conservatives attempted to capitalize on the frustration of Canadians with the "poor value" they seemed to be receiving for their tax dollars. One would think that business taxes would be most relevant to the issue of the overall investment climate, but conservatives have focused their fire on personal taxes (especially income taxes). Business taxes have in fact decreased slightly (measured as a share of pre-tax business income) during the post-war era (as discussed more fully in Chapter 11).

- *Deficits*: Deficits were the conservative issue *du jour* earlier in the 1990s, when public concern over large and unsustainable deficits resulted in unprecedented cutbacks to public programs. Business lobbyists often argued that high deficits were a source of "instability" for real businesses. This argument was vastly overstated, if indeed there is any truth to it at all. Far worse then deficits for most real businesses in Canada has been the contractionary macroeconomic effects of rapid deficit-reduction. Huge government spending cuts undermined the markets into which businesses sell their goods and services—including both direct business sales to governments and public agencies and their indirect sales which result from the general purchasing power generated by government spending. Combined deficits for all levels of government are measured here as a share of GDP. They declined rapidly in the mid-1990s, crossing over into significant government surpluses by 1997.

- *Inflation*: Once again, the allegedly negative impacts of inflation on real business activity are vastly overstated by conservative critics—mostly those in the financial community who would prefer lower inflation in any event because of the highly negative effect of inflation on financial profits. Inflation was "wrestled to the ground" in Canada, thanks to the high real interest rates first imposed in 1981. It was then pushed to the point of extinction by the further tightening of monetary policy in the early 1990s. By 1998, Canada's economy was experiencing widespread deflation in the production of domestic goods and services. Again, the fruits of this Pyrrhic victory over inflation were hollow indeed for many businesses: their markets were hammered during the transition to a zero-inflation economy, and still have yet to fully recover. Deflation is an especially ominous sign for many businesses, since it implies that the aggregate purchasing power of the economy shrinks (in dollar terms) with each passing year. We measure inflation here by the year-over-year change in the overall level of consumer prices.

- *Government Intrusion*: Business lobbyists wax long and loud about the intrusion of government and public agencies into the domain of private enterprise. One possible indication of this intervention would be the proportion of Canada's total economic output accounted for by public, quasi-public, and non-profit agencies. Interestingly, this non-business sector of Canada's economy actually declined slightly, even during the 1960s and 1970s. Despite the expansion of public services such as education and health care, the vibrant growth of the private economy during this time meant that the public sector's relative economic importance actually shrank.[5] Since 1981, of course, this gradual shrinkage has turned into a rout. The economic importance of the non-business sector in Canada has fallen by about one-quarter since 1981 in the wake of fiscal restraint by all levels of government. Apart from indicating that Canadian governments have been relegated to a very defensive, non-threatening mode of being, possessing fewer economic and political resources with which to "interfere" with the for-profit activity of private firms, this retrenchment has also opened up potentially lucrative new investment opportunities for private firms in economic activities that were previously the sole preserve of the public sector.

• *Strikes*: Businesses constantly accuse unions of disrupting the investment climate with their demands for higher wages and fairer workplace practices. No single measure captures the extent of union strength in the economy better than the frequency of strikes. Strike frequency will reflect both the organizational strength of unions (after all, you have to be in a union before you can go on strike), and also the subjective militance of union members (unions which never strike soon lose their ability to mobilize members in support of their bargaining demands). Strikes were indeed a relatively frequent thing in Canada's economy in the late 1970s (by both historical and international comparisons). Since then, however, strike frequency has declined markedly in the face of unfavourable labour market conditions and—in some provinces—anti-union shifts in labour law. Indeed, in the early 1990s strike frequency reached levels lower than at any time since Canada began collecting statistics on this subject. Some rebound in strike frequency has occurred later in the 1990s, as workers have attempted to win back, in the context of a strengthening economic recovery, some of the concessions that were extracted from them earlier in the decade. By any measure, however, labour militancy in Canada is at relatively low levels. We measure strike frequency here by the ratio of days lost in strikes and other work stoppages to the total number of days worked in the economy.

Each of these five indicators of the overall investment climate is illustrated in Figure 8-2. With the exception of the tax burden (measured as a share of total GDP), all of these indices of investment risk have declined impressively during the 1990s. And even with taxes, while the overall tax burden has increased slightly in the 1990s, the incidence of *business* taxes (which should, after all, be the most relevant to investment decisions) has not.

It is obvious strategically why conservatives have focused their fire on Canadian taxes in the late 1990s. They have succeeded in wreaking fantastic economic changes in recent years by focusing on one target after another which is held to be the source of all economic evil: first it was inflation, then it was the deficit, now it is taxes. The claim that lower taxes will fundamentally improve Canada's business climate is not credible—especially since the main priority of the tax-cut partisans is to win lower income taxes for higher-income households, rather than to reduce the tax burden on real businesses.

The five different variables illustrated above can be "boiled down" to a single index of the overall risk facing investors in Canada. This approach simply assigns an equal weighting to each component of investment risk, and then fits them to an arbitrary numerical scale (such that the average level of investment risk experienced through the period under consideration equals 100).[6] As expected, this overall measure indicates that the investment climate has improved markedly (that is, the level of risk facing investors has declined considerably) and fairly steadily since 1981.

Figure 8-2
Indices of Canada's "Business Climate"
1960-1997

Taxes as Share of GDP

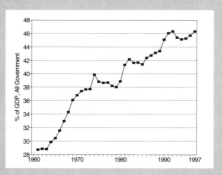

Deficits as Share of GDP

Annual CPI Inflation

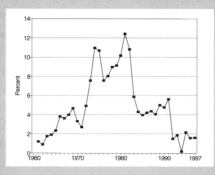

Interestingly, this composite measure of investment risk happened to reach its lowest level during the entire period in 1997. In other words, in the wake of the conservative and painful policy measures which have been imposed over the past two decades, all of which were excused by the need to make Canada a more business-friendly jurisdiction, there has never been a "better" time to invest in Canada. In this context, the still-sluggish response by real companies to this

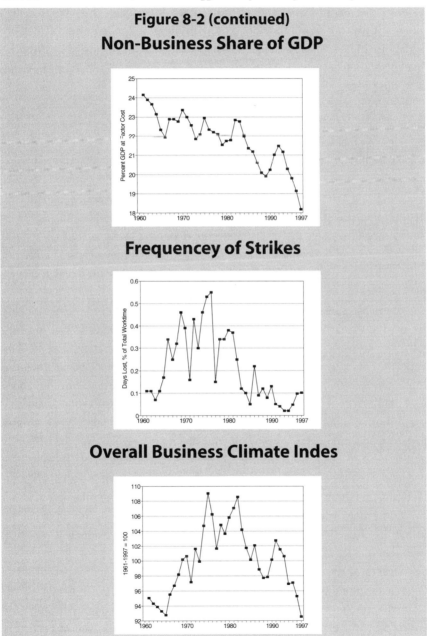

Figure 8-2 (continued)
Non-Business Share of GDP

Frequencey of Strikes

Overall Business Climate Indes

improved business climate, measured by their real investment activity, is start-ling. Surely the attempt to encourage more investment spending from compa-nies on the basis of a more business-friendly economic and institutional climate must be approaching a natural limit.

To test empirically for the significance of the investment climate in the ex-planation of post-war trends in Canadian investment activity, this composite index of investment risk was added to the "core" investment equation described above. It was not found to add anything to the descriptive power of the core equation. In fact, this test detected a slight (but statistically insignificant) *posi-tive* correlation between investment risk and real investment spending by Cana-dian businesses. This reinforces the suspicion that some of the "tough-love" policies followed over the past two decades to create a more amenable business climate (such as ultra-high interest rates and ultra-fast government spending cuts) may in fact have been counter-productive.

Experiments were also conducted by adding each individual index of invest-ment risk to the core equation; these results were similarly negative.

Despite these results, the notion that changes in the overall economic and institutional climate may affect the level of investment forthcoming from pri-vate companies should not be dismissed out of hand. Clearly, private companies will take stock of the general business climate in which they operate before de-ciding whether to put some of their hard-won capital at risk in a real and com-plex business venture.

There are some particular examples in economics where business climate factors have clearly exercised an important influence on investment. Anti-un-ion "right-to-work" laws in the Deep South states of the U.S. have clearly been important in motivating a significant migration of manufacturing investment to those states from the free-association states of the northern part of that coun-try.[7] Similar forces may be moderately impacting on the location of manufactur-ing and other more mobile forms of investment within Canada. While Alberta has stopped short (so far, anyway) of imposing right-to-work laws, the generally anti-union, pro-business institutional climate of that province does seem to have had modest success in motivating a reallocation of investment spending in manu-facturing and other "mobile" industries towards Alberta from other provinces.

Conversely, when economic institutions are threatened with fundamental instability or challenge, there is little doubt that private investors will vote with their feet and leave quickly.

Structural crises of this sort, however, have never been experienced in Canada, despite the overstated rhetoric of conservative critics. Canada has re-mained a stable, institutionally developed, pro-market economy through the entire post-war era. Businesses may or may not have approved of particular policies imposed by particular governments at particular times, but it can hardly be argued that Canada's private-dominated economy was ever "anti-business" in any fundamental sense. And, in the wake of the far-reaching changes of the last two decades, it is clearly more pro-business than ever.

"Investment climate" issues may exert a certain limited influence over the allocation of investment in certain types of facilities (such as manufacturing plants or call centres) between different provinces, but it clearly cannot explain the rise and fall of aggregate real investment spending by Canadian businesses in total. This casts fundamental doubt on the proposition that more investment could be elicited by slanting Canada's social and economic policies even further in the direction of the business community.

The Investment Slowdown and the Global Economy

The year 1996 marked a historic turning point in Canada's investment relationship with the rest of the world. That year, for the first time in Canada's history, the foreign direct investments of Canadian-based companies in other countries outweighed the total value of all foreign investments within Canada by foreign-owned firms. In other words, Canadian companies now owned more of the rest of the world than foreign companies owned of Canada. In terms of direct investment, then, Canada had become a net "creditor," rather than a net debtor.

Given the intense controversies which have accompanied the rise and fall of foreign investment in Canada during previous decades, one would have thought that this historic development might have been greeted by some kind of national

Figure 8-3
Inward and Outward Foreign Direct Investment
Canada, 1950-1997

Source: Author's calculations from Statistics Canada, *Canadian Economic Observer* and *Canada's International Investment Position*.

celebration—like a family which has paid off the last dollar of its home mortgage, or a car-owner who cracks the champagne when her vehicle's odometer clicks over the 100,000 kilometre mark. Curiously, however, this event passed largely unnoticed.

Perhaps the lack of fanfare reflects a long-standing inconsistency in the attitude of Canadians towards foreign investment: we're concerned about the implications of too much foreign control of our economy, but at the same time we're not thrilled about the prospect of those foreign investors just packing up and leaving, either. The data on foreign investment suggest that the money has been going faster than it has been coming. Is this not evidence that globalization is part of Canada's investment problem?

The historical evolution of foreign investment flows into and out of Canada is illustrated in Figure 8-3. Canada's economy has long been more reliant on foreign companies than most other developed countries. This reflects a number of different factors: our colonial heritage, our long-standing structural dependence on natural resource industries (such as mining and petroleum) in which foreign investment is important, and our early reliance on tariffs and other trade barriers to stimulate investments in domestic industry (a side-effect of which was the rise of foreign-owned "branch plants" which located in Canada to avoid the tariff).

Foreign investment was already declining sharply by the 1970s, when the issue became a hot political topic. Pressed by a rising sense of Canadian nationalism among the electorate, Liberal governments of the time introduced many restrictions on incoming foreign investment (including, most famously, the Foreign Investment Review Agency, FIRA). Most of these rules were later dismantled by the Mulroney government in the 1980s, although important sector-specific restrictions on foreign investment remain in place in several federally-regulated industries (such as transportation, communications, and banking).

Contrary to the fears of some opponents of the 1989 Canada-U.S. Free Trade Agreement, and the subsequent North American Free Trade Agreement with Mexico, continental free trade has not led to the "sell-off" of Canada to foreign investors. There has been a slight rebound in the importance of foreign direct investment (measured as a share of GDP) since the late 1980s, but nothing as dramatic as the free trade critics feared.[8] In fact, the reverse seems to have been more the case: rather than foreign companies rushing in to take advantage of a Canadian economy newly opened up to outsiders, it seems that Canadian companies have been more anxious to pack their bags and leave the country.

External foreign direct investment by Canadian firms has grown four-fold (measured as a share of our GDP) since the early 1980s. By 1996 these external investments outweighed direct investments by foreign firms in Canada, and hence

Table 8-2
The Changing Pattern of Foreign Investment
1987-1997, $ billions

By Industry

	TOTAL	High-tech Mfctrg.[1]	Finance	Energy & Mining	Service & Retail	Other
New international FDI coming in	81.6	12.4	15.8	4.5	9.9	39.0
New Canadian FDI going out	119.5	3.7	43.7	26.7	16.8	28.7
Net change, investment in Canada	-37.9	+8.8	-27.9	-22.2	-6.9	+10.3

By Region

	TOTAL	U.S.	U.K.	Other Europe	Japan	Other
New international FDI coming in	81.6	56.0	3.2	13.4	4.1	5.0
New Canadian FDI going out	119.5	51.0	14.4	15.2	2.4	36.6
Net change, investment in Canada	-37.9	+5.0	-11.1	-1.8	-1.7	-31.6

Source: Author's calculations from Statistics Canada, *Canada's International Investment Position*. Includes auto, machinery, and electronics.

the country passed the "break-even" point. [Canada's overall financial position with the rest of the world is rather different: considering forms of indirect or "portfolio" investment such as stocks, bonds, and loans, Canada's net foreign indebtedness grew quickly in the 1990s, mostly thanks to foreign ownership of a share of our public debt.]

Given the coincidence between this outflow of net foreign investment and the general slowdown in real investment expenditure in Canada (which also began in earnest in the early 1980s), it is worth considering whether Canada's closer integration into the global economy is one of the factors behind the decline of Canada's investment performance.

A closer examination of the investment outflows suggests, however, that the net negative impact of foreign investment on real investment in Canada may not be as severe as these aggregate trends suggest. Consider the data summarized in the top half of Table 8-2, which break down foreign investment inflows and outflows by industry.[9] In the all-important high-technology manufacturing sector, for which the spin-off effects of real investment are especially positive, foreign firms have invested four new dollars in Canada since 1987 for every dollar that Canadian firms have invested outside of the country. In other manufacturing sectors, as well, for which the location decisions of companies are particularly sensitive to the cost competitiveness of the host economy, Canada has been winning more incoming real investment from foreign firms than it has been losing to outmigration by Canadian firms.

It turns out that the paper economy itself is the source of most of the apparent "loss" in net foreign investment spending. Canada's booming financial and insurance providers more than tripled their foreign investments between 1987 and 1997, and the net loss of direct investment in this sector accounts for almost three-quarters of Canada's total net loss in direct investment. This outgoing investment by companies in the paper economy does not translate strongly into a loss of employment real employment and production opportunities in Canada.

Another important source of the net outflow of direct investment from Canada over the past decade is the mining and energy industry. This reflects the effort by Canadian companies (especially in the mining sector) to take advantage of lower-cost foreign resource discoveries. The outward migration of mining and energy investment has been accelerated by the adoption of very conservative, pro-investment policies in many countries (in Latin America, the former Soviet Union, and elsewhere) which used to closely regulate foreign investment.

There is also some evidence that stricter Canadian rules regarding environment protection and land reclamation may have spurred some mining firms to look abroad. While this will naturally be a worrisome trend in mining-dependent communities in Canada, it is not symptomatic of a more general unattractiveness of Canada in the eyes of investors.

Concern that global competitive pressures have undermined real investment spending in Canada are also eased somewhat by an examination of the net outflow of foreign investment according to country of origin or destination. This data is summarized in the lower half of Table 8-2. Even though the U.S. now accounts for close to 90% of Canada's foreign trade, and it has been our economic relationship with that country which has been most transformed by the free trade agreements of the past decade, Canada's investment relationship with the U.S. has been surprisingly stable.

Both inflows and outflows of foreign investment to and from the U.S. have grown in the wake of free trade, reflecting a two-way process through which companies on both sides of the border have adjusted their operations to reflect the new continental market. But the overall balance of foreign investment between the two countries has hardly changed, which is a remarkable result given the rapid restructuring of the bilateral trade relationship. Canada has picked up $5 billion in new investment, on a net basis, from the U.S. in the last decade; this is a small amount relative to the large accumulated stocks of foreign direct investment which have been built up on both sides of the border. This suggests that, in terms of our relationship with the single country that accounts for the vast majority of our international economic activity, investment in Canada has not been negatively affected by free trade and globalization at all.

Close to 85% of the net outflow of direct investment spending from Canada since 1987 has been destined, interestingly, for developing countries. Little of this outflow was experienced in industries such as manufacturing, in which low foreign wages and other production costs might be feared to lure investment away from higher-cost jurisdictions such as Canada. Most of it was concentrated in two industries—finance and mining—in which successful Canadian companies have become important global multinationals in their own right.

Mining firms are seeking out new resource bases in developing countries which have desperately remade themselves to attract incoming foreign investment. Canadian banks and other financial providers are using their strong domestic position as a platform from which to launch themselves into other lucrative markets, especially in developing economies. Both of these trends carry potentially negative implications, to be sure. For example, the heavy foreign investments of Canadian banks in lucrative but unstable developing markets could backfire on the Canadian economy if and when those investments turn sour (a problem that will be explored further in Chapter 13). But neither of these trends can be interpreted as evidence that Canada's economy is somehow fundamentally uncompetitive in the eyes of investors. In short, the investment slowdown in Canada does not seem to be the result of a decision by real investors to put their money elsewhere.

This general conclusion is reinforced by a comparison of the cost competitiveness of real investments in Canada and in competing jurisdictions. Contrary to the rhetoric of business lobbyists and conservative politicians, Canada is actually a relatively low-cost location for private companies to invest in. Figure 8-4 illustrates the evolution of one crucial measure of cost competitiveness: hourly labour costs in the manufacturing industry.

In contrast to investments in natural resource industries, which must be located near to abundant resource supplies, and in contrast to investments in most services industries, which must be located near final customers, manufacturing investments can be located just about anywhere. Falling transportation costs and the gradual elimination of tariffs and other trade barriers have allowed manufacturing firms to scout out and choose the most cost-effective locations for their new facilities. Many cost factors will enter into this decision, including the costs of land, local taxes, and energy.[10] But by far the most important cost component in manufacturing is the total cost of labour—including wages, as well as the hourly or unit cost of payroll taxes (like unemployment insurance or CPP premiums) and non-wage benefit packages (such as supplementary health insurance or pension costs).

It turns out that, on labour cost grounds, Canada fairly consistently outcompetes even the U.S. economy, which is hardly a "labour-friendly" jurisdic-

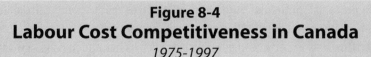

Figure 8-4
Labour Cost Competitiveness in Canada
1975-1997

Source: U.S. Department of Labor, Bureau of Labor Statistics, *International Comparisons of Hourly Compensation Costs for Production Workers in Manufacturing.*

tion. Despite stronger unions, stronger labour laws, and more generous (and hence expensive) social programs, hourly labour costs are lower in Canada once they are adjusted for the exchange rate between the Canadian dollar and its U.S. counterpart.

This somewhat surprising result is due to two main factors. The first is the Canada-U.S. exchange rate. Canada's currency has been "undervalued" on international currency markets for most of the past two decades. This means that the dollar has a lower exchange rate on those markets than should be the case given actual price levels prevailing in Canada. [Using the mumbo-jumbo language of economists, the exchange rate of the Canadian dollar is significantly lower than would be implied by the condition of "purchasing power parity."] This undervaluation means that Canadian goods and services—including the labour services of Canadian workers—appear less expensive in international markets.[11]

The exception to this general trend was a period in the late 1980s and early 1990s, when John Crow was governor of the Bank of Canada and oversaw the implementation of a tough, unilateral escalation of the war against inflation. By pushing up domestic interest rates far above the levels of our trading partners,[12] the Bank of Canada also increased the value of the dollar—which climbed above 90 cents (U.S.) at its peak. This was great for cross-border shoppers, who flocked to the U.S. to take advantage of new "bargains." But it was disastrous for Canada's economy. Indeed, this painful but temporary rise in the dollar couldn't have come at a worse time: just as Canadian industry was struggling to adapt to the new Canada-U.S. Free Trade Agreement (FTA).

In fact, the rise in the dollar was certainly more important than the free trade deal itself in explaining the rash of plant shutdowns and layoffs, concentrated especially in the manufacturing industry, which occurred during the first three years after the FTA. This level of the Canadian dollar was unsustainable, however, and the dollar fell back as the Bank of Canada (soon under new management!) was forced to cut interest rates deeply to offset the recession that its own policies had so clearly helped to cause. Barring another disastrous repeat of the experience of 1987 to 1992, the undervaluation of the Canadian dollar will continue to make Canada an attractive location for cost-sensitive investments in manufacturing and certain other industries.

A second factor which has added to the cost competitiveness of Canadian industry is Canada's socialized medical system. In the U.S., most employers must pay premiums for private health insurance coverage for their employees. This can add several dollars per hour to the total wage bill facing those employers. In Canada, most health care costs are borne collectively through public funding of Medicare. Sadly, the deinsuring of many medical services by budget-cutting provincial governments, and the failure of the Medicare system to keep up with the changing structure of total medical care (most notably including the rising costs of pharmaceutical products and home care services), means that more and more health costs are falling through the cracks of Medicare and hence may be picked up by employers.

Nevertheless, employers still shoulder a significantly smaller portion of the total health bill in Canada than is the case in the U.S., and this reinforces the cost competitiveness of real investments in Canada. This is an interesting example of how shifting a burden from businesses to individuals (that is, to the taxpayers who pay for Medicare through their personal taxes) can be quite beneficial in stimulating real investment by those companies.[13]

To test empirically for the importance of global economic pressures in explaining the slowdown in Canadian investment, the "core" econometric equation introduced earlier in this chapter was supplemented with one of two different variables reflecting the increased sensitivity of Canada's economy to global pressures. One of these measures was the degree of import penetration of Canada's overall economy. Imports have increased spectactularly as a share of GDP since the FTA was signed, and now are equivalent to about 40% of total output in Canada.[14] Has this flood of imports, some of which are low-cost products from countries with lower wages and weaker social and environmental standards, undermined the feasibility of real investment in Canada? No statistical correlation could be found between real investment and import penetration.

An alternate measure of international pressure is what economists call the "real exchange rate." As noted above, fluctuations in the exchange rate may affect investment by strengthening or weakening the cost competitiveness of a particular economy. The appropriate measure of this effect, however, is not the nominal exchange rate, measured in U.S. cents per Canadian dollar. It is more accurate to adjust that nominal exchange rate to reflect the different rates of inflation experienced in different countries.[15]

An index of the real Canada-U.S. exchange rate can thus be constructed, on the basis of data on the nominal exchange rate and relative rates of inflation in the two countries. One would expect a decline in the real exchange rate to be associated with an increase in investment in Canada, thanks to the enhanced cost-competitiveness which is the result of that depreciation. However, no statistical link between the real exchange rate and the evolution of real investment spending in Canada could be found.[16]

In short, after adjusting for the central domestic determinants of investment—economic growth, interest rates, and business profitability—no statistical evidence of an independent negative impact of globalization on capital accumulation in Canada could be identified.

There is little doubt that globalization has been an important part of the economic and political backdrop to the slowdown in real investment spending in Canada since about 1981. Efforts by particular employers to reduce production costs by shifting their operations to lower-cost foreign jurisdictions have clearly been damaging in certain industries and certain communities. It is also clearly the case that globalization limits—to some extent, in some ways—the domestic policy responses which could be implemented to reverse that slowdown. For this reason, measures which would help to insulate Canada's economy (and our capital markets in particular) from the unrestrained behaviour of global financiers will play an important role in an overall strategy to put capital back to work in Canada.

But the importance of globalization in explaining the overall decline in real investment in the Canadian economy, and hence the subsequent decline in general economic performance, has almost certainly been overstated. There is little evidence that overall investment in Canada has been undermined by a lack of competitiveness in the eyes of investors, nor by the flight of real Canadian businesses to cheaper foreign jurisdictions. In some ways, the concept of "globalization" may now be playing more of an ideological role than an economic one. The captains of industry and finance keep repeating globalization's mantra—"the world is global, there's nothing we can do, the world is global, there's nothing we can do"—in an effort to counter demands for greater social and economic responsibility on the part of private companies.

In many cases, of course, there are real international constraints which have to be identified and grappled with. But, more often than not these days, the global threat is hollow. Most of the negative developments that have contributed to the investment slowdown in Canada were implemented right here in Canada, and led by Canadians with a vested interest in a particular way of doing things. It was Canadian owners of financial wealth, not the "global economy," who demanded that the real returns on their paper investments be treated with more respect than the needs of other Canadians for real work. The constraint posed by financial globalization was one card of many in their loaded deck, but they would have been pushing powerfully for the same set of policies—zero inflation, financial stability, and deliberately restrained real growth—even if the world stopped at Canada's borders.

In short, if investment and hence job-creation are too slow in Canada, this is primarily because of the way Canadian economic and financial policies have evolved over time. And it is changes in those Canadian policies that will have to play the leading role in reversing the investment slowdown which has so undermined our economic progress.

Part III
A Recipe for Stagnation: Ingredients in the Slowdown

Chapter 9
Interest: The Impact of
Monetary Policy

A primary factor behind the slowdown in real investment spending in Canada since about 1980 has been the sea-change in Canadian macroeconomic policy that has occurred during the same time.

Through the initial post-war era, government was at least nominally committed to the goal of full employment as its No. 1 economic priority.[1] This seemed to work reasonably well during the first three decades or so after the conclusion of World War II—although the vibrant growth of private business investment during this period meant that governments didn't actually have to do very much in order to maintain low unemployment rates. Most of the "work" was already being done by a private sector that was confident, growing, and profitable.

Nevertheless, government policies reinforced the strong labour market conditions that were typical of Canada's economy during this period of steady growth and rising incomes. Very low unemployment, rapid economic growth, and steadily rising incomes made this period a "golden age" for most Canadians.[2]

Two particularly important policy levers are at the disposal of government in the area of macroeconomic management. Both of them were turned "on" through most of the golden age expansion. *Fiscal policy* refers to the government's taxation and expenditure policies. Government spending helped to offset temporary downturns in purchasing power (although, once again, there weren't any really bad downturns that needed to be offset; it wasn't until 1981 that Canada experienced its first serious postwar recession). And the growth of public sector employment through the 1960s and 1970s added to the favourable labour market trends of the time. So fiscal policy made a significant contribution to the growth and prosperity of the initial post-war era.

Monetary policy refers to the actions of the government—more specifically, the actions of its central bank, the Bank of Canada—in managing interest rates and overall credit creation in the economy. As was discussed in earlier chapters, the expansion of credit and lending is a crucial precondition for the job-creating investments that are undertaken by real businesses. Monetary policy has a huge effect on how much new credit is created, and at what price, and monetary policy was a crucial factor in both the rise and the fall of Canada's post-war economic boom.

The Great U-Turn

During the first 35 years following World War II, interest rates in Canada were maintained at stable, low levels. This fundamental policy position doubly reinforced the appeal of real investment expenditure in the eyes of private businesses. They could easily obtain credit to finance their business expansions cheaply. At the same time, any investor who wanted to generate significant profits had to undertake real investments in the real economy. In contrast to the 1990s, profits on purely financial investments were at best modest. [In the

Not Such a Bargain

"There's never been a better time to buy!" So proclaimed the slogans of real estate billboards during the late 1990s, as nominal interest rates on household mortgages fell to their lowest levels in a generation. In the wake of the tough belt-tightening of the 1980s and 1990s, it finally seemed as if Canada's economic "fundamentals" were in place. Falling mortgage rates were held out as proof that average Canadians could now share in the just rewards of our earlier economic sacrifices.

But was it really a good time to buy? Nominal rates on five-year mortgages averaged about 7% during 1998, the lowest level since Statistics Canada began gathering data on this subject. But at the same time consumer price inflation was less than 1%. That means that the *real* mortgage rate was a relatively high 6%. Incredibly, the real mortgage rate in 1998 was almost as high as had been the case in 1981, when mortgage rates averaged over 18% but inflation was running at about 11%.

Because lower nominal interest rates translate into lower monthly mortgage payments, many people conclude that a lower nominal rate means a cheaper mortgage. This is not the case for mortgages, or for any other kind of loan. It is the real interest rate, not the nominal interest rate, which determines how expensive a loan really is.

Imagine two scenarios, illustrated in Table 9-1. One captures the situation that roughly prevailed in 1998: mortgage rates of 7% and inflation of 1%. The other corresponds roughly to 1972: mortgage rates of 10% and inflation of 5%. The nominal interest rate was much lower in 1998, but the real rate was slightly higher. Nevertheless, the lower nominal rate translates into a lower monthly payment, and hence the mortgage is cheaper—right? Wrong.

Both home-buyers pay $150,000 for their home, with a $50,000 down payment. They both take out a 25-year mortgage. They both make $40,000 per year at the time of pur-

lingo of economists, the "opportunity cost" of investing money in a real business undertaking, instead of a financial investment, was relatively low.]

Fiscal policy also made a strong contribution to growth and job-creation during this time. The combination of already-vibrant private sector activity and pro-growth macroeconomic policies on the part of government produced the greatest economic expansion in the history of Canada. A similarly optimistic and expansionary economic regime prevailed during the same time in most other industrialized countries.

Interest rates remained very low throughout the "golden age" expansion. The most accurate way to measure interest rates is in "real" terms, relative to the level of inflation. Every borrower has to pay interest at the nominal interest rate specified in their loan agreement. But the real economic burden of that repayment also depends crucially on the rate of inflation.

Suppose that inflation is running at 5% per year. That implies that prices, wages, and other nominal values are rising (on average) by 5% each year. If the interest rate on a loan was also 5% per year, this would imply that lenders would ultimately receive no more back (in real purchasing-power terms) than they initially loaned out.

chase. We assume that both the resale value of the home and the home-buyer's salary increase at the rate of overall inflation.

In 1998, the lower nominal interest rate translates into a lower monthly mortgage payment: $715 per month, a saving of over $200 per month compared to the 10% mortgage. But that monthly payment is fixed in nominal dollars. In the 1998 scenario, the home-buyer's income and the market value of the house grow much more slowly than in the 1972 scenario. It takes 38% more hours of actual hard work before the 1998 buyer owns two-thirds of his or her home. It takes 22% more hours of work before the mortgage is paid off completely. The real interest rate is higher, and hence the real burden of buying the house is also higher. Maybe there was a better time to buy, after all.

Table 9-1
Don't be Fooled by Low Mortgage Rates!

	"1998" Scenario	"1972" Scenario
Purchase price of home	$150,000	$150,000
Amount and term of mortgage	$100,000, 25 years	$100,000, 25 years
Annual income of homeowner	$40,000	$40,000
Interest rate	7%	10%
Inflation rate	1%	5%
Real interest rate	6%	5%
Monthly mortgage payment	$715	$918
Hours of work until buyer owns two-thirds of home's value[1]	6,418	4,640
Hours of work until buyer pays off mortgage entirely[1]	9,827	8,074

Source: Author's calculations.
1. Assumes 2080 hours of work per year.

The happy borrowers, meanwhile, essentially received their loans for "free." They borrowed $100 one year, and paid it back with 5% interest (for a total repayment of $105) the next year. In the meantime, however, the borrowers' own income has grown by 5%, as have the prices of goods and services that they buy or sell. So in real terms, the borrowers are paying back exactly the same amount that they received—and not a penny more.

For this reason, lenders are determined to earn interest on their loans at a faster rate than general prices are increasing; otherwise there is no incentive to lend, because the real value of the loan would not increase, and might even decrease. To make a real profit from a loan, the interest rate must be higher than the inflation rate. The difference between the nominal interest rate and the inflation rate is called the *real interest rate*. (See sidebar: *Not Such a Bargain*.)

This fundamental arithmetic helps to explain why financial investors (including banks and other lenders) hate inflation with an absolute passion. Each uptick of one point in the rate of inflation translates into the erosion of 1% of the real value of their total outstanding loans, the interest rates on which are almost always specified in nominal percentage terms.

The five largest Canadian banks alone held a total portfolio of outstanding loans equal to almost $650 billion by the end of their fiscal year 1998. Imagine an increase in inflation from 1% to 2%. For most Canadians, this would hardly rate as an economic catastrophe. In fact, if the increase in inflation was the result of stronger demand and labour market conditions, the rise in inflation would be a sign of better economic tidings, not worse. For the five banks, however, any rise in inflation constitutes a significant economic blow. An unexpected one-point rise in inflation implies an ultimate real loss to the banks of 1% of their total outstanding loans: $6.5 billion per year.

Of course the banks would quickly try to readjust the nominal interest rates charged on their loans, in order to protect the real profits they make. But in the interim they lose big. No wonder the politically-powerful financial community is such a "hawk" on the subject of inflation. Any rise in inflation constitutes a significant transfer from those who own financial wealth to those who borrow it—including those who are trying to put finance to work in the real economy.

As indicated in Table 9-2, short-run interest rates, such as those set directly by the Bank of Canada, averaged less than one percentage point above inflation throughout the long post-war boom. Long-run interest rates averaged about 1.5 percentage points above inflation. Real returns on financial investments, therefore, were at best modest. During the 1970s, as inflation was accelerating in the wake of major oil price increases and other factors, real returns on many financial assets were actually negative. Investors who wanted to earn higher profits

	The "Golden Age"	The Age of "Permanent Recession"	
Table 9-2 **Then and Now:** **The Great U-turn in Canadian Economic Policy and Performance**			
	1950-1980	1981-1997	1990-1997
Policy Measures:			
Real interest rates, short-term (%)	0.9%	5.6%	5.1%
Real interest rates, long-term (%)	1.6%	6.5%	6.8%
Change gov't program spending (as % GDP)	+16.3 points	+1.1 points	-2.5 points
Performance Measures:			
Average growth real GDP (% per year)	4.7%	2.4%	1.8%
Avg. growth real GDP per person (% per year)	2.8%	1.1%	0.5%
Average growth total employment (% per year)	2.6%	1.4%	0.8%
Average unemployment rate (%)	5.4%	9.8%	10.0%
Annual growth real earnings (% per year)	+2.3%	-0.5%	+0.3%

Source: Author's calculations from Statistics Canada *Canadian Economic Observer, Historical Statistics of Canada, and Canadian Social Trends.*

were compelled to put their money "to work" in real businesses: employing real workers, hiring real machines, and producing goods or services of real value.

At the same time, government fiscal policy backstopped the overall expansion of Canada's economy, financing a dramatic increase in the scope of real public-sector activities. Total program spending by all levels of government in Canada, measured as a share of GDP, roughly doubled between 1950 and 1980.

The results of this pro-growth bias in macroeconomic policy were impressive. After inflation, Canada's real GDP grew by almost 5% per year. Not a single serious recession was experienced during the first 35 years following the end of World War II.[3] In per-person terms, real GDP grew by 2.8% per year, providing a real foundation for the greatest increase in living standards ever experienced in Canada.

Real wages increased steadily. With the unemployment rate averaging just 5% in a booming economy, workers had a strong bargaining position from which to demand and win wage increases that matched or even exceeded the rapid increase in productivity.

For a variety of reasons, the post-war golden age expansion started running out of steam by the late 1970s. On the financial side, the owners of wealth rebelled mightily and powerfully against the negative real returns which were experienced on many financial investments during the 1970s. They lobbied in a number of arenas (including the intellectual arena, where economists advocating tough anti-inflation policies came to dominate the economics profession) for a fundamental change in economic direction.

The financiers were supported, for the most part, by businesses active in the real economy. Many real businesses found their activities to be increasingly constrained by tight labour markets, labour militancy, and the economic "intrusions" of a confident, growing state (including higher taxes, a larger public sector, and more ambitious and interventionist regulatory structures). The profitability of investment in the real economy, like the paper economy, declined notably as the post-war boom carried on (this issue will be discussed in detail in Chapter 11). So financial businesses and real businesses eventually became united in their desire for a fundamental reorientation of macroeconomic policy.

This historic U-turn was engineered at the beginning of the 1980s, and no tool has been more important to its execution than monetary policy. Indeed, the sudden advent of very high real interest rates was like a cannon shot signalling the radical and historic change in macroeconomic direction.

The first shots were fired in the late 1970s in the U.K. (under the aggressive leadership of the newly-elected Margaret Thatcher) and in the U.S. (where an anti-inflation hawk, Paul Volcker, had just been appointed to head that country's central bank, the Federal Reserve). These two countries have traditionally been the most "finance-friendly" of all the developed economies, and so it was quite appropriate that the brave new world of obsessive anti-inflation policy should be introduced there.

Interest rates rose dramatically, and central banks in most other countries were forced to follow—partly by the competitive pressures unleashed in a globalized financial system (much short-run financial capital can move from one country to another in search of the highest interest rates, and this puts pressure on smaller countries to match the moves of the interest rate leaders), and partly by pressure from domestic financial and industrial interests demanding a reversal of the economic "excesses" of the 1970s.

The anti-inflation crusade arrived with a vengeance in Canada in 1981, when nominal short-term interest rates were pushed to as high as 20% (nine points higher than the 11% inflation rate). Mortgage costs skyrocketed, tens of thousands of Canadians lost their homes, and the country was pushed into a deep and long recession—the first in 35 years.

The high nominal interest rates of the early 1980s form an especially painful chapter in Canada's economic history, and most Canadians are glad that the astronomical interest rates of the time were just temporary. Unfortunately, however, the fundamental shift in monetary policy that was heralded by the crisis of

Welfare Bums

Conservatives have railed long and hard against the alleged impact of "easy public money" on the work incentive of poor Canadians. Provincial politicians of every stripe have cut welfare levels and eligibility through the 1990s. The federal unemployment insurance program has been approximately cut in half during the same period. In every case, the punitive changes are justified as breaking the omnipresent "cycle of dependency." This may hurt you, the welfare-reformers hector their unfortunate clients, but we're actually doing you a favour.

But the greatest welfare program of all is the huge safety net taxpayers have provided to financial investors in the form of high-interest government bonds. Canadian taxpayers, through their governments, spent $77 billion on interest charges in 1998: over 9% of GDP, and 20 cents of every dollar they paid in taxes. That's almost four times as much as the total cost of the welfare programs run by all ten provinces, and over six times the cost of unemployment insurance. What is the impact of this "easy public money" on the "work incentive" of investors? Knowing they can obtain returns of 6% or more, after inflation, by simply holding a piece of paper, they are sadly deterred from undertaking useful productive work. Why should they bother getting up in the morning to finance the production of a product or service of real value when they can live so well by clipping coupons from government bonds?

These unfortunate souls are locked into a "cycle of dependence." All they can think of is what they will buy when they get their next government cheque. Will it be expensive booze? A luxury car? Other wasteful forms of consumption?

What these investors need is a healthy dose of tough love. Cut their welfare benefits through lower interest rates on risk-free government bonds. If they still won't go out and get a real job, enroll them in a "workfare for capital" program: idle financial resources must contribute to community development projects in return for their income.

Perhaps we can borrow from the ideas of Ontario premier Mike Harris, as published in his 1995 election manifesto, *The Common Sense Revolution* (with all editorial changes indicated in italics!):

"We want to open up new opportunities and restore hope for *investors* by breaking the cycle of dependency...We should prepare *financial* welfare recipients to return to the *real economy* by requiring all able-bodied *capital*...either to work, or to be *reinvested in the community* in return for their benefits...Although the amount of money involved may not be large, the possibility of *community* work opens the door for *financial* welfare recipients to learn new skills, work towards full-time employment, and increase their self-esteem."

1981 was all too permanent. Figures 9-1 and 9-2 illustrate the historical evolution of real interest rates in Canada for short-term and long-term loans, respectively. In both cases, 1981 marked a break from the low real rates of the past.

While nominal interest rates on all classes of asset have declined since 1981, in step with the now-complete disappearance of inflation, real interest rates have remained at levels that can only be considered high by historical standards. Short-term rates have averaged almost 6% above inflation since 1981, and long-term rates have averaged over 6%.

Interest rates fluctuate, of course, with current economic conditions: central banks adjust short-term rates directly in an effort to moderate the ups and

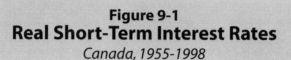

Figure 9-1
Real Short-Term Interest Rates
Canada, 1955-1998

Figure 9-2
Real Long-Term Interest Rates
Canada, 1955-1998

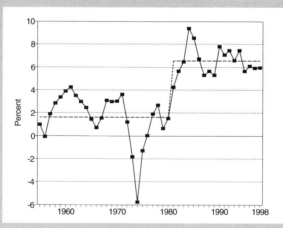

Source: Author's calculations from Statistics Canada, *Canadian Economic Observer, National Income and Financial Accounts*. Real interest rate equals nominal rate less change in GDP deflator.

downs of the economy, while longer-term rates will fluctuate to reflect both monetary policy and expectations in private financial markets. But for both classes of asset the *lowest* real interest rate experienced since 1981 is still higher than the *highest* real interest rate experienced during the preceding three decades.

The interest rate crisis of 1981 was not a temporary but painful adjustment; it marked, rather, the beginning of a permanent and equally painful new regime. Short-term real rates, on average, rose six-fold: from less than 1% before 1981 to over 5% thereafter. Real long-term rates rose four-fold: from about 1.5% before 1981 to over 6% afterwards.

The successful vanquishing of inflation, and the more recent elimination of government deficits, have not affected the level of interest rates. Indeed, in 1998—at a time when the Finance Minister and the Governor of the Bank of Canada both crowed about Canada's strong economic "fundamentals"—real interest rates still stood at about 6%, roughly equal to their post-1981 average levels.

At the same time as monetary policy was dramatically tightened, fiscal policy also shifted to a more contractionary stance.[4] During the 1980s, Canada's public sector was roughly stagnant, in terms of its share of the real economy. And during the 1990s the public sector was cut back even further. The economic effects of the shifts in fiscal and especially in monetary policy have been dramatic and painful, as summarized on the right side of Table 9-2.[5] Since 1981, real GDP growth has averaged half of its pre-1981 rate. In per capita terms, the real growth rate fell by over 60%.

Employment growth was cut in half, and unemployment, on average, doubled. The hefty annual increases in real wages that were enjoyed during the golden age have been converted into stagnation or even rollbacks since then.

Canada's real economic performance since 1990 has been particularly abject. Interest rates have remained as high in real terms as at any point during the 1980s, despite—or perhaps in part *because* of—the virtual elimination of inflation. Real government spending was cut back drastically, eliminating tens of thousands of direct jobs. Real GDP growth per capita and job-creation have both averaged less than a single percentage point per year.

The recession of 1991-92, and the unprecedented weakness of the subsequent recovery, explain a good part of the miserable performance for the decade as a whole. But even by the late 1990s, once the effects of government spending cuts had been digested and the recovery picked up steam, the performance of the real economy could only be described as lacklustre. If the purpose of the about-face in macroeconomic policies which was first imposed in 1981 had indeed been to set the stage for stronger growth and real economic progress, then those policies have clearly and profoundly failed.

The impact of high-interest-rate policies on real investment spending in Canada was severe and entirely predictable. Higher interest rates increase the cost of credit for real investors. They also cut deeply into the disposable cash flow of private businesses, which is an even more important source of investment finance. And they distract the attention of investors and entrepreneurs alike: with such lucrative gains to be made in the financial sphere, the incentive to direct one's money and one's creative energies toward the concrete task of growing the real economy is correspondingly reduced. As indicated in previous chapters, the implications of the investment slowdown for job-creation, growth, and productivity throughout the entire economy have been severe indeed.

The Permanent Recession

So perhaps laying the foundation for stronger growth was *not* really what the great post-1981 U-turn in Canadian economic policy was all about. Indeed, a crucial motivation for the change in direction seems very much to have been a deliberate effort to *restrain* economic growth, in the interests of maintaining an economic environment as conducive as possible to the profitability of both financial investments and real business enterprises.

The public personalities who are in charge of Canada's economic policies—the federal Finance Minister and the Governor of the Bank of Canada chief among them—will not admit it in public. But the facts of the matter are that the tight-money policies of the 1980s and 1990s have been largely motivated, both intellectually and economically, by a desire to ensure that unemployment does not fall too *low*.

This will strike most Canadians as excruciatingly perverse. Yet this policy of deliberately maintaining unemployment at a level considered to be "good" for business—we will call it a policy of "permanent recession"—is explicitly detailed in the more obscure research documents of the Finance Department, the Bank of Canada, and the private and academic economists who advise them.

The strange theory goes something like this. The wage increases that result when unemployment falls "too low" are the primary or even the sole source of inflation. This is harmful to financial investors. It also cuts into the profit margins of employers in the real economy. If the labour market is "too tight," inflation will accelerate continuously. It is not simply a matter of tolerating a slightly higher rate of inflation in return for a slightly lower rate of unemployment; rather, once the economy steps across the minimum acceptable level of unemployment, then the inflation rate will begin to soar without limit.

Unless government and the central bank act to pull the economy back from the abyss (through higher interest rates to slow down investment and overall economic growth), hyperinflation and financial chaos will be the ultimate result. That minimum level of unemployment below which the economy must not cross is called, in one of the most bizarre acronyms ever invented, the "NAIRU" (Non-Accelerating Inflation Rate of Unemployment). It is also known, more pejoratively, as the "natural" rate of unemployment.

The intended implication of this highly-ideological choice of language is clear: permanent unemployment is "natural," and so workers and government shouldn't bother trying to do anything about it. Vast amounts of the intellectual energy of many very smart people have been dedicated to trying to estimate the NAIRU (that point below which the unemployment rate must not be allowed to fall). It turns out, curiously, that estimates of the NAIRU tend to track the actual level of unemployment that was experienced in the recent past.[6] In other words, whatever level of unemployment happens to be prevailing is typically held to be the "natural" or non-inflationary level.

The implications of NAIRU thinking for monetary policy are clear and dangerous. The operation of competitive, deregulated labour markets alone will attain the best match between labour supply and labour demand—and hence the lowest long-run rate of unemployment compatible with stable inflation. Governments should not try to reduce unemployment by increasing demand. Rather, the role of the central bank is to focus on reducing and preferably even eliminating inflation from the system; no benefits can be derived from tolerating inflation, but clear gains result from its extinction.

Among the alleged economic benefits of low inflation claimed by its proponents: prices give more accurate economic signals, businesses have more confidence about their cost structure, and restaurants don't have to reprint their menus as often. By thus enhancing the inherent, self-regulating efficiency of free markets, monetary policy makes its biggest possible contribution to our collective well-being.

The central bank will try to guide the economy toward its natural rate of unemployment by cutting interest rates when unemployment is deemed too high. Supposedly temporary excess unemployment may need to be endured in order to bring inflation down. But in the long-run a low-inflation or even zero-inflation economy will be a more efficient and productive one.

Canada's experience with NAIRU policy has been especially disastrous, perhaps because of the unique zeal with which our policy-makers pursued the goal in the early 1990s. Under the guidance of then-Governor John Crow, the Bank of Canada was one of the first central banks in the world to set explicit targets for inflation reduction (targets which in theory would make more transparent and solid the bank's overriding commitment to inflation-control), and it even flirted publicly with the notion of aiming for a zero-inflation world.

Largely thanks to this extreme policy course, Canada experienced uniquely high interest rates between 1989 and 1992, and suffered a recession that was far worse than those experienced by its trading partners. "Natural" unemployment became a disastrous, self-fulfilling prophecy: hundreds of thousands of Canadians, thrown out of work for extended periods in the interests of bringing inflation down, found that they were unable to get a foot back into the labour market when things finally improved.

Lacking current skills and work contacts, these Canadians joined the ranks of the permanently unemployed, thereby perversely increasing the structural mismatch between labour supply and labour demand with which the NAIRU theory is supposedly concerned. Tight-money policy was extremely successful in wringing the last remnants of inflation from the system: inflation has averaged lower during the 1990s than in any other post-war decade, and by 1998 average prices were actually *falling* in Canada (a phenomenon that economists call "deflation"). Not coincidentally, Canada's real economic performance—and most notably its record of real investment—has been worse than in any other post-war decade.

NAIRU's Believe it or Not

The economics of permanent recession have truly turned the world upside down. Unemployment is a good thing, because it restrains inflation and disciplines the labour force. Too much employment is a bad thing. So are wage increases. Yes, most Canadians support themselves through wage income, and hence real wage increases are the key source of improvements in the standard of living of those same Canadians. But wage increases might mean lower profits and higher inflation. An outbreak of prosperity is to be avoided at all costs.

Once you believe in the Non-Accelerating Inflation Rate of Unemployment (NAIRU), all kinds of strange conclusions emerge. Consider the following:

- A banner headline in the *Toronto Star* of July 20, 1995 said it all:"Good news puts stocks in tailspin." The story explained that North American stock markets had tumbled in the previous day's trading on news that jobs were being created too rapidly in the U.S. This raised fears that interest rates would rise to hold back the labour market, hence reducing the appeal of stock market investments.
- This ironic world-view is evidenced repeatedly in financial headlines:"Wall Street soars on low employment figures" (*Globe and Mail*, August 3, 1996). "Good news on employment front sinks Dow" (*Globe and Mail*, July 6, 1996). "Growth a potential peril" (*Financial Post*, April 29, 1998). "Can't get enough of that bad news" (*Financial Post*, September 15, 1995). Perhaps the gold medal for upside-down thinking should go to a headline in the *Financial Post* on (appropriately) October 31, 1995:"What we really need now is a serious jolt of despair."
- It is not just the headline-writers who sum it up succinctly; market analysts can do it well, too. Consider the words of wisdom of Arve Bendiksrud, fixed

By the late 1990s, the NAIRU theory had been largely discredited in the eyes of many economists.[7] Actual experience in Canada, and especially in the U.S.— where the unemployment rate fell far below what until very recently was considered to be the minimum NAIRU level—cast huge doubt on the view that there even is a NAIRU, let alone that it poses a real binding constraint on the productive potential of the economy.

Nevertheless, monetary policy continues to emphasize the need to control inflation above all other economic goals. And we can expect that interest rates (which were still historically high, in real terms, right through the late 1990s) will be jacked up even further at the first signs of rising wages or looming inflation.

Consider the monetary policy reports which the Bank of Canada releases on a semi-annual basis. These reports no longer discuss the NAIRU explicitly, but they still rely on an estimate of what is called the "potential output" of the economy, which is theoretically equivalent. If employment grows too much, so that the economy is producing more than this potential output, inflation will accelerate.

income analyst at Toronto Dominion Securities, concerning the outlook for financial investors late in 1994:"It looks like the investment fundamentals are deteriorating more rapidly for Canada than we thought. Growth is a fair bit stronger and capacity utilization is increasing rapidly." God help us all.

• Elected officials, out of fear for their jobs, have to put the matter somewhat more delicately. For example, Finance Minister Paul Martin once wrote that "the government's reforms [to unemployment insurance and other social programs] are aimed at making sure that we never repeat the experience of the late 1980s." Between 1985 and 1990 employment grew by 2.3% per year, labour force participation rose, real per capita GDP climbed by 8%, and the poverty rate fell by 2.3 percentage points. But inflation increased from 4% to 4.8%. We can't have that, can we?

• U.S. central banker Alan Greenspan summarized the economic benefits of unemployment and insecurity in a presentation to the U.S. Senate in 1997. How could continuing low wages in the U.S. be explained, in light of growing productivity and falling unemployment? "Heightened job insecurity explains a significant part of the restraint on compensation and the consequent muted price inflation." Despite relatively low unemployment, most workers still fear being thrown into the streets—and, with little to fall back on in the way of social benefits, this fear is well-justified. This "fear factor" allows Greenspan to tolerate lower unemployment without increasing interest rates. But the moment workers start feeling a little more confident about their place in economic life, it's no more Mr. Nice Guy for the central banker. "Suppressed wage cost growth as a consequence of job insecurity can be carried only so far," Greenspan warned, and he promised to tighten monetary policy if wage growth picked up. Financial investors hate risk and insecurity—but for workers, it's economically "efficient."

In its November 1998 policy report, the Bank of Canada warned that actual output could be as little as 0.5 percentage points below its "potential," beyond which inflation would begin to accelerate without end. The official unemployment rate at the time was 8%; hence this view is consistent with an implied belief that the NAIRU is as high as 7.5%. Considering that Canada's economy was actually experiencing widespread deflation for the first time since the Great Depression (the broadest measure of prices in Canada, known as the GDP deflator, declined by 0.5% during 1998), this view would have been laughable—if it were not held by officials who have the power to slow down the whole economy merely because they *fear* inflation, whether or not they actually see it.

At a time of global financial chaos, and despite the possible advent of deflation and persistent unemployment, the November 1998 monetary policy report nevertheless focused on the ever-present danger that inflation might leap from its death bed to wreak havoc once again with the efficiency of the Canadian economy. The 29-page report mentioned "inflation" (and concepts like inflation-control and inflation expectations) a grand total of 79 times. The word "unemployment" did not appear once.

The high interest rates that have been experienced in Canada since 1981 were always justified by the need to incur temporary pain for the sake of long-term gain. By reducing inflation, tight-money policy is supposed to enhance the accuracy and efficiency with which private investors and companies conduct their business for the sake of us all. In reality, the supposed efficiency gains of operating in a low-inflation environment are generally intangible and vastly overstated, yet the lasting economic damage that has been caused by high interest rates and the chronic unemployment they have produced has been all too concrete.

No, the policies of the permanent recession were more about redistributing the economic pie, not about growing it more efficiently. Every downtick in inflation was a huge gift to financial investors: protecting their real returns, helping stock markets reach still loftier heights, and generating huge capital gains on existing bonds. And the deliberate recreation of a large and permanent pool of desperate unemployed workers has done wonders for private employers in the real economy: they can hire labour at competitive prices, and then discipline that labour to work efficiently and compliantly.

Despite the apparent elimination of inflation from the Canadian economy, monetary policy-makers remain as militant about controlling inflation as their No. 1 economic mission as they ever were. But the victories of the war against inflation are hollow, indeed, for the vast majority of Canadians.

Good Decisions

"Inflation makes it much more difficult to make good investment decisions...It is only with stability in the general price level that a sound basis can be provided for investment and lending decisions and the most efficient use will be made of the economy's resources."

—John Crow, former Governor,
Bank of Canada, March 1991

Inflation rate when John Crow was inaugurated as Governor (Feb. 1987): 4.0%
Inflation rate when he left (Dec. 1993): 1.7%
Business fixed investment (as share of GDP) in 1987: 18.6%
Business fixed investment (as share of GDP) in 1993: 14.8%

Interest Rates and Debt: Canada's Fall from the Tightrope

One especially destructive side-effect of the permanent shift to high interest rates since 1981 has been a catastrophic change in the fundamental economics of public finance in Canada. The combination of permanently higher real interest rates, with the equally permanent slowdown in real economic growth which was the (perhaps intended) result of those higher rates, led to the placement and eventual detonation of a fiscal time bomb deep within the coffers of Canadian government.

Canadians paid heavily for the shift to a tight-money regime in the form of lost jobs, chronic unemployment, and stagnant incomes—and they continue to do so. But they are also paying in the form of huge tax payments and lost public services, which were the longer-term result of the same policy shift.

High interest rates were by far the dominant cause of the slide into deficits and debt that was experienced by most Canadian governments since the early 1980s. The impact was felt directly, in the form of higher interest charges on the governments' own debts. And it was felt indirectly, through the negative impact of higher interest rates on growth and hence government revenues, and a corresponding increase in the cost of income security programs (such as unemployment and welfare, which automatically expand when the economy weakens).

The nasty arithmetic that describes the link between interest rates, growth, and government debt can be summarized in the following equation (which economists refer to as the "debt stability condition"):

Change in   =   Existing   *   (real int. rate - real growth rate) + Operating
Debt Burden   Debt Burden   Balance

In plain English, the implications of this equation can be stated as follows. Any time the real interest rate on government debt exceeds the real growth rate of the economy, then the government's existing debt burden (measured as a share of GDP) will *automatically* grow—even if the government is taking in enough tax revenues to cover the cost of all the current public and social programs it operates.

To stop the debt burden from growing in this unhappy circumstance, the government must generate a large "operating surplus." In other words, it must collect tax revenues far in excess of the cost of actually running government, in order to pay the high interest costs on accumulated debt and stop the debt burden from rising. The size of the required operating surplus grows as the gap between the interest rate and the growth rate gets larger.

If the real interest rate is lower than the real growth rate, however, then the opposite, more favourable result occurs: the government debt burden automatically *shrinks*, even if the government merely collects enough tax revenue to pay for current programs (and doesn't bother collecting taxes to pay for interest charges).

When growth rates typically exceed interest rates, the government faces an inherently stable fiscal outlook. It might incur an operating deficit in a particular year—because of a recession, for example, or perhaps because of some major public investment project—but that short slide into debt is reversed automatically as the economy resumes its growth. Interest costs on the initial debt that was incurred are more than offset by the fiscal benefits of economic growth, and the government's debt burden (measured as a share of GDP) falls all by itself.

When real interest rates exceed real growth rates, however, a dangerously unstable fiscal situation is created. If the government happens to incur a deficit in a particular year, that initial debt will subsequently grow *infinitely* as a share of GDP since interest obligations are accumulating at a pace faster than they can be offset by the benefits of economic growth.

Only if government acts quickly to set aside sufficient revenues from its operating budget—by raising taxes, cutting programs, or both—can it arrest this explosive expansion of debt. In essence, when interest rates exceed growth rates, government walks along a fiscal tightrope: one slip away from balanced budgets and the government plunges into an abyss of debt.

In essence, the shift in monetary policy that was engineered in the early 1980s pushed Canada's governments right off that tightrope. Prior to 1981, average real growth rates exceeded the real interest rates paid on federal debt. That meant an existing debt burden could be worked down over time, thanks to the powerful effects of economic growth, while still allowing the government to fully allocate its tax revenues to the provision of public and social services. Since

	Table 9-3 **Falling from the Fiscal Tightrope** *Interest rates and growth rates, 1950 to 1997*	
	"Golden Age" (1950-1980)	"Permanent Recession" (1981-1997)
Average real interest rate, federal debt[1]	3.9%	7.5%
Average annual growth, real GDP	4.7%	2.4%
Average difference	-0.8 points	+5.1 points
Operating balance consistent with a stable debt ratio[2]	$5 billion deficit	$30 billion surplus

Source: Author's calculations from Statistics Canada, *Canadian Economic Observer, Public Sector Finance.*
1. Real interest rate equals federal debt service charges divided by net debt stock, less change in GDP deflator.
2. Assumes 1998 values for net federal debt ($583 billion) and GDP ($888 billion).

1981, however, the reverse has been permanently and painfully true. Real interest rates on federal debt have averaged more than five full points above the average rate of real GDP growth. Not once since 1981 has the growth rate exceeded the interest rate.

The shift to high interest rates caused an initial burst of indebtedness in the early 1980s, due to the fiscal side-effects of the subsequent recession. But the persistence of those interest rates caused that initial debt to balloon into a full-blown debt crisis by the early 1990s: not because of irresponsible government spending on useful public programs for Canadians, but solely because of the huge fiscal cost of servicing an initial debt in a high-interest, slow-growth environment.

Canadians paid more taxes, even as government programs were being downsized, in an attempt to generate operating surpluses large enough to stabilize the debt. Apart from transferring literally hundreds of billions of dollars from taxpayers to the financial investors who hold that debt, this negative development also planted the seeds for the subsequent tax revolt by Canadians that dominated many political debates during the late 1990s. Paying more and receiving less is a sure recipe for dissatisfaction in any constituency, and Canadian taxpayers are no exception.

But it is the macroeconomics of the permanent recession, not government "waste" or "mismanagement," which is fundamentally to blame for this sorry state of affairs. If real economic growth, on average, still exceeded real interest rates by the same margin as was experienced during the golden age expansion, then the federal government of 1998 could incur a $5 billion *deficit* on its actual program operations (that is, it could collect $5 billion less in taxes than would be required to pay for all current non-interest expenses), yet still suffer no increase in its debt burden (measured as a share of GDP).

In reality, however, given a five-point gap between typical interest rates and growth rates, the federal government needs a $30 billion operating surplus just to keep the debt burden from rising.[8] The ongoing cost to taxpayers of the post-1981 shift in macroeconomic policy is huge: tens of billions of dollars of unnecessary taxes and foregone public services, year after year.

Indeed, in retrospect, high interest rates account for virtually all of the run-up in federal debt which was experienced in the wake of the onset of the permanent recession.[9] We can conduct the following thought experiment: what would have happened to federal finances had elements of the pre-1981 macroeconomic regime been retained, instead of being replaced by the deliberate adoption of high interest rates and slow growth? These simulations are presented in Figure 9-3.

The actual rise in the debt burden, measured as a share of GDP, began in earnest in the early 1980s. Accumulated federal debt rose from about 20% of GDP in 1980 to a peak of over 70 percent by 1996, when it finally began to decline. But if the federal government had paid interest on its debt at the same real rate (about 3.9 percentage points above inflation) as had been the case prior to 1981, the debt burden would have peaked at about 45% of GDP. It was the dramatic rise in the government's own interest costs, the perverse side-effect of

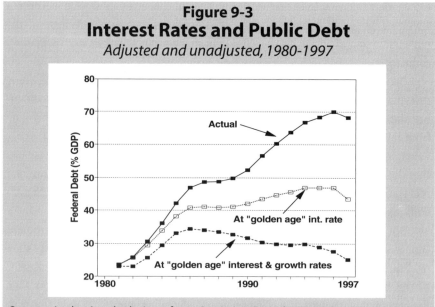

Figure 9-3
Interest Rates and Public Debt
Adjusted and unadjusted, 1980-1997

Source: Author's calculations from Statistics Canada, *Canadian Economic Observer*, and Government of Canada *Budget Plan* (various years).

its own policy of permanent recession, which drove most of the rise in the debt burden.

If we also assume that real GDP had grown at the same rate as it did during the golden age, the federal debt burden would have begun declining in 1985 (following an initial rise resulting from the large operating deficits incurred during the recession of 1981-82). And that debt burden today would be no higher than it was in 1981: slightly over 20% of GDP.

The crisis in public finance in Canada, with its huge resulting costs for Canadian taxpayers, and the damage it caused to public and social programs, has been perhaps the greatest consequence of the tight monetary policy that has been in place through most of the last two decades.

Chapter 10
Savings: Where Does
the Money Come From?

One of the most enduring controversies in all of economics involves the relationship between investment and savings. Obviously, in order to invest, an
economy must also save.

Think back to the simple example of the investment process that was introduced in the first chapter of this book: a farmer decides to expand the total
acreage of corn fields she has under cultivation. To plant additional crops (and
thus increase her total economic output), she must take some of the corn that
she might otherwise have consumed and use it instead as seed for the newly-
cultivated fields. The farmer has "saved" some corn from the current crop, and
instead of consuming it she has "invested" it in order to increase corn production next year. That unconsumed corn represents both savings and investment.

Indeed, the very design of our economic statistics reflects this identification
between savings and investment. In the national income accounts that are prepared by Statistics Canada—similar to those used in any other developed
economy—national savings and national investment will always equal one another. This is true by definition.

But a fundamental controversy in economic theory arises because the whole
process seems to involve two separate decisions: a decision by someone to save
some of their current income, and another decision by someone to take that
unconsumed income and put it into a productivity-enhancing investment. Economists agree that (when properly measured) savings always equals investment.
They disagree, however, on which causes which—in other words, which decision
comes *first*.

When the saver and the investor are the same person (like our farmer), and
when the savings and the investment are even the same physical commodity

(like her corn), the issue becomes moot. Saving and investing is one and the same act. But when savings and investment are undertaken by *different* economic actors, and when the two decisions are measured in terms of *money* rather than in terms of particular commodities, then it all gets rather complicated.

In a modern market economy, savings and investment may indeed be undertaken by different actors (although it is still often the case that the saver and the investor are one and the same, as with private companies who finance most of their investment spending from internal funds). And savings and investment are almost always measured in money (although, again, there are flows of real commodities which must ultimately correspond to those monetary values).

So sorting out the savers from the investors, and the different factors which affect these two halves of the overall process of capital accumulation, gets uncertain and controversial. But the policy implications of the controversy are huge. If the decision to save is what starts the whole ball rolling, then policies should be implemented to encourage more *saving* by individuals, companies, and governments. But if the drive to invest is the more important motive force behind capital accumulation and growth, then *investment* incentives are more appropriate—and policies which encourage investment can be quite different from, and sometimes even contradictory to, policies which encourage savings.

As a simple but powerful example, consider the impact of interest rates on saving and investment. High interest rates are supposed to stimulate savings: individuals will put more funds into their savings accounts if the payback for doing so is higher. Indeed, restoring the financial incentive to save was a key justification for the shift to high-interest-rate policies in most industrialized countries around 1980.

Investment, however, is clearly stimulated by *lower* interest rates, as was argued in detail in previous chapters of this book. Given that savings and investment are always equal by definition, one of these two arguments must be wrong. Crucial policy decisions depend on which approach is taken to this long-standing theoretical puzzle.

This chapter will review the different theoretical perspectives lying behind the different views as to whether savings or investment is the more important.

Whose Interest?

"The justification for a moderately high rate of interest has been found hitherto in the necessity of providing a sufficient inducement to save. But...the extent of effective saving is necessarily determined by the scale of investment, and that scale of investment is promoted by a *low* rate of interest."

—John Maynard Keynes
The General Theory, 1936

And it will present Canadian economic data which suggest quite conclusively that investment and growth in recent years have *not* been held back by a lack of savings. As suggested in the early chapters of this book, Canada's financial system is actually awash in money and capital. It is most definitely not a shortage of funds, or a lack of "thriftiness" on the part of Canadians, which is holding back real investment. Rather, it is a failure to put money into real economic motion—a failure to invest—that explains our post-1980 slowdown in growth, job-creation, and productivity.

The World According to Supply and Demand

Economists can be roughly divided into two broad camps on the issue of whether savings cause investment, or investment causes savings. In one corner is the traditional view that the operation of supply and demand in "free" competitive markets will naturally ensure that all economic resources possessed by a society (including all labour and capital) are efficiently put to work in real production. This theoretical model is known as *neoclassical* economics, and one of its key conclusions that economic growth is constrained by the availability (that is, by the supply) of productive inputs, including labour, capital, and raw materials.

This approach is therefore often called "supply-side" economics, since it suggests that increasing the supplies of economic resources is the key to economic growth. The neoclassical approach has been the dominant school of thought in the developed economies throughout the 20th century—except for 25 years after World War II when it was challenged, ultimately unsuccessfully, by Keynesian theories.

The implications of supply-side, free-market thinking for the savings-investment issue are clear, and are fully consistent with the thrust of the overall model. Savings of financial capital are an important input to the process of growth. We don't need to worry about those savings being actually invested in the real economy: a competitive market for capital will ensure that all available capital resources are used effectively in production. And, as described in Chapter 3, the financial industry is the intermediary—or the "matchmaker"—that mobilizes idle savings and delivers them to businesses which want to invest. What we should focus on is increasing the supply of savings.

Various policy conclusions spring from this supply-side analysis of the relationship between savings and investment. Taxes should be structured so as to encourage more personal saving. For this reason, free-market theorists have tended to support sales taxes (like Canada's GST) over traditional income taxes; since no sales tax is paid on income that is not spent, the GST thus penalizes consumption and hence should theoretically stimulate savings.

Not coincidentally, the GST also tends to shift the heaviest burden of taxation onto those households with the *least* income: since they spend virtually every dollar of their income just to get by, they also pay GST on virtually every dollar of income (unlike high-income households which "avoid" the GST through their personal savings).

Similarly, the goal of stimulating savings also motivates the various tax subsidies that are provided to personal investing and wealth ownership, such as the huge subsidies supporting RRSPs, or the special tax treatment provided to many forms of wealth-related income (including the dividend tax credit and capital gains tax exemptions).

The basic idea here is that paying taxes on future investment income will reduce the incentive for saving. For example, suppose the average return on investments is 8%. But if a high-income taxpayer has to pay income tax on the future income from those investments at a rate of (say) 50%, that cuts the effective *after-tax* rate of return in half (to just 4%). This undermines the incentive for individuals to save.

Government is targeted for special attention in supply-side explanations of the slowdown in investment and growth. Government saving (the difference between income and spending) is the opposite of a government deficit (which occurs when spending *exceeds* total income). The large deficits which Canadian governments incurred through the 1980s and the first half of the 1990s thus constituted a form of considerable dis-saving. To the extent that these deficits were financed through net foreign borrowing by those governments, this dis-saving also negatively affected national saving. And, with such a large share of domestic private savings dedicated to the financing of government deficits, the argument goes, there is little left over to fund investment activity by private companies.

In this way, government deficits "crowd out" private investment, and hence contribute to slower economic growth.[1] By reducing deficits and balancing the budget (preferably through reductions in government spending), national saving will increase and private investment will respond accordingly.

Governments can also promote faster savings, it is argued, through the design of pensions and other social programs. For example, one supposed benefit of an RRSP-type pension scheme, in which individuals are encouraged or even required to invest in the stock market, is the increased supply of savings made available to private companies (assuming, of course, that the stock market actually delivers those savings to real businesses as opposed to using them for speculative purposes). Free-market economists laud the privatized pension schemes that have been implemented in countries like Chile for their supposedly beneficial impact on overall national savings.[2]

You Do It

"Saving is a very fine thing. Especially when your parents have done it for you."

—Sir Winston Churchill

The common thread in all of these measures is the belief that "more saving is better." Yet even if an economy succeeds in increasing its savings, what ensures that these savings will be productively employed in the form of real investments? True to its free-market roots, the neoclassical theory depends on the operation of supply and demand forces to ensure that all available savings are indeed put to work in the real economy.

Interest rates play the leading role. In short, the interest rate can be thought of as the "price" of capital: it represents the cost that a borrower must pay to use a certain sum of capital for a given period (say, a year). As in any other marketplace, the price of "capital" should fluctuate until a perfect match is obtained between the supply of capital (savings) and demand for it (investment).

If savings are scarce, then the interest rate should rise (as borrowers try to outbid one another to attain some of the scarce capital). This will both inspire more savings (since people will save more in order to take advantage of high interest rates), and ensure that capital is allocated only to those projects which are the most profitable (and which hence can afford to pay a higher interest rate). The reverse should occur if there is not enough investment to use up all available savings: the interest rate falls, stimulating more borrowing, until all available savings are used up.

This model of the capital market is known as the "loanable funds" theory, and can be traced back to one of the founders of neoclassical economics, Irving Fisher (and in particular his 1930 book, *The Theory of Interest*). And it still underlies the most important macroeconomic policy prescriptions of mainstream, free-market economics.

But this supply-and-demand theory of the relationship between savings and investment misses several important features of the functioning of modern capital markets. The notion that savings and investment decisions are especially responsive to changes in interest rates—a crucial prerequisite if interest rate fluctuations are to be able to equalize savings and investment—is itself open to question. Savings, in particular, are not especially sensitive to interest rates. In fact, the savings of individuals, companies, and governments are much more dependent on income levels than on interest rates.

Personal savings increase strongly with household disposable income. Corporations save heavily out of their profits, in the form of retained earnings. And even government savings tend to rise with the level of national income: government deficits grow automatically whenever the economy enters a recession (since tax revenues decline, and the cost of social programs like unemployment insurance increases), and the reverse occurs when the economy is growing strongly. A deficit, of course, is the opposite of government saving, and thus government saving grows strongly when the economy grows rapidly.

The sensitivity of investment to the level of interest rates was analyzed in Chapter 8. Clearly, when real interest rates are high, real investment spending declines: in part because of the additional cost to companies of borrowing money for investments, in part because of the chilling effect of high interest rates on overall demand conditions, and in part because higher interest rates make many financial investments look relatively more appealing than investments in the real economy.

Nevertheless, the sensitivity of investment to interest rates is muted and takes considerable time to be fully felt. And, as described in Chapter 8, interest rates were not as important as the rate of economic growth in influencing investment. So, like savings, investment seems to depend more on income levels than on interest rates. This raises serious questions about whether fluctuations in interest rates could indeed be powerful enough to ensure equality between desired savings and real investment.

A more important problem, however, is raised by the fact that in modern economies interest rates are not actually determined by a "free-market" balance between real savings and investment flows in the first place. Instead, in a modern credit-money system, interest rates are determined primarily by the policy stance of monetary authorities—that is, by the central bank. This is especially true for shorter-term interest rates (such as overnight banking rates or 90-day Treasury bond rates). These rates are often directly administered by central banks, which set interest rates on the short-term funds which are continuously shifted around within the banking system.

But even longer-term interest rates (such as the rates on multi-year corporate or government bonds) tend to fluctuate around the levels set by monetary authorities. Longer-run interest rates do not respond immediately to shifts in shorter-run rates implemented by central bankers, especially when those shifts are a response to shorter-run economic conditions (such as a temporary interest rate cut by a central bank to offset a possible slowdown in the economy). Longer-run interest rates reveal more inertia than shorter-run rates, reflecting the longer-term expectations of lenders and borrowers about where monetary policy and related variables (such as inflation) are headed.

Another complicating factor is financial globalization. With funds better able to move from one country to another in search of the highest return, no single central bank (with the possible exception of the U.S. Federal Reserve) exerts as much influence over longer-run interest rates as may have once been the case. Instead, there is a kind of "melting pot" phenomenon in which global long-run interest rates reflect a rough average of the general policy perspectives of all central bankers. Interest rates prevailing in any particular country will be adjusted around that global average to reflect country-specific economic and risk factors (such as the rate of inflation). Nevertheless, there is no doubt that long-run interest rates are a policy-sensitive outcome. The shift towards a harsher anti-inflation monetary policy in most of the developed economies in the early 1980s was accompanied by a notable and permanent upward shift in long-real interest rates, as was described in Chapter 9. Efforts by neoclassical economists to explain this event on the basis of supposedly "free-market" forces (such as the flows of real savings and investment, or even deeper fundamental factors like the real economic productivity of capital) have not been successful.

Interest rates, both short-run and long-run, are clearly an outcome of deliberate policy, not a result of the operation of a free market for loanable funds. Thus, if interest rates are set by policy, they can hardly also be counted on to fluctuate freely in order to equate savings and investment. Some other mechanism must be fulfilling this function.

The World Beyond Supply and Demand

Enter that group of economists who place rather less faith in the ability of free, competitive markets to ensure the smooth functioning of the whole economy and the full employment of all resources (including labour and capital). Several alternative economic theories take a fundamentally different view of the relationship between savings and investment. These alternative approaches differ widely from one another, but they have one key aspect in common. They can collectively be considered as "demand-side" theories, in contrast to the "supply-side" emphasis of free-market theories.

Their shared starting assumption is the conviction that the operation of free markets alone is not sufficient to ensure that all available resources are used productively in the economy. To the contrary, the normal state of affairs in any market economy is one in which there are always pools of idle resources—and in particular pools of unemployed labour—sitting around unproductively. In this case, it is not enough to ensure that the economy is provided with adequate inputs of labour, capital, and other resources (although that is obviously important). An even greater problem may be ensuring that those inputs are actually put to use.

Numerous economic theories fall within the rubric of demand-side thinking. The best-known proponent of demand-side theories, of course, was the British economist John Maynard Keynes, who analyzed the mass unemployment experienced in most capitalist economies during the 1930s and prescribed a range of demand-stimulating measures (including lower interest rates, government spending, and public or social investment programs) to solve the problem.

Some mainstream followers of Keynes during the post-war era tended to water down his theories of unemployment and depression, treating them as a special case of an otherwise healthy free-market system. Others, however, built upon his more unorthodox insights into the behaviour and instability of private financial markets, and their impact on private investment and overall economic performance; this has come to be known as the "post-Keynesian" approach to economics.[3]

The economic thought of Karl Marx also falls within the broad category of demand-side theories. Marx was first to identify the profit-seeking investment decision by private firms as the crucial economic engine of a capitalist economy. He also explained why—contrary to the neoclassical economic theories which were developed later—the system would tend to continuously generate unemployment rather than full employment.

This is because unemployment plays a key role in maintaining the profitability of the private investment which drives the whole economy: without unemployment to continually reinforce the economic insecurity of workers, wages would tend to rise and workplace discipline would tend to erode until profitability was so undermined that investment began to decline.

Modern demand-side macroeconomists in the "structuralist" tradition combine insights from all of these schools of thought. In this approach, whose intellectual founder was probably the Polish economist Michal Kalecki (see sidebar, Chapter 4), growth and employment are determined by a complex mix of factors, including income distribution, profits, the actions of government, and the broad institutional features shaping the economic behaviour of investors and workers alike.[4]

In all of these theories, the level of employment is not fixed solely by the number of available workers, but will also depend on the number of available *jobs*—dependent, that is, on the *demand* for labour.

This seemingly simple insight has profound implications for the theory of saving and investment. In the free-market vision, any increase in investment must entail a *decrease* in consumption. Why? At any given point in time, the economy is producing as much as it is capable of producing, thanks to the miraculous guiding force of market competition. Therefore, in order to free real resources with which to make a real investment, the economy must first give up something else: it must shift resources from one sector (say, consumer goods industries like food or CDs) to another (producing investment goods like factory machinery or bulldozers). There are no idle resources, and hence more investment necessarily implies less of something else. Thus the focus on increasing savings as a prerequisite for faster investment is a logical conclusion of a model in which all resources are fully occupied at all points in time.

In a demand-constrained system, however, a certain stockpile of resources will generally be idle at any point in time due to a shortage of economic purchasing power (or demand). Economic growth can then occur either through the mobilization of new economic inputs (such as labour or capital), or through the greater employment of those inputs which the economy already possesses. Presumably, if there are resources sitting around doing nothing, they could indeed be put to work carrying out the real work of a real investment, without requiring a prior decision to set aside real savings.

The operation of the credit money system plays a crucial role in this process. Ultimately, investment is generally limited only by the willingness of businesses to invest, not by the supply of savings. Since the financial system literally creates money out of thin air in the form of credit, investing companies do not need to wait for real resources to be freed up through the thriftiness of real savers.

Thanks to credit, a company can invest now, pay later. And this financial independence allows the investment decision to take on a whole new economic importance. The initial and autonomous decision to spend more on investment is financed through the credit creation capacity of banks and other financial suppliers. Hence, all of the demand-side theories described above tend to emphasize the investment decisions of private firms as the independent, leading force of economic growth and development in a capitalist economy. Understandably, all of these theories also tend to focus on the closely related issue of the link between real investment and the operation of the financial system.

For these reasons, the direction of causation between savings and investment in demand-side economic theories is the reverse of that implied by the neoclassical approach. This contrast is summarized in Figure 10-1.

The neoclassical chain of command is pictured on the left side of the figure. Unemployment is not an issue; supply and demand forces should ensure the optimal utilization of all resources, including labour. The output of the economy is limited only by the supply of inputs, and by the efficiency with which they are used. To invest more, individuals in the economy must make a personal decision to save more. An efficient free market for capital (or, more precisely, for loanable funds) will ensure that those savings are optimally allocated to productive firms.

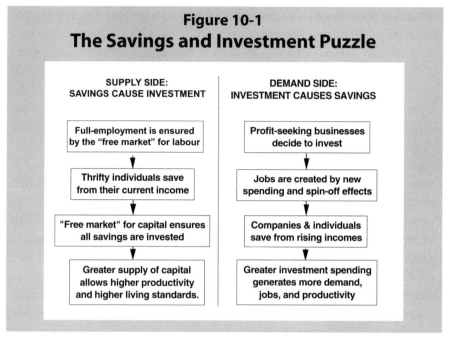

Figure 10-1

The Savings and Investment Puzzle

With more capital in use, the economy will be more productive, and the standard of living of its citizens will rise.

It is important to understand that there are no *demand-side* benefits to faster investment, according to this theory. More investment means more growth and a higher standard of living for supply-side reasons alone—because, with a larger stock of capital employed in the economy, average labour productivity will be higher.

In the alternative demand-side vision (pictured on the right side of Figure 10-1), not only is the direction of causation reversed: investment "causes" savings, rather than the other way around. Just as important, there is a whole new set of beneficial side-effects produced by faster investment. Now the level of employment depends on the strength of purchasing power in the economy. More investment generates more demand, both directly (by the investing firm) and indirectly (by the spin-off effects of that spending elsewhere in the economy, generated by the investment multiplier process that was described in Chapter 4).

Rising incomes throughout the economy allow for greater savings by both individuals and (more importantly) corporations. As in the neoclassical model, the use of more capital in production allows for greater productivity and hence higher incomes. But the more immediate benefit of stronger investment is that it allows more individuals to find work in the first place.

The Experience of Savings and Investment in Canada

So far, this overview of the savings-investment process has been conducted in the realm of economic theory, with a special focus on the different assumptions and policy conclusions of the two broad competing schools of economic thought.

The Chicken or the Egg?

Economists have never been able to agree whether savings cause investment, or investment causes savings. One statistical technique that might shed some light on the controversy is called "Granger causation" analysis. Two data series are compared, to see if changes in one variable can "explain" a significant portion of the subsequent changes in the other variable.

The outcome of this test does not prove anything in and of itself. But Granger tests can provide some empirical support for a *logical* argument that one particular variable is in the "driver's seat" of the economic relationship being considered.

Granger causation tests were performed on a number of particular savings measures (including aggregate national savings, household savings, corporate savings, and government savings). These were all compared to two specific measures of investment: gross and net fixed investment in real capital assets (including both private and public investment). [It turned out that test results were not really affected by the choice of investment measure.] Details of the tests are reported in Appendix IV of this book. A summary is reported in Table 10-1.

Table 10-1	
Granger Causality Tests: Savings and Investment	
Type of Saving	Relationship to Investment
Household Saving	Investment weakly causes saving.
Corporate Saving	Saving strongly causes investment.
Government Saving	Investment strongly causes saving.
Source: Author's calculations from Statistics Canada, *National Income and Financial Accounts*.	

The Granger test results generally verify the implications of the sector-by-sector analysis of savings experience in Canada. Household saving tends to be limited by income, which itself is largely the product of the vibrancy of investment. Strong investment, therefore, tends to promote stronger household savings. The same result is visible, and even stronger, for the government sector. Strong investment, and hence a growing economy, means healthy government revenues and strong public saving.

The only sector where savings may indeed help to determine investment is within private businesses. As was discussed above, companies in Canada's real economy finance the bulk of their real investment through internal cash resources. Changes in cash flow are subsequently reflected in changes in business investment, due to the cash flow constraint that binds most business investment programs. Hence, in statistical terms, for the business community savings may indeed "cause" investment. At the same time, however, since business profits in turn depend significantly on their own *previous* investment spending (for the demand-side reasons explained in Chapter 4), even in this case it is hard to conclude that savings are a real *constraint* on investment.[10]

To put this theory into a real-world context, we will examine patterns in saving behaviour exhibited during the 1990s by the major players in Canada's real economy: individuals, companies, and governments.

Recall that the fundamental idea that investment is constrained by a shortage of disposable savings depends on the assumption that the economy's resources are fully-employed in existing production. Only under those conditions would it be impossible to mobilize real resources to undertake a new investment project, *without* first setting aside sufficient savings to pay for that project.

The dismally underutilized state of Canada's economy during virtually all of the last two decades already casts serious doubt on the proposition that a lack of savings has held back Canada's real investment performance. The macroeconomic and financial policies imposed during the last two decades—low inflation, high real interest rates, massive subsidies to financial savings and investments, and the recent sharp cutbacks in government deficits—should have greatly improved the incentives to save in Canada. If the world really operated according to supply-side principles, the resulting flood of savings should have propelled real capital accumulation to unseen heights.

In reality, however, the reverse has been the case. Savings have actually declined—particularly for Canadian households—in the wake of economic stagnation and falling real incomes. Ironically, these weak economic conditions were themselves largely the result of the same pro-finance policies that were supposed to elicit more frugality from the nation.

Canada's experience over the last two decades provides an extraordinary real-world example of Keynes's famous "paradox of thrift," discussed below. Efforts to push more savings into the economy from the supply side, without measures to ensure that the demand for real investment expands accordingly, can turn out to be fruitless, or even counterproductive. A much more effective means of promoting Canadian savings would be to reverse the contractionary policies which have dominated the economic landscape for two decades.

Personal Saving

The omnipresent cultural symbols of personal investing—RRSP ads, street-corner stock market displays, endless (and useless) business news bulletins on radio and TV—would suggest that Canadian households must truly be a thrifty, parsimonious lot. How surprising, then, that total household savings in Canada have actually declined precipitously right through the 1980s and especially the 1990s, just as the paper boom was gathering such steam.

Indeed, in the summer of 1998, a truly historic point was reached: for the first time in post-war history, Canadian personal savings were actually *negative*.

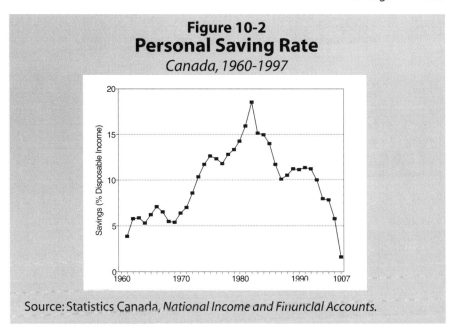

Figure 10-2
Personal Saving Rate
Canada, 1960-1997

Source: Statistics Canada, *National Income and Financial Accounts.*

In other words, Canadian households spent more on personal spending than they had available in personal disposable income. The savings rate (which measures savings as a proportion of after-tax household income) declined to below zero during the third quarter of 1998.

Compare that to personal savings which rose steadily through the 1970s, and peaked at over 18% of disposable income in 1981 (see Figure 10-2). That was when most Canadians had never *heard* of a mutual fund—and it was also when the supposedly "fundamental" economic conditions of personal investing were rather less appealing than they are now (inflation was high, stock markets were performing poorly, real after-inflation returns on many financial assets were actually negative). It is strange that, even after Canada's whole economy was extensively restructured to reinforce the incentive to accumulate financial wealth, Canadian households in effect gave up saving altogether.

There is nothing mysterious about the drastic decline in personal savings in Canada. Personal saving equals that share of household disposable income that is not spent on current consumption. It is, in other words, the thin "wedge" between after-tax income and total household spending. The problem is that, since about 1981, when the great "U-turn" in Canadian economic policy first began to be implemented, that wedge has been squeezed literally out of existence.

This trend has been especially dramatic in the 1990s, as the personal savings rate collapsed from around 12% at the beginning of the decade to near-zero by its end. The squeeze on household saving is broken down in Table 10-1. From the bottom, the average level of personal consumption spending has continued to

	Personal Income	Personal Taxes	Consumer Spending	Saving	Saving Rate[1]
Table 10-2 **Household Incomes, Spending, and Saving** *1990 versus 1997 (1992 dollars per capita)*					
1990	$22,491	$5,107	$15,450	$1,934	11.1%
1997	$21,362	$5,284	$15,816	$262	1.6%
Change:	-$1,129	+$177	+$366	-$1,672	-9.5 pts.
Proportion of decline in savings accounted for by:[2]	68%	11%	22%		

Source: Author's calculations from Statistics Canada, *National Income and Financial Accounts*.
1. Saving as proportion of disposable (after-tax) income.
2. Total does not equal 100% due to rounding.

grow, albeit modestly; Canadians have quite naturally expected that their living standards should grow at least modestly in the wake of continuing economic growth and productivity. Between 1990 and 1997, real personal spending per capita grew by about 4%, or about $350 (in 1992 dollar terms). This stubborn effort by Canadians to maintain or slightly improve their real consumption levels, despite the decline in their real incomes, thus accounted for about one-fifth of the total decline in personal savings between 1990 and 1997.

The bigger squeeze, however, has been applied from the "top". Average after-inflation personal disposable incomes were no higher in 1997 than they were in 1980, and they declined by over 7% between 1990 and 1997. This development is popularly ascribed to higher taxes, and they have clearly played a role. Average personal taxes per capita rose by 4%, in real terms, between 1990 to 1997, or by about $177 for every Canadian. This relatively modest tax increase imposed on Canadians during the 1990s does not, however, come close to justifying the hysterical rhetoric of the tax revolt movement. Higher taxes account for barely one-tenth of the total squeeze on personal savings in Canada during the 1990s.

A far more important cause of the decline in disposable income has been the decline of *before-tax* incomes since 1990. In the face of growing unemployment, stagnant or falling wages, and big reductions in government transfer payments (like unemployment insurance and welfare programs), real personal incomes declined by over $1,100 per person between 1990 and 1997 (or over 5%). This decline in before-tax incomes accounts for the lion's share—almost 70%—of the total decline in personal savings experienced during the same period.

It is clearly the failure of the Canadian economy to provide Canadians with income, not the failure of individuals to save from that income, that is the dominant force behind the collapse of household savings. This evidence clearly reinforces the conclusion of the "demand-side" theorists surveyed above: savings depend more strongly on incomes than on interest rates and investment returns. If income growth could be revived through expansionary economic policies (and particularly through strong investment spending), there is little doubt that savings would rebound accordingly.

The decline in personal savings in the 1990s is often ascribed to the boom in the valuations of stock markets and other financial assets. If Canadians with financial wealth see the paper value of their portfolio growing all on its own, then they will be less concerned with setting aside more savings for the future out of their current income, and they may even spend some of their stock market gains on additional current consumption.[5] For this reason, many conservative commentators find little to worry about in the apparent disappearance of personal savings in Canada; ironically, these are the same commentators who pressed so hard for "savings-friendly" economic policies (low inflation, high real interest rates, lower taxes on investment income) in the first place.

There is certainly some truth to the argument that booming stock markets have contributed to lower savings, especially in light of the fact that the bulk of personal savings is undertaken by precisely the same elite that happens to own most of the paper wealth whose value has exploded so impressively during the 1990s. [The lopsided pattern of ownership of financial wealth will be considered in Chapter 12.]

It would be wrong, however, to ascribe most of the collapse in personal saving to the boom in financial valuations, and it would be equally wrong to then conclude that the disappearance of household savings is nothing to worry about. In the first place, if it was the paper boom that caused the collapse of savings, then we would expect the decline in savings to be offset by higher consumption spending. As we saw in Table 10-1, however, higher spending accounts for just one-fifth of the disappearance of personal saving between 1990 and 1997.

Moreover, in supply-side economic theory, higher investment returns are supposed to elicit *more* savings from thrifty households anxious to share in those profits, not less.[6]

At any rate, if consumers (or at least a lucky elite of well-off consumers) have indeed stopped saving because of the booming paper economy, they—and indeed the whole economy—could be in for a nasty surprise when financial markets inevitably turn down. Those who were counting on their paper wealth to see them through retirement will be disappointed. Worse yet, if they respond to a financial downturn by suddenly trying to save more out of their current income, the consequent decline in consumer spending would turn that paper downturn into a real recession.

Corporate Saving

As far as real investment spending is concerned, Canada's corporate sector is the most important saver in the country. As described in Chapter 3, real businesses in Canada pay for the vast majority of their own real investment spending from internal savings. This "self-financing" ratio (which was depicted in Figure 3-1) has averaged between 90% and 100% throughout the postwar era.

Internal corporate saving includes retained earnings: the share of corporate profits which is not handed back to individual shareholders in the form of dividend cheques. A more important source of corporate saving, however, is depreciation charges. These charges represent the value that accountants ascribe to the annual wear-and-tear on a company's existing stock of real capital assets (including factories, offices, machinery, computers, and other tools and equipment). Depreciation costs are deducted from a company's income in order to calculate final profit, even though a company does not actually pay out any cold hard cash to reflect that depreciation.

In accounting terms, it is right to deduct depreciation costs to paint a more accurate picture of a firm's real sustainable viability. If a company was generating "money" largely or solely by simply wearing down its stock of capital, then that company would be gradually going out of business, and its financial statements should reflect that trend accordingly. From the perspective of the company's internal cash balance, however, depreciation charges are purely imaginary. They are not paid to anyone, but rather are retained within the firm's coffers. The idea is that the company should be using these funds to replace its capital facilities on an ongoing basis. And for the most part, that is exactly what companies do.

Internal corporate saving by non-financial businesses accounted for an average of about 50% of total national gross saving in Canada between 1990 and 1997, and covered 92% of total non-financial investments by those same companies. In turn, almost 90% of the total savings of non-financial companies during this time was accounted for by depreciation charges.

There are several interesting implications of this important internal saving by real businesses. The first, stressed in Chapter 3, is that it immediately casts doubt on the self-stated importance of private financial institutions as sources of finance for real investment spending. Companies generate most of the funds to finance their own investment activity right within their own four walls. At best, the costly and unstable process of private financial intermediation plays a role at the "margin": providing funds for the extra investment spending of especially ambitious companies that want to grow faster than their internal funds will allow. This may be important for particular companies at particular points in time; but the overall role of high finance in the concrete process of real economic growth is clearly secondary.

Secondly, anything which impacts on internal corporate cash flow will have important implications for real investment spending, and hence growth and job-creation. Generally, if companies have more money in hand, they will tend to spend it. [This is not always the case, of course, and any policy measures taken by government to enhance corporate cash flow should be conditional on real investment performance; more on this in Chapter 14.]

Corporate profits are particularly sensitive to the repetitive cycles of expansion and contraction which have dominated Canada's economy during the past 20 years. The collapse of profits during recession results in a shrinkage of cash resources available for investment; the resulting decline in investment makes the recession all the worse. Business taxes also affect corporate cash flow, of course. The average corporate tax rate has declined slightly through most of the post-war era in Canada, so it is hard to attach too much blame to taxes for the decline in business investment spending.

Another crucial component of a company's cash flow equation is the proportion of its after-tax profits it pays out to its shareholders in the form of dividends. Between 1994 and 1998, non-financial companies paid out almost 80% of their total net income in dividends. Indeed, during the four years ending in 1993, non-financial companies actually paid out *more* in dividends than they generated in profits; corporate executives are loath to cut dividend payments, even when profits are low, and hence they had to dip into their internal cash reserves to maintain dividend payouts when profits plunged during the recession.

The proportion of corporate profits paid out in dividends to shareholders has grown in recent years, reflecting the enhanced sensitivity of corporate executives to share prices and shareholder interests. This rise in the "dividend payout ratio" has accentuated the squeeze on corporate cash flow, as illustrated in Figure 10-3. Even though 1998 was a relatively good year for Canadian corporations, net income for non-financial businesses was still lower in dollar terms

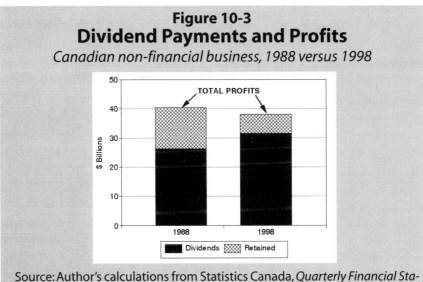

Figure 10-3
Dividend Payments and Profits
Canadian non-financial business, 1988 versus 1998

Source: Author's calculations from Statistics Canada, *Quarterly Financial Statistics for Enterprises.*

than was the case a decade earlier. At the same time, however, dividend payments increased from 65% of after-tax profits to over 80%.

Corporate retained earnings, a crucial source of finance for real business investments, are thus doubly constrained: caught between the rock of stagnant profits and the hard place of shareholders' demands for dividend payouts.

The implications for real investment and real growth are clearly negative. But the rising importance of dividends has clearly contributed to the enormous financial gains of wealth-owners during this time. Dividends are an important additional source of profits for financial investors, supplementing the capital gains (obtained from rising share prices) which are usually the main attraction of stock market investments. Dividends for the largest companies traded on the Toronto Stock Exchange typically equal about 2% of their share price; for certain companies (such as the major banks) dividends are even more lucrative.

Dividend payouts have become even more popular with corporate executives in the booming 1990s, because of their positive impact on share prices. If a company increases its dividend payment, its share price will normally rise by a multiple factor as investors react to the increased yield on this investment. A range of factors has enhanced the degree to which executives are preoccupied with the share price performance of their companies (not the least of which is the huge personal holdings those executives typically maintain of their own companies' shares). Executives are thus considerably more "dividend-friendly" than was the case in past years, when the stock market exercised a less decisive influence over corporate decision-making.

Canada's tax policy further enhances the appeal of dividend payouts, since the dividend tax credit means that dividend income is taxed at a lower rate than other forms of income. But every dollar paid out to a firm's shareholders in dividends translates into one dollar less of available cash resources with which to finance real investment spending. From the perspective of stimulating real capital accumulation, therefore, dividend payouts should be minimized. Shareholders and stockbrokers of course, would object mightily to such a change in direction. The policy implications of dividend payouts will be considered further in Chapter 14.

Government Saving

Without doubt, the sector that takes the award for Canadian parsimony in the 1990s is government. From a position of large net dis-saving in the early portion of the decade, as Canada's economy staggered through a prolonged slump, Canada's federal and provincial governments transformed themselves incredibly quickly into admirable savers.

The official turning point was reached in the first quarter of 1997. That was when, according to the most common measurement of government saving (the

Figure 10-4
Government Saving and National Saving
Canada, 1993 versus 1997

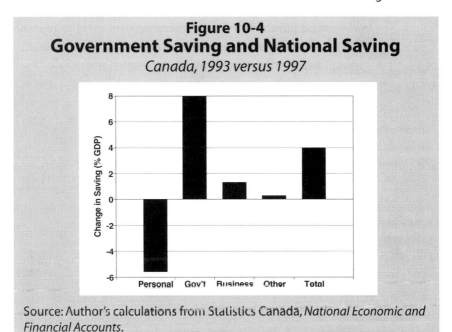

Source: Author's calculations from Statistics Canada, *National Economic and Financial Accounts*.

"national accounts" definition),[7] the total government sector of the economy (including all levels of government, hospitals, and the Canada Pension Plan) climbed back into the black after years of swimming in red ink. By mid-1998, the government sector was running up huge surpluses: over $15 billion in 1998, equal to 2% of GDP.

Despite this rapid and seemingly successful deficit-reduction campaign, however, the bottom-line impact of the huge improvement in government savings on the overall level of national savings in Canada is far from clear. As discussed above, personal savings in Canada declined precipitously through the 1990s. Indeed, personal savings in Canada fell by a total of 5.6 percentage points of GDP between 1993 and 1997: exactly the same period during which government savings *grew* by 7.9% of GDP (see Figure 10-4).

The decline in personal savings, therefore, directly and immediately offset 70% of the improvement in government savings. By 1997, Canadian governments were saving more than Canadian households, in breathtaking contrast to both the popular stereotype of governments as wasteful and irresponsible and the inflated Bay Street myth about the frugality of personal investors. In fact, Canadian governments are a very frugal lot; it is Canadian households (for the concrete reasons discussed above) who have a hard time balancing their chequebooks. And indeed, when we consider the means by which deficits were eliminated, this strange result should come as no surprise.

Government transfer payments to persons—programs like unemployment insurance, welfare, and public pensions—declined by two full percentage points of GDP between 1993 and 1997, and they have declined still further since. Personal taxes have also increased, although more modestly than the shrill spokespersons of the tax revolt movement would have us believe.

Governments have increased their own savings, therefore, largely through an outright transfer of fiscal costs onto the household sector. Less transfer income and higher taxes show up immediately in less personal disposable income and hence less personal saving. Robbing Peter to pay Paul hardly translates into improved savings performance at the national level.

The indirect impacts of government cutbacks on the savings of the personal and corporate sectors may be even more important. The unprecedentedly severe fiscal stance of Canadian governments through the second half of the 1990s knocked the wind out of the sails of an economy that was already advancing

In Love With Debt

The financial industry was long the most outspoken critic of chronic government deficits. For years financial commentators warned of impending catastrophe if government didn't "get its house in order." Apart from building up an unsustainable debt burden, they argued, governments were also sucking up too much of the hard-won savings of Canadians, thus "crowding out" more productive investment by private companies.

How quickly the tune changed, however, once government did exactly what the financiers had been demanding: quick, painful deficit elimination. Suddenly there was much hand-wringing on Bay Street over Canada's "looming shortage of government bonds." Financial analysts worried about the evaporating supply of these stable, low-risk assets, which had long provided a solid underpinning for the overall portfolios of the investing public.

Even Sherry Cooper, the notoriously conservative chief economist for the Bank of Montreal's brokerage, Nesbitt Burns, warned against reducing debt too quickly in 1998. "We'd be facing a massive market disruption," she warned. "It's dangerous." Suddenly it is not government debt that is financially threatening, it is the *repayment* of debt!

One 1997 article in the *Globe and Mail* accidentally provided a fascinating and rare insight into the true feelings of the financial markets about government debts and deficits. First a fund manager complained that bond investors will now "have to do a little more credit analysis because, with the federal government, there's actually no credit analysis. It's risk-free." So sad that these well-paid analysts will actually have to work for their money. And so much for the idea that high interest rates in Canada reflected a "risk premium" that had to be paid to investors frightened by large government debt. It turns out that it is corporate debt, not government debt, that is risky.

The article then reported that "there aren't enough quality equity investments in Canada for the money that is pouring into retirement funds." So much for the

sluggishly at best. This produced prolonged unemployment, stagnant incomes, and a generally pessimistic and defensive attitude on the part of consumers and many businesses. Income levels for the economy as a whole grew slowly, if at all, with consequent negative implications for both savings and investment.

Contrary to the predictions of many free-market economists that the elimination of government deficits would unleash a flood of private-sector saving and investing,[8] rapid government downsizing (and the consequent revival of government saving) has, if anything, contributed to the continuing stagnation of real investment and real growth.

The Paradox of Thrift

A market economy is an incredibly complex and unpredictable thing. When economic outcomes are the product of the uncoordinated decisions of millions

idea that investment in Canada is constrained by a shortage of savings (itself the result of government overspending). It is not a shortage of money, but the failure of private investors to put that money to work, that explains stagnant investment in Canada.

Finally, another investment representative stated frankly that "it's not an alternative to say, 'Oh well, we can't find any Canada bonds, so we'll just invest in small businesses.'" With the easy, risk-free profits of government bonds now harder to come by, Canadians could hardly expect their financial professionals to actually put money to work in "real" investments—the kind that produce concrete goods and services, and create real paying jobs.

Canada's chartered banks have done particularly well thanks to the slide of Canada's governments into deep debt during the 1990s. Bank holdings of federal government debt alone almost quadrupled from less than $20 billion in 1990 to nearly $80 billion by the end of 1997.

The banks benefit from these holdings in more than one way. They obtain lucrative, risk-free interest income (worth some $6 billion or more annually by 1997). And the market value of federal bonds soared during the late 1990s as nominal interest rates fell. Most important of all, these bonds form a bedrock-solid foundation for the overall balance sheets of the banks. Holding such large amounts of virtually risk-free government debt allows these banks to expand their lending to other less credit-worthy clients—literally creating profit-generating new credit out of thin air.

It is increasingly clear that—doomsday proclamations notwithstanding—the financial community hardly loses sleep over Canada's public debt. In fact, we can imagine the reaction on Bay Street if $600 billion in hard currency were to fall like manna into Finance Minister Paul Martin's hands, allowing him to pay off the entire federal debt with one big cheque. Far from leaping for joy at the disappearance of the debt burden and its associated "risk" and "uncertainty," brokers would be jumping from their skyscrapers over the sudden loss of such a lucrative and risk-free investment outlet.

of different individual players, the economy may respond to new circumstances in ways quite contrary to what simple intuition might suggest. What may seem like a rational act for numerous individual participants in the economy may ultimately hold irrational or destructive consequences for the system as a whole.

Logicians call this curious possibility a "fallacy of composition": just because something may be true for individual members of a community doesn't make it necessarily true for the community as a whole. Modern capitalism is full of these fallacies. An individual concerned about the security of their deposits at some shaky financial institution would be quite rational in rushing to that institution to withdraw all their funds. But if enough people behave in precisely this seemingly "rational" way, the bank surely collapses—a damaging, preventible, and hence "irrational" outcome.

Perhaps the most famous example of the potentially irrational collective behaviour of a market economy is the "paradox of thrift," first discovered by the British economist John Maynard Keynes. In a demand-constrained economy, employment, production, and hence incomes all depend on the amount of purchasing power coursing through the economy. Suppose that individuals decide they want to save more, perhaps to accumulate more financial wealth for retirement. Those individuals all must spend less from their current incomes in order to save more. Less spending, however, means less demand for the products of the companies which were supplying those now-miserly consumers. Those companies lay off workers, who in turn spend even less, and the whole economy slides into recession. Incomes fall, and hence so does personal saving—despite the well-intentioned efforts of households to save *more*, not less.

The only condition under which an increase in savings does not translate into falling demand and income is when the rise in savings is accompanied by a full and immediate corresponding increase in investment. But there is nothing in an unregulated market economy which can ensure that this will be the case.

This problem is more than a theoretical curiosity; it holds important real-world policy implications. Think of the massive public subsidies aimed at encouraging more personal financial investments by those Canadians who have

Futile Savings

"For most individuals, an attempt to save more means actual reduction in consumption spending...[Thus] the increased saving of the individual saver is offset by the decreased income and saving of vendors...Reduced income eventually results in reduced consumption purchases, GDP, and aggregate saving. Incentives may indeed result in some individuals increasing their saving, but only at the expense of reducing the savings of others by even more."
—William Vickrey
Nobel Prize Winner in Economics, 1997

enough money to save. If those incentives are effective, so that total savings actually rise,[9] they may have a counter-productive impact on total output and income in the economy, and hence, ironically, on savings.

It is out of recognition of this possibility that politicians and even business leaders are always so concerned with the intangible level of "confidence" in the economy. If enough consumers or investors, worried about a possible future slowdown in the economy, start socking away disposable income as a reserve fund for a rainy day, the resulting decline in spending can actually make that dreaded rainy day a reality. That's why political and economic leaders typically respond to bad economic news with a unanimous appeal to consumers and businesses to "stay calm." Like a panicked response to the discovery of fire in a crowded theatre, the hunkering-down of consumers and investors in the face of apprehended bad times can have far worse effects than the initial problem.

In its December 1998 edition, the *Report on Business Magazine* ran a feature story dealing with the response of middle class families to the financial turbulence that had wracked global markets during the preceding 12 months. The article described a "leery, recession-conscious middle class... that is ready to tighten its collective belt." It reported survey results showing that 41% of middle-class consumers planned to reduce their spending in 1999, and 56% planned to increase their saving, motivated by fear of a coming downturn.

We can only hope that the surveyed Canadians do not put their money where their mouths are. If 41% of middle-class households in Canada really did significantly reduce their consumer spending, the certain outcome of this seeming prudence would be the very recession that those households feared. In short, in a modern market economy, the simple-minded wisdom promoted by the guardians of our financial stability—a penny saved is a penny earned—can be the greatest threat to stability of all.

Chapter 11
Profits:
The Shrinking Carrot
for Real Investment

Imagine life as the President and Chief Executive Officer of Canadian Airlines International, Canada's second national airline. Kevin Benson started this job just months before the late-1996 onset of a financial crisis that catapulted the company into the headlines for months. Canadian had lost a cumulative total of $1.5 billion during an eight-year string of consecutive red ink. Despite a series of government bail-outs and wage concessions from workers, the company was running out of money—and fast. So the company demanded still more wage concessions and tax subsidies, threatening imminent bankruptcy if governments and unions were not forthcoming.

After weeks of high-pressure bargaining, the federal government eventually invoked a never-used section of emergency labour law to help force through the wage concession (although union resistance was effective in reducing the size of that concession). And the company lived to see another day.

Indeed, on the strength of a robust economy and growing airline travel, and helped along by emergency aid from government and its own workforce, Canadian Airlines finally declared a profit in 1997—its first since Canada's airline industry was opened up to "free" competition a decade earlier.

The size of this profit: all of $5.4 million, or less than one-fifth of 1% of the company's total $3 billion annual revenue. A tiny increase in the cost of any of the company's inputs—say, a 1% increase in the price of fuel—would wipe out this profit overnight. Indeed, business got back to normal for Canadian Airlines in 1998: the company lost another $137 million. The company's long-term survival, and the job security of its 16,000 employees, are as much in doubt as ever. And after three years on the job, CEO Benson was probably wishing he'd gone into real estate. Sure, he earned $317,500 in 1997—10 times as much as the average

Canadian worker—but that was barely enough to crack the *Financial Post Magazine*'s list of the 200 best-paid executives in Canada. Yet Benson would surely place among the top 10 CEOs ranked by the number of business headaches experienced.

The point of this anecdote is not to evoke sympathy for Canadian Airlines, nor for its top executive. Far from it. Bad business decisions by management have certainly played an important part in the company's woes. And Benson's personal role in the 1996 crisis was especially lamentable: he unnecessarily raised the stakes by publicly threatening bankruptcy early on, in a shallow effort to manipulate Canadian's unions into accepting more wage rollbacks. But this sent travellers and creditors alike fleeing for the exits, making the company's problems all the worse.

Rather, the sorry tale of Canadian Airlines is related here simply to illustrate just exactly how hard it can be to make money as a private company in the real Canadian economy of the 1990s. Kevin Benson has ultimate responsibility for the hiring, training, assignment and supervision of 16,000 workers. He and his managers need to coordinate the purchase or rental, scheduling, maintenance and operation of 140 technologically complex pieces of expensive capital equipment: Canadian's airplanes. These aircraft service over 500 destinations around the world, and transport over 12 million passengers per year.

The company takes in $3 billion in revenue each year, and pays out the same amount (unfortunately, usually a little bit more) for its expenses. It operates in an unpredictable and fiercely competitive industry, in which its major competitors—smelling blood—are literally trying to drive it out of business. The reward for all these trials and tribulations: one profitable year in 10, and a profit so small it almost added to the company's embarrassment to even bother reporting it. The company's shareholders would have been infinitely better-off to keep their money in a low-interest savings account at their neighbourhood bank.

Running an airline is a particularly difficult undertaking. Even Canadian's stronger competitor, Air Canada, is on shaky financial footing. The federal government's misguided policies of airline deregulation have made a unique contribution to the financial suffering of airlines and their owners. So Canadian's story is not fully representative of the state of Canada's real business sector as a whole.

But neither is it especially atypical. Like Canadian Airlines, other companies trying to produce and sell real goods and services have been hammered by poor macroeconomic conditions: high unemployment and stagnant market demand. Like Canadian Airlines, other real businesses have also had to pay out exorbitant interest payments on the money they borrowed from financiers to fund their day-to-day activities. And, again like Canadian Airlines, most real businesses in Canada have faced unprecedented competitive pressure from other firms, as

Canada's economy shifted increasingly toward a dog-eat-dog, unregulated, law-of-the-jungle system.

Government policy has obviously promoted this trend, with far-reaching initiatives in areas such as deregulation and international trade liberalization. And even though these policies were almost uniformly supported by the business community, they have also made life considerably more difficult for most of those same businesses. In theory, heightened competitiveness is supposed to translate into higher productivity and rising incomes. In practice, it has produced endless downsizing, a perpetual tight-fistedness on the part of corporations, slow real investment, and permanent insecurity for employees.

It was popular in the 1960s and 1970s to think of corporations as vast, powerful "monopolies," whose entrenched market power made the capturing of huge profits almost as certain and lucrative as if they held a license to print money This stereotype was always overstated, and it is clearly inaccurate in the economy of the 1990s. Even huge companies like Canadian Airlines are locked in a day-to-day battle for survival. Their actions are fundamentally limited by competitive pressures and other economic constraints.

It is a huge irony that, even as Canada's economy has become more business-friendly and competitive, the average profitability of real investments in companies operating in the real economy has fairly steadily declined. And, as was shown in Chapter 8, this fall in profitability has been a significant factor in explaining the decline of real investment in Canada.

Many progressive-minded Canadians will be intensely uncomfortable with the discussion presented in this chapter. Campaigns for social and economic justice have often highlighted the contrast between the huge profits reported by particular companies (especially those in the financial sphere, like Canada's super-profitable banks) and the falling living standards of most Canadians. The demand for a more just society is often phrased in terms of "taking" something from super-profitable companies (in the form of higher taxes, or higher wage payments) and "giving" it to the rest of the population. In reality, however, the fundamental problems with Canada's economy are not nearly so simple as to be solvable by direct redistribution of this sort.

By any measure, the businesses which make up most of Canada's real economy have less profits to pass around, not more. Social-justice activists are quite right to focus attention on the incredible profitability of financial institutions—as well as on certain companies in the real economy which still enjoy especially favourable financial conditions, but are not giving back social benefits to match the profits they are earning. Think of General Motors, for example, which earned so much profit in Canada (probably in excess of $2 billion in

1997) that it stopped publicly reporting its financial results, even as it was eliminating or outsourcing thousands of auto jobs in Ontario and Quebec.

This glaring juxtaposition of private enrichment with social destruction must be challenged. But most of Canada's private sector does not remotely resemble General Motors or the major banks. Throughout most of the real economy, companies are scrabbling just to survive. The fall-out of that never-ending battle is marginal profitability, endless downward pressure on wages and working conditions, and sluggish investment in the real capital our economy needs.

Many progressives also fear that highlighting the declining profitability of real business in Canada will heighten pressure to adopt even more pro-business policies and concessions, such as wage roll-backs, tax cuts for corporations, or the weakening of labour and environmental regulations. But this is far from being the only conclusion that can be drawn from a recognition of the decline of business profitability. As was highlighted in the discussion of Chapter 4 (and especially in Table 4-2), Canada has become an incredibly business-friendly jurisdiction. Yet profitability has not improved; indeed, the heightened competitive pressures which businesses face as a result of free trade and deregulation may have actually undermined profits. It is hard to imagine how even more pro-business policy shifts could improve the situation—just as it is impossible that further wage cuts by the employees of Canadian Airlines could fundamentally improve that company's prospects of survival.

Indeed, this analogy is a fitting one. Any hope that repeated wage concessions could strengthen the bottom line of Canadian Airlines was frustrated by subsequent and predictable developments in the airline industry. In the context of a battle-to-the-death competition between airlines, lower wages for Canadian's workforce were quickly translated into lower ticket prices and more rapid capacity expansion by a company desperate to protect and expand its share of the market. Meanwhile, the company's competitors pushed to extract wage concessions from *their* employees (as Air Canada did in the early 1990s), and the circle was completed.

Airlines remain as hard-pressed financially as ever; the only real change has been a fall in the wages of airline workers, despite their soaring labour productivity. Even more far-fetched was the hope that government aid (such as the tax cuts on airline fuel granted by some provincial governments as their contribution to the 1996 aid package for Canadian) could make any difference to the company's plight. In this case, similar benefits were also handed over to Canadian Airlines' competitors. Canadian Airlines enjoys marginally lower fuel costs, but so does Air Canada. Since Canadian Airlines' financial crisis was caused not by high fuel prices, but by the outcome of a process of destructive and inefficient competition within the airline industry, how could the fuel tax cut make any possible difference to the company's survival?

Very similar outcomes are produced by pro-business measures in the economy as a whole. Making it easier for one company to make a profit also makes it easier for its many competitors to make a profit. Like siblings who have a tug-of-war over a favourite toy until the toy rips apart, the bitter rivalry between companies eventually erodes the bottom-line value of whatever favour was granted to them—and nobody comes out ahead.

Far from reinforcing the case for more concessions to the business community, the unimpressive state of corporate profits in Canada actually points toward a more far-reaching critique of an economy which is fundamentally oriented around the pursuit of private profit. And indeed, by documenting and trying to understand the decline in business profitability in Canada, we shift attention away from the greed or misbehaviour of particular companies or investors and onto the more fundamental dynamics of the economic system itself.

Despite important shifts in policy purportedly aimed at strengthening the private sector, profitability has actually continued to fall. If the pro-business remaking of Canada's economy since 1981 hasn't restored business profitability, it is hard to know what will. As will be explored in this chapter and in Chapter 14, there are certain policy measures that could help to restore the financial incentive for private real investment, without undermining the well-being of workers and communities. But it may also be time to reconsider our overarching reliance on the profit motive of private investors as the dominant driving force of our whole economy.

Many progressives often lament the rise of "corporate power" in Canada over the 1980s and 1990s. To be sure, Canada's social and economic policies have demonstrated a distinctly pro-business tilt: high interest rates, free trade, deregulation, government budget-cutting. The business community has become notably more aggressive, even desperate, in its efforts to get rid of any social obstacle to its drive for profit-maximization. But does this trend really indicate a heightened degree of business *power*? Or alternatively, does it stem from a fundamental *weakness* of private business, a consistent *failure* to deliver the goods to shareholders?

Compare the current plight of Canada's businesses with the regime that prevailed during the heyday of the post-war expansion. In earlier decades, companies could well afford to grant steady real wage increases for workers, and pay for a share of a quickly growing apparatus of social protections and public services, while still "doing their thing" as private businesses: namely, making money. Productivity rose quickly, investment was strong, and profits were healthy, even as social conditions improved dramatically. Today, in contrast, business is ag-

Which Way is Up?

"Lefties" can get tied in ideological knots over the decline in business profits in Canada. If all social evil is the result of greedy corporations who refuse to share the wealth, then why is it that those greedy corporations seem to have *less* to spread around—not more?

But the issue can send conservatives into contortions, as well. The hunger for profits, after all, is supposed to be the primeval force which causes the sun to rise and the world to rotate. If businesses can't make money in Canada's free-wheeling, market-dominated economy, then what's wrong with them? And when *will* they make a buck?

The implications, when you think about it, are worrisome. Which is probably why conservatives don't talk about profitability much—a surprising silence, in light of their general focus on the need to create a more business-friendly economic environment.

Consider Andrew Coyne, arch-conservative columnist for the *National Post* and other Conrad Black newspapers. In 1991, before he hit the national stage, Coyne penned a curious article for *Canadian Business* magazine which reviewed the long-term decline in Canadian corporate profitability. He listed several factors contributing to falling profits (higher inflation, rising labour costs, stiff competition between firms). But he concluded his review with a surprisingly sanguine, what-me-worry attitude.

There's "no cause for alarm," Coyne wrote. "It may be that this is even a good thing."

Andrew Coyne thinks low profits are healthy? Put that one in your scrapbook, kids.

Jock Finlayson is another prominent conservative: vice-president of the Business Council of British Columbia and a loud critic of the NDP governments which ruled that province through most of the 1990s. In a 1998 article, Finlayson lambasted media and labour critics for falsely highlighting "record" corporate profits. In fact, Finlayson (correctly) pointed out, by any meaningful measure profitability in Canada has declined. He hectored governments to build "an economic environment that encourages Canadian companies to strive for superior results and to earn a competitive return for their shareholders."

But how does Finlayson explain the fall in profitability? "The simplest and most compelling explanation is that the domestic and foreign markets served by Canadian companies have become more competitive over time," thanks to deregulation, free trade, and globalization—in other words, the very policies that Finlayson and his business allies have been demanding for the last two decades.

So let's get this straight. Governments should create a pro-profit business environment. But pro-business policies like free trade and deregulation have reduced profitability. It seems, therefore, that governments, for the sake of profits, should do exactly the *opposite* of what the profit-hungry business lobbyists are calling for.

Business, in short, must be saved from itself.

gressive and dictatorial in its demands for concessions from communities, governments, and workers: give us what we need, or you are economically dead. Social conditions deteriorate, real wages stagnate, payrolls are downsized. Yet business still can't generate profits that would be considered barely acceptable in previous eras. So is business strong, or is business weak?

Advocates of a more equal and inclusive society will naturally respond defensively to attempts by business lobbyists to reverse so many of the social and economic gains that were made during the post-war expansion. But at the same time they should understand that the demands of the business community are not always issued from a position of strength.

In any economy dominated by the decisions of private profit-seeking firms, private profitability creates a fundamental economic constraint that can't be ignored. The difficulty for progressives is how to identify and acknowledge that constraint, without letting it undermine and sidetrack efforts to attain better social and economic outcomes, and to enforce a higher degree of accountability on the part of those private investors. This is a tricky balancing act, indeed. The discussion in this chapter will highlight the causes and consequences of the squeeze on profits in Canada's economy, and begin to explore the various policy conclusions that are suggested.

The Great Canadian Profit Squeeze

Canada's business sector enjoyed a "record" year in 1997, with a total of $83 billion in pre-tax corporate profits. In other words, corporate profits—in dollars—were higher than in any previous year in Canadian history. But in the context of an economy that is constantly growing—in real output, in population, in price levels—this is hardly a meaningful measure. Indeed, by this same standard, Canadian workers seem to have enjoyed "record-breaking" wages every year since 1946: that is, the total amount paid out in wages in Canada's economy, measured in dollars, has grown every single year since the end of the Second World War. But we all know that the 1990s have hardly been record-breaking years for workers.

A meaningful measure of labour income is not total dollars paid out, but rather the real purchasing power that can be earned as the result of a certain period of work (an hour's wage, say, or a month's salary). By this criteria, workers in Canada are worse off than they were 15 years ago. Perhaps surprisingly, by any meaningful economic measure, corporations have done even more poorly.[1]

The falling profitability of real businesses in Canada can be measured in a number of ways. One of the most common is to measure profits as a share of total economic output. This measure, called the *profit share*, indicates the portion of an economy's output that is reflected in the profits of businesses. As indicated in Figure 11-1, the profit share in Canada has declined fairly steadily in Canada throughout the post-war era: from typical levels of 20% or more of GDP in the 1950s and 1960s to an average of just 12.7% during the 1990s.

The decline in profits has been experienced by large corporations and small businesses alike. The share of corporate profits in total GDP has declined by about five percentage points over the post-war period, while the share of small business profits (excluding farms) has fallen by about four percentage points. It is important to note that this measure is conducted on a *before-tax* basis. After payment of corporate and small business taxes, the final net income of private business in Canada is at least one-third smaller than indicated in Figure 11-1: an average of just 8% of Canadian GDP during the tough 1990s.

The shrinking share of small business profits is especially surprising in light of the significant rise of self-employment and other small business activity as a proportion of total employment in the economy. This evidence reinforces the discussion presented in Chapter 6, regarding the tight economic squeeze that most small businesses find themselves in. Small companies tend to face the most competitive market pressures, they rely more heavily on relatively low-technology and low-productivity production methods, and hence their profitability is marginal at best. This in turn reinforces the low productivity of the small-business sector, since most small companies do not generate enough prof-

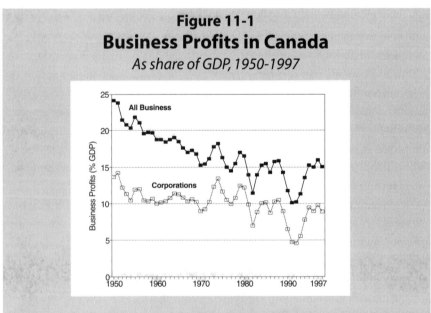

Figure 11-1
Business Profits in Canada
As share of GDP, 1950-1997

Source: Author's calculations from Statistics Canada, *National Economic and Financial Accounts.*

its to provide much if any disposable funds to finance real reinvestments in machinery or other capital assets.

Before-tax small business profits equalled $53 billion in 1997 (another
"record"!). There were 2.5 million Canadian workers who qualified as "self-employed" that same year, most of whom operate unincorporated businesses (some
high-end personal businesses, such as professional practices, are formally incorporated and hence their net incomes are lumped in with corporate profits).
That works out to an average profit from self-employment of barely $21,000 per
self-employed business operator; that is $10,000 less than the average wages
and salaries earned that year by paid workers.[2]

Indeed, if small business operators paid themselves a "normal" wage for the
time and energy they put into their businesses, the "pure" profit on the small
business itself would be zero or negative in most cases. These businesses survive solely because of the willingness of their owners (and often their owners'
spouses and children) to continue subsidizing their companies with long hours
for little or no pay.

Most investors are less concerned with their "share" of total output than
they are with the "rate" of profit which they receive in return for a particular
investment. So an alternative means of measuring the profitability of business is
to calculate the *profit rate*: profits as a share of the capital that has been invested in production.

There are numerous different ways to measure the profit rate, depending
on which particular measure is chosen for the capital stock of business: the total
assets of a business, the net capital employed in a business (adjusted for factors
such as depreciation), or the pure equity of shareholders (which excludes the
value of loans from banks and bond-holders which supplement the initial capital
of a company's actual owners).

Unfortunately, consistent long-term data on most of these measures of the
capital stock of business are difficult to obtain due to measurement problems
and other statistical difficulties. Reasonably reliable measures are available for
the total assets of business in Canada, including both their total assets and non-
financial (or tangible) assets only. Figure 11-2 illustrates total business profits
(again on a before-tax basis) as a percentage of total invested capital.

As a share of total business assets (bottom line), this rate of profit has declined by about half since 1960, to an average of less than 3% during the 1990s.
But this measure will tend to overstate the decline in the true profitability of
business investment. Earlier chapters of this book described the rising intensity
of financial intermediation in Canada: each dollar of real investment is now likely
to have far more "finance" lurking behind it than was the case in previous dec-

Figure 11-2
Business Profits as a Share of Assets
1960-1997

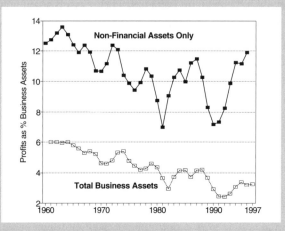

Source: Author's calculations from Statistics Canada, *National Economic and Financial Accounts, National Balance Sheet Accounts.*

ades. Including both financial and non-financial assets in this calculation, therefore, will result in some "double-counting" (since a given sum of capital may show up both as a financial asset, such as a stock or a bond, and a real asset, if a real company eventually invests that money in the form of real capital). This will imply a lower rate of profit than is really the case.

On the other hand, the top line in Figure 11-2 shows total business profit as a share of non-financial assets only.[3] Profitability measured as a share of non-financial assets has declined less markedly: by about three or four percentage points over the post-war era to an average of some 9% during the 1990s. This measure, however, will *underestimate* the decline in the profitability of real business investments. A large portion of total business profits during the era of the paper boom has been earned purely from the creation, purchase, and sale of financial assets alone, with no connection to real investment in the real economy. Measuring total profits as a share of non-financial assets only thus overstates the profitability of real investment.[4]

The true extent of the decline in the profitability of real investment in Canada therefore probably falls somewhere between the two lines illustrated in Figure 11-2.

Another perspective on the profitability of Canadian businesses is provided by the rate of profit on the equity of shareholders. These data are illustrated in Figure 11-3. Unfortunately, consistent data are not available prior to 1980, so less reliable long-term conclusions can be drawn than was the case with other data sources. Return on equity is an after-tax measure. It considers only corporate profits, not small businesses.

The corporate return on equity has declined significantly in Canada over the past 20 years: from an average of just over 10% during the 1980s to barely half that during the 1990s. Even when the economy finally climbed out of its long recession after 1995 and corporate profits recovered somewhat, profits on equity remained about one-third lower than the peak levels experienced during the expansion of the late 1980s, which in turn were lower than the peak profit levels enjoyed prior to the recession of 1981-82. And corporate profitability turned down during 1998, which is often a sign of coming recession.

Measurement problems and definitional issues make it difficult to develop an accurate picture of the longer-run trend in business profitability in Canada. Nevertheless, all of the indicators surveyed above seem to point to a similar conclusion: the profitability of business investment has eroded over time. This has especially been the case for businesses active in the real economy, since the profitability measures provided above all include the super-profits that have been earned in recent years by banks and other purely financial corporations.

Lower returns on real investment obviously reduce the incentive for companies to undertake such investments, especially when the returns on purely financial investments are becoming more attractive at the same time. Lower profitability also reduces the financial resources available to firms that want to undertake further investments.

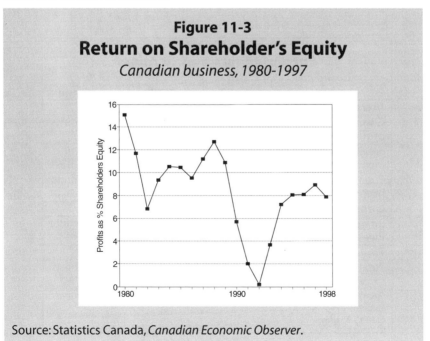

Figure 11-3
Return on Shareholder's Equity
Canadian business, 1980-1997

Source: Statistics Canada, *Canadian Economic Observer*.

The evidence presented in Chapter 8 indicated that falling profitability has not been the most important cause of the decline in real investment expenditure by Canadian businesses, but it has nevertheless been a significant one.

Explaining the Profit Squeeze

The long slide in business profitability in Canada (a trend which was mirrored in most other advanced industrial economies during the same time) has a wide range of different potential explanations. Several of these factors will be considered here.

Interest Rates

The sharp and sustained increase in real interest rates that was imposed in Canada after 1981 not only hurt consumers and governments. It also bit deeply into the pockets of companies in the real economy. Virtually all companies carry an ongoing stock of debt (financed through bank loans, bond issues, or other vehicles); a certain level of indebtedness is considered an economically efficient means of financing corporate growth. Higher interest costs, however, increase the cost of carrying that debt. To some extent, real companies have responded to a high-interest economic environment by reducing their average debt levels, especially during the 1990s. But interest costs still bite deeply into the corporate bottom line.

Table 11-1 **Entrepreneurs and Rentiers** *Capital income, percent of GDP, 1950s versus 1990s*			
	1950s	**1990s**[1]	**Change**
Users of Capital:			
Corporate profits	11.7%	6.9%	-4.8 points
Small business net income	9.5%	5.7%	-3.8 points
Total before-tax profits	21.3%	12.7%	-8.6 points
Owners of Capital:			
Interest and investment income	2.5%	6.9%	+4.5 points
Total Capital Share:			
Total return to capital	23.7%	19.6%	-4.1 points
Source: Author's calculations from Statistics Canada, *National Economic and Financial Accounts.* 1. 1990-97 only.			

In fact, over one-half of the slide in business profitability during the post-war era can be ascribed to a shift in the distribution of final income from the companies which put capital into motion in the real economy toward the owners of the financial capital (both debt and equity) that was advanced to finance those investments. In contrast to the falling share of business profits in total GDP, the share of investment income (including interest payments, dividends, and other current investment income, but excluding capital gains) in the total economic pie has more than doubled. The decline in the total economic return to *capital* in the economy has therefore been considerably less marked than the decline in the return to *business*.

The key problem, from the perspective of real investment and job-creation, is that more of this income is going to the owners of financial capital (also known as the *rentiers*), and less to those who actually set it into economic motion.

Stagnant Macroeconomic Conditions

All of the profitability measures pictured in the preceding figures show a very close relationship between business profits and the state of the overall economy. In economic terms, business profits are strongly *pro-cyclical*. Like Mother Goose's "girl with a curl in the middle of her forehead," profits do very well when the general economy is doing well. But when the general economy is bad, profits are horrid. One reason that average profit rates were so low during the 1980s and 1990s is the steep and lasting recessions that were experienced at the beginning of each of these decades. Indeed, corporate profits virtually disappeared in Canada in 1992: before-tax corporate profits equalled just 4.5% of GDP, and the average after-tax return on equity was a measly 0.18%.

Profits are ultra-sensitive to the state of the general economy because they reflect a relatively fine balance between incomes and expenses; many expenses can't be adjusted downward when business slows (at least not immediately), and hence even a relatively small decline in sales resulting from an economic slowdown is sufficient to start the red ink flowing. In fact, a downturn in corporate profits is usually one of the first signs of a coming recession.

On average during the post-war period, each increase of one percentage point in after-inflation GDP tends to translate into an increase in the *share* of profits in GDP of about one-fifth of a percentage point. So the slow and sluggish economic expansion that has been too typical of the era of permanent recession in Canada has contributed to the slide in business profitability—which is especially ironic since it was concern over business profits that partly motivated the shift toward restrictive macroeconomic policies in the first place.

The negative impact of slow growth on business profits has therefore offset much (or even all) of the benefits business might have expected from the great post-1981 U-turn in economic policy. For financial investors, however, the gains of high real interest rates and low inflation have been entirely beneficial.

Not too much should be made of the cyclical link between economic growth and business profits. Given time, businesses can adjust their capacity to reflect a slow-growth outlook, thus allowing for the recovery of profits despite generally stagnant demand conditions. And even during times of relatively stronger growth (such as the late 1980s, or the more recent expansion between 1995 and 1998), each cycle-peak level of profitability experienced in Canada was lower than the peak reached during the previous expansion. So there is clearly evidence of a structural problem in business profits, not just a cyclical one.

Business Taxes

Business lobbyists complain mightily, of course, that government has undermined the profitability of private enterprise through intrusive taxes. This is a hard claim to swallow. Business taxes declined slightly, measured as a proportion of before-tax business profits, through most of the post-war era.

Like profits themselves, the rate of effective business income tax also tends to vary with the state of the economy. Thanks to lags in the reporting and payment of corporate taxes, the tax rate will seem to rise during recessions (as corporations submit income taxes on previous years' profit even as their current profits fall). This explains the steep but temporary rise in apparent business tax rates during the last recession. Similarly, the rate will tend to decline in the

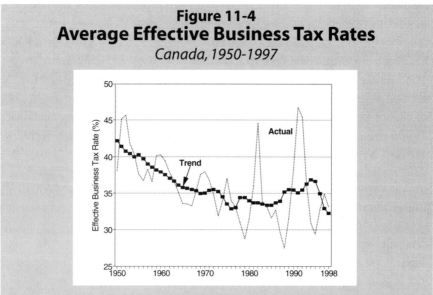

Figure 11-4
Average Effective Business Tax Rates
Canada, 1950-1997

Source: Author's calculations from Statistics Canada, *National Economic and Financial Accounts*.

early years of a recovery, as current tax liabilities are offset by losses carried forward from previous years.

On average, however, the corporate tax rate has remained fairly stable at about 35% of pre-tax profits since the 1970s. Certain changes in corporate tax policy might help to enhance the incentive for real investment spending by business (as will be discussed in the next section and in Chapter 14). But it is difficult to pin the blame for the general fall in business profitability on taxes.[5]

Competition and Competitiveness

As was discussed above, Canada's private sector has become a markedly less forgiving, more dog-eat-dog environment during the 1980s and 1990s, thanks to a range of pro-competition policies invoked by government. Trade liberalization and the widespread deregulation of many industries (including finance, energy, transportation, and telecommunications) has produced an environment in which firms battle with each more fiercely than ever for market share.

Advances in information processing, technology, and perhaps management skills have also enhanced the degree to which companies are willing and able to challenge their competitors for a profitable business niche or unexploited business opportunity. This increase in the general intensity of competition provides some explanation for the decline in profit margins.[6]

Is the heightened competitiveness of the Canadian economy a good thing? Free-market economists argue that, by forcing firms to become more efficient, prices will be lower, and consumers will benefit. They also argue that lower profit margins should also translate into lower prices for consumers. Competition can clearly produce economic benefits in certain cases, but neither is it a one-size-fits-all solution to all economic problems.

Too much competition can produce huge waste, when companies dedicate real resources to the competition itself rather than to the more efficient production of concretely valuable goods. The money wasted on advertising, on many cosmetic and pointless phony "innovations," and on the maintenance of permanent excess physical capacity as a tool for increasing market share: these are all economic costs that result from too much competition, not too little.

When companies are unconstrained by social, legal, or labour restrictions, they will often respond to intense competition through social and economic "dumping": cutting costs through straight wage-cutting or other transfers of costs onto their workers and their communities, rather than by inventing truly more useful products or truly more efficient processes. This outcome of competition is clearly destructive.

From the perspective of real capital accumulation, another potential drawback of too much competition is that it can starve market participants of the financial resources and economic space they need to invest in more sophisticated and capital-intensive production techniques, and to improve the quality of their output.

Think of the following analogy. It is well-known that if taxi service in a major city is completely unregulated—allowing for the unrestrained entry of taxi suppliers and fierce competition between them for fares—the following results tend to obtain. First, the income of taxi drivers falls significantly. Because driving a cab is a relatively "accessible" occupation (all you need is a car and a license), too many suppliers join the industry, driving down incomes.

Secondly, huge economic resources are wasted by cab drivers competing with one another for fares. Instead of designing an economically rational system for matching fares with available cabs, cab drivers waste untold hours cruising the streets or waiting in lines at airports. This activity does not increase the total output of this industry; it merely increases the chances that a particular cabbie will get a higher share of the fares available. The costs of this wasteful activity are built into cab fares, so it isn't clear that the consumer even benefits from the desperation and low incomes of the cab drivers.

Thirdly, the quality of cab service can actually deteriorate. Drivers work 18-hour days on the strength of caffeine and barbituates, and are cranky and often unsafe as a result; they have little spare cash with which to maintain and upgrade their vehicles.

Is competition "efficient" in the taxi industry? Clearly not, which is why civic authorities almost universally try to regulate the industry (with varying degrees of intensity and varying degrees of success). Extend this analogy to the economy as a whole. Unregulated dog-eat-dog competition in many industries will produce a "taxicab" economy: fiercely competitive, low-quality, labour-intensive, and low-wage.

Distributional Conflict

A final and especially challenging factor behind the long post-war decline of profits in Canada is rooted in an inevitable conflict that occurs within society over the distribution of the economic pie. During the decades of the "golden age" post-war expansion, Canadian workers were clearly winning that conflict. The share of total GDP paid out in wages and fringe benefits grew from just over 45% after World War II to a peak of 56% in 1977.

Thanks to relatively tight labour markets, low unemployment, the rise of unions and labour militancy, and the rapid expansion of the network of social programs, workers were able to win increases in real income that even exceeded, on average, the already-impressive rise in their own productivity. Hence the proportion of total national income paid to workers tended to grow, even as Canada's economy was becoming more capital-intensive.

Changes of a few percentage points in income shares might not seem important. But, given the tightly balanced relationship between costs and revenues for most corporations, and their already-small share of the total economic pie, the difference between a 45% wage share and a 55% wage share can definitely mean the difference between rich profitability and marginal viability.

Labour's share of the pie has fallen back somewhat since the 1970s, in the wake of the tough pro-business policies which have been imposed since then— although not by as much as one might think. Labour's ability to expand its share of total output was thus a key factor both in the dramatic rise in living standards which most workers enjoyed during the "golden age" boom, but also in the correspondingly marked decline of profitability during the same period.

Indeed, the desire by businesses operating in the real economy to turn back the clock on labour's post-war gains was an important part of the political motivation for the adoption of restrictive economic policies, beginning especially in the early 1980s. To be sure, the collapse of real returns for *financial* investors during the 1970s was probably the primary factor behind the implementation of high interest rates and other pro-business policies. But the deteriorating conditions faced by real businesses were also important in forging the powerful political coalition between finance and industry that forced through those policies, and that has continued to support them.

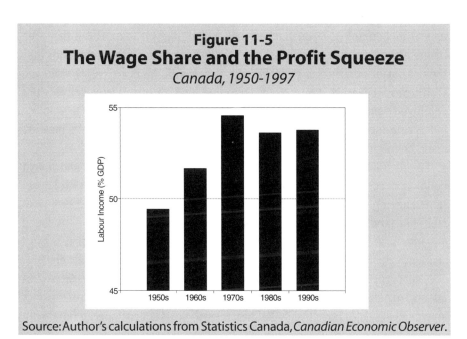

Figure 11-5
The Wage Share and the Profit Squeeze
Canada, 1950-1997

Source: Author's calculations from Statistics Canada, *Canadian Economic Observer*.

Table 11-2 **Labour Relations: Before and After the Permanent Recession** *Canada, 1970s versus 1990s*		
	1970s	**1990s**[1]
Average unemployment rate	6.7%	10.0%
Average unemployment duration	14 weeks	22.5 weeks
"Cost of job loss"	10 weeks pay	18 weeks pay
Approximate unionization	30% and rising	30% and falling
Strike frequency	0.37% total working days	0.06% total working days
Average annual change, real earnings	+1.4%	+0.3%

Source: Author's calculations from Statistics Canada, *Canadian Economic Observer*, *Historical Statistics of Canada*, and *Labour Force Historical Review*, and Bureau of Labour Information, *Collective Bargaining Review*
1. 1990 to 1997 only.

Imagine, for example, what life was like for a Canadian employer by the late 1970s (see Table 11-2). Unemployment was low, real wages were rising steadily, yet workers were still a rather demanding bunch: union activity was expanding strongly, and strike frequency was high (by both historical and international standards).

A relatively generous social safety net exacerbated the weakness of the employer's bargaining position. If worse came to worst, and a worker was fired—perhaps for trying to organize a union—it was relatively easy to find another job, and social benefits covered much of the income that was lost. This is captured by the estimated "cost of job loss" reported in Table 11-2. This number indicates the net out-of-pocket cost to an average worker who loses an average job, and then takes an average amount of time to find another one. Virtually every unemployed worker (even someone who was fired) could qualify for unemployment insurance payments which paid at least some of the bills until a new job could be found—a process which took, on average, about 14 weeks.

By the 1990s, however, all this had changed. The cost of job loss had almost doubled, to something like 18 weeks of pay—partly due to a longer average duration of unemployment (in the jobless 1990s it takes a lot longer to find a replacement job), and partly due to the erosion of social protections. Most unemployed Canadians no longer qualify for any unemployment benefits whatsoever. Consequently, losing a job in the 1990s entails a much larger financial burden.

Not surprisingly, then, worker militancy has abated considerably. Strike frequency, in particular, has fallen sharply, averaging less than one-sixth of its 1970s levels. Real wages have barely held their own, despite continued productivity gains in many sectors of the economy.

In the 1970s, Canadian workers showed up at the job and demanded fair treatment. In the 1990s, they are more likely to get down on their knees in thanks that they still have a job. The best efforts of union activists and other social justice campaigners have defended many of the gains made by workers earlier in the post-war era; but the harsh economic circumstances most workers have faced in this gloomy decade have had a chilling effect on their willingness to fight for their rights. Indeed, that was largely the point of the whole exercise.

This description of the labour relations problem faced by Canadian firms—like the litany of Canadian Airlines' financial difficulties which opened this chapter—is provided not to elicit sympathy for the poor, maligned Canadian employers, nor to suggest that workers were somehow "excessive" in their demands during the turbulent 1970s. The goal, rather, is simply to indicate that the gains labour was able to win during the vigorous expansion of the post-war era began to encounter some inherent economic limits.

The successful effort by workers to extract a greater share of the economic pie from their employers eventually came into contradiction with the continued fundamental dependence of workers on the initial profit-seeking investments of those employers. Private investment remained the crucial first link in a chain of events which set the whole economy into motion in the first place.

An old social-democratic cliché summed up the implicit *entente* which guided post-war reform strategies: "Let the capitalists take charge of production, but socialists will look after a fairer distribution." The problem, eventually encountered, is that production and distribution cannot long be separated. The success of workers in winning higher incomes, helped along by the expansion of the public sector and social programs, contributed to a long-term squeeze on the profitability of private business. To build on the significant gains of the first post-war decades, therefore, and perhaps even to hang onto them, workers had to go another step. They had to be willing to recognize the limit placed on their

Full-Employment Sickness

"Lasting full employment is not at all to [business leaders'] liking. The workers would get 'out of hand' and the 'captains of industry' would be anxious 'to teach them a lesson.' Moreover, the price increase in the upswing is to the disadvantage of small and big rentiers and makes them 'boom tired'...In this situation a powerful bloc is likely to be formed between big business and the rentier interests, and they would probably find more than one economist to declare that the situation was manifestly unsound. The pressure of all of these forces, and in particular of big business, would most probably induce the government to return to the orthodox policy."

—Michal Kalecki
Selected Essays on the Dynamics of the Capitalist Economy, 1971

demands by the continued central importance of private investment in the economy, and start to think about more far-reaching measures that might offset that dependence.

Implications of the Profit Squeeze

We know that real investment is a dominant factor in economic growth and job-creation. And we know that real investment spending by business has been undermined through the post-war era by a fairly steady decline in business profitability—which reduces both the motive for investment and the financial resources with which most companies in the real economy undertake it.

This would seem to suggest two possible courses of action. One would be to take measures to reverse the decline in business profits, hoping that investment will respond accordingly. Another would be to find alternative vehicles through which real investment expenditure can be pumped into the economy, for reasons quite separate from the hope of a private investor for private profit.

In other words, the crucial dependence of the economy on profit-seeking private real investment could be supplemented with other types of investment motivated by other types of economic and social goals. In practice, both strategies are likely to be important in reviving real capital accumulation in Canada.

The danger of suggesting that business profits need to be higher, of course, is that it opens the door to all sorts of self-serving and short-sighted demands by business for a range of economic concessions from both government and workers. If only wages were lower, the business lobbyists cry. If only workers were more disciplined and less coddled by a "nanny state." If only taxes were cut. If only environmental and safety regulations were relaxed. Then business could go about its task of fuelling real growth, while still making a buck in the process.

It was argued earlier, however, that most of these concessions would be unlikely to result in any lasting improvement in the bottom-line situation of business profits. To the extent that shrinking profits are the result of overly-intense competition between firms, then the benefits of tax or wage concessions are likely to be frittered away in a never-ending battle for market share.

There is also a self-defeating quality to the call for more concessions to business. The real living standard of most Canadians depends on the income they or someone in their family obtains through employment. The consumption of public services, financed in part with taxes on corporations, is also an important component of living standards. What is the point of sacrificing your standard of living (through lower wages and cuts in public services) in order to promote investment and growth, when the whole point of investment and growth is supposed to be to *improve* your standard of living?

Swimming Against the Tide

"Wielding power in the interest of profits is expensive. The reason, in a nutshell, is that effective use of the main instruments of capitalist power (such as the tools for disciplining labour...) entail operating the economy at low levels of output and with high real rates of interest...Capitalist power may be increased—but only at the cost of movements in capacity utilization and/or the real interest rate adversely affecting either profits or investment."

— Samuel Bowles, David M. Gordon,
and Thomas J. Weisskopf
*Beyond the Waste Land: A Democratic
Alternative to Economic Decline*, 1990

In economic terms, there is a similar seed of self-contradiction lurking within conservative demands for a more restrictive, disciplined macroeconomic environment. To be sure, the recreation of a permanent pool of unemployed, desperate workers—the central achievement of the era of tight-money anti-inflation policy—marks a fundamental improvement in the business environment facing real employers. Labour is cheaper and more compliant than would otherwise be the case; productivity is boosted,[7] unit labour costs fall, and the inherent underlying "share" of business profit in each unit of final output should grow.

This progress for employers, however, is achieved at a steep cost. High interest rates and government fiscal restraint both undermine the aggregate demand conditions which are so important to business sales and profits. High interest rates and sluggish sales also reduce the discretionary funds available for productivity-enhancing real investment expenditures.

Companies may hope that by targeting export markets they can sidestep the negative macroeconomic consequences of permanent recession in the domestic economy. Indeed, by far the strongest investment and profitability performance by corporate Canada during the 1990s (excluding the financial industry) was turned in by export-oriented manufacturing companies that sold into foreign markets which were unaffected by the "tough-love" policies being implemented at home. But export-led growth can only carry an economy so far; most business investment and production is still oriented toward domestic markets, despite the rhetoric of globalization. At any rate, if similarly restrictive policies are being followed in *foreign* countries, then exports will also be constrained by a lack of demand.

Even if profits do recover thanks to more restrictive macroeconomic policies, the positive impact of that recovery on real investment spending may be limited. International comparisons confirm that there has been at least a modest recovery in profits in most advanced industrial economies since the advent of anti-inflation monetary policies and the adoption of pro-competitive structural changes in labour market and social policies. Indeed, profits increased most in countries where unemployment increased most and where labour cost competitiveness was consequently the most improved.

But the response of investors to this improved environment is generally lacklustre, at best. For the OECD as a whole, fixed investment spending averaged 20% of GDP during the first half of the 1990s—less than in the 1980s when average profitability was lower. The continuing negative effects of sluggish demand and (in many countries) high real interest rates still seem to outweigh the pro-accumulation effects of higher profits.

Even in the U.S. economy, which enjoys the most stable and pro-business economic regime in the OECD, and where profitability has recovered strongly thanks to the right-wing policies of the 1980s and 1990s, investment performance has been less than stunning. Total fixed investment by business averaged just 13.5% of GDP between 1990 and 1997, down significantly from 16% in the 1980s. The weakness of real investment spending in the U.S., despite apparently positive economic conditions there, helps to explain the surprisingly slow American rate of productivity growth and the continuing reliance there on relatively low-wage jobs.[8]

It would be a mistake, however, to underestimate the potential of the right-wing shift in macroeconomic policy to restore—at great human cost—the conditions for profitable investment and production in the real economy. The U.S. experience is insightful in this regard. The different trajectories taken by profit rates in Canada and the U.S. raise an interesting and as yet unanswered question. Why has the right-wing recipe for rehabilitating private sector profitability been so successful in the U.S., yet so muted in its impact on profits in Canada?

Business return on equity has averaged over 10% in the U.S. during the 1990s, twice as high as in Canada. The U.S. economy is being led by a dynamic private sector that is more profitable than at any time in the last three decades. Fifteen years after Ronald Reagan was elected on a promise to remake America in a free-market vision, the U.S. economy of the late 1990s became a prototype for how lower taxes, social cutbacks, anti-union laws, and deregulation can indeed restore the vibrancy of capitalism.

Of course, the benefits of this profit-led growth for the real economic and human condition of Americans should not be overstated. U.S. economic growth has not been especially strong by historical standards, despite the revival of corporate profitability: real GDP per capita grew by about 1% per year in the 1990s, half the pace of its pre-1980 expansion. Productivity growth, despite the much-ballyhooed efficiency of U.S.-style free markets, has actually lagged most European countries. And real wages and living standards for many (or even most) Americans have stagnated, in large part precisely because of the same

God Bless America

"Increases in hourly compensation...have continued to fall far short of what they would have been had historical relationships between compensation gains and the degree of labor market tightness held...As I see it, heightened job insecurity explains a significant part of the restraint on compensation and the consequent muted price inflation...The continued reluctance of workers to leave their jobs to seek other employment as the labor market has tightened provides further evidence of such concern, as does the tendency toward longer labor union contracts...The low level of work stoppages of recent years also attests to concern about job security...The continued decline in the share of the private workforce in labor unions has likely made wages more responsive to market forces...Owing in part to the subdued behavior of wages, profits and rates of return on capital have risen to high levels."

—Alan Greenspan, Chairman,
U.S. Federal Reserve Board,
January 1997

pro-employer policies (labour market deregulation and cuts in an already-weak social safety net) which so effectively restored profitability.

Despite these drawbacks, however, the strong profitability of private business has recreated an important dynamism within the U.S. economy which helps to explain why it has done so much better than Canada's during this decade.

What factors explain the revival of business profits in the U.S., compared to their relative sluggishness in Canada? More vibrant aggregate demand conditions in the U.S. have clearly been important. Despite a consistently tough line by the central bank against any rise in inflation that would threaten real financial returns, U.S. interest rates in real terms were significantly lower through most of the 1990s than they were in Canada. Importantly, the central bank there never flirted with radical notions of zero inflation or binding inflation targets; it satisfied itself with a more flexible approach to inflation-control, and tolerated inflation rates that averaged a full percentage point higher than in Canada through the decade.

Cutbacks in government program spending were a fraction of the size, proportionately, of those that were imposed in Canada, so U.S. fiscal policy was also more amenable to growth. [Mind you, U.S. public spending was much lower than Canada's to start with, so there wasn't as much to cut!]

Tax policies may also have been important to the restoration of U.S. profitability. Average effective corporate taxes are somewhat lower in the U.S. than in Canada, and corporate tax cuts in the U.S. have played a significant (although secondary) role in restoring the after-tax profitability of U.S. business.[9]

Finally, the pro-employer shifts in labour market and social policies have clearly gone much further in the U.S. than has been the case—so far, anyway—in

Canada. Unions, minimum wages, wage-replacing social programs, and other institutional factors still retain much greater economic influence in Canada than south of the border. This largely explains why Canadian workers managed to increase their own wages, in real terms, more in the 1990s despite the horrendous economic conditions which prevailed here, than did their counterparts in the booming U.S.

Official unemployment averaged 10% between 1990 and 1997 in Canada, yet average hourly wages actually grew slightly, after inflation, during the same time: by about 2% in total. In the U.S., the official unemployment rate averaged just 6% over the same period, yet real hourly wages remained unchanged.

Once again, therefore, the socially destructive consequences of the U.S. recipe caution strongly against its adoption as a model for Canadian economic revitalization. Ironically, the U.S. economy has clearly done "better" than Canada's, yet most Canadians have done better than most Americans. Nevertheless, the success of U.S. free-market policies in recreating a vibrant and internally consistent pattern of profit-led growth is sure to result in ever-stronger pressure for similar policies in Canada.

There may be some policies which would help to shore up the bottom-line profitability of real businesses, without requiring the socially and macroeconomically destructive measures that have played such an important role in the American "success" story. These should be considered as a part of any progressive economic strategy for revitalizing real investment and real growth.

For example, as indicated in Table 11-1, the transfer of income from the users of capital (real companies) to its owners (financial rentiers) accounted for at least one-half of the total decline in real business profitability over the post-war era. Reversing that transfer—first and foremost through the adoption of lower real interest rates as a central feature of macroeconomic policy—would restore some of the lost lustre to real investment undertakings, without undermining the economic position of workers or governments. The more vibrant macroeconomic conditions accompanying such a move would further boost corporate profitability, through higher sales and capacity utilization.[10]

Similarly, measures might be considered to shift some of the burden of taxation from the users of capital (corporate income taxes) to its owners (in the form of higher taxes on personal dividend and investment income). The most effective tax measure for stimulating new investment expenditure would be targeted tax incentives tied to real investment expenditures (such as an investment tax credit for companies that increase their real investment spending). A general cut in corporate income taxes would be less effective, though even it might help to increase both the motive for real investment and the cash resources with which real companies finance it.[11]

Tax measures which discouraged dividend payments—either by eliminating the current preferential treatment of dividends in the personal income tax system, or by designing differential income tax rates for corporations (through which retained earnings were taxed less heavily than profits distributed through dividend cheques)—might also boost investment by increasing the share of total profits that is kept within corporate coffers.

These proposals to provide tax incentives for real investment undertakings may be controversial with social justice campaigners who view *higher* corporate taxes as a potential means of financing needed social programs. But the preceding overview of the decline in corporate profitability and its negative impact on real investment suggests that these activists may be barking up the wrong tree. At minimum, they need to be wary of the potential economic impacts of higher corporate taxes on real investment expenditure.

Interestingly, the disproportionate attention given to calls for higher corporate taxes by social justice activists is matched by a disproportionate *lack* of attention given to corporate tax issues by the conservative anti-tax campaigners who have taken up so much air space in Canada's political arena of the late 1990s. Of all taxes collected in Canada, it is almost certainly income taxes on companies in the real economy which have the largest negative impact on capital accumulation, growth, and hence productivity and incomes. Yet the full fire of the tax revolt has been turned against personal income taxes, especially those paid by higher-income households.

If the tax revolt partisans were truly concerned about productivity and growth, they would call for lower corporate taxes—first and foremost. Yet corporate income taxes are rarely mentioned, even in passing, by the stalwarts of a low-tax future. This suggests that the tax revolt is truly motivated more by a desire to redistribute the economic pie (from bottom to top) than by a concern to grow the pie, notwithstanding the movement's loud rhetoric about productivity and efficiency.

To sum up, then, it seems that the tax justice campaigners of the left should focus *less* on corporate taxes, while the anti-tax crusaders of the right should focus *more* on corporate taxes.

In conclusion, the bottom-line profitability of real business investment might be partially amenable to restoration through measures which reduce the share of rentiers in the total economic pie, and which expand the aggregate demand constraint which limits business profitability. Ultimately, however, the pay-off from these policies in terms of enhanced real investment expenditure by business is likely to be relatively modest. And the active resistance of the financial community to these same measures will be intense.

Moreover, profitability may be ultimately constrained by a fundamental social conflict over distribution that can't be mediated or "finessed" through shifts in monetary and tax policy. Therefore, coincident with monitoring the state of corporate profitability, and proposing certain measures (where possible and socially desirable) to enhance the bottom-line well-being of companies in the real economy, progressives will also want to think about developing policies which offset society's near-total dependence on profit-seeking private investment as the spark-plug for economic growth.

The model of social investment presented in the concluding chapter of this book might be one such approach.

Chapter 12
Ownership:
The Myth of People's Capitalism

Many personal finance advisors no doubt chuckled at a public opinion poll released in early 1999, just as Canada's annual rite of midwinter—RRSP season—was getting into full swing. The Canadian Imperial Bank of Commerce asked Canadians how they planned to pay for their retirement. Incredibly, a full 10% of Canadians (and 19% of those earning less than $30,000 per year) replied that lottery winnings would play a significant role in financing their retirement.

This finding was viewed with smug hilarity in the financial brokerages of the nation. Of course, only a tiny handful of Canadians will win enough money in a lottery to finance their retirements. The rest of us have to do it the slow-but-steady way. Count your pennies. Put aside a little bit each month. Pay yourself first. Have faith in the long-run magic of principles like "compound interest" and "dollar cost averaging." Memorize the advice of *The Wealthy Barber* and other bibles of the get-rich-slow movement.

Then you won't need to win the lottery to retire as a millionaire—you'll already be one, thanks to discipline, frugality, and (of course) picking the right mutual fund. You'll also bring lots of new business to the booming money management industry.

The poll in question did indeed raise some jarring questions about the financial literacy of the investing public. [So did another poll, released about the same time, which showed that barely one-quarter of mutual fund investors could correctly identify "management expense ratio" as the hefty annual deduction from their accounts which pays the salaries of money managers.] And it probably reinforced a sense of mission among financial advisors. "That's why they need us," they could affirm, clapping each other on the back after the markets have closed for another day. "Someone has to teach them that winning the lottery is no way to plan for your retirement."

Indeed, the sponsors of the poll were quick to seize on this spin, in hopes of spurring more RRSP business. "Quick fixes and short-term strategies don't work," hectored Samuel Cukierman, CIBC's vice-president of wealth management. "Slow and steady wins the race."

But perhaps the joke was really on the brokers, not on the hopelessly optimistic Canadians who responded to the poll. After all, it is the mutual fund industry which beleaguers the public with constant reminders about the incredible sums which are required to pay for a decent private pension. According to RRSP promotional material, a typical Canadian would need hundreds of thousands of dollars of accumulated savings to independently fund a comfortable pension.

For example, the Web sites of many financial institutions now feature "retirement planning calculators," with which prospective retirees can figure out how much money they will need to save by the time they call it quits. Imagine a 35-year old earning $50,000 per year, who aims to replace 75% of their income (the pension industry benchmark) after retirement at age 65. About 30% of that pension income will come from public pensions, but the retiree will have to take personal responsibility for the rest (unless they are among the lucky minority of Canadians who still enjoy workplace pension coverage).

Make typical assumptions about inflation (3%), investment returns (8%), and post-retirement lifespan (20 years), and we can then estimate the nest egg that must be accumulated if our retiree is to meet their pension income target. According to the online pension calculators of Canada Trust and CIBC, our 35-year-old must save an incredible $845,000 over the next 30 years. Scotiabank's guess is even more daunting: $955,000. In the face of a financial outlook this intimidating, our future retiree could hardly be blamed for wondering: "Why bother? I'll just buy another lottery ticket and hope for the best."

Perhaps because of this unintended and undesired response, most mutual fund companies no longer explicitly use frightening numbers like these in their advertising. The heavy-handed approach of past ad campaigns may have inadvertently promoted fatalistic thrill-seeking behaviour on the part of the very individuals who were meant to be scared into perpetual thriftiness.

The modern approach is more subtle and self-reflective. "What are YOUR retirement goals?" we are asked hundreds of times over each January and February. "Discover YOUR risk tolerance." Indeed, there is now a tendency for the industry to try to downplay the sums that must be accumulated, so as not to scare away business from the small-time investors who will never save $845,000, no matter how early they start.

"By and large, I think people are overestimating the amount they need to save," said Malcolm Hamilton, a pension specialist at William M. Mercer Ltd., in a 1999 RRSP round-table discussion. He and other experts went to great lengths to stress that it's never too late to start saving, despite the daunting task of trying to self-finance a pension.

In short, it may be a perfectly logical response by many Canadians of modest means, after wading through the annual barrage of intimidating RRSP ads, to shrug philosophically and conclude that their only hope is to win the lottery. How else could a lower-income or even middle-income Canadian ever hope to accumulate $845,000—no matter how frugal their habits, or how prescient their stock picks? Despite the self-righteous mantras of the personal investing movement—think frugal, think regular, think for the long-term—the cold facts of the matter are that the majority of Canadians will never own significant stores of personal financial wealth, and the vast majority of net wealth will continue to be concentrated in the hands of a small minority at the top.

This reality raises serious questions about any pension system (like Canada's RRSP system) which depends on the personal accumulation of individual stockpiles of wealth. Such a system seems sure to consign a significant share of the retiring public to spending their final years in poverty. And it also casts serious doubt on the oft-made claim of the financial industry that it services a whole society of personal investors, and not just a rich elite.

A myth has arisen in recent years that we now live in an era of "people's capitalism." The seeming omnipresence of the culture of personal investing—mutual fund scores in the morning paper, stock market tickers flashing on every screen, monotonous market updates interrupting every radio program—has contributed to this myth. The apparent size and financial power of newer financial

Rational Awareness

In a 1999 article provocatively titled "How irrational behaviour can get investors into trouble," renowned mutual fund expert Gordon Pape took personal investors to task for being too conservative in their investment decisions.

According to Pape, the failing of many personal investors is that "they're too acutely aware that these monies represent their lifetime savings." This begs the question, of course: why would truly rational investors gamble with their life's savings on a stock market prone to dramatic ups and downs of market sentiment unrelated to economic fundamentals and beyond the control of any investor?

When teenagers take stupid risks (such as driving too fast or engaging in unprotected sex), we punish them and encourage them to think of the "long term." But when fully-grown adults refuse to put their life's savings into play in a financial casino, they are deemed "irrational."

institutions such as mutual funds and workplace pension funds have also reinforced the notion that every Canadian now has a stake in the markets.

Even government itself has joined the rush; more and more government programs are being integrated with the operations of private financial markets. There have always been generous public subsidies for the private financial industry (with the $15 billion annual federal-provincial subsidy to the RRSP program being by far the largest among them). But there is a more recent and perhaps even more worrying trend to organize the provision of important public programs and services around investments in those same markets.

The federal government, for example, announced in 1997 that its new Millennium Scholarship program to assist university students would be funded from the interest on a multi-billion dollar investment in commercially traded bonds, with the whole investment program administered by private bond trading houses. And part of the upcoming reform of the financially-strapped Canada Pension Plan will involve the commercial investment of up to $75 billion in taxpayers' money in Canadian financial markets by the year 2010.

For all their oft-stated concerns about government intrusion into private sector activities, brokers must be leaping for joy in anticipation of the impact of this huge new inflow of public money on the selling prices of Canadian stocks and bonds. Together, these and other initiatives amount to nothing less than the stock-marketization of Canadian social programs.

Why on earth does the federal government, with annual revenues of $150 billion, need to hire commercial bond traders to manage a modest university scholarship program (one which will issue only about $300 million worth of scholarships each year)? Clearly the government is attempting to tap into the symbolic political and cultural power of securitization: if it's got stocks and bonds behind it, then it must be good.

This portrait of financial markets as the economic equivalent of the neighbourhood playground—something that's there for any child to play in regardless of their socio-economic status—is actually quite wrong. The vast majority of company shares are not owned through mutual funds, pension funds, or other quasi-"collective" forms of ownership. Most are owned the old-fashioned way: directly by individuals. And among those individual investors, the vast majority of shares is owned by a surprisingly small elite of very well-off families.

The myth of people's capitalism is a convenient one for those who have so much at stake in the sustenance of the paper boom. They miss no opportunity to remind the public that what's good for the stock market must be good for Canada, too. But in reality the community of financiers is not an inclusive one at all. Indeed, the highly unequal distribution of ownership of financial wealth has distorted the operation of Canada's financial system, leading to an emphasis on

macroeconomic and social policies that enhance the value of narrowly-held financial wealth at the expense of growth and job-creation in the real economy.

Even more importantly, the *form* of most financial investment in Canada, in
easily-traded securities like stocks and bonds which require no lasting relationship between the owners of financial capital and the real enterprises which put
capital to work, also discourages real investment and real growth.

Hot on the Trail of Wealth

Who owns the financial wealth of a country is an incredibly important social and
economic issue. Thus, it is astounding that Canada does not collect official statistics on the comparative ownership of wealth (including financial wealth) across
different categories of household. Statistics Canada used to conduct a biennial
survey on this matter, but the last edition of this important research was published in 1984; subsequent surveys were cancelled as part of the Mulroney government's budget cuts to the agency.

Fifteen years later, Statistics Canada is finally implementing a new survey of
household wealth, the first results of which are scheduled to be reported in the
year 2000. In the meantime, however, we can only guess at the true distribution
of wealth on the basis of less official and complete sources of data.

Before the Statistics Canada wealth survey was cancelled, it already painted
a surprising picture of a dangerously unbalanced pattern of wealth ownership in
Canada. The results of the 1984 survey are summarized in Table 12-1. The richest
one-fifth of all Canadian households (termed the top "quintile" by the statisticians) owned over two-thirds of all household wealth. Excluding the value of
residences, land, and other real assets, the top quintile's share of *financial* wealth
was even larger: the top fifth of households owned an incredible three-quarters
of all net financial wealth. The bottom 60% households, on the other hand, together accounted for just 6% of net financial wealth—one-tenth of its share of
the population. Not surprisingly, the poorest segments of society actually reported *negative* net financial wealth.

Table 12-1 Distribution of Wealth in Canada, 1984		
Household Category	**Share of all Household Wealth**	**Share of Net Financial Assets**
1st Quintile (bottom 20%)	-0.3%	-3.5%
2nd Quintile	2.4%	2.2%
3rd Quintile (middle 20%)	9.3%	7.3%
4th Quintile	19.8%	19.3%
5th Quintile (top 20%)	68.8%	74.7%
Source: Statistics Canada, *Changes in the Distribution of Wealth in Canada, 1970-1984,* June 1987.		

It is important to note that the distribution of financial wealth (stocks, bonds, and other financial assets) is consistently more uneven than the distribution of total wealth. While the ownership of some real assets, primary residences in particular, is reasonably widespread in Canadian society, the ownership of financial wealth is not. The growing relative importance of *financial* wealth in the overall wealth of Canada, therefore, likely coincides with the growing maldistribution of that overall wealth.

Has the evenness of the distribution of wealth improved since the last official survey on this subject in 1984? Not likely. Canada's real economy since the early 1980s has demonstrated an ongoing pattern of underperformance, as policy-makers shifted their emphasis from reducing unemployment and spurring real growth in favour of controlling inflation and reducing the size of government. Chronic unemployment has increased, and so has the poverty rate, which reached 18% in 1997 compared to a low point of 13% in 1977.

Incomes at the top end of society, meanwhile, have grown. The top quintile of households is the only segment which enjoyed higher income, after inflation, in the 1990s. And indeed, very high returns on financial assets during the low-inflation 1980s and 1990s explain a good part of the economic success that the higher-income brackets have enjoyed. It is hard to believe that the distribution of wealth in Canada could possibly have become more equal, even as poverty, hardship, and inequality were growing steadily all around us.

Despite the absence of official statistics, several clues are available that hint at the extent to which financial wealth has become concentrated in the hands of the wealthiest households in the land. In each case, this evidence contrasts sharply with the stereotype advanced by the financial industry that Canada is now a nation of personal investors—a community filled with frugal financiers, happily accumulating for the good of both themselves and the economy.

The self-serving nature of the mythology of people's capitalism is clear: don't question any policies or decisions that may seem to be enhancing the economic prospects of a lucky few at the expense of the many, because in fact we *all* have a stake in the paper boom.

Concerned about incredible bank profits? Don't worry, the executives say: one in two Canadians owns at least one share of those banks through their mutual funds or pension funds, so in essence we all benefit from those profits. [Of course, it might take slightly more than one share before the benefits of being a bank "owner" offset the costs of being a bank consumer, but that's another matter.]

Concerned about more layoffs at a company like CN Rail, which cut its workforce by 30% between 1994 and 1998, yet more than doubled its profits? It's been great for shareholders (the price of CN shares tripled between its initial privatization in 1995 and the most recent announced round of layoffs late in 1998), and that means it's good for you and me.[1]

Concerned about economic and fiscal policies that have placed far more importance on maximizing the profitability of financial investments (through low inflation, high real interest rates, and financial deregulation) than on stimulating real growth and job-creation? According to the theory of people's capitalism, everyone is both a worker and an investor. You might lose out in the workplace due to layoffs and downsizing, but you'll be a winner on the stock market.

In reality, about one-half of Canadians own no stake in the stock market whatsoever, and the total holdings of most of those who do own shares are economically trivial. Here are a few of the "clues" which help to reveal the extent to which financial wealth has become concentrated in the hands of a surprisingly small group of families clustered at the top of the income ladder in Canada.

Individuals and Institutions

The largest single players in Canada's financial markets are now the "institutional investors": organizations such as mutual funds or pension funds which represent the pooled assets of numerous smaller investors. These institutional investors control huge sums of capital. The largest private pension fund in Canada, the Ontario Teachers' Pension Plan, held $55 billion in assets at the end of 1997. The largest mutual fund in Canada, the Templeton Growth Fund, controlled some $10 billion in assets at the end of 1998.

These large pools of accumulated capital naturally imply a degree of concentrated decision-making power much larger than for other market players. Company executives regularly make the rounds of the important institutional investors, detailing their earnings forecasts and business plans, and working hard to maintain the good-will of these most powerful of financiers.

Yet the large size and high visibility of particular institutional investors does not necessarily imply that wealth ownership in this new era has somehow become more diverse and even-handed. These institutional investors, despite their large individual size, still account for only a minority of total equity ownership. Figure 12-1 indicates the total ownership of corporate equities in Canada, as described by the national wealth accounting system of Statistics Canada.

Despite their visibility and concentrated decision-making power, pension funds owned just 12% of all equities as of the end of 1997. Mutual funds, which represent the pooled purchase of assets by individual investors, account for another 9%. The large majority of all equities—60% as of the end of 1997—is still owned by Canadians who purchase company shares directly. Other assorted

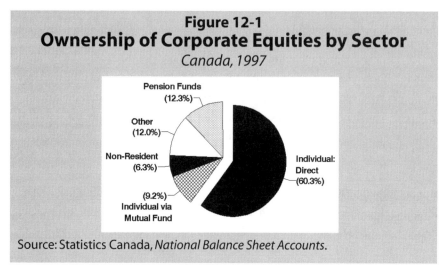

Figure 12-1
Ownership of Corporate Equities by Sector
Canada, 1997

Pension Funds (12.3%)

Other (12.0%)

Non-Resident (6.3%)

(9.2%) Individual via Mutual Fund

Individual: Direct (60.3%)

Source: Statistics Canada, *National Balance Sheet Accounts.*

investors—including non-residents, banks, insurance companies, and governments—hold the remaining 18% of equities.

So the direct ownership of shares by individuals is still the dominant form of corporate ownership in Canada. And there is some evidence that this dominance may become more marked in the future, not less. For example, the proportion of Canadian workers who are covered by workplace pension plans has actually declined in recent years—from 45% in 1993 to 42% in 1997. This reflects the growth of various forms of employment (such as part-time work, contract and temporary positions, small business jobs, and burgeoning self-employment) which are unlikely to provide pension coverage and other standard occupational benefits. So it is unlikely that the collective importance of pension funds in equity markets will grow in coming years, and it may even shrink.

Most company shares are owned directly by individuals, yet ironically the direct ownership of corporate shares is one of the least common forms of financial investment in Canada. A 1996 survey sponsored by the Toronto Stock Exchange indicated that just 21% of adult Canadians own any corporate shares directly (and only 37% of Canadians own any shares whatsoever, whether directly or through a mutual fund).

The more burdensome information requirements, transactions costs, and risks associated with purchasing the shares of individual companies have made mutual funds the equity investment vehicle of choice for most personal investors. This already hints at the extent to which financial wealth in Canada is concentrated among a small share of the population: only about one-fifth of households own any corporate shares directly, but those direct holdings alone collectively account for 60% of all equity ownership (not even counting the shares owned by these same households through indirect means, such as mutual funds).

In short, it is the rare personal investor indeed who possesses the knowledge and resources to investigate comparative investment opportunities, hire brokers to make the necessary ongoing transactions, and maintain stockpiles of specific equities and other assets stored away in their safety deposit boxes. Yet it is precisely these investors who account for the lion's share of individual ownership of equities.

Perhaps the "typical" personal investor of today bears a closer resemblance to Mr. Moneybags—the top-hatted capitalist of Karl Marx's writings—than to the unpretentious millionaire-next-door emphasized in the modern-day lore of the personal investing movement.

Income Tax Data

Canada does not collect official statistics on the distribution of *wealth*. But we have ample official data on the distribution of *income*, including the distribution of different types of income (from work, from government sources, and from the ownership of financial wealth). An ongoing stockpile of wealth generates annual flows of income which individuals (in theory) declare on their tax returns. Of course, unlike taxes collected from workers (which are almost always deducted at source long before the workers ever see their pay-cheques), taxes on most investment income must be declared and paid voluntarily by the taxpayer; this raises a problem of the possible under-reporting of investment income, which would distort any data on this subject derived from income tax statistics.

Nevertheless, the income tax system provides one of the better sources of data regarding the distribution of investment income (which in turn is an indirect indicator of the distribution of those investments). Investment income can include interest on savings accounts or government bonds, dividends paid to

Table 12-2
Investment Income by Level of Total Income
1995 Tax Returns

Income level	Under $20,000	Under $50,000	Over $50,000	Over $100,000
Number of tax-filers	10.8 million	18.1 million	2.4 million	300,000
Share of all tax-filers	52.7%	88.3%	11.7%	1.5%
Sources of Investment Income:				
Share of dividend income	4.5%	29.1%	70.9%	45.3%
Share of capital gains	4.0%	14.7%	85.3%	70.2%
Share of other investment income	24.1%	63.6%	36.4%	16.8%
Share of total investment income[1]	15.7%	46.2%	53.8%	33.6%
Investment-Related Tax Subsidies:				
Dividend tax credit	4.5%	29.1%	70.9%	45.3%
Capital gains tax exemption	0.8%	7.0%	93.0%	80.6%
Carrying charges	7.4%	31.0%	69.0%	41.6%

Source: Author's calculations from Revenue Canada, *Tax Statistics on Individuals*, 1995 Tax Year.
1. Excludes retirement income such as RRSPs and annuities.

shareholders of a company, net income from investment properties (such as rented apartments), and capital gains resulting from the sale of some asset (such as a stock, a bond, or a home) for a price greater than was paid for it.

Income tax data describing a range of investment income indicators are summarized in Table 12-2. We consider three broad sources of investment income: dividends, capital gains, and "other investment income" (which includes income received from savings deposits, bonds, rental properties, and other investments). The top 11.7% of Canadian individuals in 1995 (those earning more than $50,000) accounted for 54% of all investment income—roughly five times greater than their share of the population. Just the top 1.5% of taxpayers (those earning over $100,000 in 1995) accounted for an incredible 34% of all investment income—22 times their share of the population.

In contrast, the bottom 88% of individuals accounted for 46% of all investment income—about one-half its share of the population. And the bottom 53% of Canadians (those earning less than $20,000 in 1995) received only about 15% of all investment income.

When investment income is disaggregated into its components, it becomes clear that income derived from stock market investments, mutual funds, and other securities is much more concentrated than common savings deposits, savings bonds, and other run-of-the-mill interest-bearing assets. For example, the top 11.7% of households claimed 71% of all dividend income, and 85% of all reported capital gains. The elite earning over $100,000 (accounting for just 1.5% of taxpayers) claimed 45% of all dividends, and 70% of all capital gains. In contrast, the bottom nine-tenths of taxpayers accounted for less than 30% of all dividend income, and only 15% of all capital gains.

The conclusion that financial wealth is particularly concentrated in the upper end of the income ladder is reaffirmed by an analysis of claims for tax deductions related to stock market and other investments. These are summarized in the lower part of Table 12-2. The most common investment-related tax claims are the dividend tax credit (which refunds a portion of the taxes paid on dividend income), the capital gains deduction (through which taxpayers pay tax on only a portion of the capital gains income earned from the purchase and subsequent resale of various assets), and the deduction of carrying charges (interest payments, brokerage fees, and other expenses) which investors incur in the course of generating their investment income.

As indicated in the table, these various tax subsidies are even more concentrated at the upper end of the income ladder than is investment income itself. The distribution of the dividend tax credits mirrors the distribution of dividend income (since the credit is allocated proportionately to total dividend income); 45% of the credits were claimed by just the top 1.5% of individuals. Similarly, 93%

of capital gains deductions were claimed by the top 11.7% of taxpayers—and a phenomenal 81% by just the top 1.5% alone. Finally, 69% of all carrying charges were deducted by those earning above $50,000, close to two-thirds of that by those earning over $100,000.

Why are investment-related tax deductions even more concentrated in high-income households than investment income itself? Lower-income households may not know about the tax deductions that are available, and, given their much smaller holdings of financial wealth, they may not incur a proportionate share of carrying charges, or they may simply not go through the trouble of claiming the deductions.

The conclusion is clear, however: the generous tax subsidies that support various forms of private investment activity deliver the huge majority of their benefits to upper-income households. Moreover, in the case of carrying charges and other deductions, the value of each dollar deducted is ironically higher for the high-income taxpayers who claim most of the deductions anyway, by virtue of the fact that they are paying income tax at a higher rate than their less well-heeled counterparts. So an even greater share of the total public cost of the tax deductions is concentrated at the top end of the income ladder than is implied by the already-startling data provided in Table 12-2.

RRSP Contributions

Canada's RRSP program may qualify as the most "democratic" form of private financial investment in our economy. But this does not imply that RRSPs are especially fair: the majority of RRSP funds are owned by high-income Canadians, while most lower- and middle-income households own economically trivial amounts, or no RRSPs at all. And RRSP tax subsidies are distributed to households in a perverse manner: the RRSP holdings of high-income investors are actually subsidized at a higher rate than those of other Canadians, because of the manner in which these subsidies are calculated.

Unlike many other tax subsidy programs (such as the child tax credit for poor families), the RRSP subsidy is calculated as a tax *deduction* (in which the legal amount of RRSP contributions is deducted from income before the investor's tax bill is calculated), rather than as a tax *credit* (in which the subsidy is added back in at the end of the income tax form, after the individual's taxes have already been calculated). The value of a tax deduction depends on the rate of tax which the investor would otherwise be paying on the income that is deducted. Higher-income taxpayers pay a higher rate of tax, hence the RRSP deduction is worth proportionately more to them, and hence they receive a sweeter subsidy for their RRSP investments.

For years, progressive tax reformers have called for the conversion of the RRSP deduction into a fairer RRSP tax credit (in which all taxpayers, regardless of their income level, would receive the same rate of subsidy). But the RRSP deductions are so treasured by the influential high-income community which derives the most benefits from them that no government has dared to implement this change.

Despite these ironies, however, the fact that RRSP investments are subsidized, and that the total tax-subsidized contribution is limited (at present to a maximum of 18% of the previous year's earned income, to a ceiling of $75,000), means that RRSP investments are distributed far more equally across households than are other financial investments.

Most working and middle-income Canadians do not come close to using up the total value of RRSP subsidies available to them. In 1997, Canadians contributed more to RRSPs than in any other year in history: a record $27 billion. But this staggering total represented just 13% of what Canadians *could* have contributed if each taxpayer had used up the full RRSP "room" available to them. Only about 15% of Canadian taxpayers contributed the maximum allowed to their RRSPs.

Fat Cats

"This is not for fat cats."
—Tom Hockin, President
Investment Funds Institute of Canada
re government limits on RRSP foreign investment
September 28, 1998

"Contrary to popular belief, this is not a rich man's issue."
—Tom Hockin
November 12, 1998

"This is not a Bay Street issue."
—Tom Hockin
January 29, 1999

Share of RRSP contributions made by top 11.7% of taxpayers, 1995: 50%.

Share of total RRSP contribution-year subsidies collected by the top 11.7% of taxpayers, 1995: about 60%.

Share of RRSP contributions accounted for by the top 1.5% of taxpayers, 1995: 14%.

Share of total RRSP contribution-year subsidies collected by the top 1.5% of taxpayers, 1995: about 18%

Table 12-3
RRSP Investments by Level of Total Income
1995 Tax Returns

Income level	Under $20,000	Under $50,000	Over $50,000	Over $100,000
Number of tax-filers	10.8 million	18.1 million	2.4 million	300,000
Share of all tax-filers	52.7%	88.3%	11.7%	1.5%
Proportion who invested in RRSPs	8.4%	22.4%	69.4%	76.6%
Average RRSP contribution	$1,610	$2,598	$6,369	$12,326
Share of total RRSP contributions	6.9%	49.9%	50.1%	13.6%
Approx. share total RRSP subsidies[1]	3%	35%	65%	18%

Source: Author's calculations from Revenue Canada, *Tax Statistics on Individuals*, 1995 Tax Year, and unpublished Revenue Canada data.
1. Current-year subsidy to new investments only; excludes value of tax-sheltering for accumulated funds.

Most of the unused RRSP room is concentrated at the bottom of the income spectrum, where a shortage of disposable income constrains household saving potential.

For those who can afford it, contributing the maximum allowable into an RRSP is the first commandment of personal investing: virtually every financial advisor demands that "maxing out" their RRSP accounts is among the very first things that personal investors should do with discretionary funds. So almost all personal financial wealth held by lower- and middle-income Canadians (such as it is) is held within RRSPs. But for high-income households which have exhausted their RRSP contribution room, RRSPs will represent just a portion (and sometimes just a small portion) of total wealth holdings. For all of these reasons, the distribution of RRSP holdings across households is far more equal—or at least less unequal—than the distribution of financial wealth generally.

Surprisingly, then, the distribution of RRSPs is not very equal at all. There are a couple of data sources supporting this conclusion. The income tax data cited earlier break down total RRSP contributions by income category. High-income individuals are far more likely to invest in an RRSP than those with less income. Less than one-quarter of Canadians who earned less than $50,000 contributed to an RRSP in 1995, compared to 70% of those who earned over $50,000.

Needless to say, the average level of contributions also rises dramatically with income. Those earning less than $50,000 socked away just over $2,500 each in their RRSPs, compared to over $6,000 each for those earning over $50,000, and a whopping $12,000 each (more than $1,000 per *month*) for those pulling in more than $100,000. The end result: in 1995, a full 50% of RRSP contributions was claimed by just the top 11.7% of tax-filers (those earning over $50,000).

The top one-tenth of taxpayers, in other words, accounted for about five times more than their per capita share of RRSP contributions. The top 1.5% of tax-filers (those earning over $100,000 in 1995) accounted for 14% of all RRSP contributions—about 10 times greater than their share of the population.

Because of the perverse fact that these same high-income taxpayers are actually subsidized by the government at a higher rate for their personal investing, they account for an even larger proportion of the subsidies that are handed out to support new RRSP contributions.[2] It would be safe to conclude that those earning over $50,000 received 65% of total RRSP subsidies, while those earning over $100,000 received about 18%.

So even for this most "democratic" form of (subsidized) financial investment, the clear majority of wealth is concentrated in the highest-income segment of society: a group which perversely claims an even larger share of total government support for these investments.

This picture of the unbalanced pattern of RRSP investment in Canada is further confirmed by a second source of data: Statistics Canada's biennial reports on pension fund investments, including RRSPs. According to this data, those Canadians reporting 1995 total income in excess of $80,000—the top 2.7% of taxpayers that year—accounted for almost 20% of all RRSP contributions (and, once again, an even higher share of all RRSP subsidies).

In contrast, those tax-filers earning under $40,000 in 1995 (accounting for 80% of all taxfilers) contributed just one-third of all RRSP monies deposited that year, and received an even smaller share of total RRSP subsidies. So even within Canada's RRSP system, which in theory is supposed to support the retirement savings of average citizens, the ownership of financial wealth is highly concentrated. Yet the total stock of RRSPs—some $200 billion by the end of 1995—still accounts for a small share (perhaps one-eighth) of all household financial investments in Canada.

Outside of the RRSP system, wealth is distributed far more unequally; few lower- and middle-income Canadians have any financial assets at all outside of their RRSP holdings.

Public Opinion Polls and Other Data Sources

There are a few other sources of indirect data regarding the wealth holdings of different classes of Canadians, and these once again serve to contradict the myth that personal investing is now a virtually universal Canadian activity. Many financial institutions conduct their own private surveys of investment and wealth-ownership patterns, to support their wealth management and financial advising services. These surveys, when they are made public, tend to confirm the notion that, despite the pseudo-populist culture of personal investing, most Canadians sit on the sidelines of this game.

A 1996 poll conducted by the Toronto Stock Exchange confirmed that only about one-third of Canadians own any equities whatsoever (whether directly or through mutual funds). Stock ownership was especially rare among lower-income households: only 8% of families with income under $25,000 per year owned either shares or mutual funds, compared to over 70% of those with incomes above $75,000. And the total holdings of those lower-income households which do invest in equities are typically trivial in economic terms.

Another 1998 survey by Royal Trust showed that 55% of those Canadians who do possess RRSPs own less than $25,000 in total assets. One-third of re-spondents held total RRSP assets of less than $10,000. No matter how hard these personal investors had to scrimp and save in order to accumulate these nest-eggs, the hard truth of the matter is that these savings are completely insignifi-cant in the big-money world of pension funding.

Given recent interest rates and investment returns, it typically costs over $25,000 to purchase a pension annuity paying $150 per month—assuming retire-ment age of 65, guaranteed until the purchaser reached 90 years of age, but not protected against inflation. By this criteria, then, even a $25,000 RRSP would generate a monthly pension of less than $150 (or $1,800 per year). But only 45% of those Canadians who do own RRSPs have financial wealth exceeding that $25,000 threshold—and that doesn't count the roughly 50% of Canadians who own no RRSPs at all.

By this reckoning, perhaps one-fifth of Canadians possess sufficient private financial wealth to guarantee a private monthly pension equal to a measly $150.[3] Despite the hype of the RRSP industry, then, the ability of most Canadians to pay for their own pensions is negligible—and will almost certainly remain so.

Rules of Thumb

All of these data sources provide only indirect information regarding the distri-bution of financial wealth in Canadian society. It would be far preferable to have a complete and accurate survey of the subject, and it is hoped that Statis-tics Canada's upcoming wealth survey will provide precisely that. This informa-tion is keenly awaited, and will shed tremendous light on the extent to which the benefits of the paper boom of the 1990s have indeed been shared broadly within Canadian society—or, rather, are primarily the preserve of a lucky elite.

The preceding data sources all paint a fairly consistent picture, however, one that is unlikely to be refuted by official data in the future. The notion that financial investment is a universal, almost democratic phenomenon in Canadian society is clearly invalid. The clear majority of Canadians own no significant stockpiles of personal financial wealth whatsoever. And the clear majority of finan-cial wealth is owned by a relatively small group at the top of the income ladder.

Approximate, conservative rules of thumb can be constructed, based on the preceding data sources. The top 10% of Canadian society probably owns about 50% of all wealth (including real assets such as homes), and something closer to

Taxing the Poor

Despite the exploding popularity of personal investing, most Canadians will retire with either no personal savings or with portfolios that are too small to fund anything more than the most trivial of private pensions—$150 per month or less. An even greater irony is that many of those small-time investors will actually end up paying taxes on their puny holdings at a rate *greater* than is paid by many millionaires!

The effective marginal income tax rate for low-income senior citizens is perversely one of the highest paid by any group of Canadians. [The *marginal* tax rate is the amount of each *additional* dollar in income that is lost to taxes.] Since 1967, low-income seniors have received a supplemental pension called the Guaranteed Income Supplement (GIS). As of mid-1997, single low-income seniors could receive a maximum GIS payment of about $500 per month, in addition to regular Old Age Security pensions of about $400 per month; individual payments to married seniors were somewhat lower.

The GIS program has been a very effective tool of social policy: poverty rates among the elderly have fallen considerably since its introduction (although unmarried or widowed women still face a significant chance of ending their years in poverty). But the program is expensive: over $5 billion per year as of 1997, paid out to nearly 1.5 million Canadians (or almost 40% of those Canadians over 65).

To reduce the cost of the program, a senior's GIS income is cut back by one dollar for every two dollars of other income (including both public and private pension income) that the senior receives.

Any senior whose total income (including GIS and OAS) is less than about $12,000, therefore, effectively pays a 50% tax (in the form of forgone GIS income) on each dollar of private income they receive—including, for example, income from their own RRSPs. Add on other taxes, and those seniors can pay taxes at rates approaching 60%. In most Canadian provinces, even millionaires don't pay income tax at such high marginal rates.

Apart from the obvious ethical issue raised by this anomaly, it raises a strategic question for Canadians who might end up in that low-income group of seniors who must pay tax at such a high rate. Unless they are fairly sure that they can save enough in their RRSPs to push them well above the GIS cut-off level (of about $12,000 per year), they probably shouldn't bother trying to sock away a personal investment portfolio at all, since most of what they save will be offset by reductions in their public pension benefits.

70% of all financial wealth. The top 1% of society probably owns about one-quarter of all wealth, and something approaching 40% of all financial wealth.

These surprisingly exclusive constituencies are the ones that have enjoyed most of the benefits of the spectacular boom in private finance which has dominated Canada's economy during this entire decade.

Wealth and Income

Journalist Linda McQuaig uses a powerful analogy to describe the difference between the distribution of income and the distribution of wealth.[4] Imagine a parade, she suggests, in which Canadians are lined up in order of their increasing
annual income, and the height of each participant reflects that annual income.
A household with average income is symbolized by a marcher of "average" height—
say, something less than 6 feet tall. The parade takes one hour to pass the viewing grandstand.

This "income parade" reveals the shocking inequality of income between
families in Canada. For the first few minutes, some extremely tiny people march
by—less than a foot tall. After 18 minutes of the parade marching by, the marchers are still only three feet tall. At the halfway mark of the hour-long parade, the
marchers are still only five feet tall.

After a few more minutes, Canadians of normal adult height finally begin to
march by.

As the parade nears its end, the marchers become really tall: with six minutes left in the parade, the marchers are 14 feet tall, with 25 seconds left they are
25 feet tall, and the last persons in the parade are towering giants, hundreds of
feet tall.

This is shocking enough, but then McQuaig has us imagine a second, similar
parade: the "wealth parade." Once again Canadians line up, but this time in
order of their increasing accumulated wealth. Again the parade takes one hour
to pass the viewing area.

This time, the first marchers in the parade are actually *under the ground*—
that is, they do not have any wealth, and in fact carry net debts. It isn't until 10
minutes later that the first "break-even" Canadian marches by: the first Canadian who carries no debt, but owns no net wealth either, and hence marches by
exactly at ground-level. After 15 minutes, we see the first dwarves, standing just
three feet tall.

During the last minute of the wealth parade, marchers are as tall as Toronto's CN Tower, over one thousand feet tall. And in the last second of the parade,
the truly lopsided nature of wealth ownership in Canada is stunningly revealed:
the very last marchers in this parade are supernatural giants, towering some 200
miles above the rest of the parade.

If anything, McQuaig's description is conservative, in that it still relies on
raw data from the last Statistics Canada survey of wealth in 1984, and things
have probably become even more unequal since then.

This story provides a vivid introduction to the incredibly unequal distribution of financial wealth in Canada, which is far more unequal than the distribu-

tion of annual income (a concept with which most Canadians are more familiar). How is it that an initial imbalance in income distribution can become so amplified in the far more unequal distribution of accumulated wealth?

If every Canadian started from a position of zero savings, saved an equal proportion of their income, no matter how much they made, and if they invested those savings in equally profitable personal investments, then the distribution of wealth would perfectly match the distribution of income: no more equal, no less equal.

None of those conditions, however, prevails in reality. In the first place, most wealthy households inherited a significant proportion of their total wealth from their parents or other relatives. Secondly, higher-income investors probably obtain slightly higher average returns on their investments, simply because they tend to have more financial knowledge and more resources with which to pursue sophisticated investment opportunities. Finally and most importantly, high-income households are able to allocate a much larger share of their initial income to savings and wealth accumulation than most other households.

To be sure, higher-income households also spend larger sums of money on various types of consumption—housing and furnishings, cars, clothing, entertainment, travel—than do their less well-heeled counterparts. But it is a fundamental economic truth that this personal consumption spending tends to grow with income at a *less-than-proportional* rate. Hence, the proportion of income allocated to savings tends to increase with the level of a household's income.

The reasoning behind this observation is simple. There are certain simple necessities of life that must be paid for as a condition of basic subsistence, regardless of an individual's income level. Everyone must eat, be clothed, and housed. If their current income is inadequate to cover even these basic necessities, individuals must dip into their savings or go into debt. Rich people spend more on food than poor people, obviously, but there are limits to how much they can eat, and even to how much they can spend on luxury food products. Thus someone who earns $200,000 per year will spend more on food than someone earning $20,000—but not ten times as much.

After paying for the necessities of life (and even the non-necessities), higher-income households have more income left over after the bills are paid, and hence a higher savings rate, than those with lower income. This relationship is dramatized in Figures 12-2 and 12-3.

Figure 12-2 indicates the distribution of income across different income groups in Canadian society. This distribution in painfully uneven. The top one-fifth of households takes in more than 43% of total income (including government transfer payments such as pensions and welfare benefits), or about 8.5 times as much as the lowest fifth. This inequality is moderated somewhat as a result of Cana-

Figure 12-2
The Distribution of Income in Canada
By Household Quintile, 1996

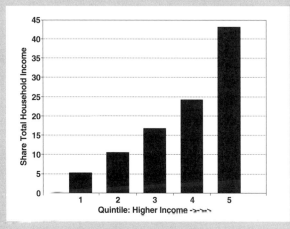

Source: Statistics Canada, *Family Expenditure in Canada*, 1996.

Figure 12-3
The Distribution of Savings in Canada
By Household Quintile, 1996

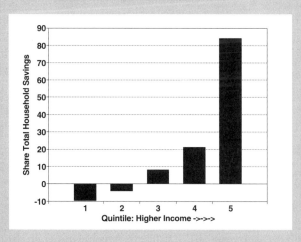

Source: Statistics Canada, *Family Expenditure in Canada*, 1996.

da's tax system (since high-income earners pay a higher-than-proportional share of total taxes), and hence the distribution of after-tax income is somewhat more equal than the distribution of before-tax income. Still, the top one-fifth of households takes in about 40% of all after-tax income.

That same top tier of households, however, accounts for "only" about one-third of total current personal expenditure by Canadian families: significantly less than their share of total income. It seems that there's only so much that these households can buy with their higher incomes. The top tier enjoys average incomes 8.5 times as large as the lowest tier, but only spends about four times as much on personal consumption. As a result, the top one-fifth of households accounts for a very large share of total Canadian *savings*—an incredible 84% (Figure 12-3).

Lower- and even middle-income Canadians have no savings whatever: their modest incomes are barely sufficient to pay for current costs, with nothing left over for RRSPs or mutual funds. These households therefore experience negative savings rates, either drawing down existing assets or (more likely) going deeper into debt.

It isn't until we reach the middle quintile of society—those earning an average of about $45,000 per year in 1995—that any positive savings are generated. Moreover, most of those middle-class savings take the form of gradual decreases in the outstanding balances of residential mortgages. [In accounting terms, paying off a long-term debt like a mortgage is equivalent to positive saving.] Virtually all of the net *financial* savings of Canadian households, therefore, takes place within the top 40% of households, and the great bulk of that is accounted for by the top tier. Since they account for the vast majority of savings, year in and year out, before long these households also account for the vast majority of accumulated wealth.

The important fact that most personal saving is undertaken by the richest minority of households also sheds light on other current economic issues. It explains, for example, why consumption or sales taxes (like Canada's GST) are *regressive*—that is, they collect a higher rate of tax from lower-income households, the ones who can least afford to pay. Since lower- and middle-income households consume virtually every dollar they earn—not because they are short-sighted or irresponsible, but simply because their income is barely sufficient to cover current costs—they pay GST on every dollar of their income. Higher-income households, however, pay less GST as a proportion of their income, simply because they have discretionary money to sock away in mutual funds (which, not coincidentally, are GST-free).

For similar reasons, the redistribution of income from rich to poor can have stimulative effects on the economy. Lower-income households spend every available dollar on current consumption, while their better-heeled counterparts have relatively high savings rates. Taking $100 from a rich household and giving it to a poor one, therefore, will tend to increase the total amount of consumption spending (since the rich family might have spent only $50 of the $100, while the poor family will almost certainly spend all of it).

This extra consumption spending in turn generates new demand and new jobs throughout the economy.[5] Income tax reductions for high-income earners, by the same logic, can actually have a dampening effect on economic growth. Higher-income households pay most of Canada's income taxes—and hence they receive the greatest share of the benefits from any general income tax cut.[6] But they subsequently spend only a portion of their tax savings on goods and services, and allocate the rest to their growing stockpiles of financial wealth.

Especially in the case in which tax cuts are offset by equivalent reductions in government spending on various public services and social programs (as was the case under the Mike Harris government in Ontario, for example), the overall effect is to *dampen* demand, growth, and employment.

The concentration of private savings in Canada in the hands of the highest-income elite has led to an inevitable concentration of financial wealth in those same hands. The political power represented by these well-off sectors of society has in turn promoted the adoption of policies which have generally rewarded savings and financial investment, often at the expense of real investment, growth, and job-creation.

These policies have included the introduction of the GST, the shift in the relative tax burden from progressive personal income taxes to regressive sales taxes, the payment of juicy tax subsidies for personal savings and investment, and of course the broader macroeconomic policies (such as high real interest rates and cutbacks in government spending) which have generally helped to fuel Canada's paper boom.

Ships Passing in the Night

This lopsided concentration of financial wealth among a small elite of Canadian society is a cause for concern on numerous grounds. It seems immediately unfair on ethical grounds. It provides a jarring refutation to the whole ideology of people's capitalism, an ideology which pretends that personal investing has become virtually as universal as suffrage itself. And the concentration of wealth has also created a dangerous and destructive political dynamic.

A small but powerful constituency of financial investors has been able to lobby for the implementation of policies that have clearly enhanced the value and profitability of finance, but at the expense of real growth and job-creation. Think of many of the policy debates which have occurred in recent years. How hard should we crack down on inflation? How should we reduce government deficits, and how fast? Should we try more aggressively to prop up the Canadian dollar? In case after case, the fundamental issue seems to boil down to a clash between those who own or manage significant quantities of financial wealth (and hence demand low inflation, less debt, a strong currency, and a free-wheeling financial market) and those who do not (and who thus would benefit from policies that emphasized job-creation, rather than the protection of financial returns).

For those who own and control finance, the stakes are huge in cementing the general direction that Canadian economic policies have followed over the past 15 years. Financiers will never forget the 1970s when the value of their stockpiles of wealth was badly eroded by inflation, falling stock market prices, unprecedented labour militancy, and negative real interest rates.

Some have described the period of deliberately restrictive, pro-finance economic policy that has been experienced in most Western economies in the wake of this turbulent time as the "revenge of the rentiers." The rentier class—those who live off the proceeds of accumulated wealth rather than the sweat of current labour activity—organized itself effectively to shift economic policy in a fundamentally different direction, to ensure that the horror of the 1970s never repeated itself.

For the rest of us, in retrospect, the 1970s were actually not so bad, despite accelerating inflation and moderate financial instability. Real wages in Canada grew by an average of about 1.5% per year during the decade, and the unemployment rate averaged just 5.9%, barely half its level during the "financially responsible" 1990s. But the fact that most Canadians have clearly been harmed economically by the pro-finance policies of the 1980s and 1990s has hardly affected the speed and determination with which this policy agenda continues to be implemented.

In short, there is little doubt that the concentration of financial wealth in Canada is also leading to a concentration of political influence and a disturbing tendency for our democracy to be governed more by the sentiments of the "markets" rather than the sentiments of the voters—even though the "market," of course, is nothing other than a symbolic representation of the vested economic interests of one small but powerful constituency of society. The motto of "one dollar, one vote" seems to be replacing the more traditional principle of "one person, one vote."

In terms of its impact on the pace and nature of real investment and capital accumulation, however, the distribution of wealth ownership in Canada may not

Just in Case

"I am not saying markets are perfect by any means. Markets sometimes do crazy things. But we don't control those markets. So it's best to stay on the good side of them."

—John McCallum, Chief Economist,
Royal Bank of Canada, January 27, 1999

ultimately be as important as the forms in which financial wealth is owned. In other words, *who* owns wealth in Canada may be less of a problem than *how* it is owned. It is not at all clear, for example, that merely redistributing financial wealth more equally in Canada would in any fundamental way improve Canada's lacklustre record in terms of putting that financial capital into motion in the real economy.

Indeed, imagine what would occur if all the existing shares in Canada's stock market were simply expropriated and then divided up on an equal per-capita basis (providing each Canadian with some $40,000 worth of corporate equities). Wealth would no longer be concentrated in the hands of the top 10% of the population, and this would have some immediate benefits, such as a better distribution of income, and perhaps more importantly a better distribution of political and economic decision-making power. But the stock market would play just as large (and just as unproductive) a role in our economy.

In fact, the wider base of share ownership in society would probably enhance the visibility and importance of the stock market, as virtually every man, woman, and child in the country turned to the financial pages each morning to see how much their $40,000 expanded or shrank in the previous day's trading. Yet all this new, superficial interest in the stock market would hardly improve the very limited extent to which financial capital is put into motion in the real economy through its frantic activities.

In fact, the reverse might actually occur. As we have seen, the majority of corporate equities are still owned the old-fashioned way: by families, often very rich ones, who have direct stakes in individual companies rather than acting through intermediaries such as pension funds or mutual funds. Of necessity, these owners cannot turn over their shares with the same frequency as the money managers do. For the truly rich families at the pinnacle of Canada's economic heap, private blocks of shares are simply too large to allow for significant buying and selling on an ongoing basis.

Imagine trying to move the Bombardier family's 62% share of the company with the same name, or the Thomson family's 72% share of its newspaper and publishing conglomerate, or the Bronfman family's 36% of distillery giant Seagram, or the Weston family's 60% stake in Weston foods, or the Desmarais family's 65% stake in Power Corp., or the Stronach Trust's 64% share of Magna Corp. These huge blocks of equity in some of Canada's largest corporations would swamp the normal supply-and-demand patterns of the stock market.

But more important is the fact that these ultra-rich controlling shareholders are not primarily interested in buying and selling financial assets for capital or speculative gains. Like the famous Remington man of television commercial fame, they literally "own the company." These shareholders have a much deeper con-

Rich and Richer

Total dividend income declared in 1995 by the bottom 9.7 million Canadian tax-filers (47% of all those submitting tax returns): $310 million.

Estimated dividend income received by the Thomson family in 1995 from its 72% ownership share of the Thomson Corporation and its 22% ownership share of the Hudson's Bay Company: $310 million.

nection to the real business and the long-term prospects of their companies than does the typical money manager or personal investor. That is why it is a rare event indeed for one of Canada's mega-shareholders to move any significant portion of their shares in open stock-market trading.

To be sure, the rising share prices of their companies have mightily enhanced the paper value of their large holdings. The apparent worth of families like the Thomsons[7] and the Bombardiers soared with share prices during the roaring 1990s, but most of these investors have no intention of ever selling out. And, perhaps somewhat ironically, this is probably a good thing from the perspective of the real growth potential of their companies.

When control of a corporation rests with a small group of individuals directly and personally committed to the real expansion of the business, rather than with a group of investors primarily interested in the resale price and market liquidity of the company's paper assets, it is quite possible that the company is better able to keep its eyes on the prize of real growth and investment, rather than fleeting changes in market valuations. How else do we explain the prevalence of family-controlled empires among the leading industrial corporations in Canada?

Excluding Canadian subsidiaries of foreign corporations, 11 of Canada's largest 20 corporations ranked by revenue are controlled by a single or family shareholder. The fundamental idea behind tradeable equities and stock markets is that they are supposed to make it easier for real companies to raise capital. We saw in Chapter 3 that stock markets actually have very little to do with raising capital for real business; and now we see that companies which have largely *bypassed* Canada's sophisticated stock market seem to be disproportionately successful. Perhaps this is precisely because they have been allowed to focus on the longer-run task of building a real business, rather than the day-to-day myopia of maximizing stock market valuations.

This long-term stability in the structure of ownership of many of Canada's largest corporations actually helps to limit the speculative activity and instability of the overall stock market. It is estimated that privately-held shares of companies listed on the TSE are nine times less likely to be bought and sold in a given year than shares held by pension funds and mutual funds (see discussion in the next chapter).

The large proportion of wealth represented by these controlling shareholders explains much of this result: huge blocks of shares in many of Canada's largest corporations literally never cross the trading room floor. And their general absence from the day-to-day marketplace helps to limit the booms of hyperoptimism and the busts of collapsing confidence that so disrupt both financial markets and the broader economy.

In this light, it would be naive to expect that merely redistributing wealth in Canada might somehow improve the stock market's poor record of channelling ever-greater floods of financial investment into job-creating investments in the real economy. If anything, the dilution of control and perspective that would necessarily accompany such a redistribution could make the stock market an even *less* effective tool for facilitating real growth.

This is not to imply that the concentration of financial wealth in the hands of a few powerful families is a good thing. To the contrary, this concentration is a major factor explaining the inequality of both income and political influence in Canada. But the continuing success of huge family-controlled corporations in Canada does accidentally reveal the extent to which the much-vaunted financial intermediation of stock markets and related institutions in Canada is economically irrelevant, if not downright counterproductive. Where saving and investment is undertaken by one and the same actors—such as through the business decisions of the wealthy families which control such a surprising share of Canada's economy—the process of putting money into real economic motion may actually occur more effectively and successfully. No intermediation is required, thank you very much.

In fact, then, the fundamental problem behind sluggish real investment may be the stock market itself, rather than the disproportionate wealth of certain stock market players. Any time a financial investment is embodied in a tradeable *security*—that is, a piece of paper which can be bought and sold in its own right, quite independently from the real economic purpose which it supposedly helps to finance—then a door is opened through which that security can leave to take on a life of its own. Entire industries, whole legions of managers and analysts, and incredible entrepreneurial creativity end up being dedicated to finding new securities to invent and market, and new ways of profiting from the endless gyrations in the prices of those securities.

The purported point of the whole exercise—raising capital and using it to do something useful in the real economy—is quickly forgotten. Virtually any type of investment can be "securitized," by converting it into bite-size paper assets destined for sale and resale on an appropriate market. And Canada's financial professionals are without doubt world leaders in developing new and cutting-edge forms of securitization.

Home mortgages, long the epitome of a close and consistent personal relationship between a banker and his or her clients, are now securitized: converted into mortgage bonds or debentures which are tradeable and whose changing prices will instantaneously reflect any outside factor, ranging from interest rate expectations to the unemployment rate. Even rock musicians and other high-paid artists are getting in on the act, converting their future streams of income into up-front bonds that can be traded on securities markets; David Bowie, Rod Stewart, and heavy metal rockers Iron Maiden are now counted among this most unlikely group of financial intermediaries.

Securitization creates a distant, arms-length relationship between the supplier of financial capital and its end-user. In theory, securitization is supposed to increase the supply of capital by reducing the time commitment required of any particular investor, and hence its risk: since securities can be sold at any time, investors can theoretically get their money back from the market long before the actual company or borrower is in a position to pay it back directly.

In practice, however, securitization introduces all sorts of new risks associated with instability in security prices and the possibility of default or mismanagement at any single link in the long chain of financial middlemen who are now involved in even the simplest of financial transactions. And untold resources are redirected from directly productive activity to the task of finding new ways to earn commissions from the issuance and trading of securities, and speculative profits from endless fluctuations in securities prices.

Even the fact that, thanks to the stock market and other securities exchanges, investors can permanently turn their backs on a company at a moment's notice may not be such an economically useful innovation. It clearly promotes short-term, speculative behaviour by investors more concerned with whether a company's share price will rise or fall over the next days or weeks than with whether the company is undertaking a fundamentally useful and viable line of business.

After the failed experiments with "free love" in the 1960s, it was discovered that too much "liquidity" could be bad for human relationships. Instead of sticking with a relationship and trying to solve its problems, participants (usually the men!) would simply head for the exits. The same pattern is promoted, in financial terms, by a stock market that reduces the relationship between financial investors and the companies they supposedly bankroll to the "no-strings" status of a one-night stand.

Other financial relationships that are less liquid may actually be more amenable to a longer-term, cooperative working-out of problems, and to the adoption of longer-term planning horizons on the part of both investors and company managers. In particular, stock markets in continental Europe are relatively unimportant compared to the size of their respective economies. The Europeans (and to a lesser extent the Japanese) rely on a system in which large banks channel household savings into equity placements in various companies. This seems to allow for a longer-term outlook on the part of company management, which is less constrained by fear that short-term declines in share prices will slash executive compensation or spark revolt among shareholders.

In conclusion, it is clear that problems in the structure of financial ownership in Canada—both its concentration among a well-off elite of households, and its predominant existence in the form of tradeable securities that bear no direct relationship to the real investment projects which are supposedly the end goal of the whole process—have contributed importantly to the failure of Canada's financial system to put money into real economic motion.

The attention of that narrow segment of society which owns significant financial wealth has been distracted from the all-important task of facilitating real investment projects and hence fuelling real growth and job-creation, in favour of generating often-illusory profits from the buying and selling of paper assets.

The next chapter will now consider the implications of the chronic fragility of those paper markets for the rest of the economy.

Chapter 13
Fragility: The Booms and
Busts of the Casino Economy

Hyman Minsky was an American economist in the Keynesian tradition, who first coined the concept of "financial fragility." In a 1982 book provocatively titled *Can 'It' Happen Again?*, Minsky described the precise mechanics of the market's seemingly perpetual boom-and-bust cycle. He showed how stock markets can feed on their own momentum to reach heights completely unjustified by the fundamental conditions of the underlying real economy—and then how the process can quickly and destructively reverse itself, leading to financial collapse and real economic contraction.

Minsky revisited the experience of the 1929 market panic and the subsequent Great Depression. He concluded that, despite the improvements in financial regulation and management techniques that have been implemented since 1929, "it" (namely, financial market crisis followed by deep recession) could and most likely *would* happen again.[1]

Minsky died in 1996, an outsider within the economics profession despite the creativity and relevance of his research. Ironically, his name—and his theories—would be invoked more in the two years following his death than they were during his entire professional career. Within a few months of his death, the Asian financial crisis had begun in earnest, its arrival heralded by the devaluation of Thailand's currency in July 1997. Within a few more months, the crisis had become clearly global in nature: Russian default, Brazilian devaluation, and chaotic uncertainty in other financial markets.

With one-third of the world economy in a finance-induced recession, and many countries (such as Indonesia, South Korea, Russia, and Brazil) experiencing contractions in output as severe as was experienced in North America during the 1930s, "it" had clearly happened again.[2] Minsky had not lived to be able to say, "I told you so"—not that he would have taken any pleasure in doing so, given the enormous human toll of this most spectacular failure of private finance in 60 years. But even if he were still alive, it's not at all clear that the barons of finance would be any more receptive to his ideas and arguments. Even as national economies in Asia, Latin America, and Eastern Europe were falling like dominoes, U.S. stock markets continued to reach for record highs.

Indeed, for a while it seemed that nothing could faze the markets, not even sober words from the chairman of the U.S. Federal Reserve, Alan Greenspan. Greenspan had sparked a one-day worldwide stock market crash in December 1996 when he decried the "irrational exuberance" that seemed to be propelling stock markets to levels completely out of touch with the concrete economic circumstances of the companies listed on them. Investors had feared that Greenspan would back up his words with actions—in the form of higher interest rates—to prick the stock market bubble.

Later on, Greenspan almost single-handedly prevented a truly global financial catastrophe by cutting interest rates three times in six weeks late in 1998, slowing down the massive flows of financial capital into the U.S. economy that were rocking markets and currencies around the planet. He took this action despite "tight" labour market conditions in the U.S. (the unemployment rate had fallen to just above 4% at the time, sparking concern in many quarters about future inflation), which is usually a sure indication that interest rates will be increased, not cut.

Then, in January 1999, Greenspan appeared before the influential Ways and Means Committee of the U.S. House of Representatives, and warned once again that share prices were unsustainable. With a central banker's typical reserve, Greenspan warned that "the level of equity prices would appear to envision substantially greater growth of profits than has been experienced of late." Greenspan even likened investments in soaring Internet-related stocks to a lottery. This time, however, the markets treated Greenspan like the boy who cried wolf: not a peep from investors, who continued to buy and sell shares of companies at prices that could never possibly be justified by the concrete earnings potential of their real-world operations.

Greed had truly vanquished fear. As long as investors kept faith that prices would continue to rise, new funds poured into the stock exchanges and—lo and behold—prices kept rising. But how long can markets continue to ascend to new heights on the sole strength of the optimism of investors that markets will continue to rise? The entire process is suspended by its own bootstraps. How long can traders in New York and other developed financial centres continue to blissfully ignore spreading misery and hardship in vast portions of the globe? And when the whole process turns around, what will be the consequences for the *real* economy?

The Inherent Logic of Boom and Bust

The general concept of "financial fragility" can be described as follows: The rise (and fall) of asset market valuations can become detached from the market's real economic underpinnings, yet also can have important real economic consequences. Stock markets and other asset markets alternate between booms inspired by hope, faith, and greed on the part of investors betting on a continued rise in asset prices, and subsequent crises of confidence on the part of those same investors when it appears that asset prices might fall.

This boom-and-bust process can occur independently of the underlying economic fundamentals of the particular companies involved, yet ironically the cycle can have important effects that extend beyond the paper economy to the real investment of real capital and the real production of goods and services. The financial ups and downs are entangled in a complex, dynamic web of relationships between asset prices (like stock and bond prices), interest rates, and the subjective confidence of company managers and consumers in the real economy. Economic growth itself becomes subject to the whims of the markets.

A potential for financial crisis arises any time a gap emerges between the concrete value of real-world wealth (including capital equipment, buildings, factories, homes, infrastructure, and land) and the financial representations of that wealth (embodied in the value of stocks, bonds, and other paper assets). As was described in Chapter 2, the paper economy and the real economy in Canada have travelled in fundamentally different directions since about 1981. The paper economy was spurred on by anti-inflation policy, steady real financial returns, government retrenchment, and financial industry deregulation. But the real economy staggered in the face of exactly the same factors: high interest rates, government downsizing, and stagnant consumer purchasing power.

As financial valuations become increasingly out-of-touch with their real underpinnings, the risk grows that those valuations might suddenly and painfully come back to earth. How this *potential* for financial crisis is converted into the *reality* of paper boom and bust was the object of Hyman Minsky's inquiries. So we will examine in somewhat more detail the concrete mechanics of how financial balloons expand, how they eventually burst—and the consequences of this boom-and-bust cycle for investment and growth in the real economy.

How can such intangible factors as swings in the mood of investors carry such dramatic consequences for financial markets, and for the real economies which depend on them? The answer lies in the very nature of easily-traded financial assets whose prices fluctuate on a day-to-day basis. Financial assets turn over at a remarkable pace: on average, each stock, bond, or currency is bought and sold dozens of times in its lifetime. The potential profits that can be captured through this eternal buying and selling often become more important than the original purpose of the financial asset in the first place: to finance some real economic activity by a company or a government.

Buying low and selling high becomes the prime motive force for financial market activity, rather than the raising and allocating of capital for real economic purposes that is stressed in the economics textbooks. By buying assets in the hope that their prices will increase (allowing them to sell at a later point for a profit), financial investors can set in motion a self-fulfilling and circular chain of events that culminates in a financial bubble. If it seems that the price of an asset (a particular company's shares, or the value of a specific currency) is on its way up, more investors buy it. This, in and of itself, pushes the price up even further, motivating still greater investor interest.

Figure 13-1 illustrates the various chains of causation that together can help to inflate a financial bubble. The mere fact of an initial rise in asset prices will spark investor interest. It almost doesn't matter what caused that initial rise in prices—whether a real factor (such as lower interest rates, which makes the ownership of stocks seem more appealing, or higher corporate profits) or a purely subjective one (like the seemingly metaphysical faith in the value of Internet companies which propelled the U.S. Nasdaq stock market to truly ludicrous heights, completely unjustified on grounds of real corporate profitability, in the late 1990s).

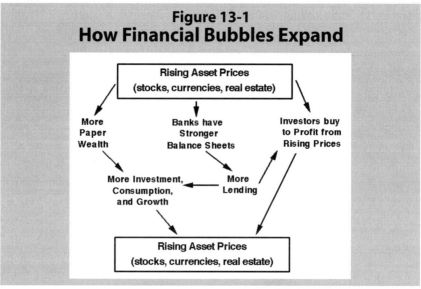

Figure 13-1
How Financial Bubbles Expand

All that matters is that prices rose, and some group of initial investors became wealthier (at least on paper). Those investors, encouraged by capital gains earned from rising prices, keep on buying—and that buying, in and of itself, pushes prices up higher. More importantly, other investors then want to get in on the act.

The unprecedented degree of transparency and competitiveness in the financial industry has clearly contributed to a herd mentality on the part of investors. Many personal investors check their mutual fund scores daily. If it seems that their fund is lagging others, perhaps because its managers were slow to jump on the latest market bandwagon, they will start to think about moving their money elsewhere. The pressure on fund managers is intense not to miss the next "big score": the next Yahoo! Inc., or Amazon.Com, or America Online Inc., companies whose exponential growth in market value single-handedly propelled those mutual funds which picked them as winners early on into the highest ranks of the industry.

Studies suggest that many money managers will invest in trendy market prospects in spite of their own skepticism about their genuine economic value, solely out of fear that their apparent performance relative to other money managers would be dragged down by having missed out on the spectacular rise of particular stocks.[3]

This self-fulfilling process of pure asset market speculation is represented on the far right side of Figure 13-1. If the price of an asset is rising, investors will buy it to profit from that price rise, and that sends the price soaring even higher. But there is much more to the rise or fall of market bubbles than just this simple process of self-feeding speculation. Indeed, if the manias and panics of financial markets were limited in their causes and consequences to merely the participants of those markets, then the problem of financial instability would not be nearly as great as it is. Investors who purchased a share purely on faith that its price would rise would sooner or later be burned when that expectation turned out to be wrong. Some investors would win (generally those who were ahead of the mass movements of the market in general), others would lose (those who, like forlorn puppies, followed the rest of the market one step behind, and one step too late). But the overall process would be a self-contained, zero-sum casino. Those who refuse to bet their life savings on such a silly, unproductive game could be forgiven for saying, "So what?" Like paramutual betting or slot machines, if some people want to waste their money on pure gambling, let them.

In fact, however, there are important channels which link asset market valuations (and the speculative behaviour they inspire) to the decision-making that drives real investment and the real production of real goods and services. And a complex process of feedback between the real economy and the paper economy both fuels the manic behaviour of the financial investors and explains why their actions have important consequences that extend well beyond the trading floors. These feedback links are also illustrated in Figure 13-1.

For example, rising market values mean that market participants—both individuals and companies—look wealthier, at least on paper. To a certain extent, the growth of *apparent* paper wealth in the accounts of those individuals and companies will encourage them to spend more on real investment projects or consumer goods. This leads to expanding business, new growth and investment, and higher corporate profits. But higher corporate profits in turn lead to a further rise in asset values, and the circular process repeats itself. Rising stock markets in the mid- and late-1990s, for example, seem to have had a significant "wealth effect" in inspiring more household spending by some consumers (at least by those fortunate enough to possess large financial portfolios).

The private banking system also plays an important role in both facilitating financial expansion and channelling the impacts of that expansion into the real economy. Indeed, one of Minsky's key insights was that modern, ultra-sophisticated financial institutions actually *worsen* the problem of financial fragility by flexibly providing resources to fuel the rise of bubbles, but then withdrawing those resources in immediate and damaging ways when the bubbles inevitably collapse.

As described in Chapter 3, private banks are literally allowed to create money in the form of new loans to their customers. But how much money they are allowed to create depends on their own internal financial reserves. If a bank is financially strong (with ample cash reserves, and a valuable portfolio of good loans and other assets), it is allowed to expand its lending. This in turn injects newly-created credit into the real economy, fuelling spending, demand, and job-creation. But if a bank is financially weak, it must cut back on its lending (lest worried customers start a "run" on the bank). This translates into less spending, stagnant demand, and unemployment.

During periods of financial expansion, private banks literally have more money than they know what to do with. Rising stock market values enhance the apparent worth of the banks' own reserve assets. They also make the banks' clients appear more credit-worthy, since both individual and corporate borrowers have more apparent wealth in the market to hold up as collateral. In boom times, banks will even lend to speculators who use the credit to buy financial assets, thus driving up markets even further. Low interest rates and an expanding economy reduce the likelihood of defaults, bankruptcies, and non-performing loans. The bottom-line result is that the balance-sheet strength of private banks improves spectacularly with rising asset market prices, and this encourages profit-seeking banks to expand their lending even more.

Figure 13-2
How Financial Bubbles Collapse

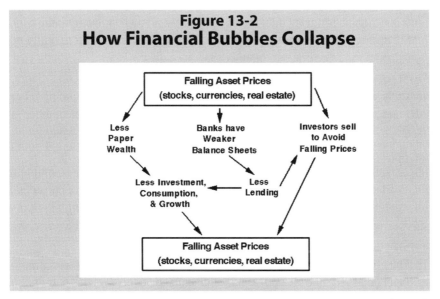

This positive mechanism came neatly into play in Canada through the mid-to late-1990s, as Canada's banks responded to strong financial market conditions with an unprecedented expansion of private credit. According to the broadest measures, total credit in Canada's economy grew by an average of over 10% per year between 1992 and 1997—far faster than the expansion of real output. This explosion of lending boosted both the profits of the banks (who, after all, earn money from the interest rate differential charged on each new loan) and the Canadian economy in general (which badly needed injections of credit-financed spending power in the wake of ongoing government and corporate downsizing). The only hitch is that the whole credit creation engine can be quickly slammed into reverse once the financial economy starts to turn down.

Indeed, as illustrated in Figure 13-2, all avenues of causation in the Minskian model of financial fragility work just as powerfully on the way down as they do on the way up. If asset prices start to fall, investors bail out. This creates a self-fulfilling prophecy: the mere *fear* that asset prices might fall can single-handedly *cause* them to fall. Big losses for those investors who didn't jump ship immediately accelerate the outward rush of capital. Money managers are pressed to join the stampede for the exits, regardless of whether the new market lows are justified by economic fundamentals, because they will score abysmally in the mutual fund scorecards if they don't.

As the former paper wealth which companies and individuals *thought* they possessed suddenly disappears, they in turn cut back on their real investment and consumer spending. Ironically, this slows down the real economy, reducing real corporate profits and hence further undermining asset prices. The "wealth effect" on consumption spending can have a particularly counterproductive influence during times of financial downturn. Personal investors who see much of the value of their portfolio suddenly disappear might suddenly conclude that they'd better start saving for retirement again (rather than counting on inflating stock markets to do the job for them). Household consumption spending is cut back, and personal savings may grow even as income levels and employment are starting to decline.

The ironic and destructive outcome may be Keynes's famous "paradox of thrift," which was introduced in Chapter 10: the simultaneous efforts by millions of individuals to save more money may collectively backfire. Reduced consumption spending translates into falling demand, higher unemployment, lower incomes, and hence lower savings—even for the same households that were trying desperately to increase their savings.

The private banking system, too, adds momentum to the downward spiral of the paper economy, and also powerfully transmits the consequences of that spiral to actors in the real economy. When markets contract, banks retrench in order to conserve their internal reserves. This creates a "credit crunch" that sends shock waves through the whole economy. Banks attempt to maximize their survival chances during a downturn by slowing new lending, and even pulling back some existing loans. Consumers and companies are left with less to spend on real goods and services. This contributes to a downturn in real economic activity, which ironically increases the likelihood of defaults on bank loans. Perversely, then, a risk-averse response to financial contraction by individual banks—who stop lending to protect reserves—actually *increases* the general default risk that the banks collectively face. Once again the seemingly rational and self-serving acts of individual market players produces perverse and irrational consequences in the aggregate.

Speculators also face a credit crunch as a consequence of financial implosion, and their ability to borrow money to play the markets is sharply constrained. This can further accelerate the collapse of asset prices. Perhaps the most spectacular example of the role of private banking in fuelling financial speculation was the rise and fall of Long Term Capital Management, a U.S.-based hedge fund (run by two winners of the Nobel Prize in Economics, no less). Through bank borrowing and other loans, the company leveraged initial equity investments of

Panic in an Orderly Fashion, Please

"A balloon that has been punctured does not deflate in an orderly way."
—John Kenneth Galbraith,
The Great Crash, 1929

$5 billion (U.S.) into a total war chest for speculative bets that many observers believed totalled an incredible $1 trillion (U.S.).

When the fund collapsed in September 1998 because of a huge wrong bet placed on interest rate differentials between bond issues in different countries, it threatened to bring down several major U.S. financial institutions with it: banks which had loaned unsecured credit to these high-tech gamblers, in many cases probably not even knowing what the money was being used for.

The U.S. Federal Reserve arranged for a high-powered private-sector bail-out of Long Term Capital Management and its lenders, and this probably helped to avoid a real financial catastrophe. But it simultaneously undermined the credibility of standard U.S. arguments that the Asian financial crisis was the result of "crony capitalism" and other non-arm's-length banking practices. Smug American regulators initially claimed that Asian-style financial difficulties would never occur in the U.S. system, since financial transactions in the U.S. economy are dominated by arm's-length, bottom line transactions rather than the complex institutionally and culturally mediated links between lenders and borrowers that characterized many Asian economies (especially prior to the financial deregulation of those economies in the early 1990s).

But the rise to prominence of Long Term Capital Management, as well as its ultimate rescue, typified U.S. crony capitalism at its finest. Perhaps there is something in the fundamental structure of speculative finance, rather than the nationality of its practitioners, which is at the root of the problem.

In all of these ways, the behaviour of a private for-profit banking system may be the greatest source of the real economic damage that is caused by the bursting of financial bubbles.

Minsky's Lessons

The analytical conclusions of Hyman Minsky's model of financial fragility can be summarized in the following three insights. First, wealth itself is a macroeconomic *variable* in any system in which that wealth is stored in the form of financial assets with instantaneously variable prices. This in itself is a rather startling admission. We usually think of "wealth" as a steady stockpile of accumulated value: a reliable reserve to fall back on during tough times. But when wealth consists largely of marketable securities that are held not for their inherent worth, but because they can be sold later for capital gains, then wealth itself becomes something that rises and falls with the other economic tides. Far from being a cushion which helps to smooth out fluctuations in income, employment, or production, sudden shifts in the market value of that wealth actually *contribute* to those fluctuations.

Second, financial intermediation—the actions of banks, brokers, speculators, and money managers—actually intensifies the swings of asset markets driven by the fickle and subjective sentiments of investors. Like a cash machine installed in the lobby of a casino, the financial system makes massive new resources available to gamblers desperate to cash in on the hoped-for profits of the paper boom. But as soon as the banks and other financial intermediaries begin to fear that their loans may not be repaid, those financial resources are snatched back. The automatic teller machine starts flashing: "No funds available." The resulting contraction of liquidity and purchasing power is a heavy blow to an economy that was already staggering.

Finally, Minsky's most worrisome conclusion was to note that financial instability carries important real economic consequences. Financial markets are not quarantined casinos. Both their manias and their crises have powerful consequences for the real economy, where real people work to produce real goods and services of real value. When financial markets are on their way up, those channels of influence tend to be benign, or even positive: more spending, more optimism, more liquidity to finance the investing activities of actual businesses. On the way down, however, financial fragility implies negative and potentially severe outcomes in the real economy.

As noted, the evaporating paper wealth of individual market players throws cold water over their personal spending. The willingness of financial suppliers to issue new equities or bonds to finance real investment projects by non-financial businesses can also quickly disappear. Combined with a credit crunch within the private banking system, this can severely hamper the efforts of companies to put money into motion in the real economy. Investors and consumers alike may suffer a general blow to their subjective confidence levels. If enough of them respond to that blow by deciding to sock spare cash away for a rainy day, that defensive response alone can be enough to make the dreaded rainy day a reality.

Government can play a positive or negative role in times of financial crisis, either adding to or offsetting the contraction in private-sector economic activity that is the expected result of financial downturn. Some short-sighted governments will respond to financial market turbulence by battening down their own fiscal hatches, fearing the effects of economic slowdown on the government's own financial situation. As described in Chapter 9, any economic slowdown automatically causes a worsening of the government's budget balance, due both to falling tax revenues and to expanded payments for programs such as unemployment insurance. If governments are committed to avoiding deficits at all costs—and this seems to have been the unfortunate and myopic political legacy

Market as Beast

"What curious, hyper-sensitive beasts the financial markets can be."
—Douglas Goold, *Globe and Mail* financial columnist
February 22, 1996

"Bond markets are volatile creatures that can wreak havoc."
—Andrew Willis, *Globe and Mail* financial columnist
March 12, 1996

"This is kind of like throwing raw meat to a wild animal."
—Robert Brusca, Chief Economist, Nikko Securities
re U.S. plan to invest pension funds on stock market
January 20, 1998

Does society *really* want to cede control over its economic destiny to hyper-sensitive beasts, volatile creatures, and wild animals?

of a decade of radical budget-cutting in Canada—then it will be tempted to respond to a private-sector slowdown with its *own* belt-tightening.

This, of course, will only deepen the recession: now the layoffs of private-sector workers are supplemented by cuts in public service jobs, and the decline of consumer spending power and confidence is made all the worse. Governments which behave in this manner actually exacerbate the boom-and-bust pattern of private markets, by cutting back public spending to balance the books when times are already tough, but loosening the fiscal taps when the private economy is doing relatively well.[4]

Sadly, Canada's federal government took this tack in the wake of the Asian-led financial meltdown of the late 1990s. Finance Minister Paul Martin maintained a strict cap on new spending initiatives, even though his government was generating significant financial surpluses beginning in fiscal 1996. In his October 1998 fiscal update, Martin pointed to the unexpected impact of the Asian crisis as justification for this continuing caution: "The dramatic downward revision in [growth] forecasts illustrates more clearly than anything why this government must stick to its careful approach to budget planning." In fact, the government went on to rake in a financial surplus for fiscal 1998 of some $10 billion, despite the economic slowdown that year, and thus the fiscal stinginess of Martin and his government was both unnecessary and counterproductive.

Other economists would argue that it is precisely when the private-sector economy encounters turbulence that government should do its bit to support employment and purchasing power. By putting too much emphasis on balancing its budget, every year, at all costs, government can cause more harm than good. Indeed, perhaps the greatest single policy conclusion that Minsky himself drew from his research was the need for aggressive counter-cyclical behaviour on the part of governments and, even more crucially, by central bankers.

To limit the damage caused by the changing moods of financial investors, governments need to step in with offsetting and countervailing measures. Deficit-financed government spending can help to support output and employment during times of financial contraction. And aggressive cuts in interest rates and other forms of monetary stimulus by central bankers can play a similarly important role in limiting and reversing the crunch in private credit that is a usual consequence of financial implosion. Fortunately, U.S. central banker Alan Greenspan seems to have read more of Minsky than has Paul Martin. It was Greenspan's aggressive loosening of monetary policy in the autumn of 1998 that helped to shake some sense back into panicked financial markets. Mind you, it was also Greenspan's earlier pro-active *tightening* of monetary policy, when he hiked U.S. interest rates on the mere apprehension of an uptick in inflation, that helped to send the whole system careening off the rails; so the man shouldn't be nominated for economic sainthood just yet.

Several other sometimes startling policy conclusions can also be drawn from a Minskian understanding of the causes and consequences of financial fragility. For example, one response to the persistent and painful instability of private finance might be to increase the economic scope of *public* finance, which is not likely to be as prone to flights of subjective fancy among gain-seeking investors. Interestingly, this provides an argument for maintaining a certain ongoing share of total financial wealth in the form of government bonds, and hence for maintaining a permanent level of government indebtedness within the economy.

This runs contrary to the apparent conclusion of the balanced-budget militants who so strongly influenced Canadian fiscal policy during the 1990s: namely, that the best level of government debt is no debt at all. They want governments to pay off the existing debt as quickly as possible through the maintenance of significant annual budget surpluses. Even the less militant fall-back position of fiscal conservatives—that the budget should be balanced, year in and year out, regardless of the state of the overall economy—implies a debt burden that shrinks steadily toward zero (measured as a share of GDP); when budgets are balanced so that the cash value of outstanding debt stops growing, the relative economic importance of the debt must inevitably decline as the economy grows. In other words, for conservatives the "optimal debt level" of government is zero.

Why governments should be so inherently different from other economic actors—such as companies and home-owners, all of whom normally maintain a certain level of debt in order to finance efficient investment activity—is not clear. And an understanding of the mechanics and consequences of financial panics suggests that having a significant stockpile of government debt on hand at all times may actually be a good thing. To be sure, the prices of government bonds rise and fall with investor expectations regarding interest rates, the credit-worthiness of governments, and other factors. But in general the market for government debt is far more stable and predictable than other asset markets (like stock markets or foreign exchange markets). And, by relying more on "grassroots" forms of debt-financing (such as Canada Savings Bonds), those debt markets could be made even less volatile.

Moreover, government bonds provide a calming "safe haven" for investors during times of financial market panic. Fearing a market meltdown, many investors will park their money in government bonds during times of crisis, which is why bond prices may actually *rise* during the panic, especially if central banks cut interest rates in response to financial market turbulence.[5] The damage caused by regular outbreaks of private financial chaos will therefore be limited if a larger proportion of financial wealth is owned in forms (such as government bonds) which are less susceptible to that chaos.

The potentially positive role of government debt in these circumstances was illustrated vividly during the global crisis of 1998. Driven by fear of plunging asset values in many emerging markets, as well as a desire to profit from the subsequent rise in the U.S. dollar, financial investors around the world snapped up U.S. government bonds in record volumes. Resale prices of those bonds soared, accentuating the downward pressure on U.S. interest rates (the decline in which was itself a major stabilizing influence on the global economy).

Imagine what would have occurred if the U.S. government had followed the advice of fiscal conservatives throughout the 1970s and 1980s, and had maintained balanced budgets instead of running large and chronic deficits. The huge stockpile of government debt which helped to calm global markets in 1998 would not have existed, in essence closing the gates to an important safe harbour just as financial investors needed it most. The flight into safe Canadian bonds on the part of financial investors was also significant, although somewhat less dramatic, during the same period. How ironic that financial investors should look upon government debt as the safest asset to hold, after years of (falsely) proclaiming that spendthrift governments were teetering on the verge of bankruptcy!

So the chronic fragility of private financial markets provides a strong argument for maintaining a significant stock of government debt as a tool for stabilizing and lubricating financial market functioning. Interestingly, this debt should optimally be measured in relation to the overall stock of financial assets in an economy (as would be suggested by a school of financial economics known as "portfolio theory"). This is different from how economists typically measure the economic significance of government debt, which is as a ratio of debt to a coun-

Lies and Damned Lies

"The markets do not lie."

> —Sherry Cooper
> Chief Economist, Nesbitt Burns
> January 17, 1999

Stock market valuation of SkyMall Inc., December 24, 1998: $58.5 million (U.S.)
Stock market valuation of SkyMall Inc., December 28, 1998: $320 million (U.S.)

TSE share price, Cartaway Resources Corp., May 8, 1996: $4
TSE share price, Cartaway Resources Corp., May 17, 1996: $23
TSE share price, Cartaway Resources Corp., May 21, 1996: $2

NASDAQ share price, Navarre Corp., 9:30 am, November 30, 1998: $27 (U.S.)
NASDAQ share price, Navarre Corp., 10:45 am, November 30, 1998: $13 (U.S.)
NASDAQ share price, Navarre Corp., 12:30 pm, November 30, 1998: $21 (U.S.)
NASDAQ share price, Navarre Corp., 4:00 pm, November 30, 1998: $15 (U.S.)

try's GDP. The debt-to-GDP ratio is an appropriate way of measuring a country's ability to service its debt and the relative importance of debt-servicing charges. But an alternative ratio, the "debt-to-wealth" ratio, may be more relevant for the issue of financial fragility and government's potential role in calming it.

As of the end of 1997, for example, government debt of various kinds accounted for less than 15% of total financial wealth in Canada. Indeed, this proportion was already falling significantly during the latter half of the 1990s, as most Canadian governments balanced their budgets and stopped issuing new debt, while the total value of private financial assets continued to boom. In the interests of financial stability, this "debt-to-wealth" ratio should probably not fall much further. As the supply of government bonds available to financial investors continues to dry up, investors will place more and more of their available funds into instruments—especially equities—that are vulnerable to a fundamentally higher degree of market instability. Indeed, the diversion of new funds from now-shrinking bond markets into stock markets has been a factor in driving those stock markets to dizzying heights, and this only increases the risk of subsequent financial implosion.

It is almost jarring to compare this potentially *stabilizing* function of government debt with the traditional view that government indebtedness is a huge source of market uncertainty. This claim was always overstated—especially during the deficit-ridden early 1990s, when many conservatives warned hysterically about Canada "hitting the debt wall" or even having our finances taken over by the International Monetary Fund (IMF). As it turns out, it is the instability of private financial markets, not the "fiscal irresponsibility" of governments, that is the source of our greater structural difficulties.

The maintenance of consistent volumes of government debt, measured as a proportion of total financial assets, need not imply ongoing profligacy on the part of Canadian finance ministers (although it certainly suggests that governments have more fiscal leeway, especially during tough economic times, than is typically supposed in the post-deficit political landscape). Governments could carry a *gross* stockpile of debt, while simultaneously maintaining a strong *net* financial position, if some of that debt is offset by government investments in other lasting assets (including both other financial assets and real economic assets, such as Crown corporations, public infrastructure, and social facilities). This would allow government to continue to play a significant and stabilizing role in financial markets, without incurring the large net interest expenses and other problems associated with a large *net* debt burden.[6]

There are other ways in which the scope of public finance could be expanded in Canada, as a means of limiting the importance of the private asset markets whose fragility poses increasing economic dangers. For example, Chapter 16 of this book will argue that a public system for financing investment projects in the real economy (including non-profit and community-based projects) would be more efficient than the complex and incredibly expensive network of private financial intermediation as a means of putting money into economic motion.

In addition to expanding the sphere of public or non-profit financial intermediation, government can also take measures to limit the economic (and social) scope of private asset markets. For example, the whole "stock-marketization" of many Canadian social programs during the 1990s—reflected in the growth of private RRSPs instead of public pensions, and the use of securitized investments and private RESPs (Registered Education Savings Plans) to support university students—represents a regrettable and unnecessary subsidy to the realm of private finance.

Quite apart from the dubious social and distributional consequences of this approach to social policy (since any program rooted in private investments, like RRSPs and RESPs, will inevitably benefit high-income earners at the expense of those Canadians whose portfolios are small or non-existent), it may also increase the vulnerability of society in general to financial panics. Subsidized financial investments, including those conducted in the name of social policy, initially help to push asset prices skyward. But during the inevitable contraction that must follow, even such matters as retirement security and access to higher education become contingent on the state of the markets.

Many other important measures can be taken to regulate and stabilize markets which, left to their own devices, repeatedly produce cycles of unjustified expansion followed by dramatic and painful collapse. Several of these policy issues will be considered in the final chapters of this book.

Profiting from Volatility[7]

One of the most disturbing aspects of the inherent fragility of private asset markets is the extent to which the constant volatility of asset prices has attracted the creative attention of financial entrepreneurs intent on finding new and ever-more sophisticated means of profiting from that volatility. The real economic purposes to which the resources represented by these paper assets are supposed to be dedicated fade so far into the background as to become virtually invisible. The main interest of the financiers is focused instead on how to profit from the ongoing market churning of those paper assets.

In order to make speculative gains from changes in asset prices, it really doesn't matter whether prices are rising or falling—as long as they aren't standing still. And, ironically, the incredible technical innovations which have been developed to help traders capture speculative gains seem to have intensified the underlying volatility of the markets being played. So the entire process, like so many others in the realm of the paper economy, becomes self-fulfilling: the interest of traders in profiting from price changes actually makes those price changes more frequent and dramatic, which in turn further piques the desire of traders to profit from that now-amplified volatility.

The tools and techniques used in the course of betting on the markets have become truly mind-boggling. Much of the action occurs not in the direct markets for stocks and bonds, but rather in the markets for various associated *derivative* products: financial assets, typically quite short-term in nature, whose value is linked to the prices of corporate equities, bonds, interest rates, exchange rates, or any other economic variable.[8] The general category called derivatives includes a wide range of specific assets such as futures, options, forwards, and swaps. What they have in common is that none represents the actual ownership of an asset (like a stock or a bond). Rather, they represent an agreement between two parties on some subsequent exchange of money or assets, the terms of which will depend on intervening changes in asset prices, interest rates, or exchange rates.

For example, a "futures" contract represents an agreement by an individual or company to sell a specified quantity of some commodity or asset at a specified price at a specified future date. The futures contract itself then takes on a financial life of its own—quite independent of the actual future delivery of the commodity or the asset in question—since its resale value depends on the difference between the agreed-upon price and the price that actually prevails on the date when the real exchange takes place. Some time prior to the contract date, the futures contract is extinguished through payment of this difference. Like a spawning salmon at the end of its upstream journey, the futures contract has finally fulfilled its life's purpose: the securitization of uncertainty regarding a certain asset price. The futures contract then dies.

Similarly, an "option" represents the right to purchase an asset or a commodity at some date in the future, at a certain specified price. Stock options are now commonly used as an important incentive in executive compensation. By issuing an option to purchase its own shares at, say, $25 each, a company creates a powerful incentive for its executives to do everything in their power to increase share prices above the $25 level, since the value of the option will equal the excess of the market price prevailing when the option is exercised, over the pre-set option price.

If a CEO succeeds in pushing the share price up to $30, each option allows her to buy $30 worth of shares for $25, and hence carries a $5 value.[9] Considering that CEOs are regularly provided with hundreds of thousands or even millions of stock options as part of their overall compensation, stock options are a powerful way of ensuring that executives keep the shareholders' interests paramount—instead of being distracted by other concerns such as community welfare or employment security for workers.

Derivatives can be combined in different complicated ways which amplify the sums that can potentially be earned (or lost) from the ongoing volatility of the markets. The only limit is the imagination of the clever analysts and traders whose job it is to invent new instruments and new ways of trading them. For example, "knock-out" options are a special form of option contract in which the option to buy the asset in question becomes invalid if the price of the asset moves outside of a specified range. This can lead to sudden and dramatic shifts in asset markets when a set of options is "knocked-out," because investors are forced to make sudden portfolio adjustments to protect themselves. Volatility breeds volatility.

Similarly, a "straddle" option involves betting that a stock or other asset will trade outside of a previously specified price range. If the price rises above or falls below the range, the bet pays off: the investor need not care whether the market rises or falls, as long as it does something—and the more dramatic the better. Like a jittery, impatient three-year-old, the paper economy can handle anything except inactivity and quiescence. By focusing leveraged sums of money on narrowly defined bets on otherwise innocuous price movements, speculators can reap huge gains when markets move the right way or the right amount. But the losses can be equally huge, even limitless, if the unexpected occurs.

Even the weather itself has sparked new high-tech forms of derivative trading. "Investors" can place bets on whether a particular winter will be cold or warm. The weather is economically relevant, of course, since it affects the real prospects of companies whose businesses are in one way or another weather-dependent (such as heating oil companies, snowboard and snowmobile manufacturers, and even shopping malls). And, true to form, clever financial professionals have devised a financial instrument, called a "weather derivative," which can be bought and sold on the "weather market," and whose value will fluctuate according to the weather patterns which actually entail.

Many of the participants in the weather derivatives market are real businesses, not speculators, who are attempting to use market hedging techniques as a complicated way of buying insurance against weather-related risks. What is new, however, is the extent to which these weather-related factors can now become economically embodied in the form of a tradeable security, opening up interesting and lucrative new opportunities for profit-making—whether from changes in prices of the "weather assets" themselves, or at least from the commissions which are charged on each trade.

In the modern paper economy, it seems, any source of change or uncertainty, even the weather itself, holds great potential as a new arena of securitization. The whole game is premised on an inability to predict the future. God help the derivatives traders if anyone ever invents an accurate crystal ball—or, worse yet, if deliberate regulations or policies should ever impart stability and predictability to the operation of financial markets. Fear of the unknown is the energy which fuels this ongoing fire. If the unknown should become known, then the game would be over.

How ironic, then, that derivative markets supposedly premised on fear of the unknown—such as the risks associated with the weather—have themselves introduced so much uncertainty and risk into the economic system. And how perverse that some of the most creative and intelligent people in society have devoted themselves to the lucrative yet ultimately unproductive task of inventing still more convoluted ways of profiting from uncertainty and insecurity.

It must be noted that not all of the investors who participate in this hyperactive process of financial roulette are "gamblers" in the pure sense of the word. In fact, only a relatively small group of the buyers and sellers of financial assets and derivatives are short-term speculators in the strictest sense of the word—that is, investors who are intent on buying and selling an asset or derivative in short order purely to profit from a price change in the interim. Many derivative investments are undertaken by other investors and even by real businesses who wish to protect themselves against unforeseen changes in the prices of assets or commodities which are crucial to their financial well-being.

For example, most oil companies participate in derivatives markets as a means of "hedging" their bets on future unforeseen changes in the price of oil; through the skillful use of futures contracts and other derivatives, oil producers can "lock in" certain prices for their future output, and hence insure themselves against unforseen declines in oil prices. The same practice is common in other industries.

This defensive use of derivatives does not imply, however, that these ultra-sophisticated financial instruments are therefore serving a productive and efficiency-enhancing purpose. Even non-speculative participants in derivatives markets are attempting to protect themselves against the effects of market fragility. Yet the expansion of financial intermediation, represented in the extreme by the design and trading of multi-layered derivatives, is itself a major cause of that fragility. The mere fact that the consequences of financial turbulence are so severe that more and more agents are drawn to derivatives, simply to protect themselves against that same turbulence, is but one more absurd manifestation of the circular, self-consuming nature of the entire system.

Gangsters, too, can often enlist the participation of honest merchants in their protection rackets, collecting "insurance premiums" to ensure that no unexpected "disasters" befall local businesses. But this does not imply that, by offering protection against these purely contrived and preventable disasters, the gangsters are serving a legitimate insurance function. The legitimate "need" for derivatives would largely disappear if the underlying risks of financial fragility abated, yet the booming markets for derivatives (the total outstanding value of which surpassed an incredible $30 trillion by 1998) are themselves part and parcel of that fragility.

Tea Leaves

As the financial economy has become more and more obsessed with zero-sum speculative trading gains, it becomes more and more important for brokers and

Think Big

"The challenge facing any hedge fund is to profit on very small price movements. The solution is to make very large bets."
—Andrew Willis, *Globe and Mail* financial columnist
September 30, 1998

Total capital actually invested in Long Term Capital Management, September 1998: About $5 billion (U.S.)

Total bets placed by Long Term Capital Management, September 1998: About $1 trillion (U.S.)

money managers to try to predict the moods and future actions of *other* market participants. This is why the thousands of economists and analysts employed within the industry spend less time analyzing the real economic factors which should in theory affect the market price of an asset (like the real productivity and profitability of a company, for instance), and more time trying to anticipate the next moves of other investors. All kinds of outlandish and superstitious notions come into play in this guessing game, which comes to resemble an "infinite loop" in a poorly-designed computer program: investors are trying to predict the actions of other investors, who in turn are trying to predict the actions of the original investors, and around and around it goes.

For example, many market analysts believe that October is typically a bad month for stock prices. It is quite irrelevant whether there is any real economic justification for this belief; if enough market analysts are convinced that October is a bad month for stock prices, then October *will* be a bad month for stock prices. In a process driven fundamentally by subjective emotion, any emotion carries a self-fulfilling potential.

The industry of analyzing and predicting shifts in those emotions runs the gamut from the pseudo-rational to the utterly preposterous. The mathematical gurus of "technical analysis" paint themselves as the high priests of this guessing game. Technical analysts analyze historical data on asset prices, trying to predict when a longer-run turning point (either up or down) may have been reached. They don't bother examining the real economic variables that may be germane to the asset price in question. Like the reading of tea leaves, the clues are hidden in the charts and tables describing past price movements, and only the analyst knows where to look.

Economic studies have repeatedly suggested that there is no scientific or empirical value whatsoever to so-called technical analysis.[10] Yet thousands of professionals are paid good salaries to mark up pictures of previous share price movements in the futile hope that the past reveals the future, and financial newspapers dedicate acres of newsprint to coverage of this pastime. The advice of technical analysts tends to be steeped in metaphysical language which may impress the uninitiated, but is fundamentally devoid of content. For example, one technical analyst was quoted in the *Globe and Mail* delivering the following all-too-typical words of wisdom: "When you break the short-term moving average, then you're into a corrective phase on the stock." This is just a pompous way of saying, "When a stock is really falling, then that stock is really falling." Incredibly, though, if enough market participants believe that technical analysis works, then it *can* work.

And the same is true of other even more far-fetched theories of market behaviour. Arch Crawford, head of a New York investment counselling firm, warned clients in a summer 1998 newsletter to sell their holdings before August 28 of that year because of the astronomical line-up of three heavenly bodies. "August 28, Sun, Mars, Pluto. Grave dangers, empires topple." He was one day off: the Dow Jones index lost over 350 points—its third largest one-day fall ever—on August 27.

Other market theories which have been reported by otherwise-reputable financial newspapers include: the 31st of the month is the luckiest day to invest; years ending in the number '8' are the most likely to experience rising markets (unfortunately, this "hot tip" can only be applied once a decade!); and if a football team with an "animal" nickname wins Canada's Grey Cup championship (like the Hamilton Tiger Cats or the B.C. Lions), there is an 85% certainty that the stock market will rise the next year.

Perhaps the creative minds at a newspaper in Fort Worth, Texas, have the best technical analysis of all. The paper's mascot is a Texas longhorn steer named Rusty. In January 1997, Rusty was let loose in a corral marked off into 100 squares, each with the name of a company. Rusty then "chose" seven stocks by defecating in their corresponding squares. At last report, the value of Rusty's portfolio had grown by twice as much as the Standard and Poor's 500-stock index.

Rusty's success is actually an accurate parable for the fleeting fame and fortune of two-legged stock-pickers. Given enough random guesses about which stocks will rise and which will fall, at least *some* money manager is guaranteed to be uncannily prescient. Their portfolio will outperform the others, and the resulting fame will attract millions of dollars in new money from investors anxious to ride the coat-tails of the latest market guru. But since it is usually pure luck—not science or insight—that determines which funds win and which ones lose, every new guru's moment of fame is inherently limited. Next year it will be someone else's random guess that will outperform the market." Indeed, an investor who shifted his or her money each year into that mutual fund which performed better than all others during the *previous* year would have underperformed the overall stock market even more surely than an investor who picked an "average" mutual fund and stuck with it (see Chapter 3).

Do What I Say, Not What I Do

In contrast to the ultra-sophisticated gambling of financial professionals, investment gurus are virtually unanimous in their advice that personal investors should never attempt to "play the markets." Rather than trying to time their interventions—buy low, sell high—to maximize speculative profits, investors should take the "long view." Invest regularly each month, don't sell out in a panic if prices should fall, and above all place your trust in the magic formulae of long-run growth and compound interest.

Funny, then, that the money managers themselves seldom follow their own advice. These powerful market insiders move quickly into action on the strength of privileged information, rumour, computerized programming instructions, or even just sheer hunch. As a result, the constant churning of stock and bond holdings by institutional investors (such as mutual funds and pension funds) accounts for a hugely disproportionate share of total financial market turnover. This adds substantially to the hefty administrative expense of running those institutions.

Institutional investors now account for about 75% of all trading on the TSE, even though they account for only about one-quarter of total share ownership. These money managers thus churn their equity holdings about nine times as often as independent investors. Some market analysts worry about the dangers posed to market liquidity and fairness by the hyper-active trading dominance of the big players. "When you've got so few players dominating three-quarters of the market, it makes it very illiquid," said one smaller financial consultant in 1995. "It produces a market that is not a very real indicator of...real value."

Why do the professionals preach one thing and practise another? Perhaps they are taking advantage of the fact that their own fast-moving speculative plays take place within a context of general passivity on the part of most individual investors. Ironically, that very passivity often stabilizes stock market volatility, particularly during downturns. For example, despite a decline in share prices of almost 25% during the third quarter of 1998, few Canadian investors dumped their equity mutual fund investments. Those redemptions which did occur were more than offset by new funds flowing into the market. A Toronto Stock Exchange survey at the time found that seven of 10 personal investors did nothing with their portfolios even as one-quarter of their paper worth evaporated. And three-quarters of those who hung tight reported that there was *no* market decline big enough to make them consider selling out. This incredible unresponsiveness on the part of individual investors was credited by many analysts as a key factor limiting the extent of the market's fall.

For professional financiers reacting at hyper-speed to news that most Canadians won't even know about until they receive the next morning's newspaper, the passivity of most investors makes for easy pickings. They can snap up hot new prospects before the rest of the world awakens to their potential—and they can dump the "dogs" on unsuspecting buyers before their share prices fall too noticeably. They can act on rumour or even on inside information—a technically illegal practice which is widespread nonetheless. Share prices will usually

Pass the Viagra

The consequences of financial market booms and busts may extend beyond the purely economic. An Israeli researcher claims that the state of financial markets is also an important determinant of male sexual performance.

"When the markets fall drastically, so does the male sexual organ," reported Dr. Alexander Oshanyesky, a specialist in blood-vessel problems, in 1997. He linked the 1993 crash of the Tel Aviv stock market to an observed rise in impotence among Israeli men.

The lines of feedback also flow both ways, the scientist indicated. "When a man is sexually impotent, he loses confidence and has trouble making financial decisions."

adjust to important new news in a matter of hours, if not minutes; most individual investors must therefore play catch-up to markets that have long since reflected the latest market sentiment. Imagine the speedy Russian national hockey team practising its power play against a pick-up squad of old-timers: the pros have scored before the amateurs have figured out which way the play is moving.

The remedy to this imbalance, however, is hardly to encourage individual investors to jump in and play the markets with the professionals. When individual investors get more actively involved in playing the market as aggressively as the money managers, is precisely when share prices tend to be the most volatile. For example, the advent of Internet-based share trading systems (through which individual investors can buy and sell their own or borrowed shares online for very low fees) has clearly exacerbated the volatility of share prices in specialized markets, especially for computer and other technology-related stocks. Nevertheless, the stock market's popular image as a place of rapid-response hyperactivity actually describes only one side of the story. There's another, larger constituency which stands calmly (or perhaps perplexedly) in the middle of the maelstrom, dazzled and stunned by the bright lights and confusing noise all around them.

Part IV
Kick Start:
Putting Money Back to Work

Chapter 14
Controlling Capital:
An Agenda for Reform

Real investment spending by Canadian companies and governments has slowed significantly during the 1980s and 1990s. The many interrelated consequences of this slowdown include slower job-creation, chronically weaker macroeconomic conditions, and sluggish improvement in productivity. Coincident with this slowdown, Canada's paper economy has experienced unprecedented expansion, prestige, and profitability. Yet the success of financial suppliers has not trickled down into the real investments which are so crucial to job-creation and productivity; and in many ways, the paper boom has disrupted and interfered with the more nitty-gritty process of putting capital to work in the real economy.

How can this unfortunate state of affairs be turned around? How can the chasm which separates financial hyperactivity from the slow-motion world of real investment and job-creation be bridged? A range of different policy measures will be required to address different facets of this broad overall problem. All of them involve attempting to exert more deliberate collective influence over the creation and behaviour of capital in our economy: influence clearly needed in the paper economy, of course, but in the real economy as well.

In fact, while it is clearly important to rein in, where possible, the unproductive wheelings and dealings of the paper economy, it may be on the real side of the investment equation that the problems of stimulating more and better injections of investment spending are more difficult. In other words, it may be easier for society to regain some collective control over financial capital, than subsequently to figure out how and what to do with that control once it is achieved.

This chapter will review, in a summary fashion, several of the policy initiatives that would limit the excesses of the paper boom, and help to facilitate the employment of capital in "real" work: producing things of value and employing job-hungry Canadians. The specific policy measures proposed fall into several different broad categories: monetary policy, tax policy, public investment policy, and policies which would strengthen and improve regulation over the financial sector (both domestically and globally). A multi-faceted approach to reviving real investment in Canada will need to include initiatives in all of these areas.

A detailed exposition of the rationale for (and effects of) each policy proposal would require, of course, another complete book (and this one is already too long!). So these policy suggestions are covered only briefly in this chapter; in many cases, it is hoped that the underlying logic behind each suggestion will have been made clear in other chapters of this book. More detailed and convincing cases for each proposal advanced here will need to be developed, over time, in the course of educating and mobilizing Canadians into campaigns for a more economically efficient and socially beneficial system of investment. Indeed, the research and educational materials of current political initiatives in

Table 14-1 An Agenda for Reform		
Policy Theme	Initiative	Description & Effect
Monetary Policy	Change the Bank of Canada's strategy	Eliminate target bands for inflation, reduce real interest rates, adopt a more balanced approach to inflation control.
	Change the Bank of Canada's structure	Improve representation in the Bank's policy decisions, and produce a more balanced approach to monetary policy.
	Use the Bank of Canada as a source of credit	Within limit, the Bank of Canada can act (like any private bank) as a source of credit for governments and businesses.
Tax Policy	Eliminate preferential tax treatment of personal investment income	Abolish deductions and credits in the personal income tax system for dividend income, capital gains, and carrying charges.
	Restrict and restructure other tax subsidies for financial investments	RRSP tax subsidies should be reduced and restructured to limit their cost and redistribute their benefits.
	Introduce a tax credit for real investments by companies	Companies which increase their stocks of real capital assets in Canada would receive a refundable tax credit worth 20% of their net capital spending.
	Provide tax support for non-profit lending	Personal investments in community or social lending institutions would receive appropriate charitable treatment for income tax purposes.
Public Investment	Increase public investment to 1960s levels	Rebuilding public investment to the same share of GDP as was experienced in the 1960s would provide an additional $20 billion per year in real investment.
	Establish a system of public & community venture investment	Develop a new institutional structure of non-profit banking and investing to finance real investments in Canadian venture projects (discussed in Chapter 16).

this area—such as the annual Alternative Federal Budget, the work of the Canadian Community Reinvestment Coalition, or the Jubilee 2000 campaign for debt forgiveness—flesh out many of the arguments presented here.

Table 14-1 summarizes the various specific policy proposals which would seem to flow from the general critique of the financial industry and the overall slowdown in real investment activity that has been documented in the first parts of this book. The policy proposals are grouped into five broad themes. The rest of this chapter will go on to discuss each of these broad themes in more detail.

Table 14-1 continued		
Domestic Financial Regulation	Develop capacity for more oversight of private credit creation	Regulators must regain some influence over credit creation by private lending institutions (through flexible reserve requirements or more direct means).
	Impose tighter rules regarding leveraged securities trading	Financial institutions (such as brokerages and hedge funds) should be strictly limited in their use of borrowed capital to finance speculative trading.
	Impose consumer performance standards on lending institutions	Banks and other lending institutions must be obliged to offer banking services to low-income Canadians and in rural areas.
	Implement community reinvestment provisions on lending institutions	Lending institutions must meet specified targets regarding their personal and business lending in the communities where they operate.
	Enhance incentives for closer links between lenders and real companies	Regulatory incentives should be developed which encourage banks and other lending institutions to take a more direct interest in the actions of the real businesses they finance.
	Improve the economic and legal environment for credit unions	A range of regulatory measures would assist credit unions to remake and rebuild their role in the broader financial industry.
	Generally limit the economic importance of private asset markets	Government policy choices in other areas (such as social policy initiatives) should support the general goal of limiting the overall economic importance of private securities markets.
International Financial Regulation	Work internationally to impose a Tobin Tax on international transactions	Collect a small tax on cross-border financial transactions which would tax speculators and possibly reduce financial turnover.
	Retain and strengthen restrictions on foreign investment of pension monies	Retain the current 20% ceiling limiting the foreign investment of tax-subsidized pension funds (including RRSPs and RPPs), and eliminate current loopholes in the rule.
	Reorient the policies and regulations of international lending agencies	Current IMF policies which require harsh fiscal and monetary restraint in developing countries should be reformed. Limits by the IMF and other international bodies on the regulatory leeway of individual countries should be lifted.

Monetary Policy

As was detailed in Chapter 9, no single factor has been more to blame for the miserable performance of the overall Canadian economy, and the consequently sluggish pace of real investment spending, than the U-turn in monetary policy that was successfully engineered in about 1981. From that point on, job-creation and full employment were no longer the top goals of macroeconomic policy: financial stability and profitability were. Interest rates soared—and in real terms, astoundingly, they have actually stayed at or near the lofty heights first reached during the interest rate crisis of 1981.

High-interest-rate policies reduced the incentive for and the financial feasibility of job-creating investments in the real economy. They sparked a historic fall in inflation rates (and more recently the advent of deflation) which did wonders for bond prices and stock markets, but which wreaked havoc on the economic opportunities of most Canadians. Clearly, a fundamental about-face in this dubious and destructive policy direction must be the first order of business in any effort to revitalize real capital investment in Canada.

How to accomplish this fundamental reorientation? A combination of changes in policy direction by the Bank of Canada as it now stands, and the implementation of certain structural reforms to the institution itself, would seem to hold the most promise. In terms of its general policy direction, the Bank clearly needs to worry less about inflation and more about job-creation and the real growth and development of the Canadian economy. This shift in emphasis should include the abandonment of the explicit targets for consumer price inflation that have guided—in theory, at least—the Bank's interest rate policies since 1991. These targets have committed the Bank to retaining consumer price inflation within a two-point band as its top goal; since 1993, this target band has been set at 1% to 3% per year.

The Bank has been surprisingly ineffective in meeting its inflation targets: it has *undershot* the band a surprising 40% of the time since the introduction of targeting in 1991.[1] The advent of deflation in Canada in 1998 revealed the bankruptcy of the targeting approach: even though consumer price inflation was consistently below the Bank's own targets, the Bank would not cut interest rates (which is what its own policy rule would seem to demand) because of the weakness of the Canadian dollar. Indeed, the Bank earlier made matters worse by unilaterally raising interest rates in 1997 and early 1998, motivated by the fear (downright silly in retrospect) that inflation, fuelled by a then-buoyant economy, might soon burst through the top of the band. The Bank thus moved to slow Canada's economy just in time for the advent of the Asian financial crisis. This single-minded obsession with preventing any uptick in inflation at any economic cost clearly exacerbated the effects of the global aftershocks which soon hit Canada.

By selecting such a transparent and unidimensional criterion on which to judge its actions, the Bank has unnecessarily raised the stakes in its ongoing war on inflation. It would be better to abandon the targets, and instead adopt a more balanced, flexible, and discreet policy strategy, in which the Bank is given leeway to adopt interest rate policies to meet the changing requirements of inflation control and job-creation. After all, the Bank's own implementing legislation—the Bank of Canada Act—specifies that it is to pursue both price stability and full employment, without giving one goal predominance over the other.

The practice of the U.S. central bank, the Federal Reserve, has been more balanced in this view: it has no explicit inflation target, it has tolerated inflation at consistently higher levels than in Canada, and thus has engineered consistently lower real interest rates. The Federal Reserve holds its cards closer to its chest than does the Bank of Canada, and this has allowed the Fed more room to manouevre in response to the ongoing fluctuations of the domestic and international economies. [Of course, the fact that the Fed presides over the largest and most powerful economy in the world has also helped!] A notably easier monetary policy is an important reason for the stronger economic conditions which the U.S. has enjoyed throughout this decade.

A range of institutional and structural reforms would support this reorientation of the Bank of Canada's general policy approach. In particular, it seems that the Bank needs to step out of the closeted world in which its decisions are currently made. The Bank is governed by a federally-appointed board on which conventional views on the benefits of low inflation and the primary importance of healthy financial returns are clearly pre-eminent. The Bank's structure should be amended to allow for the appointment of representatives to the Bank's board from different regions and different constituencies across Canada. This would help to make the Bank of Canada—perhaps the single most important economic decision-making body in the country—a more democratic and accountable institution.

Finally, a broader and more ambitious interpretation of the Bank of Canada's overall mandate would make a contribution to both the democratization of finance and the revitalization of real capital accumulation in Canada. In recent years, the Bank of Canada has fulfilled one primary function: to manage interest rates and thus control inflation. But, as a publicly-owned bank, the Bank of Canada could also fulfill a more extensive mandate. Like private banks, it has the power to create new credit, through its own lending activities as well as through its own direct control over certain components of the money supply. It can lend to governments. Indeed, as of the end of 1998, it held some $30 billion worth of federal government debt, and its ongoing buying and selling of government bonds is one of the important ways the Bank influences interest rates.

In previous years, the Bank has made much larger contributions to government finance. In the late 1970s, for example, the Bank owned about 20% of the total federal debt, compared with just 5% by the late 1990s. [Those holdings of federal debt were equivalent to about 5% of GDP in the late 1970s, versus about 3% in the late 1990s.] Larger Bank lending to governments would contribute to a reduction in the ultimate interest burden of servicing the public debt (since taxpayers would, in essence, be paying interest to their own bank, rather than to commercial banks and other private lenders), and also to a general easing of monetary conditions in the whole economy.

Adjustments to interest rates are the usual means by which the Bank of Canada attempts to regulate the overall expansion of credit. At some times, however, the interest rate mechanism loses some of its power: either because the Bank is constrained by some other factor (such as weakness in the dollar) from reducing interest rates, or because interest rate changes themselves cease to have the desired impact on borrowing and lending in the economy.

This latter problem surfaced in Japan during the late 1990s, when interest rates as low as *zero* failed to stimulate the desired expansion of lending by hard-hit Japanese banks; as a result, Japanese authorities resorted to more direct and powerful means of increasing credit, including the direct expansion of credit by the central bank. Especially during times in which private banks are unwilling or unable to create the credit the real economy needs, the Bank of Canada should be prepared to step into the void.

There are limits, of course, to the extent to which central bank credit creation can stimulate new growth and demand—limits that are often ignored by the more overambitious proponents of this general strategy. In particular, the financing of huge government deficits or other expenses through the central bank alone would promote a damaging escalation of inflation. But the dangers of this approach are also overstated by conservative critics of a more activist role for the central bank. Their stated fears that *any* expansion of central bank lending is necessarily a step toward monetization of all debts and the rapid onset of hyperinflation are just as unbelievable.

The issue is a matter of degree. The Bank of Canada currently finances a small share of public debt. It could clearly increase those holdings somewhat without sparking the end of the financial world as we know it. But equally clearly, it does not have an infinite capacity to single-handedly fund every deserving expenditure that a government might wish to undertake.

Particularly in times when the expansion of credit through traditional private channels is slow because of financial uncertainty or other problems, the central bank can step in with its own contribution to the financing of economic expansion. The Alternative Federal Budget has proposed that the Bank of Canada refinance up to 2% per year of the outstanding federal debt, macroeconomic conditions permitting, up to an additional 10% of that debt (bringing the Bank's total holdings to 15% of total debt, still significantly lower than was the case in the 1970s).[2] This seems like a reasonably balanced view, although it has drawn the expected cries of wolf from conservative financiers who would prefer that the government continue to pay high interest costs to private banks.

There is nothing, by the way, to suggest that the Bank of Canada's credit-creation role needs to be limited to governments. While it is hard to imagine that the Bank of Canada would delve into the realm of bread-and-butter consumer banking—and even harder to see what the point of such an expansion would be—it is not inconceivable that the Bank (or an appropriately structured subsidiary) could play a role in financing real investments by companies or non-profit agencies. This possibility is considered further in the model of social investment proposed in Chapter 16.

Tax Policy[3]

The importance of marginal changes in taxes in altering the behaviour of individuals and companies is often overstated. The notion that behavioural patterns that are rooted in deep structural and economic features of the economy can be fundamentally altered through "tinkering" with the incentives implicit in the tax system is usually quite wrong. Nevertheless, there are several changes to Canadian tax policy that might help to restore the incentive for job-creating investments in the real economy, while simultaneously reducing the appeal of paper speculation.

On ethical grounds, if for no other reason, Canadian governments must reduce the expensive subsidies that are currently provided to the unproductive paper-churning of the financial industry. Given the highly skewed nature of financial wealth ownership in Canada, the value of these subsidies is disproportionately pocketed by the highest-income Canadians who hardly need or deserve more government assistance. There are hundreds of more deserving uses for these public funds. Eliminating these subsidies will not significantly reduce the unproductive hyperactivity of the paper economy (nor would imposing an actual tax on financial transactions, as some well-intentioned critics of the financial industry have suggested). But at least it would free up public monies for better expenditure on other more worthy projects. Similarly, merely creating a more hospitable tax climate for real investment by companies in the real economy could not single-handedly reverse the investment slowdown; but it would help, in combination with other measures.

The first loopholes that should be closed are the numerous incentives that are provided through the personal tax system to individual financial investors. Some of these incentives were summarized in Chapter 3. (See sidebar: *The Subsidized Casino.*) We have seen throughout this book that these financial investments bear virtually no relation to the real-world processes of investment and job-creation. We have also seen the surprising concentration of financial investments in the hands of a wealthy few. Both of these trends—the paper boom and the disproportionate pocketing of its proceeds by the wealthiest segments of society—hardly need or deserve assistance from the tax paying public.

The dividend tax credit and the capital gains exemption are both justified on grounds that they will reduce the cost of capital to companies active in the real economy. We have seen that this is not the case; both these incentives should be eliminated.[4] The deducibility of certain types of carrying charges from personal investment income should also be limited. In particular, the notion that individual investors can deduct interest charges on money borrowed to subsequently reinvest in financial instruments promotes all kinds of unproductive and potentially destabilizing paper speculation; this loophole should be closed completely. Together, these measures would save the federal government over $3 billion per year.

Canada's generous subsidies to the RRSP program are the most expensive form of taxpayer support for the paper economy. Contrary to the public image of RRSPs as a form of "popular" stock market participation, in truth close to two-thirds of the total tax benefits paid out by the program are received by the top 10% of Canadian households. Figuring out how to "rein in" the RRSP program, however, is not an easy task. There are important issues of fairness within the tax system to be considered; in particular, some kind of symmetry between the tax treatment of individual RRSP investments and the more collective pension investments conducted through workplace pension plans needs to be preserved. The future growth of RRSP subsidies should be strictly curtailed; at a minimum, the ceiling on RRSP contributions should be frozen at its present level ($13,500 per year) instead of increasing over time.[5]

The federal government must also address the inequity of the current format of the RRSP program, which subsidizes the investments of high-income individuals at a higher rate than for other Canadians. Restructuring the program as a tax credit (rather than a tax deduction, as at present) would be an important improvement.

Suppose, for example, that RRSP deductions were converted into a federal tax credit, which was calculated at something like 25% of the value of contributions. This would produce a more attractive subsidy to personal savings by low-income Canadians, since the value of the credit is greater than the federal income tax rate (currently 17%) that they pay on their current income. At the same time, this approach would also reduce the degree of tax assistance given to high-income Canadians (who pay federal taxes at rates exceeding 30%, and hence would receive a smaller reduction in taxes in return for their RRSP contributions than they do at present). Numerous administrative issues involved in the implementation of such a scheme would have to be confronted, but it would nevertheless represent a positive step in both limiting the cost of the RRSP program and redistributing its total benefits further down the income ladder.

While closing tax loopholes for individual financial investors, it makes sense to consider ways to enhance the tax incentive for companies that put money into motion in the real economy. One effective way of doing this would be to offer a refundable tax credit to companies, based on their incremental investments in real capital structures and equipment. The federal government used to offer an investment tax credit, at a rate of 7% of gross fixed investment spending. It was abolished, ironically, by the Mulroney government, at the same time as it significantly reduced personal tax rates for high-income individuals.[6]

This is further evidence of how conservative tax "reforms" seem motivated more by the desire to increase the after-tax income of well-off individuals than to stimulate the real expansion of the economy. In other words, the real intent of tax "reform" is to redivide the economic pie (from bottom to top, like Robin Hood in reverse), rather than trying to grow that pie.

The federal government should consider a tax credit of 20% for net fixed investment spending by non-financial businesses in Canada. This would offset the cost to companies that decide to increase their total use of real capital assets (including machinery, equipment, and structures). The credit would be applied to net investment only, measured after the company's replacement (through depreciation charges, which are already tax-deductible) of its existing capital assets. In other words, the credit would be designed to support incremental real investment by firms rather than the ongoing investment spending that is necessary merely to preserve their existing operations.[7]

Naturally, only real net investments undertaken in Canada would qualify. Net additions to the real capital stock would be subsidized at 20%: the same rate as the federal government currently subsidizes R&D investments, and for similar reasons. Like R&D investments, the *social* benefits of real investment spending exceed the *private* benefits, and hence measures should be taken to encourage more investment than would otherwise be forthcoming from self-interested private firms.

Like the R&D subsidy, the credit would be refundable (that is, non-taxable corporations would actually receive a cash payment from the government) and taxable.[8] Such a measure would cost the federal government perhaps $5 billion per year. The cost of this measure would be fully offset by the aforementioned initiatives to close investment income loopholes in the personal tax system.

The power of this measure could be further enhanced by linking it to the decision of companies to pay out dividends to their shareholders. As described earlier, these dividend payments have grown in Canada in the 1990s, and they cut deeply into the corporate cash flow which is an important determinant of real business investment. To discourage dividend payouts at the same time as promoting investment in real capital assets, the refundable investment tax credit might be reduced by perhaps 25 cents for each dollar in dividends paid by the company. The overall rate of the tax credit could then even be increased without affecting the cost of the final subsidy.[9]

The overall effect of this measure would be to shift the corporate tax burden onto those companies most interested in accumulating cash and paying it out to shareholders, and away from those companies more concerned with growing their businesses and creating jobs.

Combined with the elimination of tax loopholes for personal investment income, this tax credit for real capital investments would result in a modest transfer of the overall tax burden from the companies that use capital in their day-to-day business (and on whose expansion the job-creation hopes of Canadians inevitably rest) to the individual owners of that capital.

There are alternate ways of achieving the same result. Instead of paying out a tax credit for investment purposes, the government could enhance the allowable capital cost write-offs which reduce the taxable income of companies undertaking real investments. Alternatively, the overall corporate tax rate could simply be reduced. The advantage of the tax credit approach over these measures is that it focuses the power of the tax incentive on those companies that are doing the most to put money into motion in the real economy.

Philosophically, one could imagine a more extreme position: perhaps companies that retain their profits internally, and reinvest those profits in the form of real capital in Canada, should not have to pay taxes on those profits at all. As long as capital is "working" in the real economy, it is generally providing economic benefits that are widely shared, and so there is no need to tax it (especially since lots of tax revenue is collected thanks to the direct and spin-off jobs and spending which were stimulated by those investments). Companies would still have to pay *non-income* taxes to cover some of the public expenses directly associated with their operations—unemployment insurance premiums, for example, or user fees for services such as public transportation facilities and regulatory administration charges—but, if their profits are reinvested in the form of new real capital, then they would avoid *income* taxes altogether.

It would only be when the owners of those companies tried to capture personal benefits from their investments (by pocketing investment income in the form of dividends, interest, or capital gains) that they would pay taxes at steeply progressive rates that reflect their privileged position and incomes. This whole approach would solve the long-standing debate over the "double taxation" of capital income (to some extent, taxes on capital are paid twice: first within a corporation, and then again by individual owners of that capital). It would also reduce the incentive for financial entrepreneurs and tax accountants to continually devise new ways of sidestepping this burden, through measures such as the income trusts which were so popular with financiers in the late 1990s.

It might seem surprising for such a proposal to emanate from the left of the political spectrum. But this book has stressed throughout the broader social benefits that clearly result from real investment spending. And it has also argued that the greatest concentration of power and wealth in Canadian society is not represented by the existence of large corporations, *per se*, but rather by the enormous accumulations of financial wealth in the hands of the individual *owners* of those corporations. The more that corporations as job-creating, productive institutions can be separated from the self-serving individual interests of their owners, the better.

In this context, measures that shift the tax burden from corporations onto their owners—even radical ones like abolishing the corporate income tax altogether—are worthy of further discussion and debate among progressives in Canada, who have often been quick to put undue emphasis on higher corporate taxes as the path to a brighter social future.

A final tax measure would provide favourable tax treatment for individuals who invest their personal savings in one of several different socially-motivated lending institutions. Numerous alternative lending funds have been developed by concerned community agencies, credit unions, and other bodies in recent years to channel low-cost capital into a variety of non-profit or community development initiatives. For example, the Calmeadow project provides micro-lending to small-scale ventures undertaken by women, immigrants, and First Nations peoples in a number of hard-hit communities across Canada. It follows the same philosophical approach that was pioneered by the Grameen movement in south Asia: it provides small sums of venture capital to groups who then work cooperatively to ensure their successful investment and repayment.

The Montreal Community Loan Association similarly supports small business and non-profit housing initiatives in the Montreal region. The Community Investment Deposit initiative of the VanCity Savings Credit Union in Vancouver supports various non-profit and community development initiatives, on the strength of funds collected from credit union members who voluntarily accept a somewhat lower interest rate on their deposits.

In all of these cases, individual investors are willingly and explicitly forgoing a certain proportion of financial profits that they could have received had they invested in conventional financial instruments. They make this sacrifice in the interests of supporting non-profit initiatives with an explicit social mandate. [In this regard, these non-profit lending initiatives differ fundamentally from the ethical mutual funds and labour-sponsored venture funds that are critically surveyed in the next chapter.] This, in essence, is a charitable act, and should be recognized as such in the personal tax system—by granting a charitable tax deduction equal to the difference between the interest rates earned on these social deposits and the going rate on financial instruments of similar risk and time commitment.

These small-scale community investment initiatives will never be major players in the overall structure of Canada's economy, and their long-run economic potential should not be overestimated. They nevertheless undertake good works, and their lenders should be duly recognized and compensated.

Public Investment

As was described in Chapter 7, the decline in public investment spending in Canada has been disproportionately important in explaining the overall slowdown in real investment activity since about 1981. Public investment in Canada reached peak levels of 5% of total GDP during the 1960s. Public investments were cut back significantly in the 1980s: the first line of defense by governments facing the terrible fiscal consequences of high interest rates, high unemployment, and slow growth.

Investment budgets were cut back further in the bleak 1990s. By 1998, public investment spending had declined to barely 2% percent of total Canadian GDP (see Figure 14-1). The social consequences of public underinvestment are readily visible in most Canadian communities: crumbling public schools, inadequate health care facilities, and potholed roads.

The achievement of balanced budgets in most jurisdictions in the mid-1990s, and the subsequent generation of large fiscal surpluses by many Canadian governments, eliminates the deficit as an excuse for the short-sighted reduction of investment budgets by governments and public agencies. Conservatives now

We Need a War

By the year 2000, Canadians will be lucky if real incomes per person are as high as they were in 1990. Thanks to a misguided war on inflation, super-fast deficit reduction by governments, and finally the outbreak of global financial chaos, this has truly been a lost decade, a decade without growth: our worst decade by far since the 1930s.

Indeed, a crucial difference between the Dirty Thirties and the Nasty Nineties is that the depression of the Thirties lasted only 10 years. We don't yet know when the current malaise will really end. By 1939 per capita output, personal incomes, and employment rates had all recovered to their levels when that decade began. The same is not true in 1999. By 1939 factories were humming and the economy was being stretched to capacity. In contrast, 1999 is marked by continuing stagnation and gloom in many parts of Canada, and an uneven recovery that is threatened by financial turmoil at home and abroad. What is the missing ingredient this time around? Clearly, we need a war.

Of course, we don't really want a war—although, with financial meltdown in nuclear-armed Russia and human misery spreading rapidly around the planet, we could very well end up with one. What we actually need is some dramatic inspiration to national action. A call to economic arms. We need a peacetime war plan that takes our idle human and natural resources and puts them to work in useful tasks—just as World War II mobilized our idle resources in 1939.

What could we do with these people and resources, instead of waging war? We should mobilize economic brigades to build a high-speed rail link between Windsor and Quebec City. We should conscript foot-soldiers to overhaul the rest of our transportation infrastructure: build a super-port in Halifax, a rail link to Pearson Airport in Toronto, a commuter system for traffic-clogged Vancouver. The federal government could rebuild our aging airports as part of this program, without even having to pester travelers for the annoying Airport Improvement Fees currently collected at many Canadian airports.

We should "rally the troops" to clean up toxic waste sites from Sydney to Swan Hills. We should "send in the marines" to finally stop the hideous flows of raw sewage that continue to foul our coastlines from Halifax to Victoria. Other investments are also urgently needed to protect the quality of our water and waterways. We should put the engineers corps to work building low-cost housing for Canada's growing army of under-housed and homeless.

By declaring this kind of peaceful war, Canadian governments could finally undertake projects that are essential to our standard of living, but which are not lucrative enough for private businesses to undertake themselves. We could patch up and send back into action huge segments of our economy that have been idled by the failure of our deregulated, zero-inflation, balanced-budget regime.

Of course, every war needs a threat, one that pulls a community together and motivates ordinary people to do extraordinary things. Sadly, the human misery now plainly visible on street-corners in virtually every city in Canada does not seem to be enough to galvanize the same kind of rapid response we can count on in times of war. But it should be.

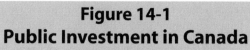

Figure 14-1
Public Investment in Canada
1950-1998

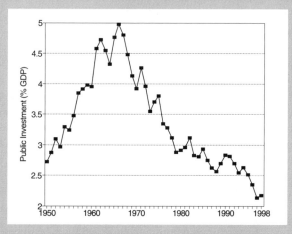

Source: Author's calculations from Statistics Canada, *National Economic and Financial Accounts*.

want to permanently undermine the fiscal capacity of the state in Canada by handing back looming surpluses in the form of big tax cuts (especially income tax cuts targeted at the well-off families that pay most income taxes). This pressure needs to be resisted: it makes far more social and economic sense to allocate future fiscal surpluses (which could easily reach $40 or 50 billion per year for all levels of Canadian government early in the next century) to rebuilding the role of public programs and services in Canada's economy. And, while providing new funds for *current* public programs such as education and health care will be a key priority in this rebuilding process, progressives should not overlook the importance of restoring the *capital* investment effort of governments and public agencies.

Governments at all levels should take advantage of the much-easier fiscal environment they will face over the next decade to substantially revamp and restore their public investment programs. Public investment spending should be rebuilt to the same share of Canada's total GDP that was experienced, on average, during the 1960s: a time when both the social and the economic infrastructure of Canada advanced by leaps and bounds.

This target would require a doubling of current public investment, resulting in new investments of $20 billion per year spread across all levels of government. Governments would easily be able to finance investment budgets of this magnitude without raising taxes or incurring deficits, in light of the huge surpluses that will be generated in most jurisdictions over the next decade. And, by so impressively stepping into the economic void created by the insufficient investment activity of private firms, governments would both stimulate growth and job-creation and tailor that growth so that it was more sensitive to the social priorities of our communities.

In the wake of decades of neglect of our public facilities and infrastructure, Canadian governments can now clearly afford to lead a dramatic effort to rebuild our public capital stock. (See sidebar: *We Need a War.*) By rehabilitating public investment as a central plank of overall economic policy, we could finally

Megaprojects, Then and Now

Every junior high school student in Canada learns about the St. Lawrence Seaway: its 15 impressive locks, its 3,700-kilometre length, its crucial role in the economic development of central Canada. Without doubt, the construction of the Seaway was a landmark in Canada's post-war economic development. Its construction employed tens of thousands of workers. Once completed, It formed an economic lifeline between the outside world and the burgeoning industrial centres of Quebec and Ontario.

Indeed, the Seaway is still important 40 years after its exuberant inauguration by Queen Eliazabeth and U.S. President Eisenhower. A revival in the global shipping industry has spurred a renewed interest in the Seaway. Ironically, in keeping with the conservative times, the federal government sold the Seaway to a non-profit committee of users and shippers in 1998.

For years, transportation enthusiasts have dreamed of building an equally ambitious transport link right alongside the shores of the Seaway: a high-speed rail transit system that would run through the high-density population corridor between Windsor, Ont., in the southwest and Québec City in the northeast.

Such a link would help to ease growing congestion on highways and in the airports of central Canada. At over 300 kilometres per hour, it could deliver passengers between downtown Toronto, Ottawa, and Montreal more quickly than air travel. And it could offer other benefits ranging from greater safety to lower pollution. Tens of thousands of jobs would be created during the construction of the project, and thousands more by its ongoing operation.

Fiscal conservatives, however, scoff at the cost of the project: $10 to $12 billion in total, over a several-year construction period. This seems outlandish in these tight-fisted times—but is it?

The St. Lawrence Seaway cost $470 million to complete. Canada's share was $330 million, plus another $30 million to resettle communities displaced by flooding. That represented a total public investment equal to 1.2% of Canada's GDP at the time, spread over a five-year construction period. A high-speed rail link between Québec City and Windsor would also require a total investment of 1.2% of GDP, and this would be spread over a longer construction period. The rail link would cost no more than the Seaway which it would parallel, and could make an equally important contribution to Canadians' economic well-being. Yet the short-sighted stinginess of the current guardians of the public purse will probably preclude its ever being built.

undertake projects that are essential to our continued standard of living, but which are not lucrative enough to enlist the participation of private businesses. Indeed, public investment is conceptually very different from private investment. It is motivated, not by the hope of private profit, but rather by the collective recognition by society (through its governments or public agencies) of a need for new facilities providing some broadly-enjoyed social benefits.

Increasing public investment therefore not only supplements the volume of real investment spending coming from private firms. More importantly, it diversifies the *criteria* on which investment is undertaken. Instead of relying on the profit motive alone as the sole economic "carrot" for crucial real investment and capital accumulation, society would begin to develop a broader and more self-reliant portfolio of investment projects, an increasing share of which would represent the marshalling of economic resources solely and explicitly because the members of a community collectively decided they needed to be marshalled.

At present, most public investment is currently limited to broader social and physical infrastructure projects that are believed to be of sufficiently universal benefit as to justify the involvement of government in their construction. Ultimately, however, we will need to expand the scope of public or non-profit investing to include other ventures which—like private firms—aim to fill more particular needs or niches in specific communities or regions. In other words, why should public investing be limited to hospitals and bridges? Why cannot society in general identify more particular projects or needs that can be undertaken through the collective, non-profit mobilization of economic resources—including capital?

Imagine a public venture investment system, which mobilized financial resources and then put them to work in a range of non-profit community or industrial development projects, even in activities that are currently dominated by for-profit private firms. This would be a crucial step towards true "community entrepreneurship," in which the responsibility for coming up with new economic ideas and organizing economic undertakings to make those ideas a reality would no longer be vested solely with those who happen to own private businesses. Instead, organizational and financial structures would be established to initiate all types of public or non-profit business ventures, matching their initial sponsors with the managerial, financial, and technological resources with which their entrepreneurial ideas could become a reality.

In this manner, the current dependence of society on the investments of profit-seeking companies for 85% of all employment could ultimately be lessened. Some specific suggestions for financing and facilitating non-profit investment are provided in the concluding chapter of this book.

Financial Regulation: Domestic

The normally arcane subject of financial regulation enjoyed an unusual but temporary period of intense public interest in Canada during the late 1990s. The federal government had commissioned a major two-year inquiry—the Task Force on the Future of the Canadian Financial Services Sector, headed by Harold MacKay—to consider the myriad of rules and regulations governing Canada's booming financial sector. Of the many topics that the task force was to consider, the most hotly contested was whether or not Canada's major banks should be allowed to merge with one another.

Four of Canada's five largest banks decided not to await the outcome of this exercise in public consultation: early in 1998, the Royal Bank and the Bank of Montreal announced their intention to merge, followed three months later by the engagement of the Toronto Dominion Bank and the Canadian Imperial Bank of Commerce. After months of speculation, during which time public opinion turned decisively against the banks, Finance Minister Paul Martin gave the thumbs down late in 1998.

The MacKay report itself, meanwhile, released in September 1998, was rather noncommittal on the subject of bank mergers: in principle, mergers should be allowed if they enhance the competitiveness of the banking industry, but the merits of each proposal should be evaluated carefully on a case-by-case basis. In other words, mergers if necessary, but not necessarily mergers. [The report could have been written by the federal Liberal cabinet.] With the proposed mergers history, the banks got back to their normal business of earning multi-billion dollar profits. And the stupefying subject of financial regulation once again dropped off the radar screens of the public's consciousness—at least until the next time two big banks decide they want to merge.

In retrospect, it is probably unfortunate that the MacKay commission's work was dominated by the fleeting issue of the proposed bank mergers. The commission's report addresses a wide range of regulatory issues that are probably of greater importance, ultimately, to the financial well-being of average Canadians than whether or not big banks should be allowed to get bigger. It is perhaps equally unfortunate that the attention of those Canadians concerned about the power and self-interest of our major financial institutions was also channeled so exclusively into opposing the bank mergers.

To be sure, the mergers raised many concerns over consumer protection and the concentrated financial power of these incredibly profitable mega-corporations. Perhaps even more importantly, the mergers—so anxiously desired by these companies—created an opportunity for greatly strengthened public leverage over their actions. But, by focusing so single-mindedly on the mergers, and opposing them on grounds that were often more symbolic than practical, attention was distracted from regulatory issues that are more crucial to the long-run goal of converting financial capital into real job-creating investments.

Often, the inadvertent impression was left that a financial system dominated by three humungous, unaccountable, and super-profitable private institutions would be completely unacceptable, but that one dominated by five humungous, unaccountable, super-profitable private institutions is quite acceptable. This whole approach very obviously missed the point of what is really wrong with Canada's financial system, and what will be truly needed to put finance back to work for Canadians.

Think of the issue of "competition" in banking. Many critics of the mergers, speaking from both the right and the left of the spectrum, expressed fear that the mergers would reduce the degree of competition in banking services and hence lead to the exploitation of consumers. In the first place, this view ignored the very fierce competition that exists in the bread-and-butter neighbourhood banking business. As explained in Chapter 3 (see section, *Can Banks Change?*), major banks (whether there are three of them or five of them) must compete with trust companies, credit unions, and many other "near-bank" institutions for the basic street-corner banking business of average Canadians. Margins in this most grassroots form of banking have been driven down as a result, which is precisely why the major banks have shifted their attentions elsewhere—most notably toward the higher-risk, higher-profit businesses of investment banking, financial trading, and wealth management.

As explained in Chapter 3, basic lending services now account for a minority of the total income of the major banks—and it was certainly not a desire to go back to the street-corner to more ruthlessly exploit the small-account customer that motivated the banks' desire to merge. Quite the contrary, the banks viewed the mergers as a convenient or even essential means of building the capital base and global networks with which to conduct their more lucrative paper chase.

More fundamentally, it is not at all clear that stronger "competition" in banking is even a good thing. Recall from Chapter 3 that banks create money because the banking laws allow them to take an initial amount of capital (the equity of the shareholders and some initial deposits) and multiply it many times over into additional loans. The banks lend out many times more money than they actually have the cash to supply, on the assumption that not all their customers will want their accounts converted into cash at the same time. If this were to happen to any bank, due to a panic among its account-holders, the bank would collapse; and a bank collapse is disastrous, not just for the bank and its customers, but for the whole economy. It creates huge uncertainty in the minds of consumers and investors, leads other banks to start calling in their loans (to shore up their own cash positions), and can single-handedly bring about a recession.

Larger, diversified banks are inherently more stable. With loans allocated to different regions of the country, different industries, and different types of customers, a large and diversified bank is less likely to be destabilized by a rash of customer defaults in any particular line of its business. And the confidence of a bank's customers (which is a real factor in determining stability) is likely to be enhanced when it is large and diversified. It could actually be disastrous to try to make the system more "competitive" by encouraging more, smaller banks to enter the industry. Countries that have smaller and hence more "competitive" banks (such as the U.S.) also have more bank failures, with resulting costs to the economy at large and to taxpayers in particular (who always end up bailing out the system).

The fact that Canada's banking system is dominated by large, diversified institutions is ironically one of the *strengths* of our financial system, not a weakness. The problem with Canada's banks is not that they are big: it is that they have no formal social accountability. The key issue is to combine the inherent efficiencies and stability of large banks with some social accountability over their operations. In short, the issue is regulation, not competition.

What sorts of regulatory measures—apart from simply prohibiting mergers between large and relatively unregulated institutions—are needed? The general goal is to enhance the degree to which the financial system acts as a stable, affordable, and accountable source of credit for real economic growth. This will require a multifaceted regulatory approach. At present, Canada has a private, virtually deregulated financial system. The management of credit creation has largely been turned over to private corporations that use their powers to generate private profits. Controls and accountability over that private credit system have been effectively dismantled (the most recent steps being taken by the Mulroney government in the early 1990s, when the regulatory distinctions between banks, insurance companies and investment dealers were largely eliminated).

Banks are thus essentially free to determine who they will lend to, at what price, and when *not* to lend. Even regulations governing the credit-worthiness and stability of the banks have been reduced: they no longer keep compulsory

Behind the Pack

"Commercial bankers are the most dangerous animals in the financial jungle because they always follow the herd."
—G. Pierre Goad, business columnist
Wall Street Journal, March 26, 1999

deposits with the Bank of Canada as insurance against bank panics, but rather must simply satisfy vague government regulations related to credit quality and asset mix.

As discussed in Chapter 3, banking is, in essence, a public utility in a modern economy. The economy needs credit to operate. If the provision of that credit is to be undertaken by private for-profit institutions (rather than by public institutions operating according to some criteria other than profit-maximization), then the whole economy depends on the profit-maximizing decisions of those companies.

Private banks may increase their lending when we don't want or need it, or for purposes (like stock market speculation) that are not socially desirable. They may restrain their lending precisely when we need it the most, because they suddenly become worried about their own credit-worthiness due to negative events in the larger economy. In fact, recent research by economists has shown that "banking cycles" (the booms and busts in private for-profit lending by banks) may be the most important factor in causing recessions. (See quote: *Behind the Pack.*) We need much more public oversight of banks: both to "protect them from themselves" (that is, to moderate their own inherent instability), and to manage the creation and management of credit in a more stable and socially beneficial manner.

What follows are several suggestions for regulatory measures that would aim to reconstruct public oversight and accountability over Canada's domestic financial system. They will need to be considered and implemented together with measures aimed at calming the global financial turbulence that has also had such a restraining influence on real capital accumulation in Canada's economy. Some of these international regulatory initiatives are considered in the following section.

Macroeconomic regulation

At present the major banks (and other financial institutions, to a lesser extent) own a huge stockpile of interest-bearing federal bonds, which act (along with equity and cash accumulations) as a risk-free foundation for their additional lending. In the past, banks were required to keep interest-free deposits with the Bank of Canada as insurance against panics. By adjusting these reserve requirements, the Bank of Canada could influence the lending behaviour of the banks (stimulating it during slow times, restricting it during boom times). Instead of paying the banks lucratively for the privilege of holding these risk-free bonds as a reserve asset, they should be required to maintain compulsory interest-free deposits with the Bank of Canada, at ratios that would vary with the state of the overall economy. This would give the Bank of Canada some additional leverage to influence credit conditions (on top of its existing ability to influence interest rates).

Other means with which the Bank of Canada and federal regulators could help to ensure a stable supply of credit in accordance with macroeconomic needs should also be explored. As described earlier, the Bank of Canada itself can act more aggressively as a source of new credit, especially during contractionary times when private banks tend to be reducing their credit creation.

The role of the deposit insurance system also needs to be updated and strengthened. Some conservative analysts have called for a watering down of deposit insurance, in favour of a "buyer-beware" approach in which it would be up to each individual depositor to ensure their funds were invested in "stable" institutions. This would mark a disastrous step backward to a free-wheeling era in which bank failures and the resulting economic and social disruption were a common event. Public concern over the risk of bank failures clearly undermines the stability of even the most prudently-managed bank, and deposit insurance is a highly effective means of reducing that public concern.

Finally, other systems of regulatory oversight over the pace and distribution of credit creation (including such proposals as more public banking, or the explicit planning of aggregate credit expansion by monetary authorities through such means as credit quotas which would be auctioned or allocated to private banks) should be considered. The key goal of this whole regulatory approach is to vest financial supervisors with more capacity to regulate and plan the expansion of credit to make it more commensurate with the needs and priorities of the whole economy, rather than just the needs and priorities of private financial institutions.

Consumer service performance requirements

To address the concern that the provision of basic banking services to Canadians (especially for poor or isolated Canadians) has been inadequate, and may get worse in the event of bank mergers, financial institutions should be required to meet certain performance standards with regard to their services for targeted groups. Institutions should be restricted from closing branches in identifiable neighbourhoods or rural communities where this closure would eliminate basic banking service.

Deposit-taking institutions should also be obliged to offer an ultra-basic package of consumer services (a chequing account with up to six cheques per month and six cash withdrawals per month) for a very low price: say, an inclusive service charge of $2 per month. This package might be available to anyone with income under, say, $25,000. Current identification requirements which also make it harder for poor people to open bank accounts (forcing them to deal with expensive cheque-cashing agencies) should be eased.

Community reinvestment

The principle of community reinvestment is intuitively appealing: banks have been granted unique powers of operation by the community, and as a cost of doing business they should be required to use those powers in ways that enhance community welfare (growth and job-creation) rather than solely their own profits. U.S. banks are subject to a Community Reinvestment Act (CRA), which mandates a greater degree of disclosure regarding lending practices than is required of Canadian banks, and also requires banks to meet certain targets for lending to homeowners and businesses in hard-hit neighbourhoods and regions. Similar measures should be considered in Canada; the Ottawa-based Canadian Community Reinvestment Coalition has been actively lobbying for such legislation.

Closer links

Banks and near-banks should be required to hold a certain proportion of their total business lending to non-financial enterprises in the form of either equity or long-term subordinated debt. [Subordinated debt ranks only above shareholders' equity on the ladder of claims against a bankrupt company; furthermore, subordinated debt cannot be "called" in by a lender before its term expires.] This target would be phased in over time. A possible initial goal might be to require the institutions to have 10% percent of their total business lending invested in this form after 10 years, rising subsequently.

   The purpose of this regulation would be to force banks to take a more direct and active interest in the operation of companies in the real economy: that is, to close some of the gap between the paper economy (which deals in securities) and the real economy (which produces goods and services). This would be an attempt to push our banking system closer to the European model, in which the link between financial and industrial capital is much closer than the arm's-length practice of "Anglo-Saxon" banking systems.

Promote credit unions

Even if all of the foregoing proposals were adopted, we would have a banking system that was somewhat more accountable to the social and economic needs of the country; but it would still be a banking system centred on the profit-seeking operations of private corporations. And so, when push comes to shove, the need of those corporations for profit and security will always outweigh the need of the domestic economy (especially during times of economic stagnation or financial uncertainty) for credit and growth. Ultimately, more ownership of (and

> ## Sacred Cow
> "My vision is a credit union system that has a standardized service and products across the country so it doesn't matter where I am doing business. However, the credit union philosophy—one member, one vote—will not change. It is a sacred cow."
>
> —Bobby McVeigh, Chair
> Credit Union Central of Canada
> July 14, 1998

hence direct control over) the financial system will need to be socialized in some form.

The creation of publicly-owned banks in specific niches of the financial system would be one important way to start to socialize ownership over finance; and some initial ideas in this regard are explored in Chapter 16. Credit unions constitute another unique and promising vehicle with which to expand democratic control over the realm of finance. Credit unions are the only sector of the paper economy which operates according to the fundamentally democratic principle of one person, one vote (*see quote*). They possess an honourable history, rooted in the struggles of groups of farmers and workers to offset the lopsided and exploitive actions of private banks.

Credit unions, however, currently face severe challenges in attempting to preserve their unique character and function as the private paper boom unfolds around them. Much of their traditional savings and loan business has been lost to the growth of mutual funds and other forms of personal investing. Many credit unions are also hampered by their small size and relatively higher overhead costs, compared to banks and other multi-branch institutions which have attained economies of scale in administration and service costs. The assets of credit unions grew half as quickly during the 1990s as did those of chartered banks.

Leaders of the movement now recognize that credit unions must act creatively and dramatically to preserve their current small role in the overall financial system (credit unions in total possessed $110 billion in assets as of the end of 1997, or about 2% of all financial assets in Canada), let alone to provide a more challenging alternative to commercial institutions. A national credit union restructuring initiative was undertaken in 1998 to consider alternative strategies for the movement. At the top of the agenda was the need to find ways to link credit unions (most of which are very small) into a more cohesive and efficient Canada-wide financial force.

Some credit union officials have responded to the challenges the movement faces by attempting to become more like the banks they are competing with. More, however, have sought to rejuvenate the energy of the credit union movement by tapping into the still-strong political and social justice roots from which the credit unions grew in the first place. Many credit unions have become more aggressive and political in challenging the actions and image of private banks. The growth, diversification, and social activism of the VanCity Savings Credit Union—Canada's largest, with $6 billion in assets—provides just one example of the potential this movement holds.[10]

The federal and provincial governments could take a number of actions that would support the restructuring and rejuvenation of Canada's credit union movement. Current provincial restrictions bar credit unions from conducting business across provincial borders; these curbs should be eased (perhaps through federal legislation allowing for the formation of a member-owned national credit-union "bank") to allow credit unions to establish a nation-wide financial network. Credit unions should also be exempted from income taxes and other levies, by virtue of their status as non-profit community-service organizations.

And current capital adequacy and deposit insurance regulations should be restructured so as to allow credit unions more leeway to expand their lending and investing activities into new venture financing and other non-traditional activities. Credit unions have typically limited most of their lending to household mortgages and other very stable types of loans. With appropriate regulatory changes, however, credit unions could become more ambitious in their own efforts to put money into motion in the real economy.

Limiting the scope of finance

Finally, the general role of private financial markets in Canadian society should simply be limited, where possible. It is doubtful that even the most far-reaching regulatory changes would ever impart a true stability and rationality to the actions of private asset markets, which will continue to be driven by speculative manias and panics. In this case, an implicit goal of general economic and social policy should be to attempt to limit the reliance of communities and governments on these asset markets in the first place. The smaller the general economic and social scope of private finance, the less the economic disruption that will be wrought when these markets go awry.

In those countries in which stock markets and other highly liquid and volatile financial structures play a smaller role—most notably in much of continental Europe—the nitty-gritty process of real investment has been less prone to financial disruption, and hence the record of real capital accumulation has been stronger.

Most importantly in Canada's case, the general "stock-marketization" of our social programs must be stopped and reversed. Perhaps entranced themselves by the aura of lucrative rationality which now surrounds anything to do with the "markets," governments have been expanding their own participation in financial trading, at the expense (and risk) of taxpayers. There is no reason for the federal government to turn to private financial markets to fund everything from pensions (RRSPs, and now even a portion of the Canada Pension Plan) to university scholarships (Registered Education Savings Plans, and the commercially-invested Millennium fund).

The Reform Party's proposal to do away with the CPP altogether, to be replaced with compulsory individual stock market accounts, represents the most extreme and potentially destructive example of this trend to securitize virtually everything in society. Apart from constituting an expansion of the already-generous public subsidies to an already-lucrative financial industry, the stock-marketization of government programs clearly also increases the general vulnerability of Canadian society to financial bubbles and panics.

Financial Regulation: International

Canada's financial system obviously operates in a global context. While some aspects of the supposed power of globalization have been overstated (see the discussion in Chapter 8), it is nevertheless certainly the case that attempts to reregulate finance from a purely domestic perspective are likely to be undermined or scuppered entirely by international financial forces. At the same time, therefore, as government acts to democratize our financial system from within and reorient it towards the facilitation of real growth rather than paper profits, it must also act—both alone and in concert with others—to attain more stability and accountability in international financial outcomes.

Tobin tax

The most commonly-advanced proposal for reregulating international finance is the idea of a so-called "Tobin tax" (named for the Nobel-prize-winning economist who first devised it, James Tobin) on international financial transactions. The general idea is to impose a tax, as small as a fraction of one percentage point, on each international transaction (such as every foreign exchange conversion). The tax would be administered by some multilateral agency (such as the International Monetary Fund, or perhaps a new body established by the United Nations), and its potentially huge proceeds would be allocated to world social and economic development projects.

For real international trade transactions and long-run real foreign investment flows, the tax would be too small to alter any economic behaviour. For short-run speculative transactions, however, which are often premised on attempts to profit from very small movements in foreign exchange rates, relative bond yields, or other asset prices, even a very small tax might be sufficient to discourage some speculative activity." The idea of a Tobin tax received a major symbolic boost in March 1999, when the Canadian Parliament approved a private member's bill, introduced by NDP member Lorne Nystrom, in favour of the multilateral introduction of such a measure. Canada's was thus the first parliament in the world to formally support the Tobin tax.

A Tobin tax would certainly be a first step towards the re-regulation of international financial flows. Its overall economic potential,however, should not be exaggerated. A Tobin tax would clearly have done little to prevent or even moderate the huge international capital flows that first pushed financial markets in several east Asian countries to undreamed-of heights, and then—by suddenly and catastrophically reversing direction—brought those markets tumbling down, leaving vast human misery in their wake.

Both the inflow of that money to Asia and its subsequent panic-stricken withdrawal were motivated by the hope or fear of gains and losses hundreds of times larger than the marginal disincentive created by any conceivable Tobin tax. Neither the awestruck investors who piled into Asia nor the horrified investors who poured out would have given such a tax even a moment's thought before committing themselves in either direction.

There is some economic evidence that small changes in transactions costs are unlikely to have any impact on overall financial market volatility; for example, the transactions costs associated with stock market buying and selling have declined significantly in recent years, thanks to the emergence of discount brokers and other institutions, yet there is no clear evidence that stock market volatility is any higher than in previous eras.

Perhaps the greatest argument for a Tobin tax is that it would at least collect some useful tax revenue from the financial investors who have wreaked such havoc in the global economy. This was the stated rationale of Finance Minister Paul Martin in March 1999 when he cast his own vote for the NDP proposal.

Foreign content limits

Some measures can be taken unilaterally to limit the extent of cross-border financial hyperactivity. One of the most important financial stabilizers, in Canada's case, is the current restriction on the foreign investment of funds invested in tax-subsidized RRSPs and Registered Pension Plans (RPPs). As has been discussed throughout this book, these funds benefit from extremely generous subsidies provided courtesy of Canadian taxpayers. The total cost of the tax incentives provided to both RRSPs and RPPs in 1999, by both the federal and provincial governments, approached an awesome $30 billion.

Given this huge degree of taxpayer support for financial investments, it hardly seems unreasonable to require that these funds at least be invested in Canada. Present rules specify that no more than 20% of these funds can be invested outside of the country. The rule is already "leaky": investors can in practice exceed the 20% limit through a number of loopholes, such as "segregated" mutual funds and labour-sponsored venture capital funds. Nevertheless, the rule is effective in forcing a significant portion of financial assets (perhaps $800 billion in RRSP and RPP investments are subject to the rule) to permanently call Canada home.

As we have seen, of course, merely investing money in a Canadian financial asset hardly ensures that a Canadian job will be created as a result. So the argument that keeping this money at home will help to create jobs here is not, on its own, especially convincing: for this to occur, we would also need measures to ensure that financial investments are more effectively put into real economic motion. Nevertheless, even in purely financial terms there are worthwhile benefits to keeping these huge stockpiles of money within the country. The fact that

Political Prisoner

"Canadian savings should be set free," screamed the headline over the *Globe and Mail* editorial of July 16, 1997. How shocking. Canadian savings are unjustly imprisoned? Where is Amnesty International when you need it?

What sparked this urgent human rights appeal on the part of Canada's leading business newspaper? The editorial called for the elimination of the foreign-content rule on RRSPs and RPPs—just one of about several hundred articles making the same case in Canadian financial publications during the late 1990s.

It turns out that Canadian savings are not quite as strictly imprisoned as, say, a labour activist in Indonesia, or a women's rights advocate in Afghanistan. Canada dismantled all restrictions on the international outflow of capital decades ago. Anyone can go to any major bank and arrange to have as much of their money as they want converted into any convertible currency and transferred to any bank anywhere in the world that will accept it.

So how is it that Canadian savings are not "free"? It is only if a financial investor willingly and voluntarily accepts a generous up-front government subsidy—worth 50% or more for high-income investors in most provinces—that he or she is obliged, as a *quid pro quo*, to keep most of their money at home. The financial editorialists rail against this government intrusion into the operation of private financial markets. But providing some $30 billion of tax assistance per year for financial investments—well, that's a form of government intrusion that Bay Street can apparently live with.

"Freedom," it seems, is in the eye of the beholder. The "freedom" of financiers to invest even more of their tax-subsidized capital in foreign countries is not really relevant to most Canadians. By the same token, the "freedom" of a homeless person to sleep under a bridge is not really relevant to most financiers.

such a significant portion of total financial assets is limited in its ability to exit considerably reduces the vulnerability of Canada, its currency, and its financial institutions to the sort of near-panic that erupted here in the summer of 1998, when the loonie plunged to an all-time record low amidst the departure of billions of dollars of "hot" money from Canadian markets.

The foreign content limit has come in for intense criticism from the financial industry and many financial investors, who bitterly resent any restrictions placed on their participation in the global paper chase (see sidebar: *Political Prisoner*). Financial lobbyists pretend that, since seemingly all Canadians have joined the personal investing bandwagon, virtually everyone would benefit from being able to capture higher foreign financial returns. The reality, of course, is that most Canadians have no significant stake in the stock market at all, and hence this regulatory change could not possibly generate measurable benefits for them.

On the other hand, the costs of further liberalizing these financial investments could be quite high. The foreign content limit on tax-subsidized pension funds should remain in place, and current loopholes in the rule should be closed.

Reforming international institutions

International financial institutions, and in particular the two Bretton Woods institutions (the International Monetary Fund and the World Bank),[12] have done little to resolve the crucial problems of global finance. In many cases, indeed, they have done far more harm than good. Canada must push for a fundamental change in direction at these bodies and at other forums overseeing the global response to seemingly endless financial crisis. The orthodox IMF recipe—high interest rates and sharp fiscal cutbacks for already hard-hit emerging economies—has proven to be disastrously counterproductive, exacerbating the negative economic and financial implications of capital flight. The IMF and the largest industrial countries should support urgent measures to sustain purchasing power and employment in the Asian and Latin American economies hardest hit by financial crisis.

Important regulatory issues also need to be pursued at the IMF and the Basel-based Bank of International Settlements (BIS). In the case of the IMF, the ongoing demand by the U.S. and some other governments that all participating nations be required to guarantee full capital account convertibility—to guarantee, in other words, the complete and absolute right of short-term financial speculators to convert their funds into any currency at any time they want—must be vigorously opposed. Recent experience has shown convincingly that individual nations must retain the right to clamp down on capital flows when those flows are socially and economically destructive.

Similarly, current BIS regulations perversely favour destabilizing short-run capital flows by exempting them from capital adequacy requirements that are imposed on longer-run capital transactions. These must be changed so that short-run investors face regulatory requirements at least as severe as those applied to long-haul investors.

Debt forgiveness

Canada needs to take the lead in writing-off accumulated debts of the hardest-hit developing economies, with private Western financial institutions bearing an appropriate share of the cost of this measure. Without debt relief, these poorest economies have literally no hope of emerging from the debt-servicing trap into which they have fallen as a result of global financial instability. The Jubilee 2000 initiative, sponsored by numerous religious and other concerned constituencies, would mark a huge step in the right direction.

Global central bank

More generally, Canada should work with other sympathetic governments in Europe and elsewhere to build support for new international financial institutions that would regulate and moderate the booms and busts of private finance. Ultimately, some form of global central bank will be required: one that imposes adjustment burdens on surplus as well as deficit countries, acts as a true lender-of-last-resort (rather than focusing on simple bail-outs of private financiers as the IMF has done), limits short-term financial flows when needed, and facilitates global growth through coordinated interest rate policies.

As national economies developed more sophisticated and integrated financial systems late in the last century and early in this one, it was discovered that the creation of powerful central banks at the national level was essential for ongoing financial stability and efficiency. Given the easy global reach of finance today, the same thing clearly needs to happen at an international level.

British economist John Maynard Keynes proposed the creation of a global central bank at the conclusion of World War II—an institution that would pump necessary liquidity into global markets and keep interest rates low to promote global employment growth. His arguments were rebuffed at the time, but are finding a new and receptive audience as the century draws to a tumultuous close.[13]

The development of a global central bank would require the solution of very difficult political and administrative problems. The formidable task of creating such an institution at just the continental level in Europe was daunting enough, despite a much closer degree of economic, political, and geographical harmonization among the participating nations. The creation of a global central bank is admittedly a long way off—but there has never been a better time to start debating and designing such an institution.

Chapter 15
A Human Face for Finance?

The discouraging state of Canada's real economy during most of the last two decades has prompted a chorus of calls for alternative investment vehicles and institutions. Stock markets, banks, and the real businesses which they finance have clearly failed in their responsibility to put Canada's huge sums of new money into motion in the real economy, creating the jobs we need and producing goods and services that we can consume.

The contrast between the paper boom of the financial industry on one hand, and the general stagnation of the real economy on the other, has motivated a widespread questioning of existing financial institutions on the part of many Canadians.

One broad response to the financial system's poor record of raising and investing funds for economically and socially useful projects has been a range of initiatives aimed at trying to redirect the flow of private finance into more con-structive (or at least less destructive) endeavours. The most noteworthy of these "activist investment" initiatives include ethical mutual funds, labour-sponsored venture capital funds, and efforts by some unions to win more say over the in-vestment of workplace pension funds.

Participants in each of these strategies aim to gain more control over the raising and investing of financial capital by becoming directly active as concerned investors; these strategies can all be described, therefore, as efforts to reform our system of financial investment "from within." This immediately raises a fun-damental question, in that we have already seen (in Chapter 12) that most Cana-dians, contrary to the hype of the mutual fund industry, are *not* investors.

The ownership of most capital, in reality, is concentrated among a small elite of very well-off households. This would seem to inherently limit the prospects of any strategy which mobilizes concerned Canadians as *investors* (rather than as citizens, taxpayers, or voters). And indeed, while each of the "activist investor" strategies surely holds some potential for effecting some change in the investment process, and enforcing a higher standard of accountability on the part of both money managers and the executives of real businesses, each also has its pitfalls which we will consider.

Ethical Mutual Funds

The most spectacularly successful activist investment initiative is the group of mutual funds in Canada which claim to base their investment decisions on ethical and social criteria, rather than just bottom-line returns. The largest ethical mutual fund sponsor in Canada is Ethical Funds Inc., conceived by the VanCity Savings Credit Union (English Canada's largest credit union) and now owned by a segment of the Canadian credit union system.

Its flagship fund, the Ethical Growth Fund, represented about $750 million in invested assets by the end of 1998, and hence ranks among the top 10% of mutual funds in Canada. Total assets contained in Ethical Funds' eight different mutual funds exceed $2 billion. Thanks to some great publicity and good financial performance (it is one of the few mutual funds which have actually matched or exceeded the average returns of the stock market during much of its history), the Ethical Growth Fund has grown exponentially in recent years. The fund was even selected as "Fund of the Year" by high-profile mutual fund analyst Gordon Pape in 1997.

More recently, sales have been spurred by a series of hard-hitting and effective television and print ads trumpeting the ethical approach to personal investing. By any standard, the company is one of the greatest success stories of the entire mutual fund industry—and yet it claims to be motivated by a higher cause than simple greed.

Other companies have also tried to cash in on the ethical investing craze. For example, the Investors' Group, one of Canada's largest mutual fund companies, with close to $20 billion under management, has its own $600 million ethical "Summa" fund. The Desjardins Trust group (associated with Quebec's credit union movement) has a $125 million "environment" fund. And several smaller, specialized funds have also sprung up, purportedly to channel investors' money into environmentally-aware companies and other worthy endeavours.

The notion of being concerned with principles—not just principal—in making investment decisions has helped the sponsors of ethical mutual funds to carve out a unique identity for themselves in a mutual fund marketplace that is cluttered with hundreds of competing providers. Indeed, while the intentions of the ethical investment pioneers who started this initiative were clearly laudable, it may not solely be a higher calling which explains their subsequent spectacular growth.

For example, the vice-president of Investors Group (which manages close to $20 billion in *non*-ethical investments in addition to its $600 million ethical fund) explained his firm's move into the ethical marketplace in the following pragmatic terms: "Based on the feedback from our sales reps, who are in touch with the public, we detect a market for this kind of product."

The ethical funds movement was initially ridiculed by investment professionals, on grounds that it could never match the rates of return generated by money managers who were not constrained by any social or ethical criteria. By artificially limiting the "universe" of investment options available to the fund's managers, the ethical investing approach would inevitably limit the returns available, too. But the ethical funds have proven these critics wrong. Returns on most ethical funds have been at least as high as average returns for other mutual funds—although, recall (as illustrated in Chapter 3) that mutual funds in general, despite their high management fees, do not match the performance of simple weighted stock market indices.

The success of the ethical funds industry, however, has raised a whole new set of controversies for the well-intentioned financiers who started it, concerns that may not be as easy for the industry to refute. Just how "ethical" is the ethical funds industry? And to what extent can individuals realistically promote a vision of social change through their mutual fund portfolios, rather than through traditional outlets for their social and political ideals?

This quandary was dramatized by an incident involving the Ethical Growth Fund in 1998. A Vancouver paper ran an exposé on how the fund—which is supposed to screen all of its investments to weed out companies associated with tobacco, military procurement, child labour, and other unsavoury practices—had invested in a strange-sounding financial beast called TIPS 35 units. These units essentially constitute a "no-brain" index-based mutual fund, in which an investor buys a portion of a bundle of different stocks constructed to precisely mirror the performance of a particular stock market.

In this case, a purchaser of TIPS 35 units would be guaranteed a return equal to the performance of the Toronto Stock Exchange's TSE 35 index, which in turn reflects the share prices of Canada's 35 largest publicly-traded companies. Investing in this type of product (or in other similar funds, such as the low-fee index funds now being sold aggressively by Canada's increasingly competitive mutual fund industry) ensures that an investor won't do any better or any worse than the market average.

Considering that most mutual funds cannot even match the performance of their respective market benchmarks, this isn't bad—although it begs another question. Why would a mutual fund buy units in a separate index fund, when the fund's clients could make that investment directly (and thus avoid the 2% annual management fees charged by actively managed mutual funds, including the Ethical Growth Fund)? As of the end of 1997, the $25 million cost of Ethical Growth's TIPS 35 units represented the fund's largest single asset purchase to date.

Whoever decided to put Ethical Growth money into the TIPS units either didn't realize that they were actually investing in all 35 of the largest companies in Canada, or else they thought that this indirect investing approach would not constitute a violation of the fund's ethical criteria. But three of the top 35 companies clearly violate the Ethical Growth fund's criteria: Imasco, which sells tobacco products, Bombardier, which is a military contractor, and Placer Dome, which had theoretically been excluded from the fund's portfolio following a disastrous mine spill in the Philippines.

After this inconsistency hit the newspapers, Ethical Growth changed its policy to prevent similar index-fund lapses in the future (in fact, the Fund had already sold its TIPS units by the time the controversy became public).[1]

End of story? Well, not exactly. The whole episode raises more fundamental doubts about the exact nature of Ethical Growth's social mandate. The outcome of the TIPS 35 controversy seems to imply that modern corporate capitalism in Canada must be a 91% ethical state of affairs, since 32 of the 35 companies (or 91%) represented in the TIPS 35 units *did* pass the fund's ethical screens. Consider a list of these companies:

- all six of Canada's largest banks
- family-run empires like Laidlaw, Seagram, and Thomson
- fiercely anti-union auto parts giant Magna International
- resource producers, including Abitibi-Consolidated, Alcan Aluminum, Barrick Gold, Inco, Macmillan Bloedel, Noranda, and Suncor
- relentless downsizers like Bell Canada, Canadian National Railway, and Northern Telecom—each of which has laid off thousands of Canadian employees during the 1990s in the search for higher profits

Even the least ambitious of social advocates would be unlikely to consider these corporate icons to represent the ethical cutting edge of Canadian society.

Perhaps the managers of Ethical Funds—not to mention the investing public—should have been less concerned with the fact that three large "unethical" corporations accidentally slipped through the fund's screening process, than with

Just A Bunch of Ethical Guys

Executive:	Peter Munk	Al Flood	Frank Stronach	Derek Burney
Company:	Barrick Gold Corp.	Canadian Imperial Bank of Commerce	Magna International Inc.	Bell Canada International Inc.
1997 executive compensation:	$3.6 million	$3.2 million	$26.1 million	$1.0 million
Famous Quote:	"That man [Augusto Pinochet, former Chilean dictator] ... had the courage to single-handedly change the direction of a whole continent."	"Austerity is not pleasant; but self-imposed austerity ... is infinitely preferable to externally-imposed austerity following disaster."	"To be in business, your first mandate is to make money, and money has no heart, soul, conscience, or homeland."	"Our much admired social safety net has led to a culture of entitlement which must be changed quickly."
Ethical Fund holdings, end-1997.	$12.8 million	$38.5 million	$34.0 million	$2.5 million

Source: Ethical Funds Inc. 1997 Annual Report, Globe and Mail, May 10, 1996 and April 18, 1998; Financial Post, March 29, 1994; Perspectives, Business Council on National Issues, Autumn 1994; New York Newsday, August 7, 1992.

the fact that even when correctly applied this screening process has virtually no impact on the composition of the fund's investments. An investment in an ethical mutual fund, for all intents and purposes, is pretty much just an investment in the broader stock market.

A small number of controversial companies is excluded from consideration on specific and narrow criteria (such as involvement in tobacco or weapons).[2] But, by and large, the ethical funds' holdings mirror those of the stock market as a whole. This will come as a jarring surprise to many well-intentioned investors who felt they were actually dedicating their money to good works. And the incredibly modest criteria applied to the funds' investment decisions contrasts strikingly with the powerful and emotional images evoked by the funds' advertising.

Stark images of dying cancer patients, chain-smoking Third World teenagers, and squads of grim commandos marching into battle: these are the emotional symbols that have moved thousands of investors to channel their money into the ethical funds' coffers. But, aside from a handful of companies directly involved in tobacco or military production, it is clear that most corporate behaviour (and most of the stock market) is quite okay, thank you, for the ethical money managers.

The heavy emphasis on investments in the major banks by the ethical mutual funds is particularly problematic in this regard. As of the end of 1997, the Ethical Growth Fund had invested a full 16% of its common equity assets in the shares of just three banks: the Bank of Montreal, the Bank of Nova Scotia, and

the Royal Bank. The fund's $33 million stake in the Bank of Nova Scotia repre-
sented its largest single investment. Its $31 million holdings of the Royal Bank
were its second-largest single investment.

Tens of millions of dollars of bank shares and bonds were also held by the
other funds in the Ethical Funds portfolio (such as its bond and income funds).
The competing Investors Summa fund was also heavily weighted in banks: its
four top holdings as of May 1998 were major banks, together accounting for 18%
of the total value of the fund.

The fantastic profitability of Canada's chartered banks during the 1990s, and
the consequent rapid appreciation of their share prices, thus contributed to the
relatively encouraging financial performance of the ethical mutual funds. For
example, the Ethical Growth Fund's 1997 total rate of return was 17.4%, higher
than the 15.0% total return on the TSE 300 stock market index that year. But,
without its significant bank holdings, the fund's total return that year would have
been just 11.7%—considerably *less* than the growth in the TSE index.

Now, it seems odd that an investment fund which bills itself as an alternative to the commercial, bottom-line-fixated financial establishment would focus
so heavily on investing in the most powerful and entrenched representatives of
that same financial establishment. What is it about Canada's major banks which
justifies their designation as a leading ethical investment opportunity?

True, banks do not have smokestacks which pollute the atmosphere, and
they do not produce military hardware. But the role played by banks in Canada's
economy can hardly be described as "ethical." The banks have benefited mightily from—and hence have energetically lobbied for—exactly the same set of conservative economic policies that have so undermined growth and job-creation,
and hobbled the ability of the state to moderate and regulate the character of
that growth.

The banks have a huge vested interest in continuing Canada's tough anti-
inflation policy, consistently high real interest rates, the wide-ranging deregulation of many economic sectors (most notably including finance itself), sharp cutbacks in government programs, and more recently the allocation of government
surpluses to debt repayment and tax cuts rather than social reinvestment.

Even in their own employment and management practices, Canada's banks
have revealed their self-interested and regressive character. They ruthlessly
smashed repeated unionization attempts in the 1980s, and continue to pay their
hourly clerical employees very low wages. Despite earning total profits in excess of $7 billion during 1997, the banking industry employed 35,000 hourly em-
ployees who earned an average of just $12 an hour (and only received 24 hours of
work per week, on average).

Canada's best-paid banker that year—John Hunkin, head of the investment banking arm of CIBC, who pulled in total compensation of $10.4 million—single-handedly took home more income in 1997 than 680 of these average bank tellers.

In short, the banks epitomize what is wrong with Canada's paper economy, not how to make it more ethical. Moreover, the practice of investing in an independently-managed lending institution punches a huge hole in the ethical wall which supposedly oversees the investment decisions of the ethical mutual funds. For some reason, chartered banks are considered sufficiently ethical to pass the screens erected by the ethical fund industry. But those banks in turn have no screens governing their own lending and investment decisions: they invest in *any* venture, including those that might have been turned down by ethical mutual funds.

If the reasoning behind the ethical mutual fund industry is to "starve" unethical ventures of new financial capital, thus limiting their expansion opportunities (in fact, this reasoning is weak, as is discussed below), then investments in banks and other unscreened financial institutions clearly undermine the whole approach.

Another example of this contradiction is the Ethical Growth Fund's $20 million stake (as of end-1997) in another mutual fund company, Investors Group. [This is the same company, ironically, which sponsors the Summa ethical fund—the Ethical Growth Fund's leading competitor.] Apart from epitomizing the bizarre and wasteful practice of mutual fund companies investing in other mutual fund companies, this investment begs another question. The Investors Group manages $20 billion in assets, the vast majority of which (apart from the $600 million Summa fund) is not screened on ethical grounds. Why invest in a mutual fund company for ethical reasons, when that company in turn invests in *another* mutual fund company which does not impose screens on its investment decisions?[3] The whole process begins to resemble a shell game, in which the appearance of acting ethically becomes more important (for advertising purposes) than whether or not the money actually ends up supporting a "good cause."

Not surprisingly for an initiative which has proclaimed such lofty goals in its advertising, the rather modest and pragmatic reality of "ethical investing" has sparked considerable controversy. Critics have complained that too many ethical fund holdings are not nearly "ethical" enough, and bristle at the dominance of establishment blue-chip corporations in the funds' portfolios.

The extensive foreign holdings of the ethical funds also sparks concern; for example, as of 1997, the Ethical Funds company had invested some $225 million of its total assets outside of Canada (both through specialized "segregated" foreign funds, and through the 20% foreign content allowed within balanced mutual funds), in the stocks of such global ethical leaders as Disney Corp., IBM, Microsoft, and private U.S. health-care providers.

The ethical fund managers respond that it is better to do something, however imperfect, than to do nothing; they argue that it is better to reward corporations which are at least trying to modify the social or environmental impacts of certain of their operations, than to abstain entirely from making ethical choices in personal investing. This debate obviously needs to continue, and recent controversies regarding some of the holdings of the ethical funds will probably ensure that it does continue. Since many ethical funds are owned by credit unions, which themselves represent a rare bastion of democracy within the financial industry, there is considerable prospect for improving the ethical performance of the industry precisely through this public debate and pressure.

There are several other tough issues, however, quite unrelated to the problems of defining what constitutes an "ethical" investment, which must also be addressed by the advocates of ethical stock market investing.

For example, the link between buying or not buying the shares of a particular company, and actually influencing the *behaviour* of that company, is generally taken for granted in the ethical investing literature. It shouldn't be. When an ethical mutual fund claims that it will put money to work in "good" companies, and not in "bad" ones, it is accepting the proposition that there is a fairly direct link between the stock market (where shares are bought and sold) and the real investment and business activities of the companies listed there. Most of this entire book, however, has been dedicated to showing that this is not the case.

When ethical mutual funds (or any other mutual funds) buy shares, they are not "giving" that money to the company whose name appears on the shares, and they are not "putting their money to work" in the real economic operations of that company. Rather, they are giving the money to whatever investor owned the share previously. Unless the share is purchased through a new issue, and unless that new issue is raising new funds for a company (rather than buying out previous insider owners of the company, or reducing the firm's debt levels), the buying and selling of shares has nothing to do with raising money for real business activities.

As described in Chapter 3, well over 95% of stock market activity—which has been fuelled frenetically in recent years by the constant churning activity of pension and mutual funds—has no connection with financing real investments. So the notion that an investor is withholding capital from a company by virtue of not purchasing its shares is economically incredible.

Ethical fund advertising has promoted the misconception that buying a company's shares is equivalent to giving that company some money, because this impression reinforces the emotional power of the desired message. For example, a powerful 1998 set of television ads for Ethical Funds featured a woman grieving for a relative lost to smoking-related cancer. After describing the woman's anger at the tobacco industry, the ads grimly report: "But every year she unknowingly sends them a donation," in the form of holding tobacco-related shares in her mutual fund. But how is purchasing a share equivalent to giving a company a donation? It is actually quite wrong to conclude that companies "get" the money that is spent on their shares. In reality, the buying and selling of mutual funds—including ethical mutual funds—has virtually no impact on the financial well-being or real business activity, good or bad, of the companies whose shares are traded like so many poker chips.

Ironically, then, this advertising theme refutes the supposed goal of investor education so espoused by the ethical money managers. As Ethical Funds president John Linthwaite puts it, "We believe that Canadians should know where their money goes." But, if this were genuinely the case, the ethical financiers should explain to clients that their money is actually going to whoever owned the shares of non-offending corporations prior to their purchase on the stock market—minus, of course, a generous 2% administration fee per year to pay for the services of the ethical money managers.

But surely, an ethically-minded personal investor might argue, selling a company's shares will have *some* negative impact on that company's real business. It is certainly true that the collapse of a company's share price is often a signal of some fundamental problem in the company's real business (although this is not always the case: see sidebar *What is Wealth?* in Chapter 2).

A company with a falling share price will face intense pressure—from its shareholders and from its lenders—to make fundamental changes in its business practices. This does not imply, however, that ethical funds could force a company to change its ways by exerting downward pressure on the price of its shares.

In the first place, ethical funds are not possibly large enough to affect share prices on Canada's stock markets: all the ethical funds together account for at most one-tenth of one percent of the total market capitalization of Canada's stock markets. Nor are they likely to ever become large enough to do so. Recall from Chapter 12 that the majority of financial wealth in Canada is concentrated in the hands of a small proportion of well-off families. These families are unlikely to start making many of their decisions on ethical grounds, rather than profit-maximizing grounds. [If they were, they might have given away some of their accumulated wealth!]

In this sense, ethical investing faces far greater barriers than other consumer activist campaigns. Consider the past effectiveness of consumer boycotts in changing the behaviour of certain companies—consumer pressure on the tuna industry to adopt dolphin-safe fishing practices, for example. The fact that billionaire Ken Thomson may not personally support this cause should not greatly affect its chances for success: it is unlikely that the Thomson family consumes any more tuna than the typical Canadian household (indeed, it probably consumes less). Hence Thomson's abstention or opposition is not significant to a campaign based on attracting support from a large number of tuna eaters.

The fact, however, that the Thomson family probably possesses as much stock market wealth as the bottom 50% of the Canadian population clearly *does* undermine the chances for success of the ethical investing movement. In a democratic realm, in which decisions are made one voter (or even one consumer) at a time, it is possible to imagine how powerful movements can be built one person at a time. But, as soon as we enter the realm of private finance, which operates according to the maxim of "one dollar, one vote" (not "one person, one vote"), then the concentrated power of the rich and the super-rich becomes a fundamental obstacle to change.

Even in the unlikely event that the ethical funds movement could mobilize enough support on the basis of "one dollar, one vote" politics to spark a significant sell-off of a particular company's shares, what would happen next? The ethical funds would then face the counteracting influence of investors who are *not* motivated by ethical consideration. They would rush to purchase the affected company's shares, which are now trading at a lower multiple to its expected future earnings than would otherwise be the case.

Remember that a pure ethically-inspired sell-off is not motivated by fear over a company's profits, but rather by ethical concerns.[4] Most investors are not motivated by ethical criteria: they are making decisions based on expectations of bottom-line returns, pure and simple (and this is likely to always be the dominant motivator for private investment decisions). Note that these investors do not have to be *anti-ethical* in order to frustrate the effects of the ethical funds movement; they merely have to be "agnostic." [An anti-ethical investor would be someone who purchased an unethical company's shares despite expectation of a *lower* return.] In other words, they merely have to be neutral on the issue of a company's ethical performance.

The ethically-inspired sell-off of a company's shares perversely *increases* the relative attractiveness of those shares according to traditional investment criteria, since the share price is now temporarily lower than would otherwise be justified, given the expected future profits and dividends of the company. Agnostic investors will snap up the shares, and the share price should return to its original level, with the only permanent effect being a one-time transfer of wealth from ethical investors (who sold low on ethical grounds) to agnostic investors (who purchased shares in a still-profitable company at an artificially low price).[5]

In short, the economic intuition underlying the notion that ethical invest-ment decisions can impact corporate behaviour is incredibly muddled. This prob-ably explains why this intuition is rarely, if ever, spelled out.

Many ethical investors point to the pressure that can be brought to bear on corporate executives through actions launched by concerned shareholders: le-gal suits, publicity campaigns, the raising of controversial issues at sharehold-ers' meetings, approaching other shareholders to express their concerns, and so on. To be sure, these forms of pressure and lobbying can be quite successful in modifying some of the worst practices of private businesses, especially when combined with pressure levied against the firm from outside the shareholders' community (from workers, communities, or governments). Shareholder activ-ism has played an important role in many important social change initiatives in Canada; it was particularly notable in the successful efforts to force Canadian banks to divest some of their holdings in apartheid South Africa, Pinochet's Chile, and other notorious jurisdictions. But it has been the *activism* of shareholders in these instances, not their ownership of shares, which has been influential in changing corporate behaviour. Indeed, many or most of the activists in Cana-dian corporate responsibility campaigns (many of which were launched by reli-gious organizations) had purchased just a single token share of the offending company—so as to gain admittance to shareholders' meetings and position them-selves as "insiders" in the debate. It was the loudness of their voices and the persistence of their organizing, not the market value of their portfolios, which made these activists so effective.

Incredibly, however, the ethical money managers have betrayed this legacy of shareholder activism with their explicit decision to remain purely *passive* play-ers in the companies represented in their portfolios. Far from using its shareholdings to pressure companies to improve their practices, the ethical funds movement has explicitly limited its role strictly to buying or not buying a compa-ny's shares. As Ethical Funds president John Linthwaite puts it, "It is not within our mandate to take an activist stance on specific issues." This will come as a surprising disappointment to many whose hopes were raised precisely by the prospect of using their money to promote activist goals. Even when an ethical fund takes the rare step of dumping its holdings in an offending company, it does so quietly and without fanfare (usually for legal reasons, and to avoid burning bridges within the tightly-knit community of private financiers), rather than making a high-profile statement of protest which might reinforce the efforts of non-shareholding parties to enforce a higher standard of accountability on the offending business.

Sadly, in some cases the ethical funds have even helped to defeat these expressions of genuine shareholder activism. For example, the Ethical Growth fund cast its proxy votes with management in defeating a motion to limit CEO compensation to no more than 20 times the salary of an average bank employee, introduced by activist shareholders at the 1997 annual meeting of the Royal Bank. President John Linthwaite, justifying the fund's stand on this issue, said: "This ... was very much a corporate governance issue, where we normally adopt a policy of voting in favour of anything that enhances shareholder value." [6]

In general, the statements and actions of the ethical mutual fund industry might be characterized as well-intentioned but overstated. The industry's effective advertizing has raised the expectations of ethically-minded individual investors far higher than is justifiable given both the very cautious, pragmatic nature of the funds' actual screening processes, and the industry's refusal to become an active insider in the struggle for more socially responsible corporate behaviour. In this context, the funds can be rightly criticized for not doing as much "good" as they imply with their advertizing, but surely they are at least moving in the right direction.

In some respects, however, the ethical funds' promotion campaigns may actually undermine the longer-role goal of reforming and regulating the financial industry. Nowhere is this more the case than with the ethical funds' oft-repeated claim that there is no contradiction between earning a high rate of profit and being true to one's principles. "Performance without compromise," crows the Ethical Funds prospectus. "At Ethical Funds, we believe that in order to achieve superior financial returns, you don't have to sacrifice your principles," explains another brochure. "Time and time again, we've found that progressive, ethically-managed companies are more profitable that their less conscientious counterparts." The ethical funds industry has gone to great lengths to make the point that its clients need not forego *any* profit in order to make a social statement with their mutual fund investments. And this case seems to have been proven by the relatively good financial performance of the major ethical funds.

But this whole approach can lead to some strange and worrisome political conclusions. First, if a private financial investor can earn a high rate of return from an ethical mutual fund, does this not seem to imply that the profits earned by those lucky Canadians who own significant quantities of financial wealth are somehow fundamentally "ethical"? We have seen that most financial wealth in Canada is owned by a small elite of society. Is there not some ethical problem with the very fact that someone receives large amounts of new money by sole virtue of the fact that they owned large amounts of money in the first place? Apparently not, in the world of ethical investing.

The Ethical North American Equity fund earned a one-year return of 42 percent in 1997. An investor with, say, $100,000 in that fund ended the year with

$42,000 more than they started, in return for doing nothing more strenuous than writing a cheque and reading quarterly statements. In comparison, the average Canadian worker earned just $31,000 in 1997 as compensation for an entire year's labour. One doesn't have to agree with Shakespeare ("Neither a borrower nor a lender be!") to wonder if this is really an ethical state of affairs. Yet by so aggressively promoting the supposed ethical value of personal investment decisions, and leading us to the conclusion that—yes—financiers can be ethical, too, the ethical mutual funds may leave Canadians less inclined to question the fundamental ethics of private finance, not more.

The ubiquitous claim that ethics and profits can indeed go hand-in-hand also promotes a naive, Pollyanna view of the workings of the real economy. Well-managed companies are both ethical and profitable, the argument goes, and hence by screening companies on social grounds the ethical funds coincidentally pick out the most profitable ones.

In some superficial sense, this may be true. Managers who regularize and standardize operating procedures and are generally respectful of their legal and regulatory responsibilities will be managers who tend to avoid certain ethical problems (such as mine disasters, workplace safety problems, or other potentially litigious quagmires) while simultaneously running productive and profitable operations. Moreover, profitable companies tend to be precisely the ones with discretionary resources to dedicate to goals such as charitable donations, affirmative action hiring practices, or even (to some extent) better employee compensation. In this sense, it is higher profits which "cause" better ethics, not the other way around.

Canada's banks, which have relatively good reputations on many "corporate citizenship" subjects (such as charitable donations), exemplify this reverse direction of causation. Companies which are highly profitable typically strive doubly hard to act (or at least appear to act) ethically, as a matter of good public relations, if for nothing else. But none of this implies that ethics and profits are indeed consistent, or even mutually supportive. And in the real-world environment in which they must constantly try to survive, companies face regular and very fundamental trade-offs between profitability and any significant conception of responsibility to their employees, the communities in which they operate, or the natural environment. By aggressively promoting its claim that good ethics and healthy profits are fully consistent, the ethical mutual fund industry is obscuring these fundamental economic and social trade-offs.

For example, any business in Canada faces a central incentive to minimize the amount of labour which it hires to perform needed tasks, and to minimize what it pays for that labour. This is a fundamental feature of an economic system in which the bottom-line profits of a business are siphoned off to the private owners of that business: the more costs can be reduced (including the costs of human resources), the greater are the profits left at the end of the day. An owner need not be merely greedy in order to be motivated in this manner. More often than not, they are forced into relentless cost-cutting by competitive pressure from companies which are more aggressively economizing on all inputs (including labour) and hence reducing costs more quickly.

What has been the collective result of all of these corporate-level efforts to reduce costs and maximize profits? Combined with conservative, pro-business economic policies on the macro level (such as high interest rates to restrain growth), the outcome has been endless corporate downsizing in the context of a generally lacklustre labour market. Unemployment and underemployment have remained high, while wages have stagnated—even as the productivity of those lucky enough to keep their jobs has grown. The number of "good" jobs with profitable, productive corporations declines steadily, while displaced workers are forced into marginal employment or self-employment to support themselves.

There is a fundamental ethical dimension to every one of these corporate downsizing decisions. In each case, the interests of the firm's owners for profits results in the displacement, unemployment, and reduced economic prospects of those who earn their living from work instead of from the ownership of financial wealth. The life prospects of many displaced workers are literally shattered.

Minimizing employment, ruthlessly shedding surplus workers, and cutting compensation to the minimum level necessary in the light of general labour market conditions: these are the imperatives of doing business successfully in modern capitalism, and they raise fundamental issues about the ethical structure of our society. Virtually any company which refused to follow the cost-cutting mantra would eventually be driven out of business. This makes it very difficult for an ethical mutual fund to select companies which might genuinely put "people before profit," because those companies are not likely to be around for long. So it is not surprising that the ethical funds quite happily invest in companies which have ruthlessly downsized their way to success (like Canadian National Railway, Bell Canada, and Northern Telecom).[7]

To boycott companies which laid off workers or paid lousy wages would hardly constitute a recipe for financial success in the nitty-gritty arena of late-20th-century corporate capitalism. It is to be expected that ethical investment funds will need to make some strategic compromises in their specific portfolio decisions. But to do this while stridently denying any trade-off between ethics and profits, when virtually all of the firms in their universe are forced by the rules of the game they are playing to act in fundamentally unethical ways, is to obscure the nature of the system itself in a grotesque manner.

Always Look on the Bright Side

The managers of ethical mutual funds certainly know a good business opportunity when they see one. And the stock-marketization of Canada's social programs is generating an endless stream of new business arenas in which the tried-and-true promotional themes of the ethical investing industry can be applied over and over again.

For example, Ethical Funds Inc. was fast out of the blocks with Canada's first-ever ethical Registered Education Savings Plan (RESP). The RESP system is very similar to Canada's RRSP system: investors can shelter money in an RESP account from taxes on interest or capital gains, until such time as the funds are withdrawn to pay education expenses for the investor or for his or her children or grandchildren.

RESPs were supposedly introduced to help Canadians cover the skyrocketing cost of higher education. Tuition fees at Canadian universities tripled between 1988 and 1998, thanks to relentless government cutbacks in education budgets. Students and their families have found it increasingly difficult to pay for a university education, even as they were being lectured *ad nauseum* that getting a good education is a prerequisite to success in the brave new job market.

Unfortunately, RESPs won't do much to change this state of affairs. Like RRSPs, they deliver juicy taxpayer subsidies to those lucky Canadians who have extra money for personal investments. Adding insult to injury, the federal government announced in 1998 that it would pay a 20% cash credit (up to $400 per child per year) to RESP investors, most of whom are well-off to start with: more Robin Hood in reverse.

But, spotting a lucrative new market, Ethical Funds leaped into the fray, promising to donate a share of its RESP sales to education initiatives for children in developing countries. As the brochure stated stirringly, "We believe that education is the right of every child." Well, if that's true, Ethical Funds' managers should look long and hard at Canada's RESP program, which will subsidize higher education for families with significant investment portfolios, while simultaneously pricing public education out of reach for the rest of society.

Ethical Funds is obviously not endorsing government budget cutbacks by participating in the RESP program. And, if someone is going to invest in an RESP, it is probably better to invest with a company which donates a share of its profits to the Third World than with one which doesn't. But, by so aggressively and uncritically touting RESP investments as a tool of ethical behaviour, the Ethical Funds program adds momentum to a fundamentally regressive shift in Canada's education policies which progressive Canadians should still be fighting to reverse.

At a bare minimum, one would hope an ethical RESP brochure might say a few critical words about the nature of the RESP program and its social and economic effects, or even include a mail-in postcard with which ethical Canadians could protest the whole boondoggle. But then, that might undermine the carefully calculated feel-good emotions which seem to be the primary purpose of the ethical investment movement.

Worse yet, this ethical contortionist act undermines the efforts of those who are actually fighting to moderate corporate abuses. Think of the workers at CN Rail, fighting to save their jobs after yet another downsizing announcement (CN reduced its workforce by almost 10,000 between 1995 and 1999, even as its stock market value tripled). Along comes an ethical money manager, arguing that CN's actions are ethical enough for the company to be included in the Ethical Funds portfolio. Hence the incredible profits which CN shareholders (including the mutual fund) have enjoyed as a direct result of those layoffs must also in some genuine way be ethical.

"We have to invest in *something*," the ethical fund manager would cry. Yes, all money managers must make their choices—but the ethical funds do the entire social justice movement in Canada a disservice when they try to deny that the whole process has a seedy, ugly, and fundamentally unethical underside.

The ethical mutual fund industry was largely initiated by Canada's credit union movement. Credit unions (like other deposit-taking institutions) have been challenged by the explosion of mutual funds and the rise of personal investing. Few depositors keep much cash in simple savings accounts any more, and this has forced credit unions to change their services if they want to maintain their share of the personal banking business. [In fact, credit unions have been fighting a losing battle in this regard, with their share of total financial assets in Canada falling fairly steadily since the era of high interest rates and high finance began in 1980.]

Still, given the political and social roots of credit unions, it is not surprising that the decision to offer "crass" financial services (like mutual fund investments) might prove to be a difficult one. Thus ethical mutual funds provided credit unions with a politically correct solution to their dilemma: they could join in the paper boom that was boosting the fortunes of other financial institutions, yet still be seen to be promoting the original goals of social accountability and financial democracy which motivated the formation of credit unions in the first place.

Many individual investors probably also felt squeamish about investing personally in the stock market, even as they despaired at the historically low rates they were earning on standard savings accounts. This may have been especially true for many of the baby-boom Canadians whose RRSP accounts have powered the mutual fund industry to new heights: many no doubt experienced pangs of guilt as they invested in the same corporations they once protested against in the 1960s and 1970s.

Guilt is rarely a healthy motivator in interpersonal relationships, and the same is likely true of economic and financial ones. Individuals fortunate enough

> # I Like What I See
> "A lost job can put a smile on any shareholder's face."
> —Eric Reguly, *Globe and Mail* business columnist
> October 24, 1998

to have some spare cash to invest—and this remains a lucky minority—should probably just go ahead and invest in a mutual fund. And credit unions should probably just sell them. Investing in the stock market may seem uncomfortable to those with a social conscience, and probably for good reason. It would have been better to recognize that discomfort and accept it as an inevitable consequence of the way Canada's economy has been structured in the 1990s. But instead the founders of the ethical funds set their sights higher, trying to put an ethical stamp on an activity—private personal investing—which is inherently selfish and in many ways economically destructive.

The true motivation for most of the incredible growth of ethical mutual funds may be inadvertently captured in one of the Ethical Funds advertising slogans: "Feel good about your finances." Allowing a certain constituency of the investing public to sleep better at night is quite a different outcome from using your money to change the world. As suggested more delicately by Moira Hutchinson, former coordinator of the Task Force on the Churches and Corporate Responsibility and a pioneer of shareholder activism, "There is a danger of emphasizing too much the idea of ethical investment as a means to a clean conscience." The ethical fund industry's advertising has suggested a high calling, but its actions in practice seem to have been motivated more by a desire to foster a feel-good sentiment among its burgeoning clientele than to effect real social change.

Ethical mutual funds, especially those run by credit unions, will likely get better over time at designing and imposing stronger screens on their financial investments and clarifying their role in political campaigns focused on corporate misbehaviour. But their fundamental nature as agents for individual, private financial investors inherently limits their potential to change a world in which the concentrated ownership and destructive behaviour of financial wealth is a big part of the problem.

Labour-Sponsored Investment Funds

If ethical investment strikes some social activists as an apparent contradiction in terms, then the labour-sponsored venture capital industry must qualify as a positively Orwellian distortion of the English language. Labour-sponsored funds (LSFs) are mutual funds which specialize in investing in small and medium-sized companies. Private investors receive a range of generous tax breaks to subsidize their LSF holdings (in addition to the usual RRSP subsidies). In turn, the funds are supposed to finance the start-up and growth of job-creating small businesses. In reality, however, the LSF industry keeps about one-half of its total assets in low-risk government bonds and other "non-venture" investments.

Management costs in the LSF industry are huge, averaging close to 5% of total assets each year, yet the industry's venture investment portfolio has demonstrated average rates of return that are near-zero, or even negative. Clearly it is the generous tax subsidies—which reduce the net after-tax cost of an LSF investment for many investors to virtually zero—which drive the whole strange industry. Even the connection of the LSF industry to the labour movement whose name it carries is fuzzy and uncertain.

As of 1997, the LSF industry represented a total of over $4 billion in invested assets.[8]   About half of this total is represented by concrete investments in real small and medium-sized businesses. The other half represents investments in government bonds, T-bills, and other "paper" investments. Relative to Canada's overall financial industry, the LSF industry remains a bit player. Total LSF assets represent just over 1% of total mutual fund assets in Canada, and are equivalent to about 0.2% of the total market capitalization of Canada's major stock markets. New investments in businesses by LSFs (perhaps $350 million annually in recent years) equal about 0.25% of total business investment in Canada. LSF investments in small and medium-sized businesses account for about 0.15% of the total assets of Canada's non-financial business sector.

However, within the specialized venture capital business (which provides equity and other long-term financing to small and medium-sized businesses), the LSFs have quickly become important players. LSFs now account for over one-half of all venture capital in Canada, and have helped to deliver important sums of new financing for particular small businesses. This is not to say that these businesses could not have obtained financing elsewhere; other types of investment (bank loans, issues of new shares, or private financing) still remain the most important sources of new capital for small business. The venture capital industry in general, and the LSFs in particular, have given small businesses an additional source of finance which they typically prefer (partly because LSF investments are publicly subsidized and hence cheaper, and partly because venture capital providers may be less demanding than some other sources of capital in terms of information disclosure, constraints on management independence, and other factors). But it would be wrong to conclude that each dollar of LSF investing represents financing that otherwise could not be obtained through conventional financial channels.

Canada's LSF industry can be broken down into three general categories, as summarized in Table 15-1. Quebec's Solidarity Fund is Canada's oldest and larg-

Table 15-1
Three Categories of LSFs

Fund Category	Number of Funds	Total Assets (year-end 97)
Solidarity Fund, Quebec	1	$2.2 billion
"Rent-a-Union" Funds, Ontario	15	$1.8 billion
"True" Labour Funds, English Canada	5	$265 million
Source: Annual Reports of the funds.		

est LSF. It was founded in 1983 by the Parti Quebecois provincial government, and is sponsored by the Quebec Federation of Labour. An important feature of the Solidarity Fund is its connection to the ultimate goal of Quebec independence, a goal which is supported by most unions and social groups in Quebec. A key justification for the fund is its effort to strengthen the domestic private sector in Quebec, reducing its reliance on financial and management inputs from outside of Quebec; this is considered important in laying the economic basis for Quebec independence.

The Solidarity Fund has also demonstrated the most explicit and interventionist social mission of all LSFs in Canada. The Solidarity Fund's prospectus document speaks stirringly about the struggle for full employment and positions the Fund's mandate within that context. The Fund has established several subsidiaries which are charged with investing directly in less developed regions of the provincial economy. The Solidarity Fund also has by far the best record of investing in unionized companies: 20% of its 365 investments at the end of 1997 were in firms whose workers were at least partially represented by unions. That is a small proportion, but far higher than LSFs in English Canada (which have invested almost exclusively in non-union enterprises).

A second category of LSF includes about 15 funds established in Ontario, accounting for about $1.8 billion in assets—just under half of all LSF assets in Canada, and close to 90% of all LSF assets in English Canada. One of the strangest legacies of the former NDP government in Ontario is the unique provincial legislation creating LSFs in that province. In Ontario (unlike elsewhere in Canada), the right to establish an LSF was not limited to a major labour federation. Instead, any individual union—no matter how small or obscure—can establish a fund. The result has been the emergence of a bizarre "rent-a-union" LSF industry. Few investors in the Ontario funds have any connection to the labour movement whatsoever. Private financial consultants simply arrange for official sponsorship from some obscure union, in return for an endorsement fee that by Bay Street standards barely qualifies as petty cash. The funds can then be marketed with a union "seal of approval"—mostly to high-income investors who likely oppose the operation of unions in every other facet of the economy.

Unions involved in this industry include such prominent voices of labour as the CFL Players' Association, the Canadian Police Association, and the Professional Association of Foreign Service Officers. In many cases, private financial professionals have been explicit about their intention to use the LSF legislation to create a lucrative tax-loophole for their private clients. The result has been a flood of incoming money from private investors, so that the rent-a-union industry quickly came to rival (in aggregate) the Solidarity Fund.

A good example of the bizarre practices that occur in Ontario's LSFs (the fastest growing segment of the LSF industry in Canada) is provided by an LSF called SportFund. This fund was started by Joel Albin, a former vice-president of the Bank of Montreal. He was quite explicit about his goal, which was to generate maximum tax breaks for his wealthy clients (see sidebar). SportFund boasts a panel of "expert" investment advisors, including such notable financial professionals as Darryl Sittler (former Toronto Maple Leaf), Brad Park (former Boston Bruin), Ernie Whitt (former Toronto Blue Jay), and Franco Harris (former Pittsburgh Steeler).

The union which nominally sponsors SportFund, in return for an endorsement fee, is (who else?) the CFL Players' Association. The sorts of important social projects funded by the subsidized capital accumulated in SportFund include a sports bar, an indoor adult playground, and Don Cherry's junior hockey franchise. Ironically, SportFund boasted a higher return in 1997 than any other LSF in Canada: an impressive 17%. Several other LSFs in Ontario were also started by financial professionals who left well-paying jobs with established institutions to take advantage of the lucrative tax loopholes created by the LSF legislation.

Outside of Quebec, five LSFs enjoy official support from segments of the genuine labour movement. In B.C., Manitoba, and New Brunswick, the funds are sponsored by the provincial labour federations. In Ontario, where the Ontario Federation of Labour has refused to support the LSF concept, two funds—the First Ontario Fund and the Canadian Venture Opportunities Fund, with combined assets of about $30 million as of 1997—were started by respective coalitions of several of the more conservative private sector unions. Together, these five "true" LSFs make up the smallest part of the overall LSF industry; combined, they account for about $250 million in assets, or some 5% of all LSF assets in Canada.

The operation of the rent-a-union funds which dominate the LSF industry in English Canada has become a huge embarrassment to the LSF "true believers."

Putting Money to Work

"When I saw what the labour-sponsored vehicle offered with the tax breaks, I thought, 'Geez, if I can structure it in a way that I could get my investors those tax breaks, then why not?' It would be sort of negligent not to as a corporate finance person... [But] to qualify, I needed a union."
—Joel Albin, President and CEO, SportFund Inc.
January 23, 1995

In Name Only

"The current generation of labour-sponsored venture capital funds still stands out as the most powerful tax avoidance tool available in Canada... The labour "sponsor" receives a fee for adding its name to the enterprise, but generally plays no further role."

—Dunnery Best, Senior Vice-President,
Merrill Lynch Canada Inc.
February 13, 1999

To some extent, therefore, the sponsors of the "true" funds have tried to differentiate themselves from the rent-a-union industry; four of the five "true" funds in English Canada, for example, have formed a Labour Sponsored Investment Funds Alliance (together with the Solidarity Fund) which has adopted its own (non-binding) statement of principles on how a "true" LSF should behave. [The Canadian Venture Opportunities Fund is not a member of this Alliance.] The sponsors of the "true" LSFs will only go so far, however, in attempting to distinguish themselves from rent-a-union funds. Notably, they will not publicly criticize other funds, and have not demanded that the federal and provincial governments withhold subsidies from funds which do not meet their own criteria for constituting an LSF.

And, while Ontario's rent-a-union funds typify the worst abuses of the LSF industry, and reveal how this subsidized industry can so easily be manipulated for cynical private gain, the general weaknesses of the LSF concept are not limited to those Ontario funds. Even "true" LSFs reflect most of the weaknesses of this general approach—a reliance on individual private investors, an emphasis on tax reduction over job-creation, huge and wasteful administrative expense, poor job-creation records, and dubious political implications for unions. Some of these issues are considered below.

Subsidy and Reality

The LSF industry would not exist without massive subsidies from the federal and provincial governments. These subsidies come in many forms. The first and most direct is the LSF credit itself. The federal government will cover 15% of the cost of any LSF investment, up to an annual individual maximum of $5,000. Most provincial governments will match this subsidy, for a total credit of 30%. Individual investors have to keep their LSF shares for eight years, or they must pay back the subsidy. After eight years they can sell their shares, buy new ones (even shares in the same LSF), and claim the 30% credit all over again. Since 1992, the federal and provincial governments have spent a combined total of about $1.5 billion on the LSF credits alone. With the 1999 expansion of the maximum subsidized investment, the LSF credit will cost both levels of government up to

$300 million per year.

The effective subsidy rate for LSF contributions is enhanced by virtue of the fact that they qualify for inclusion in an individual's RRSP account. For high-income earners, this translates into an additional subsidy of about 50% (depending on the specific high-income tax rates prevailing in each province). High income earners thus get a total of 80% back from government for their investments in an LSF: 30% from the LSF credit, and 50% from the RRSP. Ironically, because of the regressive way in which the RRSP credit is designed, the effective subsidy rate for the typical Canadian worker contributing to a labour fund is actually *lower* than the subsidy paid to a high-income earner investing in exactly the same fund. [See Chapter 12 for an explanation of this feature of the RRSP system.]

There is another lesser-known but incredible additional source of subsidy for the LSF industry. LSF contributions qualify, for federal tax purposes, as a "small business" investment. Most Canadians are only allowed to invest up to 20% of their total RRSP accounts in foreign countries. As discussed in Chapter 14, the rationale for this restriction is obvious: since RRSPs are heavily subsidized by Canadian taxpayers, these funds should be invested within Canada to boost domestic growth and job-creation. But investors in "small businesses" (including owners of LSF shares) are allowed to divert more of their *other* RRSP investments to foreign countries. In general, an investor is allowed to invest three extra RRSP dollars abroad (above and beyond the normal 20% ceiling) for every RRSP dollar invested in a small business in Canada (including the LSFs).

What is this subsidy worth? The financial industry has been lobbying hard for the federal government to eliminate the 20% cap on foreign RRSP investments. They point to studies showing that the typical foreign investment earns a higher rate of return than investments within Canada—at least 0.75 percentage points of extra profit per year for each dollar invested abroad.[9] By allowing an investor to attain extra foreign profit on $3.00 of subsidized RRSP investments for each dollar contributed to an LSF, this translates into a subsidy of 2.25% per year (3 times 0.75 points), or a compounded total of about 19.5% over the eight-year period during which LSF investors are required to keep their investments in the labour fund.

Incredibly, then, for a high-income investor, this third subsidy reduces the true cost of an LSF investment almost to zero: 30% for the LSF credit, 50% for the RRSP deduction, and 19.5% for the allowable extra foreign content. This equals a total subsidy rate of 99.5%. In other words, for each $100 contributed to an LSF, a high-income investor actually pays just 50 cents.

The foreign content rule creates some uncomfortable problems for advocates of the LSF concept. Tax-savvy investors are allowed to move $3.00 of subsidized investments out of Canada for each dollar they contribute to an LSF. The net impact on investment within Canada is thus *minus* $2.00! Can these investments thus really be seen as a contribution to business investment in Canada?

Even some of the "true" LSFs have placed special emphasis on this loophole in their public advertising. For example, a promotional leaflet for B.C. Working Opportunities Fund highlighted the fund's ability to help investors avoid the statutory limit on foreign investment of RRSPs. Incredibly, the same leaflet also argued that "keeping your money in B.C." was a key reason why investors should contribute to the fund.

The accumulated cost of all of the federal and provincial subsidies to the LSF industry up to the end of 1998 is well in excess of $3 billion.[10] This represents about three-quarters of all of the assets held at that time by Canada's LSFs. And it considerably exceeds the value of the total investments by LSFs in actual small and medium sized businesses (since LSFs invest only about one-half of their funds in small businesses, with the rest being held in low-risk government bonds).

One recent study estimated that it costs government $1.35 for each dollar that LSFs invest in actual businesses.[11] Wouldn't it be more efficient for government to simply make direct public investments in deserving ventures, dispensing with the expensive charade of private money managers and private investors?

The problem with any investment strategy that exists primarily on the basis of tax subsidies offered to private individuals or companies is that all sorts of grotesque and unintended consequences are produced, thanks to the creative efforts of these same individuals and companies to avoid income taxes. This difficulty has been illustrated vividly by past failed Canadian investment policies that were similarly structured. For example, the huge subsidies offered to frontier oil exploration and Canadian TV and film production in the 1980s motivated the creation of entire industries whose existence was predicated solely on assisting individuals and companies to maximize the value of these tax breaks—quite apart from whether any oil was discovered or any film of cultural or economic value was actually produced.

The lesson of these fiascoes is that, to be efficient, investment subsidies to private agents must be tied to concrete results: actual investments in real endeavours with real social benefits. Canada's LSF policy is repeating this same error. Like the exploration grants of the National Energy Policy or the failed TV and movie subsidies, the appeal of the LSF industry to its investors and managers has everything to do with tax breaks and little to do with real productivity and economic growth.

Subsidized T-Bills

Another disturbing aspect of the LSF industry is the small proportion of total assets that is actually invested in small and medium-sized businesses in Canada. Federal law requires only that 60% of an established LSF (one that has been in existence for five years or more) be invested in actual venture stakes in real businesses. Most LSFs do not meet this target, either because they have not yet operated for five years, or because they are simply in outright violation of the rule.

For example, the large Working Ventures fund, nominally sponsored by the now-defunct Canadian Federation of Labour, held just one-third of its $828 million total capital at the end of 1997 in actual venture investments, even though the fund was created in 1986. Other funds had attained venture investing shares ranging between 35% and 55% by the end of 1997. Established funds which consistently break the 60% rule can be fined; however, these fines are refundable if the LSF subsequently meets the venture vesting target, and the degree of enforcement of the 60% rule has so far been questionable.

Even the nature of the subsequent punishment can be quite bizarre. For example, to avoid being fined for its low venture investment activity, in 1996 the Working Ventures fund committed $15 million to an Ontario government fund (the Community Small Business Fund) which provides risk capital to small businesses. By so doing, the fund avoided a $30 million fine it was supposed to have paid because of its poor record of venture investing.

The whole justification for the private-sector approach to investment embodied in the LSF industry is that private financiers are somehow supposed to be more efficient than government in allocating capital and supervising investment projects. Yet, when the second-largest LSF in Canada fails to meet the 60% investment target, it avoids major fines by paying into an alternative provincial government investment agency. Millions of dollars of taxpayers' money would be saved if the huge subsidies were simply given directly to a public investment bank (like the one in Ontario, or similar funds operating in other provinces), dispensing altogether with the hungry middlemen who run the LSF industry.

The LSF industry was initially given the right to invest in low-risk money-market instruments because it was felt that private funds could not be fully invested in actual business ventures without creating unacceptable difficulties of risk and illiquidity for the individuals who invest in the fund. A fund with all its money invested in real businesses might face temporary cash-flow difficulties, or be too vulnerable to poor performance in a few of its supported business ventures. Therefore, the government allowed these funds to keep a large share of their subsidized capital in low-risk non-business assets, as a necessary condition of making these funds (despite the high subsidy rate) acceptable to private investors.

The astonishing fact that the federal and provincial governments are subsidizing over $2 billion in low-risk investments in Treasury bills and other bonds is a direct result, therefore, of the choice of private, competitive financial firms as the delivery vehicle for this subsidized venture capital. If, instead of establishing an elaborate network of private funds, supported by private investors, and staffed by private money managers, government had established a genuine public investment bank, there would be no need to keep a huge supply of subsidized T-bills on hand.

Management Expenses

The LSF industry as a whole spends at least $75 million per year on deadweight administrative costs—a large amount for an industry which has invested at most $2 billion in real business projects. LSFs typically have higher management fees (measured as a proportion of their assets) than other types of mutual funds. Whereas bond-based mutual funds report typical expense ratios of about 1% of assets per year, and equity-based funds about 2% of assets per year, many LSFs report management expenses equal to 5% of assets per year, or even more.

Again, it was expected that LSFs would have higher administration costs than other investment funds, in theory because of the inherent costs involved in brokering and supervising investments with numerous small companies. Nevertheless, it is worth noting that over the eight years for which investors are required to hold their LSF shares in order to keep the 30% credit, even just a 3.3% annual management fee compounds to a full 30% of the initial investment. In other words, the high overhead cost of running a typical LSF eats up the full value of the 30% LSF credit.

In fact, the true cost of administering the LSFs is actually much greater than the stated management expense ratios, again because of the fact that these funds maintain one-half of their assets in low-risk Treasury-bills and other bonds. It is not expensive to manage a simple portfolio of bonds. In fact, two of the "true" LSFs—the First Ontario Fund and New Brunswick's Workers Investment Fund—have outsourced management of their non-venture assets to private investment agencies, in both cases for an annual fee equal to 0.2% of those assets.

So, if we deduct a share of total LSF management costs equal to 0.2% of their bond holdings, the remaining management expenses can be considered a fair estimate of the "pure" overhead cost of running the actual venture capital business. The results are startling. After controlling for the fact that LSFs maintain one-half their capital in low-risk, relatively low-cost bonds and Treasury-bills, the true management expense ratios for the pure small business portion of their assets soar by anywhere between 75% and 400% from the apparent expense ratios reported by the funds.

Many funds—even some of the "true" LSFs (such as Manitoba's Crocus Fund and the First Ontario Fund)—are collecting expenses on their actual venture investments in excess of 10% or more per year of the total value of their small business investments. No wonder it is so difficult for these venture investments to show any positive return whatsoever, when the whole process is dragged down by such an expensive administrative superstructure.

These huge management costs drag down the financial performance of the funds. On average, LSFs generated negative bottom-line returns during 1998, and average returns of only about 3% per year during the booming 1990s as a whole—despite the sure profits which the funds earn on their large holdings of low-risk bonds. Without their public subsidies, most private investors would never tolerate such high management expenses, or such low bottom-line returns. Now, in principle, there is nothing wrong with a public investment program which generates a small or even zero return on its assets—so long as those investments are socially mandated and meet clearly specified and measured social goals. But, if Canadian taxpayers are going to subsidize an investment program with zero or negative returns, it would be far better to support public or social projects with explicit social goals—low-cost housing, non-profit community development projects, public infrastructure—rather than paying for an elaborate and costly network of private financiers and accepting the notion that private companies motivated by private profit are the best agents to organize economic growth and job-creation.

Venture Investment Criteria

As with the ethical mutual fund industry, controversies have also erupted over the criteria on which LSF assets are invested in the private companies which are supposed to be the ultimate beneficiaries of this strange investment system. Even though the LSF industry is often advanced as a form of "social" investment, there are actually no binding social, ethical, or labour criteria on which the funds are allocated to recipient companies.

The only restriction is that these companies have less than 500 employees and less than $50 million in total assets. Beyond that, the LSFs are legally free to invest in any company that they wish. Since most funds (including the "true" funds in English Canada) are committed explicitly and legally to maximizing the value of shareholder assets, this means selecting companies on the basis of high expected profitability and low expected risk. This, in and of itself, is rather strange for a subsidized investment system ostensibly designed to serve social goals.

Some of the results of this virtually unconstrained approach to venture investment are quite bizarre. For example, many LSFs invest in small businesses by purchasing a portion of new shares that these companies issue through an initial public offering (IPO) or other conventional equity offering. This constitutes a blatant abuse of the stated purpose of the LSF industry. The subsidies to this industry are justified on grounds that unconventional sources of finance are required by small businesses which simply cannot access conventional stock markets. So why are the funds permitted to place subsidized capital in vehicles (such as IPOs) which are readily snapped up by non-subsidized investors?

Other issues are raised by the types of companies that benefit from LSF placements. One would think that a "labour-sponsored" industry would be sensitive to the labour relations practices of the companies in which it invests. Yet, the question of whether a company is unionized, and whether it treats its workers fairly, are not normally relevant to the investment decisions of LSFs. The vast majority of LSF-supported companies (including those financed by the "true" LSFs) are non-union firms.

Indeed, many of the companies which have benefited from the subsidized capital offered by the LSF industry are some of the worst violators of the principles which the labour movement otherwise promotes. For example, the Working Ventures fund has invested heavily in an Alberta-based "short-line" railway. Short-line railways take advantage of a deliberate labour loophole in most provinces, under which union representation is annulled when ownership is transferred from a unionized national railway (governed by federal jurisdiction) to a provincially-chartered short-line. The economic *raison d'être* of these companies is that this loophole allows them to sidestep a union and thus pay drastically lower wages.

The growth of short-line railways represents a direct attack on the jobs and working conditions of union members in the railway industry. Yet a major LSF, in the name of "labour," is actually financing this attack.

Other questionable LSF investments:

- The Canadian Medical Discoveries Fund invested in a company trying to develop Canada's first private hospital in Calgary.
- Numerous funds (including several of the "true" funds) have investments in private hotels, restaurants, tour companies, and other hospitality industries. Some of these "small businesses" are actually franchises of established international chains.
- Working Ventures invested in a company which operates a network of video lottery terminals in Atlantic Canada.

- One of the largest LSF placements ever was a $7 million investment by Working Ventures in an elite golf and country club near Saskatoon, Sask.

In these and other cases, it is extremely hard to consider the company in question as holding sufficient social value to justify injections of publicly subsidized capital.

One particular example illustrates vividly the potential ironies of using public funds to subsidize private investments without attaching binding performance criteria to those investments. Working Ventures has invested several million dollars in Indigo Books, a firm competing in the new mega-bookstore market. Indigo is the creation of Heather Reisman, a well-connected Toronto executive, formerly a senior manager at Cott Corp. Ms. Reisman is married to Gerry Schwartz, CEO and majority owner of Onex Corp., a leveraged buy-out firm with assets of about $6 billion. Schwartz was the second-best paid CEO in Canada in 1997, with total compensation (including exercised stock options) of just under $19 million.

Indigo's flagship store in Toronto was the site of a special 1998 birthday party for Ms. Reisman. The aisles of books were rearranged to make room for a glamorous soirée attended by luminaries such as Conrad Black and Brian Mulroney. Reisman recently managed to defeat a union organizing drive launched by the Union of Needle, Industrial and Textile Employees (UNITE—which ironically co-sponsors a competing LSF, the Canadian Venture Opportunities Fund). In the wake of employees being fired for having a bad attitude and other forms of arbitrary treatment, enough workers signed cards to force a certification vote. After typical management pressure leading up to the vote, UNITE lost by six votes.[12]

The notion that this well-heeled, well-connected, anti-union book retailer located in a tony Toronto neighbourhood should be the recipient of millions of dollars of publicly subsidized capital at all—let alone that this capital should be advanced in the name of "labour"—surely constitutes one of the most outrageous chapters in the strange saga of Canadian LSFs.

Embarrassed by the strange and counterproductive nature of some LSF investments, the "true" LSFs claim to adhere to a social code in their investment decisions. But the wording of these commitments is deliberately vague, and no binding ethical or social screens are actually imposed. For example, the charter of the Labour Sponsored Investment Funds Alliance calls for "ethical employment practices and cooperative labour relations." Yet the vast majority of companies supported by the funds are non-union.

How do the labour unions sponsoring these funds expect that labour relations will be "ethical" and "cooperative" if workers remain unorganized? Indeed, if labour relations in non-union companies can be sufficiently "ethical" and "co-operative" to justify investments of the "workers' money," why do workers need unions in the first place? B.C.'s Working Opportunity Fund actually stresses in its promotional literature that "whether a company is unionized or not does not enter into consideration when making investment decisions." Similarly, the prospectus document of Manitoba's Crocus Fund states explicitly that "the fund's investments are not to be influenced by whether the business is non-unionized or unionized."

All LSFs in English Canada (including the "true" funds) commit to maximizing long-run returns as their dominant investment objective, and none list social or ethical criteria as among the top factors guiding investment decisions. In short, despite some overtures to the contrary, there is no fundamental difference between the criteria governing LSF investments—namely, high profits and low risk—and those governing the decision-making of any other private investment agency.

LSFs and Job-Creation

The LSF industry claims to have "created or maintained" a total of 100,000 jobs in Canada, or about 1% of all private-sector paid employment. This claim is not credible, however, and rests on a single and highly implausible assumption. To arrive at this job total, LSF managers simply add up all of the workers on the payroll of all of the companies which have received financing from one or more of the LSFs. Underlying this approach is the assumption that every one of those companies would have become completely and permanently bankrupt, with no jobs retained in any successor firm, were it not for the infusion of capital from an LSF.

Since virtually all LSF placements take the form of minority holdings in sponsored companies, it is hardly fair for the LSFs to claim credit for all of the employees on the payroll.[13] Moreover, while the LSF industry has probably generated some genuinely new funds for small business ventures, much of the financing channeled through LSFs would have occurred even without the labour funds (obtained through banks, equity markets, or traditional unsubsidized venture capital funds).

In other words, many of the investments made by LSFs would have occurred through alternative vehicles in past years. Thanks to generous tax subsidies, however, the LSF vehicle has become a preferred choice for both private investors and the supported companies. A large share of the demand for LSF financing, therefore, has simply been *diverted* from other investment sources, and cannot be considered to be creating net new jobs.

Obviously, some jobs have been created or maintained as a result of LSF investments, and the workers in those companies are understandably grateful.

What is a fairer estimate of the total employment impact of the LSF industry? It might be assumed that the LSFs' share of total business job-creation is proportional to their share of total business investment, or of the total business capital stock. In this case, the LSF industry might account for between 0.15% and 0.25% of total private sector paid employment in Canada—or between 15,000 and 25,000 jobs in total. Even 15,000-25,000 jobs is nothing to scoff at, of course, in the context of a chronically depressed labour market, but nevertheless this is not an impressive job-creation record in light of the total public subsidies exceeding $3 billion that have been received by the industry.

A Profile of LSF Investors

The sponsors of LSFs like to claim that they are vehicles for directing the savings of average union members and other working people toward more socially useful projects. This claim is one of the justifications for the involvement of certain unions and labour federations in the industry. After all, it is not entirely clear why unions were chosen to oversee the LSF vehicle in the first place, since the LSF industry exists to funnel the subsidized investments of private individuals into placements with private, usually non-union companies. Why were unions given the responsibility for (at least nominally) overseeing the industry in the first place? The idea that these funds somehow represent "labour's capital" is hence one of the political justifications for the involvement of unions. In reality, however, the clear majority of LSF investors have no connection whatsoever to unions—even those who have invested in the "true" LSFs.

The typical LSF investor is very similar to the typical RRSP investor. As discussed in detail in Chapter 12, most Canadian households simply do not have disposable income to devote to personal financial investments, no matter how generous are the public subsidies to those investments. And hence LSF investments, like all other personal investments, are disproportionately concentrated in high-income households, most of whom probably oppose the operation of unions in other spheres of the economy, but who happily participate in "labour's" investment scheme because of the generous tax subsidies involved.

Data on the income levels of LSF investors are available from Revenue Canada, which oversees the payout of the federal tax credit to these investors (see Table 15-2). About 375,000 Canadians contributed to an LSF in the 1995 tax year, or just 1.8% of all Canadians who filed tax returns. Among those who earned over $50,000 (and accounted for just over 10% of all tax-filers that year), about 7% of tax-filers invested in an LSF.

Average contribution rates, not surprisingly, also grow with income. LSF contributors who earned less than $50,000 put, on average, about $3,350 into their LSF accounts. The average LSF contribution for investors earning between

Table 15-2			
LSF Contributions by Income Category			
1995 Tax Returns			
Income level	Under $50,000	$50,000 - $100,000	Over $100,000
Share of all taxfilers	88.3%	10.2%	1.5%
Proportion who contributed to an LSF	1.2%	6.9%	6.3%
Share of all LSF contributors	56%	39%	5%
Average LSF contribution	$3,350	$4,585	$7,550
Share of total LSF contributions	46%	44%	10%

Source: Author's calculations from Revenue Canada, *Tax Statistics on Individuals*, 1995 Tax Year, and unpublished Revenue Canada data.

$50,000 and $100,000 rose to $4,585, while those earning over $100,000 contributed an average of over $7,500. In total, tax-filers who earned less than $50,000 in 1995 (almost 90% of tax-filers that year) contributed just 46% of total LSF investments. On the other hand, those earning over $50,000 (about 11% of all tax filers) accounted for 54% of LSF investments.

LSF contributions are thus slightly *more* concentrated among high-income investors than are tax-subsidized RRSP contributions in general. Recall from Chapter 12 that those earning under $50,000 accounted for 49% of all RRSP contributions in 1995, compared with 46% of all LSF contributions.

Implications for the Labour Movement

Perhaps the biggest difficulty with the LSF industry for the unions that nominally gave it birth cannot be described with economic statistics. By positioning themselves as investors in small businesses (most of which are not unionized), participating unions compromise their activity and credibility as *unions* in a number of worrisome ways.

For example, the LSF industry is premised on the claim that small business is the main engine of growth and job-creation in Canada's economy. But, as was described in detail in Chapter 5, the net job creation of Canada's small business sector is vastly overstated in misleading statistics which ignore the rapid rate of job destruction and turnover in this same sector. The real driving forces behind economic expansion, for the most part, are larger companies (which account for the bulk of investment and export demand) and government. Generally, the small business sector is dependent on the investment decisions of these more dominant economic players.

Moreover, small business is perhaps the most conservative political sector in Canadian society today with respect to most of the legal and political issues confronted by unions. Small business lobbyists regularly call for smaller government, lower taxes, further cutbacks in unemployment insurance, and weaker health and safety laws. Small businesses, on average, pay lower wages, offer

fewer employment benefits, are more resistant to unionization, are less productive, and invest less in real capital than larger businesses.

Not all small businesses share these views and reflect these bad practices,
of course, but most do, driven to desperation as they are by their efforts to stay
afloat in their fiercely competitive, marginally viable industries. How do unions
oppose the counterproductive views and practices of the small business sector,
while at the same time holding up small business as not only the engine of economic growth, but as a worthy recipient of publicly subsidized capital?

Similarly, the LSF industry, whether deliberately or inadvertently, has clearly
helped to promote the ideology of "people's capitalism" that is so effectively
propagated by the financial industry. In reality, as was discussed in detail in
Chapter 12, financial wealth in Canada is incredibly concentrated in the hands of
a tiny elite. Yet the financial industry has always tried to position itself as somehow representative of society as a whole. The advertising and lobbying claims
of the LSF industry serve to further reinforce the false notion that workers are
important investors.

Moreover, virtually any union initiative that involves the solicitation and
management of private investment contributions from individuals creates a huge
potential internal conflict over those issues for which the interests of workers
and the interests of investors diverge. There are many real-world instances in
which this potential conflict of interest could become politically debilitating.

For example, as described above, many LSFs aggressively promote their investments as a convenient means of avoiding the federal government's 20% ceiling on foreign investment of tax-subsidized pension funds. This positions "labour's capital" on exactly the opposite side of the fence from the labour movement itself, which has called energetically for the maintenance, and even the
tightening, of the 20% rule.

This is not to suggest that the labour movement should not be concerned
with investment. Quite the contrary. Unions need to understand and challenge
the power of private finance and private investors if they are ever to effectively
redirect economic policy. But this challenge is not likely to occur through the
positioning of union members as important private investors in and of their own
right, especially in the context of an investment vehicle that is as individualistic
and profit-oriented as are the labour-sponsored funds.

Pension Fund Activism

A third focus for efforts aimed at reforming the nature of private financial decisions has been the huge pools of capital represented by workplace pension funds.
These funds represent some of the largest single financial pools in Canada.

Trusteed workplace pension plans held total assets at the end of 1997 of close to $400 billion, representing about 7.5% of all financial wealth in Canada. Corporate shares account for close to one-third of the funds' assets; the rest are held in government bonds and other investments. Pension funds thus control about 12% of all equity ownership.

It is likely that the relative importance of these pension funds will gradually decline in coming years, as a result of the falling proportion of Canada's workforce which enjoys workplace pension coverage. More Canadian workers are employed in smaller businesses which do not provide pension benefits; a growing number of others are self-employed. Employees in unionized workplaces are 2.5 times more likely than their non-union counterparts to enjoy workplace pension benefits; union members thus make up the clear majority of Canadians with workplace pension coverage, even though they account for just one-third of all Canadians workers. The slight erosion of unionization rates during the 1990s has therefore clearly limited the growth of trusteed pension funds.

Even where pension benefits are provided, there is a shift toward individual RRSP-style pension coverage, under which the employer contributes a fixed sum each month to each worker's RRSP account. Those workers are then usually free to invest those funds as they see fit. These "defined-contribution" pension plans have the advantage of lower administration costs than traditional "defined-benefit" plans (which specify the value of monthly pensions that must be paid when a worker retires). Their drawback, however, is that the pension a retired worker ultimately receives depends on numerous unknowns, such as the performance of the stock market and each individual worker's investment decisions. From the standpoint of the activist investment movement, the growing popularity of defined-contribution plans will further limit the financial power represented by workplace pension funds.

Indeed, the importance of these pension funds is often exaggerated. It is often claimed that modern capitalism is moving toward a form of collective ownership, in which workers own their companies through their pension funds. Futurist Peter Drucker even titled his 1975 book on this subject, *The Unseen Revolution: Pension Fund Socialism in America*. This implies a revolutionary potential for pension fund activism that is clearly not justified. Despite the importance of particular large funds, pension funds in general account for only a small share of total financial wealth in Canada, and that share is likely to decline somewhat in coming years.

Nevertheless, the concentrated power and high profile of particular pension funds make them very important players in Canada's overall financial landscape. The largest workplace pension fund, the Ontario Teachers Pension Plan, held some $55 billion in assets at year-end 1997. This makes it the largest single financial investor in Canada, larger even than the Canada Pension Plan (which at present maintains only a relatively small "reserve" fund of about $40 billion).[14]

The Ontario teachers' fund also symbolizes the ethical and political dilemmas raised by the decision-making power and investing activities of large pension funds. Prior to 1990, the fund was only permitted to invest in low-interest government bonds—a source of great outrage among Ontario teachers. Legal changes that year allowed the fund to invest more freely and aggressively in order to generate higher returns. The teachers' fund has since become one of the most "activist" of institutional investors in Canada, shaking up the cozy atmosphere of Canadian corporate boardrooms with demands for greater corporate accountability (and greater profitability).

The fund's investment strategy has included taking large minority positions in real estate developments and other non-traditional investments. Its relentless search for higher returns has certainly paid off in financial terms: it is one of the few institutional pools of capital in Canada whose returns have consistently exceeded the performance of the overall stock market. But it has also raised eyebrows among those, including many Ontario teachers, who believe the financial power of the fund should be put to work in the interests of better social outcomes, not just bottom-line returns.

For example, the teachers' fund owns about one-quarter of Maple Leaf Foods, majority ownership of which was purchased in 1995 by the McCain food empire. In 1998, Maple Leaf declared war against its unionized workers (most of whom belong to the United Food and Commercial Workers' union, the UFCW), demanding huge wage concessions backed up by the threat of plant closures. Maple Leaf actually shut its Edmonton factory after workers there went on strike against the wage rollbacks. Other UFCW units eventually accepted the wage cuts, but at huge cost to both the standard of living of their members and the credibility of their union.

In Winnipeg, for example, UFCW members burned their collective agreements and shouted down their union leaders after reluctantly accepting an incredible seven-year contract in September 1998 that contained huge wage rollbacks. One 13-year employee of the plant saw his wages fall from $17.50 to just $9.25 an hour, a cut of almost 50%. It is safe to say that Maple Leaf could not have undertaken such an aggressive and wrenching shift in its labour relations without the passive support of its largest minority shareholder. And hence many teachers, along with others in the union movement, were appalled at the link between the teachers' pension fund and this significant attack on the wages and working conditions of Maple Leaf employees.

Large pension funds wield economic influence in other ways, too, beyond their specific investment decisions. For example, many pension fund managers have been vocal in lobbying for looser rules governing pension investments, most specifically calling for the relaxation of federal restrictions on the foreign investment of tax-subsidized pension monies. Once again it seems the "workers' money" is being used *against* workers, instead of for them: the managers of workplace pension funds travel to Ottawa espousing exactly the opposite position to that advanced by union leaders. We can probably guess which set of lobbyists is listened to more carefully.

So the interest of many workers and union activists in attempting to influence the behaviour of workplace pension funds is understandable. And in one important respect, this form of financial activism has a clear advantage over both ethical mutual funds and labour-sponsored investment funds. Workplace pension funds are an inherently *collective* investment vehicle, in that the capital is pooled and invested on behalf of all of the members of the pension plan, rather than being held in individual accounts. Pension funds are thus one form of financial investment in which the traditional rules of democratic decision-making (one person, one vote) might hold sway, in contrast to the one dollar, one vote "democracy" of the paper economy.

Pension fund activism would seem to hold greater potential for reforming financial behaviour in a way that breaks fundamentally with the individualistic structure of other investment vehicles. At a bare minimum, it would be hoped that workers and unions could prevent at least some of the most glaring instances of the financial power of pension funds being used in direct contradiction to the broader interests of working people. At the same time, however, attempts to gain greater say in how workplace pension funds are invested raise several complex economic and strategic issues which must be carefully considered before too many eggs are placed in this basket.[15]

In the first place, it is not at all self-evident—legally, economically, or politically—that the money in a pension fund is indeed the "workers' money," let alone any particular *union's* money. A pension fund exists to ensure that an employer meets its contractual commitment to pay retirement pensions to its employees at some point in the future. Pension law requires firms to set aside adequate funds to meet those future obligations, on the basis of certain assumptions regarding life expectancy, future earnings, investment returns, inflation, and numerous other factors. Without these accumulating accounts, there could be little guarantee that an employer's promise to pay future retirement pensions would in fact be fulfilled.

Pension funds are thus the actuarial equivalent to the show-business slogan: "Show me the money!" They are supposed to be an up-front guarantee that workers' future pensions are reasonably secure, regardless of the financial fortunes of the company in question. From the narrow perspective of ensuring the integrity of those future pensions, it is quite legitimate for workers and unions to conclude that what occurs to pension funds in the interim—between the time they are set aside and the time the pensions are paid out—is not really their direct concern. Pensions are envisioned not as the outcome of an *investment*, but rather as the deferred payment of *wages* by an employer who has been forced (through collective bargaining, legislation, and/or moral suasion) into recognizing that its responsibility to the well-being of its employees extends beyond their tenure as employed, productive workers.

The act of "investing" only enters the equation because it provides a convenient and more affordable way for the employer to arrange for the payment of those future pensions. Moreover, the risk associated with those investments is borne by the employer which sponsors the plan; this is fundamentally different from individualistic RRSP-style plans, which shift that risk entirely to the individual worker.

By engaging in the co-management of pension funds, workers and unions start to muddy this division of responsibility implicit in the traditional understanding of occupational pensions, and in so doing open up a Pandora's Box of potential trade-offs and quandaries. For example, if workers and their unions are going to share in the decision-making authority over pension fund investments, it seems reasonable to expect that they will have to shoulder some of the responsibility—in the form of reduced pensions—if those investments should happen to bomb. At present, this is not the case: it is the employer's responsibility to ensure that its promise of future pensions is fulfilled, regardless of successes or failures on the stock market. How can workers demand that their employer pay a predetermined pension benefit, come hell or high water, if they are simultaneously going to tell employers how pension contributions should be invested in the intervening period?

The response of many pension fund activists to this potential quandary is to borrow a page from the ethical mutual funds hymn book, claiming that there is no contradiction between high financial returns and ethical or socially responsible behaviour. Hence, pension funds can be channeled into socially beneficial undertakings without in any way undermining the viability of those future pensions. The argument that profits and ethics can go hand-in-hand was considered above and found to be superficial and unconvincing. An obvious question is begged: why do companies and investors engage in seemingly destructive or regressive forms of economic behaviour, if not to enhance their returns? Was there some motive other than higher profits—perhaps a simple, irrational hatred of organized labour—which inspired Maple Leaf Foods to launch its 1998 attack on its unions? And was there some similarly non-pecuniary motive which elicited the (at least passive) support of the Ontario teachers' fund in that conflict?

The Maple Leaf battle typifies the fundamental trade-off between profitability and social well-being that is inherent in a system of unregulated competition between private firms and private investors. For every example of a profitable firm which demonstrates its social responsibility in relatively trivial ways—perhaps a bank which scores high on the ethical scorecards because of its generous charitable donations—there is another company whose profit-seeking actions undermine the economic and social well-being of its employees and their communities in far more fundamental ways. And, if good corporate behaviour is indeed so profitable, then it should be enough to highlight this information for the benefit of existing fund managers whose mandate is limited to maximizing financial returns: their own profit-maximizing impulse should then kick into gear, without requiring an added "push" from socially-concerned pension fund activists.

Indeed, it is not clear why the stock market would not recognize and appropriately reward successful efforts by a company to implement business strategies that are simultaneously socially responsible and profit-enhancing. Many advocates of socially-responsible investing argue that good corporate behaviour (a better commitment to workers, communities, and the environment) pays off in higher long-run profits. If this were true, why wouldn't the stock market (and hence purely bottom-line-focused money managers) reward those companies accordingly?

Financial investors may be many things, but they generally aren't stupid or (at an individual level) irrational. If a company can indeed become more profitable by valuing its other "stakeholders" (workers, communities, the environment) and building longer-term relationships with them, then the talented analysts who are paid big money to identify prospects for future profits would be sure to seize upon that firm's longer-run potential. The notion that the stock market is too impatient to wait for the longer-run payoffs that are supposedly produced by these kinder, gentler strategies is not believable. More likely, the stock market has come to a different and more realistic conclusion: namely, companies which go "softer" on their workers and other "stakeholders" are likely to be *less* profitable than their competitors, not more, given the intensely competitive markets in which most of them operate.

For that reason, it would be more honest for the advocates of pension fund activism to acknowledge the existence of a trade-off (or at least a potential trade-off) between profitability and social responsibility. By then demanding that their pension fund managers put more priority on the social responsibility part of the equation, these advocates are putting their money where their mouths are, instead of pretending that they can have their financial cake and eat it ethically, too.

Pension funds obviously need to generate adequate and positive returns in order to fulfill their obligation to current and future retirees. But pension fund activists can make a convincing case that the financial solvency of a pension fund need not be undermined by investments which generate an *adequate* return, as opposed to the *maximum* returns sought in a socially-unconstrained investment approach.[16] In other words, socially-responsible investments can be pursued which allow for the financial viability of the plan in question, while forgoing the higher returns that would be earned by an unconstrained investment mandate.

Once this trade-off is explicitly acknowledged, however, other challenging but tractable problems emerge. In the first place, the goal of socially responsible investing is constrained by existing legal requirements imposed on pension fund trustees—namely, that they fulfill a "fiduciary responsibility" to future pensioners by investing the entrusted funds solely according to the criteria of maximum return. This provision allows no diversion of pension monies to good but less profitable causes. It also helps to prevent against outright pension fund corruption of the type associated with the U.S. Teamsters and other unions in previous decades.

To some extent, this conflict between the social and financial objectives of pension fund managers can be "finessed" through the careful design of alternative investment projects. [Greystone Properties Ltd., discussed further below, provides one example of how this can occur.] As long as a pension fund investment can be expected to earn adequate returns, in light of actuarial assumptions, to guarantee the payment of the proscribed future pensions of plan members, then managers should be able to win some ethical and social leeway in making their investment decisions.

U.S. experience has shown that the requirement of fiduciary responsibility on pension trustees can still allow a fair degree of leeway for trustees to support socially-mandated projects. Efforts to obtain legal and legislative clarity on this issue in Canada should be pursued.

The notion of investing pension monies on grounds other than bottom-line profitability will also cause obvious controversy within the ranks of the workers whose pensions depend on those investments. Hence the overall strategy presupposes an ongoing grassroots education and political campaign to convince rank-and-file plan members that adequate (albeit not maximum) returns can be earned while utilizing pension monies in more constructive (or at least less destructive) ways. And the outcome of that ongoing debate is by no means clear. It may very well turn out that greater control by union members over the investment of pension funds produces a *greater*, not lesser, focus on maximizing financial returns.

For most of these individuals, their per capita share of an accumulated pension fund represents by far the largest sum of money they will ever "own." To inform them that their union is trying to win more control over that money in order to invest it for the social good will be fiercely controversial. It was suggested in Chapter 12 that merely allowing more Canadians to "play the markets" is no guarantee that the priorities and outcomes of those markets will somehow become more socially beneficial. Similarly, if the outcome of greater worker control over pension fund investments is the accidental creation of a whole new constituency of profit-seeking, individualistic investors, then the effort will clearly have done more harm than good.

Indeed, it is no coincidence that the most independent and aggressive union pension funds—such as the Ontario teachers' fund in Canada, or the California public employees' fund (CALPERS) in the U.S., with total assets of $130 billion (U.S.) at the end of 1997—have been precisely the institutional investors most intent and most successful in forcing a more explicit bottom-line focus by company managers on the maximization of shareholder values, regardless of the consequences for the employees of those companies and their communities.

The most notable outcomes to date of the more "activist" approach on the part of pension plan managers have nothing to do with "social" goals. They have been, rather, the success of these managers in limiting the use of "poison pill" provisions and other cozy management practices which protect the interests of company executives at the possible expense of share values. CALPERS and other major U.S. pension funds have been expanding their "activism" more recently to address some ethical and social issues. But there is little doubt that the dominant effect so far of their more interventionist approach to investing has been to *enhance* the extent to which companies are subject to the bottom-line discipline of the stock market, not to moderate it.

There is a final cautionary note that must be considered by the pension fund activists. Pension funds have attracted attention from the socially responsible investment constituency because of their large individual size and their rare status as institutions of collective (rather than individual) financial decision-making. We have already noted that the aggregate economic importance of pension funds should not be exaggerated: despite the huge size of particular funds, pension funds are small in the context of the overall paper economy. Equally important, the funds' status as large pools of capital potentially subject to some degree of democratic oversight should not single them out for particular performance requirements that are not imposed on other financial investors. Pension funds own about 12% of all Canadian equities. It is politically and strategically risky to require them to adhere to a higher ethical and social standard (which, if we are honest, implies some sacrifice in terms of financial returns), when the other 88% of the stock market is allowed to run roughshod over the social and economic landscape. Apart from the fact that this proposed "solution" to the failings of the financial system actually misses 88% of the problem, this strategy could have the unintended result of undermining support among workers for collective defined-benefit pension plans in the first place. Individualistic, unconstrained RRSP-style plans may start to look quite appealing to those who hunger for a piece of the paper boom.

So, for both economic and strategic reasons, it is problematic to single out workplace pension funds for regulatory or performance burdens which are not—at least eventually—intended to be imposed on *all* financial investors. In this context, an analogy can be made to the history of union efforts to negotiate important non-wage benefits (including pension benefits!) for their members. Progressive unions have always phrased those bargaining demands as being a first step toward winning better social protections for all members of society, not just unionized workers. Benefit programs which were first negotiated in a few key industries could then be proposed as publicly-run benefit or insurance programs (such as extended health care, pharmacare, or dental insurance) available to everyone.

The same should be true of efforts to impose social conditions on pension fund investments. These efforts must always be positioned as part of a much broader effort to impose higher standards of social accountability on the financial system as a whole, through regulations and policies of the sort described in Chapters 14 and 16.

With all of these caveats in mind, then, it is quite right that Canadian unions are carefully beginning to explore the possibilities of imposing certain conditions on the investment of workplace pension funds (through negotiation with employers or through outright co-management of the funds). There are many examples of initiatives in this area, and their experimentation and experience over the coming years will help to fill in some of the questions regarding the extent to which pension fund activism can indeed be a fruitful avenue for financial reform.

Several public-sector unions, including the Canadian Union of Public Employees, have recently won formal representation on public-sector pension boards in several provinces, and these union representatives are now exploring ways of effectively influencing pension fund investments. Pension funds in several private-sector industries (such as construction) have long allowed for joint union-management trusteeship, and union-side trustees are beginning to expand the criteria on which their investment decisions are made. A recent B.C.-based initiative to enlist the power of union pension funds in pressing department stores and other companies to crack down on the sale of products made with child labour is an encouraging example of the potential for coordinating pension fund activism with broader social and political campaigns.

The Canadian Auto Workers (CAW) negotiated an agreement with the major auto-makers in 1993 to dedicate a certain proportion of pension premiums to the construction of non-profit housing in auto-dependent communities. This provision, unfortunately, was struck down by Ontario regulators, but future refinements to contract language could conceivably solve this difficulty. At any rate, the CAW approach provides an example of how certain conditions can be imposed on the investment of pension monies through the collective bargaining process, without the union taking on explicit joint responsibility for co-management of the pension fund (a move which opens up the Pandora's Box of issues discussed above).

Progressive teachers in Ontario are also organizing and lobbying for the imposition of clear social criteria governing the investment decisions of the mightiest of pension funds, the Ontario teachers' fund.

These varied initiatives should carry on cautiously but ambitiously. At a bare minimum, all unions must be concerned at the current extent to which the economic power of the capital pooled in these funds—a power which exists solely because of union successes in winning pension benefits for their members in the first place—is used to undermine the broader economic interests of those workers and their unions.

One particularly interesting initiative could provide a model for future progress in this area. Greystone Properties Inc. is a non-profit real-estate development company based in Vancouver, which was funded through investments made by several pension funds which were co-managed by unions. The company has specialized in the construction of low-cost non-profit housing in the tight Vancouver housing market. It requires all of its projects to be undertaken by unionized contractors. Greystone thus goes far beyond being simply a passive owner and investor of financial capital, to intervene in influencing the way in which that money is actually put into motion in the real economy. In other words, Greystone steps outside of the realm of financial investment decisions, to become actively involved in the real investment process.

Both the end-product of those investments (low-cost housing) and the method by which they are carried out (creating unionized construction jobs) result in explicit and beneficial social impacts. Greystone's early experience suggests that pension fund investments with the company have generated returns at least as attractive as those produced by other placements, thus avoiding (for now) the difficult profits-versus-ethics debate. Whether this will remain the case even in the wake of Vancouver's economic slump (and the consequent cooling of the housing market there) is an important issue. So, too, is the question of whether the Greystone approach is transferable to other economic sectors which may have less economic space for non-profit, union-wage suppliers of goods and services.[17] Nevertheless, the Greystone initiative is a very important one, and demonstrates the potential for democratically-controlled capital to make a real difference in the real economy.

Conclusion: Investors or Citizens?

Perhaps there is a single, common difficulty encountered by all of the preceding efforts to channel financial investment in more socially constructive directions. Each attempts to exert some degree of social control over financial investments from within a general system of private and very unequal ownership of capital. In this context, the "basis to claim" of the partisans in each initiative is their legal ownership of the capital in question—whether as individual investors in a mutual fund or labour-sponsored investment fund, or as members of a workplace which is collectively covered by a particular pension fund. It is their status as investors, in other words, rather than their status as citizens, which constitutes the platform from which their call for greater social accountability is issued.

The Ethical IMF

Any "activist investor" strategy can entrap well-meaning investors in dilemmas which trade-off their interests as *investors* against their interests as workers, union members, neighbours, and citizens. A telling example of this risk was provided by the corporate response of the Ethical Funds company to the 1997-98 financial meltdown in Asia and elsewhere.

In the wake of that global chaos, the Ethical Pacific Rim Fund lost almost 40% of its value in 1997. [One might wonder why it is considered "ethical" in the first place to invest tax-subsidized money in places like Singapore and Indonesia—but that is another story.]

Following this catastrophic loss, Ethical Funds managers moved quickly to reassure investors. This is standard operating procedure for mutual fund managers during times of market turbulence. Instead of asking why financial markets are so turbulent, and questioning whether these paragons of instability should really be entrusted with such economic importance, the key goal of mutual fund managers during market "corrections" is to stop their clients from withdrawing their money. Ethical Funds responded like any other mutual fund provider in this context. Think about the long-term, its brochures urged soothingly. Stay the course. Slow and steady wins the race. Panic only makes things worse.

But the real surprise was the Ethical Funds' endorsement of the ultra-conservative policy response to the Asian crisis that was designed and imposed by the International Monetary Fund (IMF). To try to staunch the flood of financial capital that was catastrophically fleeing the Asian economies, the IMF imposed harsh and contractionary measures, including sharp increases in interest rates (to 50% or higher) and dramatic cutbacks in government spending. The provision of short-term IMF

In these bleak economic times, of course, activists must take advantage of every platform they can clamber onto. And so it is quite natural that, where progressive-minded citizens also happen to be investors, they should want to use that status to reinforce their overall demands for greater social equality and prosperity.

But this attempt to reform the investment process from within should come stamped with a prominent warning label: *Use with extreme caution!* In attempting to fashion a social change movement within a generally tight and self-interested community of financial investors, these activist investment initiatives risk endorsing and reinforcing the same structures they are opposing. They introduce a variety of potential conflicts of interest between the non-investment concerns and priorities of sponsoring organizations (such as credit unions or trade unions) and their bottom-line interest in the financial profitability of their own investments. They tend to underestimate the degree to which control over financial capital is concentrated in the hands of a small private elite which is quite insulated from any of the ethical or social imperatives which the activist investor movement attempts to propagate. And, worst of all, they may inadvertently contribute to the dangerous notion that the ultimate decision-making power over

credits, essential if the complete collapse of the Asian financial system was to be avoided, was tied to these measures.

Led by American officials, the IMF also seized on the crisis as an opportune moment to demand Western-style "reforms" to the previously tightly-regulated Asian financial system, demanding less control over international capital flows, and more powerful and free-wheeling stock markets.

A growing chorus of economists has denounced the IMF measures as disastrous. They clearly contributed to the catastrophic collapse of output and employment in Asia, and hence will exacerbate and prolong the financial crisis. Far better would have been measures to limit capital flows directly (as were adopted by the Malaysian government), combined with expansionary interest rate and budgetary policies to offset the destruction of private credit and maintain output and employment levels.

What was the official Ethical Funds view on this crucial subject? President John Linthwaite wrote diplomatically in the 1997 annual report, "We are encouraged by the prompt response of the IMF to stabilize Asian economies and the receptiveness of Asian countries to proposed economic reforms." In a choice between policies that keep people at work and policies which protect the market valuations of financial assets, even the ethical mutual funds come down on the side of investors. This irony is especially bitter in light of the fact that British Columbia—home of the Ethical Funds head office—experienced more economic fall-out from the Asian crisis than any other province, with thousands of jobs lost in forestry, mining, and other industries which depend heavily on Asian markets. The bitter IMF policies probably contributed to the unemployment of thousands of B.C. workers, to say nothing of the mass human hardship experienced throughout Asia. But as long as they help to restore all-important levels of investor confidence, they win the ethical funds' stamp of approval.

what is done with capital should indeed rest with the owners of that capital (be they individual or institutional).

The flip side of this coin is that, if you're not an investor, then what happens with investment is none of your business. Yet the broader goal of democratizing and regulating finance is premised precisely on the notion that investors must be held accountable to the entire communities in which they accumulate and reinvest their capital. In other words, a truly democratic financial system is one in which all citizens have a voice, not just those who own capital.

Credit unions constitute one remaining outpost within the broader financial industry which still respects this now-radical notion that democracy works according to "one person, one vote," rather than "one dollar, one vote." Indeed, the most ethical thing about ethical mutual funds and some of the labour-sponsored investment funds may very well be the fact that they are sold through credit unions. These vehicles thus channel a small share of financial business (the commissions paid on mutual fund and LSF sales) through institutions that genuinely challenge many of the structures and assumptions of private finance.

Any business that can be conducted through credit unions instead of commercial financial institutions definitely makes a small contribution to the preservation and perhaps the expansion of true financial democracy. For that small segment of the Canadian population which happens to possess both disposable cash and a social conscience, the clearest stand they can take is to deal with a credit union instead of a bank. Even better would be to become actively involved in the collective and democratic management of that credit union, thus helping to ensure that it remains both effectively administered and true to the progressive founding principles of the credit union movement.

Beyond the clear choice of dealing with and getting involved in a credit union, conscientious individuals concerned with the ethical and social implications of their personal financial choices will face continuing and difficult personal dilemmas—and this is probably a good thing.

The crucial problems in the financial system are rooted in the structures of concentrated private ownership and the fundamental dynamics of self-interested financial markets, rather than in the choices made by individual investors. To attempt to focus the attention of progressive-minded Canadians on that small proportion of investment decisions which may be amenable to popular suasion—union pension fund investments and the mutual fund holdings of sympathetic individuals—would be to divert attention from the real problem. The financial industry will be reformed not through appeals to the hearts and minds of financial investors themselves, but through social and political pressure which imposes a greater degree of accountability and oversight over the realm of finance, in the name of society at large.

In the meantime, of course, concerned individual investors will want their own investments to somehow be part of the solution (or at least not so much a part of the problem). They can consider various options. Ethical mutual funds and labour-sponsored investment funds have been reviewed and found wanting, but many concerned investors will still support them as imperfect steps in the right direction. Investors can also support numerous community or social investment funds which have been established by credit unions, religious organizations, and other groups. These funds explicitly offer a lower rate of return than commercial financial instruments (thus raising the spectre of a profits versus ethics trade-off that is so feared by the ethical mutual fund industry), but they channel the funds directly into worthy community development projects, both in Canada and in developing countries.[18]

Finally, a socially-concerned personal investor who still hungered for the seductive returns of stock markets and other mainstream financial instruments might even adopt the following strategy. First, accept the fact that personal investment choices alone can make no measurable difference to the behaviour and outcomes of the economy. Invest, if desired, in a no-fee index-based mutual fund which will mirror the financial performance of the overall stock market, but without paying the inflated salaries of well-off money managers who oversee active mutual funds (including the well-off money-managers who run the ethical mutual funds).[19] Make this investment through a credit union, where possible. Finally, take an amount equal to roughly 2% of the total sum invested (representing the management fees that *would* have been paid on any actively-managed mutual fund) and donate it to social change and political action projects (including those, like the Canadian Centre for Policy Alternatives, the Council of Canadians or the Canadian Coalition for Community Reinvestment, all based in Ottawa, which are fighting for progressive reforms to the financial system).

This investor will end up with a financial return roughly equal to those who invested in actively managed mutual funds (since history shows that most mutual funds don't match overall market returns, despite their expensive management fees). But they will have supported social change activism with their 2% "tithes," instead of the unproductive market-churning of overpaid financial professionals. And that is definitely a reason to sleep well at night.

Chapter 16
Doing it Differently:
A Model of Social Investment and Community Entrepreneurship

Previous chapters of this book have identified and explored the various factors that have contributed to the slowdown of real investment and real capital accumulation in Canada. Persistently high interest rates, the legacy of the about-face in macroeconomic policy which was engineered in the early 1980s, have been a crucial factor. So, too, have been the chronic sluggishness of demand and purchasing power in the wake of the policies of "permanent recession."

The falling profitability of real business investment has reduced the incentive for companies to undertake expansion of their capital facilities—especially when the returns on purely financial investments have been so consistently high. Ironically, the U-turn in economic and social policies experienced in Canada since 1981, motivated in large part by a desire to resuscitate that profitability, has done little if anything to enhance the motivation for real investment by real businesses, despite the obvious and growing social costs of the new policy regime.

The never-ending march to "securitize" all forms of wealth in the form of easily-traded paper assets, and the inherent fragility of the markets which buy and sell those securities, have also contributed importantly to the slowdown. And the securitization of wealth has made our whole economy—now even including many of our social programs—precariously vulnerable to the mood swings of financiers.

Chapter 14 of the book mapped out a wide-ranging agenda of economic and financial reforms which would help to reverse some of these negative trends. Lower interest rates, expansionary macroeconomic policies, and a greater tolerance for moderate inflation (the greatest of all economic evils, as far as the owners of financial wealth are concerned, but more like an inconvenience for the rest of us) would help a lot.

Various measures to shift the burden of taxation from the users to the owners of capital, and to encourage firms to retain more of their profits internally (rather than distributing them to shareholders), would also help to stimulate stronger investment performance by companies.

Rebuilding public investment spending would be an important component of the overall recovery in real investment spending.

And a range of possible financial reforms might help to channel the vast sums of financial capital which have been accumulating in our banks and stock brokerages more effectively into real, productivity-enhancing investments in the real economy. At minimum, these financial reforms would be important in reducing the vulnerability of the real economy to the chronic manias and panics of the financial realm.

Together, these measures would make an important contribution to reversing the negative economic and social trends evidenced in Canada's economy in the 1980s, and especially the 1990s. They would help to put financial capital back to work in real jobs. They would stimulate growth, job-creation, and rising incomes. But even the reforms proposed in Chapter 14 are still probably inadequate to ensure the vitality of capital accumulation in the long-run.

Optimistically, the range of reforms proposed in Chapter 14 would undo many of the damaging changes of the last two decades. They would re-elevate employment above financial returns in the pecking order of economic policy, and would stimulate an important but probably temporary period of stronger growth and job-creation. Sooner rather than later, however, this expansionary strategy is likely to face problems similar to those that Canada experienced in the 1970s— like *déja vu* all over again.

The economy would begin to strain at its true capacity limits for the first time in a generation. Backed up by stronger labour markets and (presumably) progressive changes in labour law and social policies, workers would try to win back what they have lost since 1981. Despite enjoying the benefits of stronger purchasing power throughout the economy, private companies would simultaneously begin to feel a pinch from re-energized labour markets and re-energized state activity (including public investment, a reconstruction of social programs, and presumably a more ambitious approach to the regulation of private-sector activity).

Needless to say, financiers would also frantically resist the sort of policy agenda mapped out in Chapter 14; lower interest rates plus modestly higher inflation imply a two-sided decline in financial profitability that would be mirrored by declines in stock markets and other asset prices.

In short, society would quickly be into a period of fairly fundamental conflict over the structure of economic decision-making power and the very direction of economic development: a brouhaha of political-economy, a bench-clearing brawl over who's in charge of accumulation, production, and distribution.

A fundamental shift in policy direction of the sort mapped out in Chapter 14 would face incredible opposition from those who have done so well during the 1980s, and especially the 1990s, particularly from financial investors. But, even if that initial fierce opposition could be overcome, and a progressive policy agenda actually implemented, this would really mark just the opening salvoes in an increasingly bitter tug-of-war over whose economic interests will be most protected as the economy progresses, and whose won't.

We can't pretend that undoing the regressive macroeconomic and social policy changes of the last two decades would somehow be universally beneficial, and hence acceptable. Indeed, it is the vested interest of business—both financiers and real employers—in the policies of "permanent recession" that explains both why these seemingly counterproductive policies were implemented, and why it will be hard to replace them.

In criticizing the policy direction of the last two decades, many progressives imply that the fault for our current morass lies with a mistaken belief in faulty right-wing economic ideas. But, despite the seemingly irrational social consequences of the policies of permanent recession, it is quite wrong to ascribe the huge post-1981 U-turn to a lack of correct understanding on the part of policymakers, their advisors, or the business community. Financiers and employers have powerful vested interests at stake in the direction of macroeconomic policy. They act in a sophisticated and self-interested manner. They know what side their bread is buttered on. And they have marshalled a huge array of intellectual and political resources (including much of the economics profession) to support their case for restraint in the real economy combined with full-speed-ahead in the paper economy.

An argument can be made that a return to expansionary, full-employment monetary and fiscal policies might not be as bad for the business community (especially for businesses producing real goods and services, especially those selling into the domestic market, and especially in the shorter-term) as business lobbyists typically argue. At the same time, however, we can't be naive that these expansionary, pro-jobs policies will somehow benefit "everybody."[1] If so, why haven't they been implemented? Indeed, why were they removed in the first place?

The resistance of real businesses to the undoing of the neoconservative policy revolution of the 1980s and 1990s would be expressed in many ways. Inflation could result from their efforts to protect shrinking profit margins through higher prices. More intense workplace conflicts would certainly erupt over working conditions and pay. The business community would issue increasingly strident political demands for a restoration of a pro-business economic and institutional climate. And, sooner or later, they will start to back up those demands with damaging cutbacks in their real investment spending—cutbacks which, as we have stressed throughout this book, would hold serious consequences for over-all growth and job-creation.

In short, many real investors are likely to do what unionized workers also do when their demands are not being heeded: they will go "on strike," and either reallocate their investment spending to more profit-friendly jurisdictions abroad, or else simply stop investing altogether. Unless society has been able to collectively reduce its reliance on those private investors as the "spark plug" of the whole economy, that strike will have devastating economic and political implications. And the whole circle of the 1980s and 1990s would be repeated again. To really win back what has been lost over the past two harsh decades, and then to hang onto it, society needs to be prepared to fundamentally take on some of the economic functions—and in particular the task of mobilizing and investing real capital—that has currently been assigned to a narrow sub-set of the population (the capitalists).

In other words, whole communities have to be prepared to step up to the plate, and say: "If private companies are not willing to supply the real investment that a high-wage, egalitarian economy needs in order to maintain growth and job-creation, then we will do it ourselves."

This process of entire communities and even nations collectively undertaking capital accumulation is called the *socialization of investment.* Instead of real investment being an economic function assigned primarily to profit-seeking private firms, it becomes a central economic task that is undertaken more broadly by public or community-controlled institutions and enterprises.

Various forms of social investment will ultimately need to be developed to supplement or ultimately replace the economy's reliance on injections of private investment expenditure as the leading force in economic growth and job-creation.[2] The process of social investment will obviously require a range of institutional and regulatory initiatives aimed at winning more public and democratic control over finance. But it will also require the even more ambitious development of our collective capacities to take that finance and do something economically useful with it—putting it into motion in the real economy, creating jobs, and producing goods and services of real value.

This parallel process of learning to conceive and carry out real investment projects on a public or non-profit basis might be called *community entrepreneurship.* In economic theory, the "entrepreneur" is identified as the agent responsible for assembling the various inputs to an economic process (including workers, machines, technology, and raw materials), and then overseeing their

Done Its Work

"The rentier aspect of capitalism [is] a transitional phase which will disappear when it has done its work.... It seems unlikely that the influence of banking policy on the rate of interest will be sufficient by itself to determine an optimum rate of investment. I conceive, therefore, that a somewhat comprehensive socialization of investment will prove the only means of securing an approximation to full employment."

—John Maynard Keynes
The General Theory, 1936

activity in a creative and productive manner. At present, entrepreneurship is a process which largely occurs within private companies (although the *entrepreneur* is not necessarily the *owner* of the company, as witnessed by the legions of salaried researchers and managers who work for large corporations which they do not own).

For investment to become socialized in the real sense, not just the financial sense, this entrepreneurship function needs to become the broader responsibility of entire communities, organized through public and non-profit enterprises, agencies, or other ventures. Ultimately, society needs to become less reliant on the private investor to decide what needs to be produced, and how it will be done, and more willing to fulfill this function itself.

Socialized Investment, Then and Now

There is nothing new about this insight that communities or nations will eventually need to take collective responsibility for the mobilization and management of real capital accumulation. Economists and activists alike have long recognized that at some point fundamental changes would be required in the structures of ownership and control over real capital in order to ensure that capital accumulation continues—and, just as importantly, that it works for the betterment of average citizens, rather than their impoverishment.

Karl Marx, of course, believed that the internal dynamism of profit-led capital accumulation would eventually run up against limits imposed by falling profitability and worker demands for economic justice. From a different perspective, John Maynard Keynes believed that government fine-tuning could eliminate mass unemployment—but he also accepted that at some point government would need to go further, undertaking the socialization of investment itself to ensure sufficient injections of investment spending to ensure the continuation of full employment (see quote).

Keynes' contemporary, Michal Kalecki, understood more clearly the long-term dangers posed by regulated full-employment to an economic system that

Full-Employment Jeopardy

"Full employment capitalism will have, of course, to develop new social and political institutions which will reflect the increased power of the working class. If capitalism can adjust itself to full employment, a fundamental reform will have been incorporated within it. If not, it will show itself an outmoded system which must be scrapped."
—Michal Kalecki
"Political aspects of full employment," 1971

was still rooted in the profit-seeking behaviour of private companies. He predicted—all too accurately, in retrospect—that Keynesian-style demand-management policies would founder on the rocks of increasingly desperate opposition from private investors (both real and financial) anxious to recreate an economic environment more amenable to private profit. Kalecki identified a need for far-reaching institutional changes governing the investment process, if the gains of full-employment macroeconomic policy were to be solidified and protected (see quote).

These and other theoretical insights inspired a range of political and economic strategies that were undertaken in different developed market economies over the post-war period. All were motivated by a common recognition that it will be increasingly difficult to "bribe" private firms into investing sufficient new real capital, expended in the right economic sectors, to create and maintain a high-wage, structurally balanced, fully-employed economy.

This recognition would seem to require the construction of new investment structures and vehicles to deliver investment spending on a non-profit and more democratically accountable basis. Many of the European social-democratic parties that came to power in the first decades following the conclusion of World War II initiated the wide-ranging nationalization of important industries (including mining, heavy industry, and transportation). In some countries—such as France and Scandinavia—these publicly-owned industrial networks are still central pillars of the economy.

In Canada, public investment grew dramatically during the post-war boom—and not just in the form of expanded public and human services. Crown corporations in important industries like electric utilities, telecommunications, transportation, and energy accounted for up to 20% of all business assets in Canada by the late 1970s.

Many experiments were undertaken in Canada and elsewhere with alternative financial institutions for delivering credit and finance to undertakings that might be economically or socially beneficial, but which will not be granted sufficient financial support by commercial financiers alone. Some of these alternative structures remain in place today—including Canadian initiatives such as the

Business Development Bank, the Export Development Corporation, and a range of public venture capital investment agencies established in provinces such as Quebec, Ontario, B.C., and Saskatchewan.

In general, however, recent economic and political developments have not been kind to these past attempts to develop and implement models of social investment. The collapse of centrally-planned economies in Eastern Europe certainly seemed to undermine the case that economies could be made more dynamic and efficient through the conscious regulation of investment and production, rather than through the self-interested decisions of private investors and firms.

The stagnation and chronic inefficiency associated with many (but certainly not all) nationalized industries in Europe and Canada, combined with the increasingly tight fiscal constraints facing the governments of those countries in the wake of the restrictive macroeconomic policies of the 1980s and 1990s, sparked a wave of privatization that significantly reduced the role of public companies in traditionally private-dominated industries.

In Canada, the assets of Crown corporations, measured as a share of the total non-financial business sector, shrank by one-third during the 1980s and 1990s; this could fall further if current suggestions to privatize provincial electric utilities and other remaining Crown corporations become a reality. Public investments in Crown corporations are now more commonly associated with cost overruns, chronic losses, and an inability to make difficult decisions, than with the goals of job-creation and economic accountability which motivated those investments in the first place.

Public financial institutions, too, have often not lived up to their mandate. Recent controversies regarding the Alberta Treasury Branch—which was founded in the midst of populist prairie opposition to the power of private banks during the 1930s, and which remains Canada's largest publicly-owned bank—are a bitter example of this legacy. In the wake of alleged inefficiency and political cronyism in its lending operations, the provincial government of Ralph Klein (hardly sympathetic to the principle of non-profit economic undertakings in the first place) wants to privatize it.

Indeed, "privatize it" now seems to be a one-size-fits-all response to the problems of Crown corporations or public agencies. [In fact, privatization is even proposed for profitable, successful Crown corporations as often as it is for the chronic loss-makers.] It does not really matter whether privatization results in any subsequent improvement in the agency's economic performance. What really matters is that the problem stops being a headache for politically sensitive governments.

Political expediency is the clear motive, for example, behind the planned 1999 privatization of the Cape Breton Development Corporation, which operates two troubled coal mines in the depressed Cape Breton region of Nova Scotia. Whatever company ultimately buys the mines, assuming that the federal government can find a buyer at all, is likely to shut them both down. Why doesn't the government simply drop the axe itself, thus avoiding the expensive charade of privatization and "rationalization"? Because elected officials fear the political fall-out that would result, and hence they hive off the responsibility to private investors who face no such political pressures.

In many cases like this one, endless jargon about the "efficiency" of private firms is a blatant smokescreen: what matters is not that private companies are *efficient*, but rather that they are *unaccountable* to the communities in which they operate, and hence can be the bearers of bad news without suffering repercussions.

Strangely, thanks to the widespread attitude that private market decisions are somehow "neutral," "natural," or "inevitable," many people will accept things from private companies that they wouldn't tolerate from their elected leaders. Hence privatization becomes a convenient tool for making an end-run around the public anger that accompanies layoffs, closures, and downsizing.

Even apparently "successful" privatizations are often rooted in exactly the same strange political dynamic. For example, the privatization of CN Rail in 1995 is often heralded as a fantastically successful economic initiative. To be sure, the private company has been a hit with investors, whose share values tripled in the three years after privatization. The federal government, meanwhile, earned a billion dollars towards its deficit-reduction priority (not much in the grand fiscal scheme). But in actual operational and economic terms, has the privatized company really been so successful?

In 1998, the company hauled barely as much freight as it did in 1994 (before privatization), and it actually earned less in total revenue. Its real investment in new machinery and railway structures has declined substantially under private ownership. But the company did all this with 10,000 fewer workers—the sole reason for its transformation from "basket case" into "profit machine."

Eliminating 10,000 well-paying jobs at a time of chronic unemployment and falling incomes is hardly a positive achievement in the big picture. By imposing painful downsizing that politically accountable governments shied away from, the company earned big money for its owners, and made a modest contribution to the elimination of the federal deficit. That is something quite different, however, from making a real contribution to national economic progress.

Despite the hollow and often destructive legacy of the privatization movement, "nationalization" and "public ownership" remain dirty words, even on many parts of the left. It is time to start washing them off and shining them up. Public investment through creative, innovative, and accountable Crown corporations could once again make a significant contribution to the total investment effort undertaken in the Canadian economy, as well as to the production of goods and (more likely) services which are not forthcoming from the private sector.[3]

Important challenges in the funding and operation of Crown corporations need to be addressed, if they are to be revitalized as a creative and efficient force in economic development. Crown corporations work best when they are given both a clear mandate and explicit and binding financial targets. Obviously, the mandates of Crown corporations need to be broader than simply to "make money." If that were the goal, private firms would do the job much better. But neither can their goal be to simply "lose money."

Crown mandates need to be particularly carefully considered when a Crown corporation is established in an industry where it will compete directly with private firms This often raises unrealistic expectations that the Crown corporation will provide the product or service in question more cheaply than its private counterparts do, or use production or management methods that are somehow more socially acceptable (showing more care for the environment, or keeping more workers on staff).

Many Canadians, for example, hoped that publicly-owned Petro-Canada, formed at the height of the 1970s oil shocks, would sell gasoline more cheaply than the "greedy" private oil companies, and mandate confusion dogged the company until its subsequent privatization (at which point its mandate became crystal clear: to make money for its shareholders).[4]

These naive expectations about the role of Crown corporations, especially those which compete with private firms, ignore the fundamental power of private competition in shaping and constraining the actions of companies which operate in competitive markets. If the production and sale of a product is to be conducted in a deregulated, competitive setting, this will exert a generally harmonizing influence on the business decisions of all players who want to survive in that industry—regardless of who their owner is.

The traditional practice of requiring Crown corporations to fulfill economically impossible mandates, without the economic or political resources required to do the job, explains much of the poor financial performance of many (but not most) Crown corporations.

The managers of Crown corporations should face budget constraints that are as binding as those experienced in the private sector. This is not to imply that every activity undertaken by a Crown corporation must be self-financing or profitable. But, if a public subsidy is to be provided to a Crown activity, on the basis of some calculation that the social benefits of such a subsidy would exceed its costs, then this should be done explicitly and with budget constraints that truly "bite."

If a Crown corporation cannot meet the task required of it within the budgetary limit set for it, then the managers should be fired (if it is a case of mismanagement) or the mandate should be revised or abandoned. The practice of tolerating chronic losses and underperformance from Crown corporations reflects more the failure of political leadership and corporate management to face facts and make tough decisions, than it does any inherent inefficiency in public enterprise *per se*.

Disasters and Other Good Things

It is curious, but true: natural disasters are often *good* for the economy.

For example, in the wake of the devastating ice-storm experienced in early 1998, the province of Québec undertook a rebuilding program which propelled it to the top of the Canadian charts in terms of economic growth and job-creation during the following year. Other natural disasters—floods, hurricanes, earthquakes—can have similar effects, motivating investment, reconstruction, and job-creation that would not have occurred otherwise.

Even purely man-made disasters can have beneficial impacts. Many economists, for example, noted that the spin-off effects of the huge investments in computer technology undertaken to forestall year-2000-related computer problems added measurably to total investment spending and hence job-creation during the late 1990s. At time of this writing, it is not known if the Y2K bug will prove to be a gigantic anti-climax or the onset of social breakdown. In the meantime, however, its looming arrival has created a lot of new jobs for computer programmers—whose spending in turn has stimulated additional job-creation and growth.

Disasters themselves, of course, cause often deadly human hardship, and we obviously want less of them, not more. But what is it about disasters that stimulates the mini-booms which follow in their wake? The key conceptual feature is that the disaster forces society in general (and insurance companies, in particular!) to *spend*. Disasters motivate follow-up economic activity, including major public and private real investment spending, that in turn produces jobs and can actually raise incomes.

As a society, can't we capture those beneficial effects of a disaster, without actually having to incur one? If we can spend money and put idle resources to work after a disaster, why can't we do the same without incurring the hardship and tragedy of a disaster in the first place?

Disasters force individuals, companies, and institutions to spend money that they didn't think they wanted to spend in the first place. That involuntary imperative to invest in rebuilding ironically produces an outbreak of job-creation and prosperity.[1] The trick is to find ways of compelling new investment spending, when private profit-seeking agents would not otherwise do so. In this way, the problem relates to the distinction between profit-led private investment and socially-mandated public investment that is explored in this chapter.

Managers of private companies which were similarly slow to face hard economic facts would be driven out of business, if they weren't fired first by disgruntled shareholders. We do not have to accept the same *criteria* as private financial markets for the imposition of this type of discipline—quite the contrary: the whole rationale for Crown corporations is the recognition that some economic projects need to be undertaken for reasons other than the maximization of private profits. But we should nevertheless accept the *need* for this discipline.

Consider the economic implications of pollution. The modern global economy faces a looming disaster in the form of numerous environmental problems associated with fossil fuels consumption—most acutely the problem of global warming. To respond to this disaster will require the expenditure of vast quantities of money to adjust a huge range of economic activities so that they become more environmentally sustainable.

Is this a good thing or a bad thing? In a world in which investment spending is driven by private profit alone, it seems to be a bad thing. Companies have to spend more (on environmental protection) to get the same output. Even if they can pass on some of those costs to the final consumer, demand for environmentally-expensive goods and services will likely decline, and so will profits. Thus it is no surprise that most private investors in environmentally troubled industries are virulently hostile to the notion that they should be forced to undertake these expenditures. To the extent that lower profits imply less business investment, then these regulations would indeed be likely to reduce output and employment in affected industries—just as their critics threaten.

On the other hand, the vast investment expenditures required to respond to looming environmental issues could be beneficial from a social perspective—in the same way that rebuilding after a flood or rewriting computer programs to prevent a millenium bug can also be beneficial for the economy. This would be especially true if those environmental investments were simply mandated on broader social grounds, rather than being incorporated and accommodated within the existing regime of profit-led investment.

Suppose that society just came out and openly recognized that huge environmental investments need to be made, and that a fund will have to be created to pay for them (financed in part, presumably, through taxes collected on environmentally-damaging commodities). The negative impacts of the costs of environmental regulation on private profit-driven investment would be largely offset. Jobs would be created by the boom in environmental investment and its spin-offs. Society would enjoy both higher incomes and a cleaner environment.

Once society takes hold of its own economic destiny, allocating resources to things because they need to be done (rather than because they might be profitable), then even bad news can become good news.

---

[1] This effect is similar to Keynes's "paradox of thrift," explained in Chapter 10, except that it operates in reverse: by being forced to spend money, an economy can end up with more than it started with.

Part of building our broader capacities for social investment and community entrepreneurship will therefore involve the resuscitation of Crown corporations as creative and dynamic sites of economic activity. In the long run, it will likely be more successful to build up new Crown corporations oriented around the provision of new goods and services than to form Crown corporations by nationalizing existing private firms (although there are cases in which outright nationalization may be desirable for structural or strategic reasons).

The most successful examples of Crown corporations that played a truly entrepreneurial role in Canada's economic history were companies established to lead important economic and technological changes that private businesses were unable to carry out on their own. Once-pioneering companies like Ontario Hydro, Air Canada, and Canadair created jobs, mobilized capital, and contributed to the quantitative and qualitative development of Canada's economy in ways which are still proving beneficial today.

Repeating this success in other emerging industries will be the most likely means of rebuilding Crown enterprise as a dynamic and progressive economic force—rather than through the expensive and dubious buy-out of existing profitable companies in hopes that merely transferring top-level control of those corporations will somehow allow them to operate in a fundamentally different way. Emerging industries in which Crown corporations could play a similarly entrepreneurial role in future years might include:

- *New forms of health services, such as home care or pharmacare.* Imagine, for example, a Crown corporation which acted as a centralized national drug-purchase agency for provincial pharmacare plans, and even manufactured its own generic drugs where that was appropriate and feasible.
- *The renovation of Canada's transportation infrastructure.* Major public investments will clearly be required to bring about dreamed-of transportation advances such as high-speed rail transport or better commuter services in Canada's major cities, and many of these investments would be conducted most effectively through Crown corporations.
- *More accessible community data services and Internet links.* Crown enterprises could provide hardware, software, and data transmission facilities specializing in public access applications (for libraries, schools, and other public facilities).

Revitalized Crown corporations are clearly one means through which real investment and entrepreneurship could be undertaken on a not-for-profit, more democratically accountable basis. But numerous other institutional forms have also been advocated as potential vehicles for the undertaking of social investment. The idea of a public investment bank, which would channel financial resources into new ventures undertaken by a range of different types of enterprise (conventional businesses, Crown corporations, or non-profit and community-based ventures) is one proposal which continues to find widespread support.

The Canadian Labour Congress, for example, has proposed a publicly-controlled National Investment Fund to spur investment in real job-creating projects. Successive versions of the Alternative Federal Budget have made similar proposals, according to which private financial institutions would be required to keep a small portion of their assets on deposit with a public investment bank. This bank would then use these funds, along with others that it could leverage through the normal operation of the banking system, to support worthy capital investments that are not undertaken by private investors. The Economic Policy Institute has developed a similar proposal for the U.S. economy.[5]

The previous chapters of this book have hopefully reinforced an understanding of the need for this type of approach. The rest of this chapter will attempt to map out its structure and functions in more detail.

A Public Venture Investment System

The current investment regime in Canada, as described throughout this book, consists of two major parts: a financial side, which raises or creates financial capital (through banks, stock markets, and other financial institutions), and a real side which sets that finance into motion in the form of real job-creating investments.

A large part of Canada's investment problem, of course, is the weak and uncertain link between those two personalities of "investment." The whole process—both financial investment and real investment—is currently conducted mostly on private, self-interested grounds. The financial investor hopes for a paper return on a paper investment, while the owner of a real business hopes for a profit on a real investment.

Imagine if this whole process was replaced by one in which the need of the broader community for capital accumulation and job-creation explicitly motivated the chain of economic activity which culminates in a new investment in some real venture. This system of public venture investment, like the current private one, would have both a financial side and a real side. To be sure, it would require the marshalling of and control over significant financial resources. But many progressives have put an unbalanced emphasis on campaigning for more social accountability and public control in the purely financial realm (through a range of initiatives ranging from the socially-minded financial vehicles reviewed in Chapter 15, to regulations and taxes on financial institutions, to the outright nationalization of one or more major banks).[6]

As has been stressed throughout this book, a financial investment is quite distinct from a real one. Canada's weak investment performance cannot be improved by simply trying to "push" more finance into the domestic economy. Indeed, as was argued in detail in Chapter 10, our poor track record of real investment cannot be explained by a "lack of money." What is also needed are new ways to put money into economic motion in the form of real job-creating investments—in greater volume than is likely to be provided by private firms alone, and dedicated to end-goals broader than simply the generation of private profits.

Indeed, as with our current private investment regime, it is the "real" side of the investment equation that will likely prove the tougher nut to crack. Regaining more social control over finance represents a major economic and political challenge—but a readily conceivable one. Developing the institutional structures, projects, and managerial or entrepreneurial capacities which would be required to put that finance to work, in an accountable and efficient manner, will require an even more ambitious process of thought, debate, and creative experimentation.

A possible structure for a publicly-owned non-profit venture investment system is summarized in Figure 16-1. This proposal reflects the dual nature of investment: financial and real. On the financial side, the system would create a public venture investment bank. Its initial seed capital would come from the compulsory deposit by existing private financial institutions (including banks, near-banks, mutual funds, and registered pension funds) of a small share (perhaps up to one-half of one percent, once the system was fully phased in over several years) of their total assets.

At present, this would generate some $12-15 billion in initial capital for the public system, again after a phase-in period that would last several years. The compulsory deposits would be justified on grounds that these private financial institutions have been granted unique powers by the public to create and manage credit. As a cost of doing business, the institutions would be required to dedicate a share of their assets to the financing of public and community investment ventures.

Think of this requirement as the financial equivalent to requiring private broadcasters—who also operate thanks to unique powers granted by the public—to allocate a small share of their total on-air time to public service announcements and other community broadcasting.

This required deposit would be fiercely resisted by the financiers, of course, but would have a barely noticeable effect on their bottom line. Mutual funds, for example, pay out several times this amount each year for money management fees, despite the fact that these money managers (as described in Chapter 3) consistently underperform the benchmark indices of the markets in which they operate.

Additional financial resources for the bank could come from credit injections by the Bank of Canada. The rationale for the Bank of Canada to undertake a more pro-active role in financing real economic investment was described in Chapter 14; Bank of Canada injections would vary with the state of overall macroeconomic conditions (increasing in times when private credit creation is weak or uncertain, declining or stopping entirely when the private economy is growing more rapidly). In this manner, the public venture investment bank would help to expand the range of policy instruments available to the Bank of Canada to manage the all-important supply of new credit in the economy.

Governments, pension funds (including public funds like the CPP), and even individual investors could also invest in the public bank.

These voluntary deposits would be paid a decent real rate of interest: perhaps two or three percentage points above inflation. This would be less than can usually be earned in private financial investments, but still sufficient to fund a typical defined-benefit pension plan. Like other banks, the public venture bank would be able to leverage its initial injections of capital into a multiplied volume of total lending.

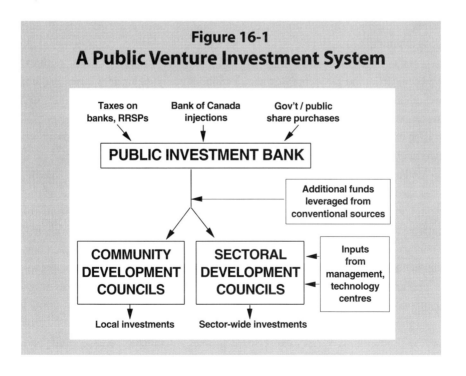

Figure 16-1
A Public Venture Investment System

On the real side of the equation, the public venture investment system would depend on two parallel institutional structures to deliver its financial resources to real job-creating ventures in Canada's economy. One structure would allocate finance to support projects in different communities and regions of Canada. Another would fund investment initiatives undertaken on a sectoral or industrial basis.

These investing institutions could be called *development councils*. They would work with interested parties on a regional or sectoral basis to identify unmet economic and social needs, conduct an inventory of available economic resources (including unemployed or underemployed labour, land and other natural resources, and the technical capacities of the region or industry), and then develop and stimulate new ventures which would put those resources to work.

The development councils would be a meeting place for the various interest groups which might play a role in undertaking new community ventures—including local and regional government agencies, labour and community groups, educational institutions and technology centres, and even private businesses which might consider participating in some joint investment initiatives.

The development councils would receive annual allotments of financial resources from the public investment bank, based on the bank's overall capital supply, macroeconomic conditions, and the past performance and future plans of each council. The councils would then act somewhat like the local loan managers of a commercial bank: receiving business plans, evaluating them, issuing funds to the most likely candidates, and then overseeing the progress of the projects undertaken.

Project submissions would be evaluated on a very different set of criteria, however, from the project reviews undertaken by private lenders. Each project would have to pass a certain "hurdle" rate of return. The overall public venture system would operate on a non-profit basis. This would require, in essence, that it earn enough from its investments to cover the modest interest costs (equal to two or three points above inflation) paid to its initial investors.[7]

All prospective projects would need to meet this criteria. Beyond that, however, profit maximization would not be the goal of the venture investments undertaken. Rather, those project applications which pass the hurdle rate-of-return test would then be ranked in order of their anticipated overall *social* return. This broader measurement of social benefits would include job-creation, taxes generated for governments, the sourcing of inputs from local and national suppliers, and projected benefits in areas such as environmental protection or affirmative action hiring.

Putting hard numbers to the social costs and benefits of a prospective investment venture is a tricky exercise, of course, and much careful planning and

Learning by Doing

"Workers surrender[ed] their capacity to do, the capacity for the creative planning and execution of goals....Hierarchical-authoritarian management systems exclude any hint of institutional forms for the running of workplaces in ways that combine efficiency and democracy. It is, for example, possible to imagine workers taking over existing technology and modifying it, but much harder to imagine... what entirely different forms of collective democratic coordination and management might look like. The democratic collective labourer is a productive force yet to be invented."
—Sam Gindin
"Socialism with sober senses," 1998

experimentation will be required to develop efficient and consistent evaluation criteria. But the evaluation of private investment projects on purely financial criteria is also an incredibly complex and inherently speculative undertaking—yet that does not stop banks and other traditional lenders from coming to their own judgments about which projects look the most attractive.

During and after the screening and approval of investment projects, the development councils will need to undertake standard due diligence procedures, exactly similar to those performed by private lenders, to ensure the viability of funded projects. Community ventures in many cases will be able to obtain supplementary investment financing from alternative sources, including existing private financial institutions.

It will not be sufficient, however, for the development councils to simply sit back and screen the prospective community entrepreneurs who come knocking at their doors. Quite the contrary: one of the key goals of the whole initiative is to assist in the development of entrepreneurial capacities within the broader communities which would be undertaking those investments. This will require pro-active efforts by the development councils to pull together economic stakeholders in particular regions or industries, identify openings for potential new investments, and marshal the resources (including the managerial and technological resources) which will be needed to make those visions a reality.

The provision of expert managerial and technical assistance to venture investments could be facilitated through the work of specialized management and technology centres, which would take a leadership role in organizing new undertakings and ensuring their feasibility.

The work of university research parks, which have been established at many universities to facilitate the economic application of technological developments achieved at those universities, is a fine example of the economic potential of these centres of managerial and technical expertise. At present, the university research parks generally focus on for-profit technology spin-offs, but this need not necessarily be the case. Indeed, the coexistence of publicly-funded research with privately-owned spin-offs is often an uneasy one: why should the commercial benefits of a research breakthrough paid for by the taxpayers be conducted solely by private firms? In the context of a broader system for financing and managing public venture investments, it would be conceivable for universities and other public research and technology centres to oversee the application of their technological advances through social rather than private investment vehicles.

Examples of some of the regional or sectoral ventures which could be undertaken through a public venture investment system are provided in Table 16-1. These examples should be considered as illustrative only; an inventory of dozens more similar potential initiatives could be assembled on the basis of detailed concrete surveys of the economic strengths and weaknesses of Canadian regions and industries.

A key common feature of the proposals introduced in Table 16-1 is that each represents a multi-dimensional effort to pool economic resources (including but not limited to capital) in order to address some major structural weakness resulting from the reliance of the region or industry in question on the purely self-interested actions of private investors and firms.

Where private companies alone are doing a good job of developing a region or sector's economy, there is less justification for the intervention of a public venture initiative. But where they are not, and where the economic potential of a region or industry is underutilized as a result, then there exists a strategic opening for community entrepreneurship to show that it can do the job better.

This does not imply that a public venture investment system should focus on "bailing-out" failing private ventures: quite the opposite, community entrepreneurship needs to be envisioned as a positive, pro-active force in developing a completely new basis on which to conduct real investment and job-creation, rather than being a source of subsidy or "Band-aids" for unviable private ventures. But where community entrepreneurship can best show its unique strengths is in the provision of goods and services, and the development of physical capital and human potential, where existing private agents are failing to do the job.

There are some real-world examples of this general approach to social investment and community entrepreneurship—but not many. The closest illustrations of how the system might work in practice are probably provided by the clusters of public and cooperative enterprises which are an important feature of the economies of central Italy, the Basque and Catalan regions of Spain, and parts of Scandinavia.[8]

These successful experiments with sophisticated forms of non-profit investing share common features which suggest a direction for future institution-building in Canada. They depend on the investment and production decisions of non-profit but fully autonomous enterprises (many but not all of which are relatively small). They maintain an ongoing focus on developing productive, efficient, and sophisticated products and production methods, rather than financing marginal or unproductive undertakings. Each initiative has a strong financial component, including the development of credit unions and other sources of democratic financial services; these institutions play a crucial role in financing non-profit enterprise in the real economy.

Finally, each initiative also draws strength from some widely shared political conviction on the part of local citizens. The precise nature of this political motivation varies from case to case: it is rooted in the progressive nationalism of the Basque and Catalan communities in Spain, and in a more explicitly socialist tradition in central Italy's "Red belt" region. But in every case the effort to develop social investment and community enterprise over time occurs in the context of a broader political movement to transform society in a more fundamental sense.

This broader political goal imparts a common direction to the actions of the individual enterprises and agencies undertaking those investments, as well as a powerful sense of motivation for the individuals whose work and dedication is crucial to their success.

The public venture investment system envisioned here has a spiritual sibling, at least, in the grass-roots community economic development (CED) projects which have been undertaken in numerous regions of Canada, usually in economically depressed areas or among especially hard-hit populations. These are laudable efforts to do at least something productive with the significant portions of the Canadian population which have simply been written-off by private market forces.

Small-scale CED ventures, however, will never be a leading force in Canada's economic development, and they should not be held out as a model of how to socialize investment and entrepreneurship. The main reason for this view is that most existing CED ventures share most of the negative features of small business that were reviewed in Chapter 6 of this book: they are typically very labour-intensive, low-productivity, and low-wage undertakings, which are very vulnerable to fluctuations in broader economic conditions (not to mention fluctuations in government subsidies!).

The motive for these non-profit CED ventures differs from that of profit-seeking small private companies, but the means and outcomes of their undertakings are very similar. Building on these CED initiatives—providing them with more capital and managerial resources, in particular—will be important in the overall effort to develop a community and culture of community entrepreneurship. But a more convincing vision of social investment will need to "think big-

Table 16-1
Public Venture Investment:
Possible Regional & Sectoral Initiatives

Sector or Region	Initiative
Auto parts, Ontario	Auto industry restructuring has required independent auto parts suppliers to design and produce increasingly complicated "sub-assemblies" for faster installation in final vehicles. With some exceptions, Canada's parts industry is not developing the domestic R&D and engineering capabilities to fully participate in this restructuring, even though Canadian engineers and workers have the necessary skills. A cooperative initiative to combine the engineering know-how of universities and research parks with the production skills of auto parts workers, backed by strategic public investments in new ventures, could better position Canada's parts industry for this new era.
Tourism, many regions	Canada has an abundance of extraordinary natural places. In many cases, however, a lack of investment in high-value, high-quality facilities and human resources has clearly undermined the extent to which the tourism potential of these places is utilized. This is clearly true in most of Atlantic Canada, much of Canada's north, and even in some of Canada's smaller but beautiful cities. A cooperative tourism investment strategy to maximize value-added tourism services, with investments in both facilities and skills, could help to turn several of Canada's beautiful but depressed tourism regions into high-value destinations on a par with the Whistlers and Myrtle Beaches of the world.
Sustainable forestry, B.C.	British Columbia's forestry and paper industries are in crisis. But the longer-run economic potential of the province's forests is still huge, especially if the industry can be reoriented toward more environmentally sustainable harvesting and processing methods. Provincial regulatory measures will play an important role in this sort of strategy (such as appropriate royalty provisions for sustainable forestry, or requiring minimum content levels for sustainable forest products in domestic construction or paper use). But a sectoral initiative to invest in alternative forestry and paper facilities would also be essential. It is not clear that for-profit forest companies have the willingness or the ability to lead the transition to a sustainable, high-value forestry industry. A sectoral restructuring initiative, based in part on public venture investment, would make a contribution to the reorientation of this still-crucial industry.

Table 16-1 cont'd	
Sector or Region	**Initiative**
Railways, Montréal	Railway deregulation and privatization have devastated many of Montréal's important railway technology and machining facilities. At the same time, the lack of an integrated regional transportation infrastructure contributes to the urban region's relative economic underperformance. Public venture investments in new commuter and freight rail facilities serving the Montréal region, combined with corresponding commitment to railway-related manufacturing and service capabilities, could revitalize rail transport in the urban region and boost the city's overall economic prospects.
Bioregional planning, Windsor	The unique climate of southwestern Ontario offers the potential for the development of numerous new agricultural and environmental industries—especially in light of ongoing restructuring in traditional agricultural industries in the region (such as tobacco). For example, the production and manufacture of hemp and hemp products (recently legalized in Canada for industrial purposes) could create jobs and make a contribution to the reduction of global warming. A regional biodiversity council would work with farmers, manufacturers, and retailers/wholesalers to identify new products and markets, and invest in their successful production.
Shipbuilding, coastal regions	Canada's shipbuilding industry needs up-front investments of capital and technology to allow Canada to produce equipment for the development of offshore oil and gas resources, to modernize the Great Lakes shipping fleet, and to restore and replace much of our aging marine infrastructure. The implementation of fairer rules regarding international shipbuilding trade would play an important role in revitalizing this strategic industry. But so would a cooperative public-private investment strategy to enhance the productive capabilities of the industry, allowing it to supply more of Canada's own marine construction requirements.[1]
Social housing, cities	Public funding for non-profit housing initiatives of all kinds (including housing co-ops) has been under attack everywhere—partly because of government budget constraints, but also because of opposition from the private housing industry (which hates the competition). Yet the private for-profit housing industry is clearly failing to supply the low-cost housing that many urban communities require. The legacy of that failure is steadily-rising housing costs in most cities, and a growing constituency of underhoused and homeless Canadians. Because of the lower levels of technological and business risk which they usually face, non-profit housing projects are among the safest and most feasible outlets for public venture investment.

[1] A detailed argument supporting a proactive industrial policy for Canada's shipbuilding sector is contained in "Reviving Canada's shipbuilding industry: A new vision," Marine Workers' Federation and CAW Canada, 1997.

ger" than is currently the case with most of Canada's CED movement. For social investment to become a true force in Canada's economy, it will need the economic and human capacity to undertake large, capital-intensive, highly productive projects that could constitute a new leading edge of future economic development—not just a low-cost, last-chance "fall-back" activity for communities which have been left out of that development.

Questions and Answers

The preceding proposal describes a completely new process for mobilizing economic resources, including capital, and putting them to work for the betterment of the members of society (not just the owners of the capital). This would represent a fundamental shift in the structure of economic decision-making authority in our economy—a clear break from society's current and near-total reliance on the decisions of private investors to set their money into motion in the real economy.

Needless to say, this is an ambitious, perhaps Utopian exercise in economic and institutional visioning. All kinds of institutional, economic, and political questions are raised by suggesting that the economic "job" currently filled by the capitalist—namely, identifying what will be done, and organizing and financing its doing—could be done instead and on explicitly different criteria by less self-interested and more socially-accountable institutional forms.

These questions are obviously not all going to be answered here. This chapter, rather, simply aims to highlight the direction that progressives need to be thinking in if we are ever to reduce our fundamental dependence on the private investor as the "team captain" of economic growth. In the wake of the failure of private enterprise to provide Canada's economy with the real investment it needs for job-creation and productivity, and the uncertain prospects for fully reversing that failure through policy reforms and regulatory initiatives, we need to start to consider how we might develop alternative investment vehicles that could eventually come to supplement private investment as the leading force in economic progress.

Nevertheless, some of the important conceptual issues and problems facing such an undertaking can at least be highlighted here. For example, one key risk faced by this sort of public venture initiative would be the temptation to use its financial and political resources to attempt to bail-out or otherwise protect existing jobs and facilities that are threatened from time to time by the decisions of private investors. To be sure, there are many cases where strategic non-profit investments can help to restructure threatened facilities, and reorient the expertise and capital assets possessed within such facilities towards alternative activities with more hopeful longer-term outlooks. These efforts, in many cases, can produce socially and economically preferable outcomes. But it would be a huge mistake to conceive of a public venture investment system solely, or even significantly, as a source of last-ditch aid for otherwise non-viable undertakings.

Even in a progressive, rapidly-growing, and dynamic macroeconomic setting, industrial restructuring will continue to take place, facilities will close, and workers will be laid-off. Obviously this process needs to be regulated to ensure fair treatment for those affected. But the process still needs to occur.[9]

Hence the general mandate of the system would need to be specified clearly and carefully. Its goal is genuine *positive* entrepreneurship: the marshalling of resources (including capital) on a non-profit basis to meet some new or unmet need, judged to be desirable on social cost-benefit grounds. This is very different indeed from using those resources to subsidize ventures which are failing because they do not meet the *private* cost-benefit criteria which rule the world of for-profit activity.

The managers of the public investment system would have to be supervised and evaluated on those criteria, and be structurally insulated from the sorts of narrow political pressure which have made a mockery out of many previous public job-creation or investment initiatives.

It is a difficult task to conceive of how a system of public investment and entrepreneurship could be designed to promote the general concept of democratic accountability on the part of economic decision-makers, but in such a way as to not have that system beholden to narrower sectional interests and pressures. The private-sector solution to this governance problem is simple: explicitly abandon any notion of democratic or community accountability whatsoever, so that all decision are made on the basis of the private interests of the company's owners. In this manner, private firms don't worry about being unduly influenced by the desires of local communities or particular groups of workers to protect their vested interests in particular facilities or jobs. Private firms don't have to care about this, and they generally don't, which is why they are much more "efficient" than other types of institutions at slashing and burning their way to prosperity.

Clearly a public venture investment system will aim to do better than this; in particular, social cost-benefit criteria will govern investment decisions, rather than narrower private ones. But that does not mean that even the managers of a public investment system will not face very tough decisions for which their ability to see a bigger picture, and their capacity to act in the interests of that picture, will be crucial.

Hence a key issue to be considered in designing a public venture investment system is how to strike that fine balance between the general goal of more social accountability over investment and the organizational independence and integrity of the public investment institution itself. We would not want the sectoral and local development councils to act like any other purely self-interested private agency. But, just as important, the councils could not become slush funds for local political or economic interests, or devolve into an easy source of funds to bail-out or forestall painful restructuring initiatives in the private sector.

Conservatives argue that this balance can never be obtained: unless someone is investing their *own* money, they will never take the necessary steps to ensure that those investments are made wisely and efficiently. This knee-jerk view is not convincing, and ignores the institutional reality of how most investment is already conducted in Canada. Local bank managers do not invest "their own" money; they invest their *employer's* money. Yet they act in a disciplined and "efficient" manner (within the goals and accountability structures which have been established to guide them). The same will need to be true of a public venture investment system. It would operate on fundamentally different criteria from the current investment regime; in particular, it would aim to maximize social returns by mobilizing capital and other resources, creating jobs, and efficiently producing goods and services that the private market cannot or will not.

The public system, however, needs to impose the same economic discipline and accountability as currently face private investors and private firms, if it is to be successful and valuable in the long-run. It needs to be democratically accountable, but free from narrow "pork-barrel" political pressures and special interests. The failure of many previous public investment initiatives can be traced to their failure to appropriately design and oversee structures of accountability and discipline to guide the decision-making of managers.

Another management challenge facing a public investment initiative would be to locate and develop the sources of entrepreneurial talent, creativity, and energy required to set a particular project in motion in the first place. In Canada today, the vast majority of individuals who possess the skills and interest for "managing" productive economic activities go into private business to satisfy that urge. [Sadly, a disproportionate share of these creative people enter the financial industry, where they dedicate their skills to the development and sale of ever-more-complex financial instruments, rather than applying themselves to inherently useful endeavours.]

Initiating, pushing for, and ultimately managing community entrepreneurial projects will require just as much creativity and management skill as any other business venture. Why would someone do it for the good of an entire community, as opposed to their personal gain as a private executive or business-owner?

Economists in the "free-market" tradition hold the knee-jerk view that selfishness is the only consistent motivation for the economic activity of human beings. This is patently wrong. Many individuals with energy, creativity, and ambition are motivated by factors which have nothing to do with their particular ownership of a business or a stock of financial capital. Hence those energies can certainly be harnessed, given appropriate institutional forms and incentive structures, within enterprises that have no private ownership of capital.

No economist studied—or celebrated—the virtues of entrepreneurship more than the eclectic Joseph Schumpeter; he was quite explicit in his view that there was no necessary link between private ownership and entrepreneurial spirit (see quote).

Indeed, the modern corporation is itself testimony to the separability of private ownership and concrete, real-world management efficiency. Most corporate managers, researchers, engineers, and other decision-makers have no significant personal stake in the ownership of the companies for which they work. This doesn't stop them from being fantastically creative and productive in what they do.

To be sure, there are ever-closer ties between the owners of corporations and their top executives, ties which have been cemented by the growing importance of stock options and other market-related incentive and evaluation schemes. But the significance of these holdings rarely penetrates below the top couple of levels of the corporate hierarchy. They are not important in motivating work effort or creativity on the part of individual decision-makers on the company's ground-floor level. Rather, stock options have proven to be fantastically effective in winning the allegiance of a company's *top* leadership to the single goal of maximizing shareholder wealth. Knowing that stock market valuation is crucial to their personal success, these executives then crack the whip in order to orient, motivate, and evaluate entire organizations to succeed on the same criteria—even though most members of those organizations have no direct personal stake in the rise and fall of their company's share price.

Get Up and Go

What motivates an entrepreneur? "First of all, there is the dream and the will to found a private kingdom, usually... also a dynasty.... Then there is the will to conquer: the impulse to fight, to prove oneself superior to others, to succeed for the sake, not of the fruits of success, but of success itself.... Finally, there is the joy of creating, of getting things done, or simply of exercising one's energy and ingenuity.... Only with the first [motive] is private property as the result of entrepreneurial activity an essential factor in making it operative. With the other two it is not.... The second and third... motives may in principle be taken care of by other social arrangements not involving private gain from economic innovation."

—Joseph Schumpeter
The Theory of Economic Development, 1934

It seems reasonable, then, that those top executives could be provided with some alternative but equally powerful and transparent overriding management objective: meeting production and delivery targets, for example, or maximizing some agreed-upon measure of social well-being. If their career paths (and their compensation) depended on meeting that objective, then they would surely be just as efficient in motivating and supervising the performance of the whole organization as any option-hungry CEO. In the case of most Crown corporations or public agencies which have experienced chronically poor financial performance, it is not any inherent inefficiency of non-profit activity which is to blame. Rather, it is the failure of those enterprises' owners to set clear targets for management, and then to enforce those targets with the same ruthlessness that modern-day shareholders demand of their corporate executives, that is at fault.

It may thus be *feasible* to recruit, hire, and motivate entrepreneurs on grounds other than the private profitability of private capital. But it will require a large cultural change within the community of entrepreneurial-minded people for this to occur. There's no inherent reason why most people with management-like skills and training should be "pro-business," but they generally are.

At the same time, there is also no reason that only "professional" or "technocratic" managers should be the ones capable of devising and implementing community-based entrepreneurial projects. Part of the management development task associated with a public investment system will therefore involve recruiting existing entrepreneurs with the promise of decently-compensated and socially-meaningful work. But part will also involve the development of management and entrepreneurial skills from *within* the communities and sectors which undertake the new public or non-profit ventures.

These problems, and many others, are fundamentally challenging issues that will need to be overcome in the development of a socially ambitious but economically viable public venture investment system. Indeed, in comparison to these difficulties, the ambitious proposal (discussed in Chapter 14) to create a global central bank to promote international financial stability, starts to look downright modest in comparison.

In the absence of both the political power and the economic capacity to implement such a public investment system on a large scale, capital accumulation in Canada will continue to be primarily reliant on the profit-seeking decisions of private companies for the foreseeable future—supplemented, hopefully, by larger injections of public investment spending, the revitalization of Crown corporations as a significant force in economic development, and growing experimentation with alternative forms of community entrepreneurship and investment.

By successfully experimenting with models of public and community venture investment, first on a small scale in particular communities or industries, and then more ambitiously as the organizational strength and political confidence of community entrepreneurs matures, the groundwork can be laid for the long-run development of a non-profit but economically sophisticated economic constituency.

Just because a policy alternative may seem far off does not imply that it is irrelevant to current discussions and debates. Having a better understanding of the fundamental roots of a problem like the investment slowdown, and at least a notion about the sorts of far-reaching measures that may ultimately be required for its solution, imparts a more informed perspective to efforts aimed at winning more modest and incremental interim measures (like lower interest rates or adjustments to existing tax policies).

The vision of social and economic change imagined here seems reminiscent of the theories of institutional competition and conflict initially developed by the Italian theorist and activist Antonio Gramsci. How do fundamental structural changes take place in a society? Not overnight, and not by simply appointing a new executive team to lead an existing institutional apparatus. Rather, a long-run process of creative and conflict-ridden institution-building is required, as groups of citizens attempt to carve out their own economic and social bases from which to offset and ultimately challenge the power of existing decision-makers.

The notion of the gradual and experimental development of a democratically-controlled system for financing and managing non-profit economic ventures would seem to fit with this model. As such a system was developed over time, its participants would learn by doing, building their capacities to undertake the whole process of investment and entrepreneurship from beginning to end, and gradually reducing their reliance on continued injections of real investment from private for-profit firms.

As their economic "independence" thus increased over time, communities would be in a better position to demand higher standards from those private investors who still wanted to play the game. One morning the citizens of a com-

Bit by Bit

"No social formation is ever destroyed before all the productive forces for which it is sufficient have been developed, and new superior relations of production never replace older ones before the material conditions for their existence have matured within the framework of the old society."
—Karl Marx,
A Contribution to the Critique of Political Economy, 1859.

munity or even a whole country would wake up and realize they were in charge of their own economic destiny: they now possessed the institutional strength, the financial resources, and the entrepreneurial experience and capabilities with which to oversee the continued accumulation of real capital and the continued qualitative and quantitative development of the economy. Now, however, this process would be conducted with the explicit goal of bettering the economic and social well-being of society in general, rather than the private gain of the few.

Endnotes

Notes to Chapter 1

[1] The total administration costs of the mutual fund industry are huge: about $7 billion per year (see Chapter 3 for more details). The fundamental efficiency of public pension administration parallels the well-known efficiency of Canada's Medicare system, which is vastly cheaper to administer than private health insurance systems such as the one in the U.S. Public health care avoids the huge overhead costs of administering hundreds of separate private plans, overseeing payouts, and enforcing numerous different sets of rules regarding fees, coverage, and premiums. Similarly, a universal pension system, in which virtually every paid worker qualifies according to a single set of common rules, avoids the administrative waste of managing millions of separate individual or workplace-based pension plans.

Notes to Chapter 2

[1] All of the statistics on the paper economy presented here exclude the real estate industry, which is sometimes lumped together with purely financial service industries but which actually has a stronger link to the real economy.

[2] In previous times, central banks would guarantee the value of a currency with gold. Now, in a non-gold monetary system, the value of money is ironically "guaranteed" with more money. In other words, the Bank of Canada will honour on demand the value of a $20 bill—by giving its owner another one in exchange! Nevertheless, in accounting terms the currency in circulation is still treated as a liability of the central bank.

[3] The net worth of Canada as a whole includes the net worth of Canadian governments and businesses, in addition to the personal net worth of individual Canadians.

[4] Data on wealth distribution was collected until 1984, when the service was discontinued under the Mulroney government. Statistics Canada is developing a new survey on household wealth which will provide more data on this crucial subject in coming years.

Notes to Chapter 3

[1] For example, see "Finance, entrepreneurship, and growth: theory and evidence," by Robert G. King and Ross Levine, *Journal of Monetary Economics* 32(3), December 1993, pp. 513-542. Their argument is unconvincing and circular: they measure the degree of financial intermediation by the relative size of the stockpile of money in an economy, and find—lo and behold—that economies with more money are those with higher standards of living!

[2] The process of converting an existing stockpile of wealth, owned within a firm, into smaller "bite-size" chunks which can be bought and sold on an asset market, is called *securitization*. See Chapter 12 for more discussion of this process.

[3] For example, shares of CN Rail were first sold for $27 in November, 1995. The market price jumped by $5 in the first day of trading, suggesting that the federal government underpriced the company by at least $400 million (or 15 percent). Within three years the price of CN shares had tripled, as the company generated record profits thanks almost purely to merciless downsizing and other forms of cost-cutting. The company's shares were especially popular with railway-savvy U.S. investors, who owned the majority of the newly-privatized company within two years of its initial sale.

[4] Important examples of this school of thought include Robert S. Chirinko and Huntley Schaller, "Why does liquidity matter in investment equations?", *Journal of Money, Credit, and Banking* 27(2), May 1995, and Steven M. Fazzari, R. Glenn Hubbard, and Bruce C. Petersen, "Financing constraints and corporate investment," *Brookings Papers on Economic Activity* (1), 1988.

[5] The difference between nominal and real interest rates is extremely important, and will be explored in Chapter 9.

[6] The author is grateful to Marc Lavoie for clarifying comments on this section of the book.

[7] This decline in the apparent interest rate spread (between the average rate charged by the bank on its loans and the average rate paid out to its own depositors) must be interpreted with caution. The declining spread is often presented as evidence that banks have become more competitive and "consumer-friendly" in their lend-

ing business.   In reality, however, other factors also influence this spread: the growing proportion of bank assets dedicated to non-loan businesses, and the decline in the nominal level of interest rates paid on both loans and deposits, have also been important.   If we calculate a sales margin on bank lending in the same manner as other businesses do—with net income expressed as a share of incoming revenue rather than as a percentage of the value of outstanding assets—then the gross profit margin on bank lending has been stable, at 30 percent or more of total interest income.

8   See Chapter 14 for more discussion of bank regulations.

9   This net borrowing from abroad translates into a deficit in Canada's international balance of payments, since that foreign borrowing is ultimately used to purchase imports of goods and services above and beyond the value of Canada's exports. Net foreign borrowing by Canada was uniquely low during the period covered by Table 3-3. Our traditionally large foreign borrowing mostly disappeared between 1995 and 1997, in the wake of a weak economy and reduced foreign borrowing by governments. Since 1997, however, large balance of payments deficits (and the foreign borrowing required to finance them) have once again reappeared.

10 This statement does not mean to suggest that Canada is an "Anglo" country, or that only its English colonial heritage is important—only that our historic links with the British Empire were influential in shaping the sorts of financial institutions which developed here.

11 Most countries have one dominant stock market, but the U.S. has two—the New York Stock Exchange and the Nasdaq—so the trading activity of both is included.

12 As will be discussed in Chapter 5, there are numerous ways to measure real investment; this is the most common.

Notes to Chapter 4

1   For example, "When will the fiscal brake be released?," by Jeff Rubin and John Lester, CIBC Wood Gundy Occasional Report #15, August 1996, singled out the macroeconomic side-effects of the spending cuts for the sudden post-1995 slowdown in growth and job-creation.

2   A huge amount of "work" is performed in society, of course, but not "counted" within the formal labour market: unpaid household and caring labour which is performed in private households (primarily by women), the volunteer community labour of concerned citizens, and other activities. The proper measurement, valuation, and consideration of that labour is crucial if we are to design social and economic policies which genuinely improve the living conditions of Canadians (including those who perform this unpaid work). Nevertheless, most Canadians need to earn money in order to survive in our market economy, and hence the state of

the *paid* labour market is obviously the central determinant of the economic well-being of working people.

[3] There are a range of different definitions of what constitutes productive "capital," which will be explored further in the next chapter.

[4] A decreasing share of total business investment is represented by the construction of actual new facilities (such as factories, mines, or office buildings), and more is represented by purchases of ever-more sophisticated machinery (assembly lines, robots, computers, and heavy equipment). Excluding the residential construction industry, business investment in structures fell from 55 percent of total investment spending in the early 1960s to 40 percent by 1997. This reflects the greater emphasis on the intensive use of technology in production, rather than traditional spending on "bricks and mortar."

[5] Wide-ranging deregulation in Canada in the 1980s and 1990s has dramatically reduced the number of industries and companies subject to price regulation. Typically, regulated industries followed a "cost-plus" pricing system, in which the regulator would examine the apparent cost of running a business, and then set prices high enough to cover those costs plus an agreed-upon profit margin for the private supplier. Attempts to regulate the prices charged by private suppliers have generally foundered in the wake of numerous difficulties, including a lack of regulatory responsiveness and flexibility, and the ease with which private suppliers are allowed to simply pass on higher costs (including hidden profits) to consumers.

[6] This discussion is implicitly assuming that the public and non-profit sectors only produce *services*, and not *goods*. There is nothing to say that this must be the case; a public or non-profit enterprise could obviously produce and distribute or sell some concrete product just as easily as it produces and delivers services. We could imagine public or non-profit entities producing textbooks, for example, or health supplies, public transit vehicles, or numerous other tangible, concrete products. For a variety of economic and political reasons, however, Canada's public and non-profit sectors are presently focused almost exclusively on the provision of services. A full 99 percent of non-business activity in Canada's economy in 1997 consisted of service delivery rather than goods production. The non-business sector accounted for over one-quarter of the value of all service industries that year, but almost none of the value of goods production.

[7] A stimulating discussion of this problem, together with ideas for possible solutions, is provided in "Democratic Citizenship and the Future of Public Management", by Greg Albo, in Greg Albo, Leo Panitch and David Langille, eds., *A Different Kind of State? Popular Power and Democratic Administration* (Toronto: Oxford University Press, 1993).

[8] The globalization of the world economy has not reduced the overall importance of the investment multiplier effect; it has merely diffused and dispersed its impacts. Within a single country, the multiplier effect is not as strong as in previous dec-

ades; but adding up the multiplier effects which are felt indirectly by that country's trading partners, the multiplier process is still very much at work. A simultaneous increase in investment in several trade-linked countries at once would be as powerful a stimulus to economic growth as ever. The key problem created by globalization in this respect is more political than economic. With the benefits of investment being more dispersed among numerous countries, the pressure on individual national government to introduce pro-investment policies is diluted.

9 There are other implications of this reliance on imported capital equipment, beyond just their negative effects on Canada's international balance of payments. Economic geographer Meric Gertler, for example, makes a convincing case that the efficiency with which new technology is implemented in practice decreases when the users of that technology (such as Canadian-based industrial companies) are located far from the producers of that technology (such as the sophisticated machinery and equipment producers located largely in Europe and Japan). See "'Being there': proximity, organization, and culture in the development and adoption of advanced manufacturing technology," by Meric Gertler, *Economic Geography* 71(1), January 1995, pp. 1-26. Canada's own machinery and equipment manufacturing industries have expanded strongly through the 1990s, so perhaps this difficulty is abating somewhat.

Notes to Chapter 5

1 This is not meant to imply that education is valuable only because it enhances economic productivity; education, of course, is also essential for personal and social development.

2 One version of this argument that is not especially convincing, however, is the notion that since these social expenditures constitute an "investment," it is somehow legitimate to fund them on a deficit-financed basis. The analogy is often made to a private company which experiences a net cash outflow at a time when it is making major real investments. Surely society can do the same, since its "investment" in education and health will also "pay off" in economic terms. The analogy breaks down, however, because unlike the private company, there is no obvious reason why the government's own future revenues can reliably be expected to be higher because of its current expenditures on education and health care. No private company can consistently spend more, year after year, than it takes in; deficit-financed investments today must be more than paid off with additional revenues in the future, or else the company quickly goes bankrupt. Chronic public deficits, therefore, cannot be justified by this analogy to the investment financing of private businesses.

3 Some fascinating research is presently being conducted on the economic effects of "social cohesion." One important collection of such research is *The Economic*

Implications of Social Cohesion, Lars Osberg, ed., (Toronto: University of Toronto Press, 1999).

4 A fifth category of non-financial investment reported in official economic statistics is investment in product inventories, mostly undertaken by private companies (such as the inventories of retail companies, or manufacturers which maintain stockpiles of spare parts). These accumulations of inventory are typically small, however, relative to the overall economy, and they do not play the same economic role as the other forms of real investment considered here. By excluding inventories from consideration, this book's definition of "real investment" is thus equivalent to what economists normally refer to as *fixed* investment.

5 Residential investment is lumped in with business investment both because it is usually private construction companies which undertake the work, and because in statistical terms the purchase of a home (even by an individual homeowner) is technically treated as an investment by a private business, which then "rents" back the home to a tenant (even if that "tenant" is the person who owns the home).

6 For more details on this argument see "Equipment investment and economic growth: how strong is the nexus?", by J. Bradford de Long and Lawrence H. Summers, *Brookings Papers on Economic Activity* (2), 1992, pp. 157-211.

7 For these reasons, some economists even argue that net investment is not really a relevant variable; it is gross investment which is of key concern. A leading example of this approach is provided in *A New View of Economic Growth*, by Maurice FitzGerald Scott (Oxford: Clarendon, 1989).

8 This use of the term "real" is likely to be confusing in the context of the earlier distinction which has been made in this book between "real" and "financial" investments. Normally, economists use the term real to denote variables (such as incomes or interest rates) which have been adjusted to reflect changes in the overall level of prices; in this sense, "real investment" would refer to annual nominal investment spending deflated by the average level of investment goods prices. We are already using the term "real investment," however, to refer to actual investment in tangible capital assets (as opposed to the purchase of purely financial assets). So we will use the term "price-adjusted" investment to capture the conceptual issue noted above.

9 The measurement of productivity is a complex and controversial subject. The discussion in this book defines productivity as the total value of output per unit of work (also known as average *labour productivity*). Some economists prefer other measures. In particular, some utilize a measure known as *total factor productivity*, which is believed to capture the efficiency with which an economy utilizes *all* of its productive inputs (including capital goods, energy, and other raw materials), and not just its labour. The measurement of total factor productivity is very difficult, however, and is usually contingent on prior assumptions about the nature of income distribution and other crucial variables. And from the perspective of the

impact of productivity on living standards, it is average labour productivity which is most important. While managers and policy-makers are obviously interested in ensuring that capital assets and other inputs are used as productively as possible, what matters for the standard of living of human beings is how much output is produced per person working.

[10] This result is exactly opposite to the expectation of many free-market economists that any government activity automatically results in the "crowding out" of an equivalent degree of private activity. For more detailed studies of the effects of public investment on private investment, see "Does public capital crowd out private capital?", by David A. Aschauer, *Journal of Monetary Economics* (24) 1989, pp. 171-188; and "Public and private investment: are there causal linkages?", by S.J. Erenburg and Mark E. Wohar, *Journal of Macroeconomics* 17(1), 1995, pp. 1-30.

[11] The classic argument regarding the benefits of strong investment for export performance was developed by the famous British economist Nicholas Kaldor. See especially his article, "The role of increasing returns, technical progress and cumulative causation in the theory of international trade and economic growth," *Economique Appliqué* (4), 1981, pp. 593-617. The notion that strong investment can spur heightened export competitiveness, which in turn stimulates still more investment, has come to be known as "Kaldor's Law." A modern version of the argument and evidence supporting it are provided in "International competitiveness," by Jan Fagerberg, *Economic Journal* 98(3), 1988, pp. 355-374.

[12] See *Capital Spending and its Implications*, by Michael Goldstein (New York: Sanford C. Bernstein & Co., 1997).

[13] Many I-told-you-so pundits blame the "over-investment" of Asian companies for the subsequent financial crisis experienced there in the later 1990s. This is not convincing; more important was the adoption of U.S.-style financial market liberalization by those same countries, which undermined the previously-regulated relationship between real companies (which carried large debt burdens as a consequence of their fast investment programmes) and the providers of often-subsidized finance. For a critique of the notion that the Asian financial crisis heralds the end of Asian-style economic development strategies, see "Understanding the Asian crisis and its implications for regional economic integration", by Brian MacLean, Paul Bowles, and Osvaldo Croci, in Alan Rugman and Gavin Boyd, eds., *Deepening Integration in the Pacific Economies* (Aldershot, U.K.: Edward Elgar, 1999).

[14] There are many curious examples of this general neglect of investment issues on the part of mainstream economic theorists. For example, conventional quantitative models of the economic impacts of free trade agreements typically do not bother to even portray real investment spending; investment is simply lumped together with other sources of demand (including consumer spending and government purchases) into a total indicator of national consumption. Considering the

crucial attention that has been paid explicitly to the liberalization of investment policies in most recent free trade agreements (including the North American Free Trade Agreement and the World Trade Organization), this approach is simply incredible. Similarly, there is a whole sub-school of economics known as "growth accounting," which attempts to explain and decompose historical patterns of economic growth in different countries. These studies typically find, equally incredibly, that investment is not especially important to economic growth. The source of most growth ends up being assigned to an undefined residual termed "technical progress"; this begs an obvious question about how the benefits of technical progress are supposed to be captured by an economy, if not through investment in technologically advanced capital equipment. The general findings of the growth accounting approach are also coloured by the underlying free-market assumptions of the theoretical model—namely, that all resources will automatically be fully-employed in the economy, and all participants in the economy will naturally be paid incomes which vary directly with their real productivity. One leading economist even came to the bizarre conclusion that the rapid, investment-driven growth of the Asian economies was actually a mirage, since it clearly resulted from rapid capital accumulation in those countries instead of from the disembodied "technical progress" residual of the growth accounting models. For this reason, then, it didn't really "count" as growth—although it certainly seemed to help the citizens of those countries to triple their standard of living within a generation! See "The myth of Asia's miracle," by Paul Krugman, *Foreign Affairs* 73(6), June 1994, pp. 62-78.

[15] Perhaps not coincidentally, those in charge of Canada's macroeconomic policies—most importantly including the Bank of Canada, which sets interest rates—actually believe that the economy *cannot* sustainably grow by more than 2.5 percent per year, and they make it their business to ensure that it doesn't (by increasing interest rates whenever growth seems "too strong"). According to official monetary policy, therefore, a sustained increase in the employment rate and a corresponding reduction in poverty are both impossible and undesirable. The negative consequences of this upside-down world-view will be explored in Chapter 9.

Notes to Chapter 6

[1] This is not to imply that higher minimum wages are irrelevant to workers in large companies, even those who make far more than minimum levels. Economic evidence suggests that higher minimum wages also tend to increase the general level of wages, as higher-income workers push to preserve the existing differentials between themselves and the legal minimum. But this effect is felt indirectly and over time, and hence the opposition of large employers to higher minimum wages is muted. Measures which are applied equitably across the board to all small busi-

nesses—such as a higher minimum wage—should not unduly affect the competitive position of any particular small firm, and hence the hysterical opposition of small businesses to these types of measures seems somewhat misplaced.

[2] The progressive potential of the small business sector should not be dismissed out of hand. Unions have a small but significant role in the sector, one that could grow with the adoption of innovative techniques such as collective bargaining for independent contract workers. In some countries (such as Italy) the small business constituency has been supportive of interventionist social and economic policies. The traditionally progressive politics of many Canadian farmers is indication that some small business operators can indeed come to a progressive analysis of the economic problems they face. Nevertheless, the fact remains that for the foreseeable future Canada's small businesses in general will remain arch opponents of exactly the sorts of policies which most progressives support. The author is grateful to Andrew Jackson for insightful suggestions regarding this discussion.

[3] Some reports on employment by type of establishment group companies according to the total size of the firm, while others use the size of the workplace as the relevant measuring stick. Large firms account for more total employment than do large workplaces (since many individuals work for large companies, but in small branch offices, restaurants, or workshops). Thus *companies* with more than 500 total employees accounted for significantly more job-creation during 1997 than this statistic implies.

[4] Of course, there is another way to reduce UI costs: simply eliminate benefits for many of the unemployed workers who would otherwise receive them. This is exactly the course that has been followed by Canadian governments in the 1990s, cheered on by businesses large and small. For more details on the relationship between job turmoil and firm size, see "An overview of permanent layoffs," by Garnett Picot, Zhengxi Lin, and W. Pyper, Statistics Canada, *Canadian Economic Observer*, February 1997.

[5] See "The self-employed," Statistics Canada, *Labour Force Update*, Autumn 1997.

[6] These averages exclude individuals with negative income from self-employment, and those who have been operating their businesses for less than 16 months. Actual average earnings for all self-employed Canadians are therefore significantly lower than reported here.

[7] A useful collection of theories on this subject is presented in "What makes an entrepreneur?", by D.G. Blanchflower and A.J. Oswald, *Journal of Labor Economics* 16(1), 1998, pp. 26-60.

[8] The push-versus-pull issue is considered in more detail in "Rising self-employment in the midst of high unemployment: an empirical analysis of recent developments in Canada," by Zhengxi Lin, Janice Yates and Garnett Picot, Analytical Studies Branch, Statistics Canada, October 1998. They find that weakness in paid employment is a significant factor in the rise of self-employment, but not the most important.

[9] Two studies which consider the link between self-employment, small business, and tax evasion in detail are "The size of the underground economy in Canada," by Gylliane Gervais, Statistics Canada Catalogue 13-603E, #2, 1994; and "Taxes, economic conditions, and recent trends in male self-employment: a Canada-U.S. comparison," by Herb Schuetze, Dept. of Economics, McMaster University, 1998.

Notes to Chapter 7

[1] If anything, the data pictured in Figure 7-3 understate the decline in the true capital-labour ratio. The measure of the capital stock utilized in that graph is deflated to 1986 dollar terms using the same methodologically flawed price indices which were introduced and criticized in Chapter 5. The phenomenal apparent decline in the price of computers and other high-technology equipment which is suggested by these price indices, implies that the "real" value of the capital stock is higher than it actually is. It is likely, therefore, that a more accurate measure of the capital-labour ratio would indicate that it has been declining even faster during the 1990s than Figure 7-3 indicates.

[2] In fact, to the extent that public investment cutbacks accentuated the economic weakness which fundamentally contributed to the emergence of public deficits in the 1980s, then these investment cutbacks actually made things worse.

[3] The breakdown between energy and non-energy investments may be relevant to the question of when the investment slowdown started in Canada. Total investment spending, measured as a share of GDP, began to decline markedly in the early 1980s. For non-energy investment spending, however, the decline seems to have commenced some years earlier. This suggests that the policy-related changes which were stressed in the earlier discussion—most notably the shift to strict anti-inflation interest-rate policy in the early 1980s—are not the only factors behind the investment slowdown. Other structural factors (including a decline in business profitability) may have been exerting an earlier negative influence on investment; this issue will be discussed further in Chapter 11.

Notes to Chapter 8

[1] The theoretical roots of these contrasting approaches to economics will be considered again in Chapter 10. Recent econometric research on the determinants of investment is surveyed in "Business fixed investment spending: modeling strategies, empirical results, and policy implications," by Robert S. Chirinko, *Journal of Economic Literature* 31(4), 1993, pp. 1875-1911. The classic contributions to the neoclassical literature on this subject are by Dale Jorgenson; see the compendium of his work in *Investment, Vols. I and II* (Cambridge, MA: MIT Press, 1996). Recent

research in the Keynesian and post-Keynesian traditions is provided in *Finance, Investment and Macroeconomics*, by Myron J. Gordon (Aldershot, U.K.: Edward Elgar, 1994), and *Can the Free Market Pick Winners?*, by Paul Davidson, ed. (Armonk, N.Y.: M.E. Sharpe, 1993). Important empirical contributions to the structuralist theory of investment are assembled in *The Macroeconomics of Saving, Finance, and Investment*, by Robert Pollin, ed. (Ann Arbor: University of Michigan Press, 1997), and *Globalization and Progressive Economic Policy*, by Dean Baker, Gerald Epstein and Robert Pollin, eds. (Cambridge, U.K.: Cambridge University Press, 1998).

[2] The importance of this factor substitutability in the production decisions of firms is clearly overemphasized in neoclassical economics; in many cases, the ratio of factor inputs is not flexible at all, but is determined rather strictly by the nature of technology in use. Some degree of factor substitutability is clearly possible, however, and hence there is no reason not to allow room for these sorts of effects.

[3] In technical terms, this methodology consists of the application of successive Wald F-tests for the statistical significance of additional variables added to the "core" equation. In addition to the tests performed on the investment climate and globalization variables that are reported in this chapter, additional unreported experiments were performed by the author to consider the possible significance of a range of other variables to the evolution of private investment spending. These other considered variables included measures of the stock market value of companies (which might be held to affect investment through a Tobin's "q" type of mechanism), various measures of private and public savings, and a measure of real wage costs. In no case were these potential additional variables found to add any significant degree of explanatory power to the "core" investment equation presented in this chapter.

[4] See *Economic Freedom of the World*, by James Gwartney, Robert Lawson, and Walter Block (Vancouver: Fraser Institute, 1996). A critique of the philosophical and economic underpinnings of the Fraser Institute's "freedom project," and an attempt to develop an alternative freedom ranking for the Canadian provinces, is provided in *Economic Freedom for the Rest of Us*, by Jim Stanford (Ottawa: Canadian Centre for Policy Alternatives, 1999).

[5] The size of all government programs did rise through most of this period, reaching a peak (as a share of GDP) in 1992, and declining rapidly since then. An increasing share of government programs, however, has been accounted for by various transfer payments (in which the government collects revenue from one group and hands it back over to another group). These transfer payments include income security programs (such as unemployment insurance or welfare) and public pensions. While they obviously play an important role in moderating the skewed distribution of income that would otherwise occur within a private economy, these transfer payments do not represent an actual intrusion by government into the production of goods and services. The strictly-defined "public sector" of the economy—meas-

ured by the proportion of GDP accounted for by goods and services production undertaken by public agencies—has declined steadily since at least 1960. If anything, the measure of public sector retrenchment depicted in the data on the public sector's share of GDP underestimates the true extent of the withdrawal by government from real economic activity, since it does not reflect the declining importance of Crown corporations. Since 1978, the proportion of total non-financial business assets accounted for by Crown corporations has fallen by one-third, to just 13 percent by 1997.

[6] The following methodology was followed in the construction of this index. Each of the five component variables was scaled so that its average value over the 1960-1997 period was 100. They were further normalized so that their average standard deviation during this time (a measure of the variability or instability of each series) was 10; this additional step is required in order to ensure that each variable exercises an equal influence on the changes in the composite index. The composite index is then simply calculated as the average of the five normalized component series.

[7] This phenomenon is described in detail in *Manufacturing on the Move*, by Robert Crandall (Washington, D.C.: Brookings Institution, 1993).

[8] There are several different possible and sometimes conflicting impacts of free trade on foreign investment patterns; for a more detailed discussion of the relationship between free trade and foreign investment in the Canadian context, see "Investment," by Jim Stanford, in *Canada Under Free Trade*, Duncan Cameron and Mel Watkins, eds. (Toronto: Lorimer, 1993).

[9] It should be noted that an inflow or outflow of foreign direct investment does not automatically translate into an inflow or outflow of an equivalent amount of real investment expenditure. Some foreign investment flows occur solely to finance the acquisition of existing companies, in which case no real investment expenditure occurs (at least not immediately). Companies do not typically purchase new foreign affiliates, however, unless they plan to maintain them as going concerns, and this will ultimately necessitate real investment expenditures of some kind. Thus there is still a close but imperfect link between the direction of foreign direct investment flows and the location of real investment spending.

[10] The discussion here has focused on labour costs. Other studies have confirmed that Canada is a notably low-cost location for investment on broader grounds. See, for example, *The Competitive Alternative: A Comparison of Business Costs in Canada and the United States* (Toronto: KPMG, 1996).

[11] The explanation of the long-term undervaluation of the Canadian currency is a complex and controversial undertaking. Conservative commentators point to policies which undermine the always-nebulous "confidence" of investors—things like high government debt or the threat of Québec separation. This view is harder and harder to accept, as the dollar continues to languish despite the sharp con-

servative shift in Canada's economic policies. Consider the dollar's fall to an all-time record low of 63 cents (U.S.) during 1998–the same year in which Canada's governments generated a combined fiscal surplus of close to $20 billion, and the Parti Quebécois provincial government suffered a decline in electoral support that probably delayed the prospect of another referendum on sovereignty for several years. More likely explanations for the undervaluation of the loonie would include its status as a "small-country currency" (which are typically more vulnerable to instability in foreign exchange markets than the currencies of large countries), and the weak performance of the real Canadian economy (in comparison to most other industrial nations) during most of the last two decades.

[12] This experience itself is a strong refutation of the oft-heard argument that Canada can do nothing to control its domestic interest rates in the context of a globalized financial system. Canada's nominal short-term interest rate in 1991 was four percentage points higher than in the U.S., even though our inflation rate was lower. According to the "globalization hypothesis," this should have sparked a massive and unsustainable inflow of financial capital to Canada until such time as the interest rate differential was eliminated. To be sure, significant funds did flow into Canada, and this helped to push up the value of the dollar to damaging levels, but the extent of the financial response was far from instantaneous and all-powerful. The same would be true of a relative *decline* in Canadian interest rates. Clearly, financial capital is more mobile than it has ever been, but it is still far from being *perfectly* mobile: important institutional, cultural, and economic factors still significantly limit the extent of financial mobility.

[13] This general strategy will be considered further in Chapter 14, which argues for a shift in the burden of *income* tax from real businesses onto the generally well-off individuals who own those businesses.

[14] This traditional way of measuring imports as a share of GDP overstates the importance of foreign trade in the bigger economic picture. When domestic industry is closely integrated with industries in other countries (in Canada's case, with industry in the U.S.), one result is the development of an extensive cross-border trade in unfinished products, spare parts, raw materials, and other "intermediate" goods. Current statistics simply add up the combined value of all imports—even those which might subsequently be re-exported in the form of some finished product. This leads to a great deal of "double-counting" in foreign trade statistics. In terms of their ultimate share of final demand or domestic consumption, imports are much less important—accounting for perhaps 20 percent of all final demand.

[15] In this manner, the real exchange rate can vary even if the nominal exchange rate does not change. For example, inflation in Canada has been consistently lower than in the U.S. through the 1990s. To maintain a constant real exchange rate, this would imply that Canada's dollar should have become stronger (since nominal prices in the U.S. are growing faster, and hence the U.S. dollar should fall relative

to Canada's to maintain a given relationship between the purchasing powers of the two currencies). In fact, however, the loonie tended to stay stable or even fall during this period. This implies that the decline in the *real* exchange rate during the 1990s was even steeper than the fall in the nominal exchange rate (measured in U.S. cents).

[16] If the empirical test was narrowed down to focus on manufacturing investments only, then the exchange rate would likely have had more statistical impact, since it is the manufacturing sector which is most sensitive to international production cost comparisons. Even this result, however, would not "prove" that globalization has contributed to the investment slowdown in Canada; given the decline in the real exchange rate of the dollar through most of the 1990s, this would in fact imply that investment here has benefitted from globalization.

Notes to Chapter 9

[1] An interesting review of the historical evolution of full-employment policy in Canada is provided in *The Full-Employment Objective in Canada, 1945-85: Historical, Conceptual, and Comparative Perspectives*, by Robert M. Campbell (Ottawa: Economic Council of Canada, 1991).

[2] This "golden age" was not golden for everyone in Canada, of course. Access to the fruits of this economic boom was not universally available—especially for women and workers of colour, who experienced disproportionate levels of unemployment or underemployment. Nevertheless, the rapid growth of total employment and income, underwritten by the expansion of public services, resulted in tremendous increases in living standards for most working households, and major reductions in the incidence of poverty.

[3] In strict terms, economists define a recession as any episode in which the country's real (after-inflation) GDP declines for two or more quarters in a row. By this definition Canada did experience three mild recessions during the golden age, but none were severe or long-lasting enough to have a major impact on unemployment or income levels. On an annual average basis, real GDP grew in every year but one (1954) in Canada between 1946 and 1981.

[4] Many observers equate an expansionary fiscal policy with the existence of large deficits; this would imply that fiscal policy was very expansionary during the 1980s and early 1990s, when Canada's deficits were huge (particularly in contrast to the roughly balanced budgets of the 1950-1980 era). This assumption is wrong. The large deficits of the post-1981 era initially arose not because of stimulative spending initiatives but rather because of the collapse in revenues that accompanied reduced economic growth, and the impact of this slowdown on the cost of existing programs (like unemployment insurance). High interest rates had a compounding effect by dramatically increasing the debt service charges incurred by now-in-

debted governments. Fiscal policy moved in an almost uniformly contractionary direction through the 1980s and especially the 1990s, swimming against the macroeconomic tides in an effort to reduce the size of deficits despite the explosive combination of slow growth and high interest rates. The persistence of those deficits until the mid-1990s, despite budget-cutting by most governments, revealed just how profoundly the economic fundamentals underlying the state of public finances had deteriorated.

5 A useful summary of the economic consequences of overzealous anti-inflation policy is provided in *Unnecessary Debts*, by Lars Osberg and Pierre Fortin, eds. (Toronto: Lorimer, 1995).

6 Numerous powerful critiques of both the theory and the empirical methodology underlying these quasi-scientific estimates of the NAIRU have been prepared. See especially "Searching for a will o' the wisp: an empirical study of the NAIRU in Canada," by Mark Setterfield, D.V. Gordon, and Lars Osberg, *European Economic Review* 36(1), 1992, pp. 119- 136.

7 The special Winter 1997 edition of the *Journal of Economic Perspectives* contains a number of broad retrospective analyses on the rise and fall of NAIRU thinking.

8 Once again, despite claims that Canada's fiscal and economic house has been put in order thanks to the tough-love treatment of the 1990s, the gap between interest and growth rates remained as large as ever. In fiscal 1998 the federal government paid interest charges equal to 7.5 percent of its outstanding debt; since prices, on average, were actually *falling* during this time, the real interest rate was closer to an incredible 8 percent. Real GDP grew during the year by about 3 percent, leaving a 5-point gap between the two—almost precisely the average that has been experienced since 1981. Far from being rewarded by financial markets for our prudence, it is clear that without a fundamental change in policy direction Canadians can simply expect more of the same.

9 This argument that high interest rates caused Canada's public debt runs counter to the claim of many conservatives that high interest rates themselves were the result of public indebtedness. Financial investors, worried about high debt levels and possible government bankruptcy, demanded high interest rates to reflect a "risk premium" on their loans to government. This argument is wrong on numerous counts. First, high interest rates were imposed in the early 1980s when Canadian debt levels were very low; moreover, high interest rates (in real terms) have persisted despite the balancing of government budgets and subsequent decline in debt levels. Economic studies have failed to find any predictable relationship between debt levels and interest rates, either over time or across countries. The policy decisions of central bankers and governments appear to be the far more dominant influence on real interest rates, even in the longer-term. For more on the links between debt and interest rates, see "Cause and effect in the relationship between budget deficits and the rate of interest," by John Smithin, *Économies et*

Sociétés 9, Jan.-Feb. 1994, pp. 151-169, and "Is there a risk premium in Canadian interest rates?" by Jim Stanford, *Canadian Business Economics* 5(4), Summer 1997, pp. 43-59.

Notes to Chapter 10

[1] There is also an argument that government spending *period*—even when it is fully funded through taxes and a balanced budget, rather than being associated with deficits—crowds out private investment and hence slow growth. Taxes reduce household disposable income, and hence reduce savings, which must in turn constrain investment.

[2] In national income accounting terms there is actually no fundamental difference between paying for a pension through a private contribution to a private pension program (like an RRSP) and payments to a government (in the form of taxes or pension premiums) for a public pension. In this sense, the Canada Pension Plan is itself a very effective incentive for "saving," since it collects compulsory levies from individuals and their employers—money which obviously cannot therefore be "spent" in other ways. From the perspective of the financial industry, however, the privatized system is a much preferred approach. In a private plan, individuals have to accumulate large stockpiles of wealth to fund post-retirement income, and these stockpiles become the raw material for the endless paper shuffling of the money managers. A public plan, on the other hand, pools both the contributions and the pension payments of the whole working population. This smooths out the "life-cycle" timing problem faced by private pension schemes (namely, that the income is earned first, but the pensions are paid out later): since a share of the population is always working while another share is retired, a public "pay-as-you-go" plan doesn't need to accumulate such a stockpile of wealth.

[3] The Canadian economist Marc Lavoie has provided a very accessible introduction to post-Keynesian theories in *Foundations of Post-Keynesian Economic Analysis* (Aldershot, U.K.: Edward Elgar, 1992).

[4] A powerful collection of structuralist-oriented writings on the crucial subject of savings and investment is provided by Robert Pollin, ed., *The Macroeconomics of Saving, Finance, and Investment* (Ann Arbor: University of Michigan Press, 1997).

[5] There is a curious measurement issue which also helps to explain the apparent link between the booming paper economy and the decline in personal savings. The personal savings rate equals current savings divided by current disposable income. But that measure of current income does not include capital gains on assets (and in particular, the huge capital gains enjoyed by financial investors in recent years). Thus the actual total income of those investors is higher than is suggested by the economic statistics. Moreover, investors have to pay taxes on those capital gains, and these taxes show up in current tax payment data (even though the income

against which they are collected does not show up in current income data). As a consequence of this measurement problem, total personal incomes appear lower than they actually are, while the burden of personal taxes appears higher than it is in reality. Both factors artificially and incorrectly reduce the *apparent* rate of personal savings.

6 If savers have a certain target for the wealth they want to acquire by a certain point in time (when they retire, for example), then a higher rate of return can allow them to meet that target with less savings. This might explain the apparently negative relationship between personal savings and stock market returns (economists refer to this anomalous result as a "backward-bending supply function"). The implication is uncomfortable for the free-market theory of the capital market: if savings are *negatively* related to returns, then it is even less likely that fluctuations in interest rates can efficiently ensure ongoing equality between savings and investment.

7 Most countries measure government deficits or surpluses on a national accounts basis, which includes all cash payments and receipts which a government incurs. Canadian governments, however, tend to use the stricter "public accounts" definition of budgetary balance; the public accounts include non-cash liabilities (such as future public service pension liabilities). On a public accounts basis, the deficit of Canada's aggregate government sector was not eliminated until 1998.

8 Some of these arguments are presented in *Deficit Reduction: What Pain, What Gain?*, by Bill Robson and William Scarth, eds. (Toronto: C.D. Howe Institute, 1994). Ironically, some free-market thinkers are also skeptical that deficit reduction will improve overall savings performance, but for very different reasons. On the basis of a truly bizarre theory known as "Ricardian equivalence," they argue that personal consumption spending will decline when governments run large deficits, because those individuals (possessing perfect foresight) understand that large deficits now must imply higher taxes in the future, and hence they will increase their savings pro-actively in order to meet personal targets for wealth accumulation despite the higher anticipated future taxes. This theory has been consistently disproved by empirical studies, yet it remains popular with some conservatives. If "Ricardian equivalence" was really at work in Canada in the late 1990s, we would have expected to see a large boom in consumer spending offsetting the rapid decline in government deficits; as illustrated in Table 10-1, however, this was not the case.

9 In fact there is considerable economic evidence to suggest that savings incentives such as Canada's RRSP program are *not* effective in increasing aggregate savings; what happens, instead, is that individuals divert savings that would have occurred anyway in other forms, into the subsidized saving vehicle.

10 Other Granger-type studies have found that even in the corporate sector, investment may "cause" savings. For example, see "Profits, investment, and causality:

an examination of alternative paradigms," by Satyadev Gupta, *Southern Economic Journal* 55(1), July 1988, pp. 9-20.

Notes to Chapter 11

[1] In 1998, total wages grew by about 4 percent—the 52nd consecutive "record-breaking" year for Canadian workers. Before-tax corporate profits, however, fell by 5 percent, an ominous sign since falling profits are often the first sign of a coming recession.

[2] This calculation will further underestimate true small business incomes to the extent that some owners of small businesses pay themselves wages from their businesses' gross income. More complete surveys suggest the average total income (including both profits and wages) of self-employed individuals to be about $30,000 per year—still lower than for paid employees. See "The self-employed," Statistics Canada *Labour Force Update*, Autumn 1997.

[3] Most of these non-financial assets, not surprisingly, are invested by non-financial businesses; as of 1997, financial companies held only 5 percent of the total tangible capital stock of the business sector in Canada, even though they accounted for almost 60 percent of total business assets.

[4] The less marked decline in profits as a share of *non-financial* assets raises several interesting questions. We have seen earlier that real or tangible capital assets have grown more slowly than financial assets. An ironic outcome of this divergence is that business profits have fallen less dramatically when measured as a proportion of those tangible assets, than when measured as a share of total assets or total GDP. Ironically, then, companies in the real economy have been able to partially preserve their profitability by investing *less* in real capital assets. Indeed, the *Wall Street Journal* article cited in Chapter 5 indicates that this is an explicit strategy now urged by many financial analysts. This may be effective for certain individual companies, but it is clearly a negative development for the entire economy—and to the extent that underinvestment by real companies undermines the growth and purchasing power of the aggregate economy (which itself is crucial to business profitability), then the strategy is self-defeating.

[5] At the same time, it is hard to believe that "corporate tax giveaways" have played a significant role in the debt-and-deficit crisis of Canadian governments, as is often alleged by many corporate critics. Figure 11-1 indicates that expressed as a share of their before-tax income, average effective business tax rates have not declined since about 1970. It is true that corporate taxes make up a much smaller share of total tax revenues in Canada than was the case in earlier decades: as little as 5 percent of total government revenues in the 1990s, versus 25 percent in the 1950s. This was not due to lower business tax rates, however. Rather, it was the result of

the steady decline in profits as a share of GDP, together with the simultaneous rise in the overall size of government and hence total tax collections.

[6] Economic historian Robert Brenner has prepared a fascinating and controversial study which locates the decline of profitability in the growing intensity of competition between different trading blocs—especially the U.S., Europe, and Japan—over the postwar era. See "Uneven development and the long downturn: the advanced capitalist economies from boom to stagnation, 1950-1998," *New Left Review* (229), May-June 1998.

[7] The impact of right-wing macroeconomic policies on labour productivity is especially controversial and difficult to measure. On the one hand, a more "disciplined" labour relations climate and a more "flexible" labour market should produce greater levels of work intensity and accountability from workers ever-fearful of losing their jobs. Employers become freer to assign labour to profit-maximizing functions unencumbered by union rules or government safety and labour regulations. On the other hand, the stagnant macroeconomic conditions which have accompanied the policies of permanent recession in Canada have clearly undermined productivity: slower real investment undermines productivity, as does the continuing existence of significant excess physical capacity. The net effect is uncertain—although Canada's miserable productivity performance during the 1990s hardly suggests that the right-wing recipe has been successful. For a classic and nuanced treatment of the economic and institutional determinants of productivity, see "Hearts and minds: a social model of U.S. productivity growth," by Thomas J. Weisskopf, Samuel Bowles, and David M. Gordon, *Brookings Papers on Economic Activity* (2) 1983, pp. 381-441.

[8] A useful and comprehensive overview of profitability trends across OECD countries, and their relationship to real investment spending by private business, is provided in "Does aggregate profitability *really* matter?" by Andrew Glyn, *Cambridge Journal of Economics* 21(3), 1997, pp. 593-619.

[9] One study estimates that reductions in U.S. corporate income taxes increased the after-tax return on equity by about two percentage points between 1960 and the 1990s. See "The revival of corporate profitability in the United States," by Richard D. Rippe, *Business Economics* 31(1), January 1996, pp. 35-42.

[10] An example of this potentially beneficial effect is provided by macroeconomic simulations of the progressive programme of the Alternative Federal Budget (a fiscal and economic document designed each year by a coalition of labour and community organizations). These Budgets aim to expand total employment through a combination of expansionary fiscal and monetary policy; macroeconomic modeling indicates that the impact of the programme on profits, in the short-term anyway, would be highly positive. For details see *Alternative Federal Budget Papers* (Ottawa: Canadian Centre for Policy Alternatives, 1997), pp. 43-46.

" One recent study suggested that the final net impact on real investment spending of a corporate tax cut is less, even under favourable circumstances, than the foregone revenues which government loses through the tax cut. This implies that the government would get more "bang for the buck" by targeting its tax subsidies more tightly on investment activity, or even by simply spending the money on real investment itself. See "The sensitivity of the corporate income tax to the statutory rate," by Peter Dungan, Steve Murphy, and Thomas A. Wilson, Working Paper 97-1, Technical Committee on Business Taxation, Department of Finance Canada.

Notes to Chapter 12

[1] In fact, the majority of CN shares are now owned in the U.S. More experience with the economics of the private railway industry led U.S. investors to spot the huge potential at CN (once it was privatized) to boost profits through relentless cost-cutting, and they snapped up the majority of shares quickly after privatization. While the benefits of higher share prices have largely been exported, therefore, the negative economic impacts of 10,000 lay-offs in 5 years have been felt closer to home.

[2] The federal government lost tax revenues of about $7 billion due to the RRSP deduction in 1998, and the provincial governments lost another $4 billion. Both levels of government provide an additional subsidy to the RRSP system by allowing interest and dividends to accumulate tax-free within RRSP shelters; this costs an additional $8 billion per year. This second type of subsidy for accumulated RRSP funds is distributed even less fairly than the subsidy for current-year contributions. Many lower- and middle-income Canadians use RRSPs not for retirement savings but as an income-averaging device: they contribute to their RRSPs during good years, and withdraw funds (at lower tax rates) in years of unemployment or underemployment. For this reason, their RRSP balances tend to rise and fall over time (rather than rising steadily as is usually the case for higher-income regular contributors). Hence their share of accumulated RRSP monies (and the government subsidies to those monies) is even smaller than their share of RRSP contributions in any single year. It should be noted that about one-fifth of the cost of the overall RRSP program—less than $4 billion per year at present—is offset by income taxes collected on withdrawals from RRSP accounts and post-retirement RRSP payouts.

[3] If 50 percent of Canadians own RRSPs, and only 45 percent of those with RRSPs own a total portfolio exceeding $25,000, then only about 22 percent of Canadians have RRSP portfolios worth more than $25,000.

[4] See McQuaig's book, *Behind Closed Doors* (Markham, Ont.: Penguin, 1987), pp. 35-40. See also her more recent book, *The Cult of Impotence* (Markham, Ont.: Penguin, 1998), pp. 134-138.

⁵ Conservatives argue that the lower aggregate savings rate resulting from this re-distribution of income would harm the economy. As discussed in Chapter 10, how-ever, the economic evidence suggests that it is a lack of investment demand, not a lack of savings, that explains Canada's poor investment performance during the 1990s.

⁶ Income tax cuts can be targeted so that more of their benefits are received by lower-income households, through such measures as increasing targeted tax cred-its (such as the GST credit or the child tax benefit), or reducing the lowest tax rate. Any general income tax cut, however (such as that implemented by the Harris government in Ontario between 1995 and 1998), will inevitably deliver most of its benefits to high-income households simply because these households pay more tax than anyone else.

⁷ For example, thanks primarily to a 33 percent rise in the share price of Thomson Corp. during 1997, Ken Thomson's estimated personal fortune grew by close to $5 billion during that year alone—and he moved up to 7th place on *Forbes* magazine's list of the wealthiest people in the world, with an estimated total fortune of $20 billion. See "Ken Thomson places 7ᵗʰ," by Brenda Dalglish, *Financial Post*, June 23, 1998, p. 14.

Notes to Chapter 13

¹ Minsky's various economic contributions are reviewed and elaborated in *Finan-cial Conditions and Macroeconomic Performance, Essays in Honour of Hyman P. Minsky*, Steven Fazzari and Dimitri Papadimitriou, eds. (Armonk, N.Y.: M.E. Sharpe, 1992).

² Strictly speaking, the claim that the global financial crisis of 1997-98 was a purely "Minskian" crisis (rooted in the rising debt burdens of private firms) is controver-sial; traditional Keynesian-style aggregate demand problems also played a crucial role. Nevertheless, the processes and consequences of the financial fragility that were exhibited during that crisis were clearly reminiscent of Minsky's overall think-ing. The author thanks Mario Seccareccia for clarifying this point. For the most succinct description of the pure Minskian chain of causation, see "A Minsky crisis," by Lance Taylor and Stephen A. O'Connell, *Quarterly Journal of Economics* 100(Supp.), 1985, pp. 871-885.

³ See "Herd on the street," *The Economist*, November 28, 1998, p. 74. In *The Econo-mist*'s judgement, this market-driven pressure to run with the pack is contributing to the overvaluation of stock markets, and hence to the risk of subsequent col-lapse. It wrote, "A fund manager is unlikely to be blamed much if a stock-market plunge damages his portfolio—so long as all his peers are hurt too. But woe betide the manager who bucks the trend and stays out of the market, only to see it soar higher still."

4 It is for this very reason that so-called "balanced budget" laws, which are intended to force governments to maintain balanced budgets, are economically destructive. Even those who believe firmly in zero deficits should at least accept that the government's budget balance will naturally rise and fall with the general state of the economy; a better approach would be to require a budget that was balanced on average over a whole economic cycle (allowing the government to incur deficits during bad years, offset by surpluses in good years). To try to suppress this natural counter-cyclical behaviour of public finances would actually amplify the underlying boom-and-bust pattern of the economy.

5 The resale price of a bond is inversely related to the level of interest rates. Because a bond specifies the value and timing of the repayment of the debt which the bond represents (including interest on that debt), its cash value over time is fixed; that is why bonds are often referred to as "fixed income" instruments. The *up-front* market value of the bond will then vary with current interest rates. If current interest rates are low, then the fixed income stream guaranteed by a particular bond will seem more attractive relative to the going returns on other assets, and hence the price of the bond will rise. Likewise, if interest rates rise, then those future specified income streams look less attractive, and the resale price of the bond falls.

6 The gross debt of a government equals all of its obligations; net debt equals its obligations minus its assets. As of 1998, Canada's federal government carried a net debt of about $580 billion; its gross debt was some $50 billion larger. There is not much difference, therefore, between the two measures in Canada's case. In some other countries (especially in continental Europe and Scandinavia), governments are much more active in investing in real businesses, Crown corporations, and other economic projects, and hence the difference between gross debt and net debt is larger.

7 The author thanks Myron Gordon for assistance with section of the discussion.

8 A useful overview of derivatives and the economic risks associated with them is provided by the U.S. General Accounting Office, *Financial Derivatives: Actions Needed to Protect the Financial System* (GAO Report GGD-94-133, May 1994).

9 If the share price should fall below $25, then the option is worthless. Incredibly, however, companies will then often issue new options to the CEO at a lower preset price (or even retroactively *reduce* the price on the outstanding and now worthless options) as a means of ensuring the continuing full loyalty of the executive to the goal of higher share prices. This reveals clearly that executive stock options have little to do with rewarding the "efficiency" of CEOs, and everything to do with conscripting their allegiance to the never-ending campaign for higher share prices— no matter how much that CEO might have screwed up in the past.

10 Financial economists have proven quite conclusively that share prices at any point in time reflect the current state of knowledge about the company in question, and

subsequent price movements reflect the market's response to new knowledge that becomes available. A recent review of this "efficient market hypothesis" is provided by Eugene F. Fama, "Market efficiency, long-term returns, and behavioural finance," *Journal of Financial Economics*, September 1998.

ⁱⁱ Many financial newspapers sponsor contests through which amateur investors can submit a hypothetical portfolio of shares, and the paper then tracks which portfolio generates the greatest returns over a certain period of time; the winner receives a cash prize. The winners of these contests, which can attract thousands of entries, invariably outperform any commercially managed mutual fund. Does this apparently surprising result imply that the amateurs can outperform the pros? Hardly. Given that there were far more random combinations and permutations of shares represented among the thousands of contest entries, than exist among the hundreds of commercially managed mutual funds, we should actually expect *some* amateur to win the contest virtually every year, based on the simple law of averages. In golf tournaments, real skill is at work, and the pros almost always beat the amateurs. Picking stock market winners, however, is fundamentally a game of chance—and hence the amateurs have at least as much hope of winning the prize jacket as the so-called professionals.

Notes to Chapter 14

ⁱ For more details see "Missing the target again," by Jim Stanford (Ottawa: Canadian Centre for Policy Alternatives, September 1998).

² For details, see *The Alternative Federal Budget Papers* (Ottawa: Canadian Centre for Policy Alternatives and Choices, 1998), pp. 58-68.

³ The advice of Neil Brooks regarding several of the following points is gratefully acknowledged.

⁴ Investors have some flexibility in the choice between collecting dividend income or collecting capital gains. Shareholders can "declare their own dividends" on holdings in companies which do not pay out large dividends, simply by selling some of their shares (on the assumption that share prices are rising to reflect the greater retained earnings of non-dividend-paying companies). For this reason it is sensible to maintain approximate equality between the rates of taxation on dividends and capital gains earned by individuals; the proposal to do away with both of these subsidies simultaneously would preserve this equality (setting the marginal rate of taxation on both forms of income at about 50 percent for high-income shareholders, versus 37.5 percent at present). See the discussion in *Report of the Technical Committee on Business Taxation*, Department of Finance Canada, December 1997, pp. 7.5-7.8.

⁵ In fact, the federal government—nervously eyeing the escalating cost of the RRSP program—did exactly this in 1996, freezing the $13,500 limit until 2003. The present

plan is to increase the maximum contributions by $1000 per year in 2004 and 2005, and by regular increments in subsequent years. The multi-year freeze in the ceiling has reduced somewhat the extravagance of the RRSP program, but the maximum contribution is still far out of reach for most Canadian taxpayers.

6 Economic studies suggest that the elimination of this investment tax credit had a modest but measurable negative impact on real investment spending by Canadian business. See, for example, "A macroeconometric analysis of the effects of taxation on financing and real investment in equipment in Canada," by Serge J. Nadeau, *Applied Economics* 26, 1994, pp. 1037-1048. The Mulroney government's tax reform also reduced the rates at which the cost of many types of real capital assets could be written off by businesses, but then reduced the overall corporate tax rate as a *quid pro quo*. The net result was no major change in the overall tax burden faced by companies, but a shift in that burden from companies which don't invest much in real capital onto those which do. This approach was ironic in light of the Mulroney government's stated view that private business investment is the leading force in economic growth. This suggests again that enriching the owners of capital, not encouraging their actual economic effort, is the primary goal behind these tax "reforms." A recent federal government committee on business taxation remained faithful to this general approach: it advocated reducing the overall corporate tax rate, while further eroding the remaining tax incentives for real investment spending (such as accelerated depreciation provisions). See the *Report of the Technical Committee on Business Taxation,* Department of Finance Canada, December 1997, Chapter 4.

7 Important measurement and definitional issues would have to be confronted in the design of such a tax—but no more so than is already the case with other components of the tax law, such as the rules regarding capital cost allowance calculation and deduction. Presumably, the depreciation of existing capital would be measured by a company's earned capital cost allowance for tax purposes. In this manner, companies which are already receiving tax assistance in the form of accelerated write-off provisions (such as most energy companies) would not be doubly subsidized by the tax credit. By focusing the tax credit on net investment only, this proposal would help to avoid a problem with other investment tax credits in the past—namely, that since they subsidize much business investment which would have occurred anyway, they don't get much "bang for the buck" in terms of new investment elicited per dollar of credit paid.

8 Important criticisms have been made of government subsidies which are embedded in the tax system (in the form of tax expenditures) rather than being explicitly paid through government programs. It is argued that tax expenditures are less transparent and subject to less accountability than equivalent "up-front" programs. In this case, the implicit tax credit proposed here could be restructured as an

explicit government subsidy to real investment spending, with no impact on its overall economic effect.

⁹ For the reasons described in note 4 to this chapter, shareholders in companies which reduced their dividend payouts as a result of such a measure can still "declare their own dividends" by selling shares and collecting capital gains, on the assumption that a company's share price would rise to reflect its retained earnings. But the actual cash cost of these "indirect" dividend payouts is borne by *other* financial investors (the ones who buy the shares from the initial investor), not from the company's internal cash reserves. In this sense, the "indirect" dividends which investors could still attain would necessitate the (indirect) raising of new capital from the stock market, rather than depleting the cash stockpiles of the firms which undertake most real business investment.

¹⁰ A history of the VanCity experience is provided in *Working Dollars: The VanCity Story*, by Herschel Hardin (Vancouver: Douglas & McIntyre, 1996).

¹¹ A thorough discussion of the Tobin tax, its merits, and implementation issues is provided from a Canadian perspective in *Good Taxes: The Case for Taxing Foreign Currency Exchange and Other Financial Transactions*, by Alex C. Michalos (Toronto: Dundurn, 1997).

¹² Named for the town in New Hampshire where they were founded after the conclusion of World War II.

¹³ One creative and pragmatic discussion of the possible shape and function of such an institution is provided in "Reforming the privatized international monetary system," by Jane d'Arista and Tom Schlesinger, *FOMC Alert* 2(7-8), December 1998, pp. 1-16.

Notes to Chapter 15

¹ For complete coverage of the controversy, see "Capitalist crunch," by Anders Hayden, *This Magazine*, July/August 1998, pp. 22-26. The TIPS controversy and its rectification also highlight an important point: the ethical funds industry is a "work-in-progress," and the policies and practices of the funds have changed and will continue to change over time in response to experience, public pressure, and other factors. Particularly for those ethical funds which are managed by credit unions, and hence are inherently more susceptible to democratic pressure than purely private financial institutions, public discussion and pressure regarding the strength of their ethical stands could quite conceivably have an impact over time on their practices and policies. In this context, many of the criticisms presented here can be taken constructively, as highlighting various ways in which the ethical funds could be made *more* ethical—although this discussion also suggests that there are several ways in which the concept of ethical mutual fund investing may be inherently perverse.

² Even when these criteria "bite," their net ethical impact is not easy to evaluate. Bombardier's military production, for example, does not constitute a large share of the company's total business. Yet Bombardier is a major producer of public transit equipment—something that an ethical investor might favour. It should be noted that in addition to "negative screens," which prohibit investment in particular companies, many ethical funds also follow a "best of sector" approach which channels their funds into companies in any industry (including ethically or environmentally questionable ones, such as mining or forestry), as long as those companies do a relatively better job of meeting ethical and social performance criteria than their peers. Proponents of the best-of-sector strategy argue that it rewards imperfect companies for at least trying to improve their record; critics suggest it even further waters down an already-lax set of ethical criteria.

³ Ethical Growth has invested in the shares of Investors Group itself, not in Investors-managed mutual funds, so the link between Ethical Growth and the ultimate companies whose shares are purchased by Investors Group is one step removed—but still of concern.

⁴ There are many instances in which both motivations for a share sell-off (concerns over ethics and concerns over profits) arise simultaneously. For example, the shares of a company might fall dramatically because of litigation threats related to some problem that is *also* a source of ethical concern (such as cancer-related actions against tobacco companies, or a mining company facing litigation because of a mine disaster or effluent flood). In these cases it will be impossible to distinguish the influence of ethical investment decisions from those of purely "agnostic" investors who may not have cared about the ethical dimension of the problem but rather were motivated by concerns over the company's future profits. The successes claimed by the ethical investing movement in forcing down the share prices of tobacco-related companies were clearly not an outcome of ethical screening of investments. Rather, these outcomes resulted from the decisions of regular, run-of-the-mill investors fleeing these companies because of concerns over future profitability. And the strategic lesson to be gained from these experiences is not that ethical investing somehow "works." What was effective, rather, were the legal and political actions which made these unethical practices unprofitable in the first place.

⁵ The growth of ethical mutual funds has actually sparked the emergence of a countervailing group of "politically incorrect" mutual funds, which specialize in the purchase of shares of tobacco companies, military contractors, and other outlaw companies on supposed grounds that their artificially-reduced share prices do not adequately reflect future profit prospects. One such fund in the U.S., titled "Morgan Funshares," outperformed average stock market indices by specializing in investments with alcohol, cigarette, and slot-machine manufacturers. It is unlikely that these offbeat funds will ever be significant players in financial markets;

but other "agnostic" financial investors, in their endless shopping around for "undervalued" companies, play exactly the same function.

[6] In the wake of the Royal Bank controversy, Ethical Funds has changed its policy to a more neutral position regarding corporate governance issues such as this one, once again demonstrating the company's responsiveness to public concern over its ethical lapses. Ethical Funds still does not play an activist role, however, in campaigns to change corporate behaviour; its role remains that of a passive financial investor.

[7] The ethical mutual funds do not typically say much about labour relations in describing their ethical screens. The most specific promise by Ethical Funds Inc. on this criteria is to require adherence by investee companies to employment equity, labour safety practices and child labour laws. This in itself constitutes a statement on the sorry state of Canadian workplaces in the 1990s: a company which merely follows the *law* can be singled out as a *good* ethical performer!

[8] See "Labour-Sponsored Funds, Examining the Evidence," by the Canadian Auto Workers Research Department, February 1999, for a more detailed critique of the labour-sponsored funds.

[9] See, for example, Ernst and Young Co., "Impact of the Foreign Property Rule," October 1997; and Conference Board of Canada, "Maximizing Choice: Economic Impacts of Increasing the Foreign Property Limit," January 1998. Other studies put the cost to investors of the 20 percent foreign content limit (and hence the benefit of the LSF foreign content loophole) much higher. For example, one report by Morgan Stanley International showed that funds invested in international equity markets received an average return 7.4 points higher each year than funds invested in Canadian equities. No wonder investors are so anxious to eliminate the foreign content rule—and so interested in loopholes such as the LSFs.

[10] As with any other public subsidy, the bottom-line fiscal cost is offset somewhat by tax revenues generated through the economic activity stimulated by the subsidy; in the case of the LSFs, how much new employment and investment has been stimulated is controversial, as will be considered below.

[11] *Adding Value: The Economic and Social Impacts of Labour-sponsored Venture Capital Corporations on their Investee Firms*, by Edward T. Jackson and Francois Lamontagne (Ottawa: Canadian Labour Market and Productivity Centre, 1995), p. iii. This estimate is probably conservative, in that the proportion of LSF assets that has been invested in real companies is lower in practice than the ratio assumed by the study, and the study does not consider the foreign content incentive. On the other hand, this study was written before the total LSF credit was reduced from 40 percent to 30 percent in 1996.

[12] The whole saga is reported by journalist Kevin Wilson in "Behind the failed Indigo drive," *NOW Magazine*, November 19 1998.

13 Following exactly this same methodology, for example, an individual investor could claim to have "created or maintained" 132,000 jobs in 1997 by spending $88.35 to purchase one share each of the new shares issued by the following five companies: Alberta Energy Company, Bell Canada Enterprises, Cadillac Fairview, Manitoba Telecom, and Sun Media.

14 The comparison is not a fair one, however, because the teachers' fund is fully-funded (meaning it must accumulate capital in advance to cover the future pension liabilities for its clients) while the CPP is structured on a "pay-as-you-go" basis, meaning most of the cost of CPP pensions is covered by the annual contributions of CPP members who are still working. Thus the CPP needs only a relatively small "reserve" fund to cover occasional mismatches between inflows of premiums and outflows of pensions, and can thus support a larger number of pensioners with a smaller permanent pool of cash. The pay-as-you-go system has its own difficulties, of course (particularly when the number of current workers paying CPP premiums declines due to demographic change or high unemployment), but its central advantage is its much smaller up-front financial requirements: it is a much less "finance-intensive" means of funding pensions.

15 A useful overview of many of these issues is provided in "Unions and Pension Fund Investments," by Bob Baldwin, Canadian Labour Congress Conference on Jobs and the Economy, February 1998, and in *Prudence, Patience, and Jobs*, by Kirk Falconer (Ottawa: Canadian Labour Market and Productivity Centre, 1999).

16 The actuarial assumptions underlying most pension plans only require a real (after inflation) rate of return on investments of about 4 percent per year—far lower than the mega-returns the funds have enjoyed during the paper boom of the 1990s. A fund could therefore make socially-mandated investments that offered a 4 percent real return and still meet its obligations. But this would require an explicit decision to forego the higher returns (of 10 percent per year after inflation, or more) that are available to unconstrained funds.

17 There are several similar approaches to socially-motivated pension investments that have been undertaken in the U.S., where the strategy is known as "economically targeted investing" (ETI). Like Greystone, these initiatives started in housing and real estate developing, but more recently have expanded into other sectors (like community economic development, insurance, and even manufacturing). The experience of these initiatives, and the extent to which they are genuinely able to stimulate more progressive forms of activity in the real economy, will be an important test of the long-run potential of pension fund activism. The author is indebted to Kirk Falconer for background information on the U.S. ETIs.

18 Several of these initiatives are conveniently described under the heading "alternative investments," in *The 1997 Canadian Ethical Money Guide*, by Eugene Ellmen (Toronto: Lorimer, 1996).

[19] The Ethical Funds company spent almost $30 million in 1997 to manage its eight different mutual funds. It is quite fair to ask whether the company would have done more to promote social change in Canada by simply donating that $30 million to progressive political causes, than by paying the expensive salaries of the money managers who oversee its respective portfolios.

Notes to Chapter 16

[1] Andrew Glyn calls this a belief in the "Keynesian free lunch"; see "Social democracy and full employment," *New Left Review* 211 (1995), pp. 33-55.

[2] By this definition, the socially-minded financial initiatives surveyed in Chapter 15— such as ethical mutual funds and labour-sponsored venture funds—clearly do not qualify as forms of social investment, since they perfectly preserve the monopoly over investment decisions that is currently held by private investors and businesses. It is thus rather misleading to refer to these initiatives, as is often done, as forms of "social investment."

[3] The Canadian economist Herschel Hardin has written convincingly about the positive role of autonomous state enterprises and other forms of what he terms "community-centred enterprise." See especially *The Privatization Putsch* (Halifax: Institute for Research on Public Policy, 1989).

[4] Actually Petro-Canada had already operated under a "commercial" mandate for some years before its ultimate privatization.

[5] For more details on these initiatives, see: "Towards democratic control of our economy: the case for a National Investment Fund," Social and Economic Policy Department, Canadian Labour Congress, June 1993; *The Alternative Federal Budget Papers* (Ottawa: Canadian Centre for Policy Alternatives, 1997), pp. 65-70; and "Back to investment: a proposal to create a capital investment fund," by Jeff Faux, Dean Baker, and Todd Schafer, Economic Policy Institute Briefing Paper, Washington, D.C., February 1994.

[6] The author is indebted to Bob Baldwin for assistance in formulating this argument.

[7] Some of those initial investors—and in particular the financial institutions required to deposit a small proportion of their assets in the bank—do not receive interest. These savings would cover the public system's administration costs and losses on failed ventures, thus allowing the bank to invest capital "at cost" (two or three points above inflation) but still break even.

[8] The Mondragon cooperative complex in Spain is probably the best-known of these initiatives; the story of the others needs to be compiled and told more widely. An interesting review of the Mondragon experience, and its potential relevance to Canada, is provided in *From Mondragon to America: Experiments in Community Economic Development*, by Greg MacLeod (Sydney, N.S.: University College of Cape Breton Press, 1997).

[9] Indeed, one of the advantages of situating the restructuring of individual companies or industries in the context of rapid growth and full employment at the macroeconomic level is that the desperate consequences currently produced by that restructuring—in which many of those affected have no hope of attaining alternate employment—are ameliorated by the rapid creation of new jobs in growing industries. That is why expansionary macroeconomic policy is so important to effective industrial restructuring.

Appendices

Appendix I
Capital: Where is It?

Table A1-1 Financial Capital by Form Canada, $Billions, end-1997	Financial Assets ($Billions)	Share of Total Financial Assets (%)
Total financial assets	$5.17 trillion	100 percent
Currency (notes in circulation)	$30.5 billion	0.6%
Corporate shares (equities)	$1 trillion	19.3%
Government bonds and Treasury-bills	$848 billion	16.4%
Corporate bonds	$365 billion	7.1%
Mortgages	$482 billion	9.3%
Other loans	$290 billion	5.6%
Chartered banks	$834 billion	16.1%
Near-banks (excl. credit unions)	$165 billion	3.2%
Mutual funds	$255 billion	4.9%
Insurance companies	$269 billion	5.2%
Social or "Democratic" Financial Institutions and Sources		
Public financial institutions[1]	$105 billion	2.0%
Governments	$351 billion	6.8%
Non-financial Crown corporations	$23 billion	0.4%
Credit unions	$110 billion	2.1%
Canada & Québec Pension Plans	$51 billion	1.0%
Trusteed pension funds	$388 billion	7.5%
Ethical mutual funds	$3 billion	0.06%
Labour-sponsored venture funds	$4 billion	0.08%
Community foundations	$1 billion	0.02%

Source: Author's calculations from Statistics Canada, *National Balance Sheet Accounts*, *Bank of Canada Review*, and misc. sources. Due to definitional differences, asset values reported here may differ from market- value figures commonly reported.
1. Includes Bank of Canada, and federal and provincial government institutions.

Table A1-2 Real Capital by Form Canada, $Billions, end-1997	Real Assets ($Billions)	Share of Total Real Assets (%)
Total real assets	**$3 trillion**	**100%**
By Type of Asset		
Residential structures	$804 billion	26.9%
Non-residential structures	$766 billion	25.6%
Machinery & equipment	$271 billion	9.1%
Land	$710 billion	23.7%
Other durable goods	$439 billion	14.7%
By Owner		
Individuals and unincorporated businesses	$1.46 trillion	48.8%
Non-financial private business	$864 billion	28.9%
Financial businesses	$61 billion	2.0%
Governments	$381 billion	12.7%
Non-financial Crown corporations	$222 billion	7.4%
Source: Author's calculations from Statistics Canada, *National Balance Sheet Accounts*.		

Appendix II
Glossary of Terms

References within a definition to other terms defined within this glossary are indicated in italics.

asset: Something which an individual or company owns, and which has a monetary value.

bank: A business which accepts deposits and lends money. In Canada, "true" banks are chartered under the terms of the Bank Act; but other financial institutions (called *near-banks*) conduct very similar activities.

Bank of Canada: Canada's *central bank*, owned by the federal government, and ultimately accountable to the Minister of Finance.

bond: A financial asset which specifies the repayment schedule of a loan with interest. Also called a "fixed income" or "fixed interest" asset.

capital: A stockpile of wealth which is used as an economic input. Capital can take *financial* or *real* forms.

capital accumulation: The process of adding to an economy's stockpile of capital. This term is usually used in the real sense, in which case capital accumulation occurs when new investment in *real capital* outweighs the loss of capital value through wear-and-tear or *depreciation*.

capital-intensive: A company or industry which employs relatively large amounts of *real capital* in production, relative to the size of its labour force; equivalently, a company or industry with a high *capital-labour ratio*.

capital-labour ratio: The value of *real capital* used in a company or industry, measured per worker employed there.

central bank: A public financial institution, usually established at the national level and controlled by a national government, which sets short-term interest rates, lends money to commercial banks and governments, and otherwise oversees the operation of the *credit* system. Also known as the "monetary authority."

credit: The ability to purchase something without immediately being able to pay for it. The "supply of credit" refers to the total value of credit available to businesses and consumers in an economy.

credit union: A cooperative financial institution which is owned by members who have each purchased one share, and who control the institution on the basis of one member, one vote.

debt: An amount of money owed by an individual, company, or other organization to someone else.

deficit: The amount by which an individual or institution's current expenses exceed its current income. Usually used in reference to government finances.

deflation: A process in which the average level of prices in an economy declines over time.

depreciation: The loss of value from an existing stockpile of *real capital* assets used by a company or an economy within a given period of time due to normal wear-and-tear and obsolescence.

derivatives: Financial assets whose market value in turn is tied to the market prices of other financial or real assets (such as interest rates, exchange rates, commodity prices, or stock market indices).

entrepreneur: An individual or group of individuals which takes overall responsibility for identifying an opportunity to produce and sell something, and the subsequent organization and supervision of the production process.

equity: The proportion of a company's total *assets* that is not owed to banks or other lenders, but rather is owned outright by the company's owners. Individual company *shares* (the price of which in theory should reflect the equity value of a company) are also known as "equities."

exchange rate: The "price" at which the currency of one country can be converted into the currency of another country.

Federal Reserve: The U.S. *central bank*, also known as "the Fed."

financial capital. A stockpile of money or other financial assets.

financial fragility: The instability in the market value of financial assets (especially *securities*) that results from swings in the subjective sentiments of investors, and the impact of that instability on the real investments and economic decisions of companies and consumers.

financial investment: The purchase of a financial asset in the hope or anticipation of receiving a higher monetary value back in the future; equivalently, an addition to an existing stockpile of financial capital.

fiscal policy: The budgetary decisions of governments, including the collection of taxes and the level of government spending.

gross domestic product (GDP): The aggregate value (usually measured at market or selling prices) of all the goods and services produced and sold within a national economy.

gross investment: The total value of new *real investment*, including the investment required to offset *depreciation*.

human capital: The economic value embodied in the skills, knowledge, and physical capacities of human beings.

inflation: A process in which the average level of prices in an economy increases over time.

infrastructure: Facilities, structures, and services which are of widespread and general usefulness to the overall operation of the economy. Usually refers to "physical infrastructure" (bridges, roads, communications facilities), but can also refer to "social infrastructure" (such as education and health services).

interest rate: The rate at which interest must be paid on an outstanding debt (see also *nominal interest rate* and *real interest rate*).

International Monetary Fund (IMF): An international financial institution established at the Bretton Woods conference in 1944, which began operations in 1947. Its responsibilities include international oversight of foreign exchange markets and financial capital flows.

intermediation: A process of acting as an agent to facilitate an economic or financial transaction between two interested parties—like a "middleman."

investment: In general, any addition to an initial stockpile of *capital*. Investment can take *financial* or *real* forms.

investment rate: *Real investment* measured as a proportion of the existing stockpile of *real capital*. The net investment rate (after depreciation) is the rate at which the capital stock is growing.

investment share: *Real investment* measured as a proportion of *GDP*.

leveraging: Usually used in reference to private companies or investors, the process of using borrowed money to expand the economic or financial activity the private firm or investor is undertaking.

liability: A monetary obligation or debt owed by an individual or company; the opposite of an *asset*.

liquidity: In a *macroeconomic* sense, liquidity refers to the extent to which new *credit* is available to finance purchases by companies and individuals. "Liquidity" is strong if new credit is readily available for those who want or need it. In a financial sense, liquidity refers to the ease with which an *asset* (financial or real) can be purchased or sold. "Liquidity" is high if it is easy to sell an asset in return for money.

macroeconomics: The overall economic performance of a country or region, as indicated by such measures as economic growth, unemployment, and investment.

macroeconomic policy: Government policies that are aimed at influencing the macroeconomic conditions of a country or region. The most important "instruments" of macroeconomic policy are *fiscal policy* and *monetary policy*.

monetary policy: Efforts by *central banks* and the governments to which they are accountable to influence interest rates and the overall levels of *credit* and *liquidity* in the economy.

mutual fund: A financial institution that pools the financial investments of its clients, and then subsequently purchases particular *securities* on their collective behalf. Mutual funds are believed to be useful in reducing the risks and administration costs faced by individual financial investors.

near-bank: A financial institution which is not a chartered bank, but which conducts very similar lending and depositing business. Examples include trust companies, household finance firms, and credit unions.

net investment: The value of new real investment, after deducting the investment required to offset *depreciation*.

net worth: The value of the total assets of an individual, institution, or economic sector, after deducting the value of total liabilities. For a corporation, net worth is equivalent to the equity of shareholders (which in strict accounting terms is also considered to be a "liability" of the firm).

nominal value: The monetary value of a stream of income or an asset, expressed in current dollar terms (see also *real value*).

nominal interest rate: The rate at which interest must be paid on an outstanding debt, measured in percentage points (see also *real interest rate*).

operating balance: In public finance, the difference between the total revenues of a government and the amount it spends on current programs and capital investments (but before the cost of interest payments on government debt). In corporate accounting, the difference between a company's total revenues and the day-to-day operating expenses of the company (but before interest costs and various forms of corporate overhead).

productivity: The efficiency with which a company or economy produces goods or services. Most commonly measured in terms of output per employed worker (or output per hour of work).

real value: The value of a stream of income or an asset, after adjusting for changes over time in the general level of prices. Real values are usually expressed in "constant dollar terms," which indicate the real purchasing power of the asset or stream of income at some base year (see also *nominal value*).

real capital: The stockpile of tangible capital assets which are used in the course of real-world economic activity (including machines, computers, transportation and construction equipment, factories, offices, other buildings and structures, and any other "tool" used in work activity).

real exchange rate: The *exchange rate* between two currencies, adjusted to reflect relative changes in the general levels of prices in the two economies. The real exchange rate is a measure of the real purchasing power of a currency.

real interest rate: The interest rate on a loan, minus the rate of *inflation*. The real interest rate measures the real purchasing power reflected in future payments on a debt obligation.

real investment: New purchases of *real capital* equipment (such as machinery, tools, buildings, and structures).

rentier: An investor whose relationship to a company or enterprise is strictly limited to the ownership of financial wealth (such as stocks or bonds) and the receipt of income on that wealth (such as dividends or interest).

return on assets: The profits of a business measured relative to the total value of capital (both real and financial) used in that business.

return on equity: The profits of a business measured relative to the shareholders' *equity* in that business—that is, the total assets of the company, less the value of obligations owed to banks and other lendors.

RPPs (Registered Pension Plans): Trusteed pension funds established at individual workplaces or groups of workplaces. Investments in these funds (by employers, employees, or both) are treated to generous tax subsidies.

RRSPs (Registered Retirement Savings Plans): Individual investments in specified qualifying financial assets; such investments receive generous tax subsidies.

securitization: The process of converting stockpiles of financial wealth into small "bite-size" *securities* that can be traded on private asset markets.

security: A financial asset that reflects a small portion of some broader stockpile of financial wealth, and that can be bought or sold among financial investors at variable prices without an immediate impact on the firm or institution which initially issued the security. Examples of securities include company *shares*, *bonds*, *derivatives*, and units in income trusts or mortgage funds.

shares: Financial securities initially issued to investors who advance equity capital to a business. The resale price of a share should thus reflect a proportionate share of the *equity* value of that business.

social capital: The economic value of "healthy" social conditions (including good levels of health and education among individuals, relatively equal income distribution, and communities that are safe, stable, and mutually supportive).

socialization of investment: The process through which responsibility and ownership of real investment is transferred from private profit-seeking firms to more broadly-controlled and accountable agencies (such as governments, Crown corporations, or community and non-profit enterprises).

speculation: The purchase of a financial asset or security purely in the hope or anticipation that its market price will increase, allowing a gain to be made on its subsequent resale.

surplus: The amount by which an individual or institution's current revenues exceed its current expenses. Usually used in reference to government finances.

wealth: The existing stockpile of accumulated worth of an individual, firm, or society. On a gross basis, wealth is equivalent to the total value of an individual's or institution's *assets*. On a net basis, after deducting the value of *liabilities*, wealth is equal to their *net worth*.

World Bank: An international financial institution established at the Bretton Woods conference in 1944, which began operations in 1946. Formally known as the International Bank for Reconstruction and Development. Its main role, in theory, is to facilitate capital flows to assist in the economic development of poor countries.

Appendix III
Data Sources

Statistics Canada is one of the premiere statistical agencies in the world, publishing an incredible range of data on all kinds of economic and social topics. By becoming more familiar and confident with these data sources, trade union members and community activists can significantly strengthen the informational content and political effectiveness of their research and educational materials.

This appendix summarizes some of the more important Statistics Canada data sources that were utilized in this book. All are available free-of-charge through any university library, major public reference library, or the Statistics Canada research libraries located in major cities.

Canadian Economic Observer (Catalogue 11-010)

This monthly publication conveniently assembles summary data from many of the more detailed data sources described below, including the national economic accounts, labour market indicators, and key financial outcomes (such as interest rates, exchange rates, and corporate profits). An annual historical supplement (Catalogue 11-210) provides longer-term annual data series for each of these variables.

National Economic and Financial Accounts (Catalogue 13-001)

Every three months Statistics Canada publishes this fundamental economic report, which indicates the growth and composition of the overall national economy. Figures on gross domestic product are reported in several ways. GDP by expenditure breaks down the total output of the economy by class of expenditure (personal consumption, public-sector consumption and investment, business investment in fixed capital and inventories, and exports and imports). GDP by income breaks down total output into the different categories of income generated by that output (wages and fringe benefits for workers, profits for corporations and small businesses, and income for financial investors).

A special category in the income account indicates the annual cost of the depreciation of real capital, which was an important issue considered in this book. Sector-by-sector income and expenditure accounts provided in this catalogue are an especially rich source of data on the financial state of Canadian households, governments, and financial and non-financial businesses, including their respective gross and net real investment expenditures.

Financial Flow Accounts (Catalogue 13-014)

A less-known and supplementary source of data on the income, expenditures, and investments of different sectors of the economy is provided in this quarterly catalogue. Tables provide details on the sources of new funds received within each sector, and the uses to which those funds are put. Rich detail is available here on subjects such as new share issues by private companies, or the detailed composition of household financial investments. A "financial market summary table" provides a useful portrait of the overall financial flows within and between different sectors of the economy.

In some cases, key indicators (such as the overall savings of each sector) presented here will differ due to definitional and measurement issues from similar series reported in the National Economic and Financial Accounts; when this is the case, the general practice adopted in this book has been to utilize the NEFA version of the data.

National Balance Sheet Accounts (Catalogue 13-214)

Where the Financial Flow Accounts describe the ongoing *flows* of financial capital between different sectors of the economy, the National Balance Sheet Accounts provide a snapshot of the accumulated stockpiles of *wealth* in Canada, broken down by type of asset and by broad sector of ownership. Again, the breakdown of the data is incredibly rich, providing a good indication of the different forms of wealth (especially distinguishing between different types of real and financial capital) and the institutions where that wealth is owned (including various categories of financial and non-financial companies).

The one shortcoming of the National Balance Sheet Accounts is its failure to provide a breakdown of wealth holdings by households, decomposed according to class of household. Its presentation of a single aggregate series on household wealth ownership thus sidesteps the important question of the distribution of that wealth between different groups of households. This is an important issue on which more light will be shed with the upcoming Statistics Canada wealth survey, the first results from which should be published in the year 2000.

Fixed Capital Stocks and flows (Catalogue 13-568)

This historical review summarizes the long-run evolution of real capital accumulation by different industries and different sectors of Canada's economy. It provides a range of different measures of annual investment flows and stockpiles of accumulated capital. Difficult measurement issues are encountered in trying to measure these important variables (such as real versus nominal valuations, and the treatment of depreciation), hence some knowledge and judgment will be required by the researcher in trying to utilize this data source.

Hard copies of the data are published only every several years (the most recent version of which, at time of writing, presented data up to the end of 1994); but updates are available on-line.

Quarterly Financial Statistics for Enterprises (Catalogue 61-008)

Quarterly data on the financial state of Canadian business is provided in this publication. Both income and expense data and balance sheet stockpiles (assets and liabilities) are reported. Data are provided for numerous industrial groupings (including financial and non-financial companies). It is a good source of information on corporate profits, dividend payouts, and methods of investment financing.

Private and Public Investment in Canada (Catalogues 61-205 and 61-206)

Timely data on new real investment spending in Canada are available from these catalogues, which are assembled on the basis of surveys of major investors. At present the structure of these catalogues is not very "user-friendly," and is more suited to economic forecasters (interested in upcoming changes in investment spending by industry or sector) than for researchers interested in a historical perspective.

Initial forecasts of investment spending are presented each year in Catalogue 61-205; a follow-up survey (titled "Revised Intentions") is reported a few months later in Catalogue 61-206. Obtaining historical data on actual investment spending by sector involves a tedious search through back issues of the catalogue; it is much easier to obtain the data through on-line sources (from Statistics Canada's CANSIM system) where that is accessible.

Canada's International Investment Position (Catalogue 67-202)

This is an annual catalogue on Canada's investment relationships with the rest of the world. It contains a breakdown of Canada's foreign investments in other countries, and foreign investments in Canada, by type of investment (direct versus portfolio, short-term versus long-term) and sector and country of ownership. Longer-term historical data on most series are also provided.

Labour Force Information (Catalogue 71-001)

Monthly data on employment, unemployment, labour force participation, earnings, and even unionization are presented in this important catalogue. Breakdowns are provided according to sector of the economy, type of employment, gender, region, age, and size of firm. The data are obtained from a monthly survey of Canadian households. Annual average data and historical series are also available. (See supplementary Catalogues 71-201 and 71-202.) Published and unpublished historical data can also be obtained from a new Statistics Canada CD-ROM based on the labour force survey.

Employment, Earnings and Hours (Catalogue 72-002)

This is a monthly publication that provides more detail regarding employment levels by detailed industry, as well as average levels of hourly wages, monthly salaries, and working hours. It is based on a monthly survey of *employers* (rather than the monthly survey of *workers* reported in Catalogue 71-001), hence some of its data will differ from that reported in the Labour Force Information survey. An annual historical supplement, with yearly averages, is also published (Catalogue 72-F002).

Non-Statistics Canada Sources

Several additional sources of information regarding the financial industry are available from non-official suppliers. The monthly journal, *The Toronto Stock Exchange Review*, provides a wealth of empirical data on the companies listed on Canada's dominant stock market.

An annual catalogue published by the Financial Post Datagroup, titled *Record of New Issues*, summarizes aggregate annual issues of new securities by Canadian companies and governments.

These and other useful sources of detailed financial data are available at the business libraries maintained by most universities and public reference libraries.

Appendix IV
Reports on Econometric Tests

This section provides more detail regarding the econometric and statistical tests that were summarized in different chapters of the book.

Chapter 4: Causality Tests, Investment and Growth

Granger causality tests were performed on annual data for fixed investment (both gross and net) and total GDP, in constant dollar terms, from 1960 to 1997. These data are published in Statistics Canada, *Canadian Economic Observer*. The tests compared first differences of natural logged series (equivalent to a comparison of proportional rates of change). Three different sets of test regressions were performed (for both gross investment and net investment), using cumulative lagged terms for both variables of one, two, and three years, respectively. The test considers whether the lagged variables of one series collectively make a statistically significant contribution to the explanation of the other series; it is thus possible for two variables to "Granger-cause" each other. The choice of investment measure (gross or net) did not affect the test results, which are summarized in Table A4-1.

Table A4-1 Granger Causality Analysis *Investment and GDP*			
Number of Lags Considered →	1	2	3
Net Investment:			
	I**	Q**	Q
Gross Investment:			
	I**	Q**	Q
I = investment causes GDP at 5% level; I** = investment causes GDP at 1% level. Q = GDP causes investment at 5% level; Q** = GDP causes investment at 1% level.			

Chapter 5: Capital-Intensity Regressions

Cross-sectional data were collected on capital-intensity, average weekly earnings, and average labour productivity in 51 Canadian industries at the two-digit level. Capital-intensity was measured as the net fixed capital stock in each industry, in current dollar terms, calculated using geometric depreciation rates, divided by total average employment in the industry, for the year 1994. Average weekly earnings equal total average wages and salaries per employee in 1994. Average labour productivity equals total GDP at factor cost in the industry in 1994 (measured in 1986 dollar terms) per total employee.

Capital stock data are published in Statistics Canada, *Fixed Capital Stocks and Flows*; employment and earnings in *Employment, Earnings and Hours*; and sectoral value-added in *Gross Domestic Product by Industry*. Least-squares regressions of earnings and productivity, respectively, were performed on the natural log of average capital-intensity. Seven outlying industries with extremely high levels of capital-intensity (oil and gas, pipelines, telecommunication carriers, electric utilities, water distribution, gas distribution, and other utilities) exert a disproportionate influence on the regression results; results are reported below both including and excluding these seven industries. The exclusion of the outlying industries strengthened the apparent link between capital-intensity and wages, but weakened the apparent link between capital-intensity and productivity. Results are reported in Tables A4-2 and A4-3.

Table A4-2		
Least Squares Regression Results		
Independent Variable: GDP at Factor Cost per Worker, 1994		
	Coefficient	T-statistic
Including 7 high capital-intensity industries		
Constant	-59.478	-2.85**
Capital-intensity (natural log)	39.559	7.64**
Adj. R^2: .534	F-Statistic: 58.304	# of Observations: 51
Excluding 7 high capital-intensity industries		
Constant	12.087	0.91
Capital-intensity (natural log)	16.134	4.21**
Adj. R^2: .280	F-Statistic: 17.73	# of Observations: 44
* indicates variable significant at 5%; ** indicates variable significant at 1%.		

Table A4-3 Least Squares Regression Results Independent Variable: Average Weekly Earnings, 1994		
	Coefficient	T-statistic
Including 7 high capital-intensity industries		
Constant	294.12	5.90**
Capital-intensity (natural log)	103.69	8.36**
Adj. R^2: .580	F-Statistic: 69.972	# of Observations: 51
Excluding 7 high capital-intensity industries		
Constant	260.54	4.19**
Capital-intensity (natural log)	114.42	6.26**
Adj. R^2: .470	F-Statistic: 39.148	# of Observations: 44
* indicates variable significant at 5%; ** indicates variable significant at 1%.		

Chapter 8: "Core" Investment Equation

The econometric tests reported in Chapter 8 utilize annual data from 1960 to 1997. The dependent variable is net private fixed investment. The three explanatory variables included in the "core" investment equation are GDP growth, the real interest rate, and business profitability. Additional variables considered for their potential significance include the investment risk index (the construction of which was described in Chapter 8), imports, and the Canada-U.S. real exchange rate (an index calculated with 1971 as the base year, on the basis of the nominal exchange rate adjusted for relative changes in consumer prices in the two countries).

All aggregate expenditure variables (including GDP itself) are normalized by measuring them as shares of potential GDP; potential GDP is calculated as the level of GDP that would be produced by a fully-employed potential labour force, calculated as the product of the working-age population in any given year and the peak historical rate of labour force participation that had been attained prior to that year. The potential output of this potential labour force is estimated as the product of the potential labour force and the level of average labour productivity that would entail given the continuance of average productivity growth rates during the decade in question. In the context of this normalization, the GDP series can be interpreted as a measure of aggregate economic capacity utilization.

The long-run interest rate utilized equals the long-run bond rate less the rate of change in the GDP deflator. Business profits equal before-tax corporate profits. The regressions are performed using first-differenced series; the combination of the previously-described normalization process plus the first-differencing also ensures that all series are stationary, as documented in Table A4-4.

Table A4-4	
Stationarity Tests	
Variables in Net Investment Regressions	
Variable[1]	**Augmented D-F Test Score[2]**
Net business fixed investment[3]	-3.378
GDP[3]	-4.793
Real long-run bond rate	-3.891
Corporate profits[3]	-5.375
Investment risk index	-4.038
Imports[3]	-7.895
Real exchange rate	-3.690

1. All variables tested and modelled in first differences.
2. Tested with constant and one lag. Critical values: 10% -2.613; 5% -2.950; 1% -3.635.
3. All aggregate demand variables tested and modelled as proportion of potential output.

Table A4-5			
Least-Squares Regression Results			
Independent Variable: Net Business Fixed Investment, 1964-1997			
	Coefficient	T-statistic	Beta Coefficient[1]
Constant	.0015	1.51	-
GDP	.521	8.20**	.785
GDP (-1)	.159	2.35*	.239
Long Int. Rate	-.0014	-2.41*	.239
Long Int. Rate (-1)	-.0017	-2.96**	.218
Profits (-2)	.235	3.06**	.282
Adj. R^2: .751		D-W Statistic: 1.906	
F-Statistic: 20.858		# of Observations: 34	

* indicates variable significant at 5%; ** indicates variable significant at 1%..
All variables modelled in first differences; aggregate demand variables expressed as share of potential output.
1. Coefficient scaled by ratio of dependent variable standard deviation to independent variable's standard deviation.

A least-squares regression of net fixed investment on the three "core" variables confirms that each is a significant determinant of business investment spending in Canada. Results of this regression are presented in Table A4-5. Because of the use of lagged explanatory variables, and the first-differencing of all variables, three observations are lost from the data set, which commences in 1964 as a result.

The right-hand column of Table A4-5 presents a "beta" statistic for each set of variables. This coefficient equals the coefficient on each explanatory variable, scaled by the ratio of the standard deviation of the dependent variable to the standard deviation of the explanatory variable in question. This coefficient thus provides a relative measure, comparable across explanatory variables, of the importance of each explanatory variable in explaining changes in investment.

The simultaneous relationship between investment and GDP might suggest the possibility of simultaneous equation bias in a least-squares regression of the former on the latter. Hence a two-stage least-squares regression was also performed on the "core" variables, using lagged independent terms, potential output, imports, the investment climate, and a measure of stock market prices as instrumental variables; none of the coefficients changed significantly in the two-stage procedure, and hence these results are not reported.

Once the initial "core" equation was established, tests were performed for the potential significance of additional explanatory variables. These tests consisted of adding these additional variables one at a time to the "core" equation, and then conducting a Wald F-test for the significance of the added variable. Variables considered included the investment risk index constructed in Chapter 8, imports, and the real exchange rate. A range of potential lag structures was also considered (ranging from the current term to a two-year lag). In every case the tests proved negative: the additional variable in question did not add significantly to the explanatory power of the equation, as summarized in Table A4-6.

Finally, on the basis of the original "core" investment equation, the cumulative change in private net fixed investment in Canada can be retroactively decomposed into its three major component causes, on the basis of the estimated

Table A4-6
Tests for Additional Variables
LS Regression, Net Business Fixed Investment

Hypothesis	Variable	Lag	F-test[1]
Investment Risk	Climate	0	.102
		1	2.218[2]
		2	.026
Globalization	Import Pen.	0	.201
		1	.537
		2	.179
	Real Ex. Rate	0	.002
		1	.000
		2	.125

1. 5% critical value is approximately 3.8.
2. Variable has opposite-to-expected sign in this test.

Table A4-7
Accounting for the Slowdown
Business Net Fixed Investment, 1980 to 1997

Variable	Change 1980-97	Resulting Change in Fixed Inv.	Percent Change in Fixed Inv.
Net Business Fixed Investment	-4.68 points	-4.68 points	100%
GDP / Capacity Utilization			
(0)	-2.21 points	-1.15 points	24.6%
(-1)	-5.44 points	-0.86 points	18.5%
			43.1%
Real Long Bond Interest Rate (0)	+4.39 points	-0.61 points	13.1%
(-1)	+5.43 points	-0.92 points	19.7%
			32.8%
Before-Tax Corporate Profits (-2)	-2.18 points	-0.51 points	10.9%
Unexplained & Error		-0.63 points	13.4%

coefficients and the cumulative changes in the explanatory variables. This decomposition is summarized in Table A4-7.

Chapter 10: Causality Tests, Savings and Investment

Granger causality tests were also performed between several different measures of domestic savings in Canada, and both gross and net fixed investment spending in Canada, using annual data series from 1960 to 1997. Savings measures chosen are gross sectoral savings, including capital cost allowance. The series are compared in terms of first differences of natural logs, and are thus equivalent to proportional rates of change. Once again, the choice of gross or net investment had little impact on the obtained results, which are summarized in Table A4-8.

Table A4-8					
Granger Causality Analysis					
Investment and Savings					
	Gross Investment			**Net Investment**		
Number of Lags Considered →	1	2	3	1	2	3
Household Savings	I			I		
Corporate Savings	S^{**}, I	S^{**}	S^{**}	S^{**}	S^{**}	S^{**}
Government Savings	S, I^{**}	I^{**}	I^{**}	S, I^{**}	I^{**}	I^{**}

I = investment causes savings at 5% level; I^{**} = investment causes savings at 1% level.
S = savings cause investment at 5% level; S^{**} = savings cause investment at 1% level.

Index

M

N

O

P

Petro-Canada 49, 89, 393
Picot, Garnett 421
Pollin, Robert 423
privatization 49, 51, 391, 392
profit rate 237
profit share 235
public investment 93, 97, 100, 107, 111, 154, 320, 323
public sector 73, 81, 189, 423
public venture investment 324
Pyper, W. 421

R

real interest rate 188
Reform Party 333
Registered Education Savings Plans (RESP) 297, 333, 353
Registered Retirement Savings Plan (RRSP) 1, 208, 255, 265, 297, 316, 334, 360, 368, 371
Reguly, Eric 355
rentiers 241, 252, 253, 276
research and development 95
residential structures 98
retained earnings 220
Rippe, Richard D. 431
Rodrik, Dani 96
Rubin, Jeff 415

S

Sawyer, Malcolm 118
Schaller, Huntley 414
Schlesinger, Tom 437
Schumpeter, Joseph 409
Seccareccia, Mario 433
securitization 48, 68, 280, 299, 414
self-employment 7, 130
Setterfield, Mark 427
small business 123, 236
small businesses 369
Smithin, John 427
social capital 94
Solidarity Fund 356
St. Lawrence Seaway 323
Stanford, Jim 423, 424, 428, 435
strike frequency 169, 246
Stronach, Frank 77, 277
structuralist economics 162, 212
Summers, Lawrence H. 418

T

Taylor, Lance 433
technical analysis 302
technological change 79
Thomson, Ken 277, 278, 348, 433
Tobin tax 54, 333
Toronto Stock Exchange (TSE) 11, 27, 43, 45, 53, 54, 55, 222, 262,
268, 304, 341

U

unemployment insurance 129, 177, 191, 210, 218, 246, 319

V

VanCity Savings Credit Union 320, 332, 340
Vickrey, William 226

W

Watkins, Mel 424
Weisskopf, Thomas J. 249, 431
Willis, Andrew 293, 301
Wilson, Kevin 439
Wilson, Thomas A. 432
Wohar, Mark E. 419
Working Ventures 362-366
World Bank 336

Y

Yates, Janice 421